Clive Oxenden
Christina Latham-Koenig

New
ENGLISH FILE

/ **LRC Stoke Park**
GUILDFORD COLLEGE

Advanced
Student's Book

OXFORD
UNIVERSITY PRESS

Contents

		Grammar	Vocabulary	Pronunciation

1

4	**A** What motivates you?	discourse markers (1): linkers	work	word stress and rhythm
8	**B** Who am I?	*have*	personality; family	rhythm and intonation
12	**C** Whose language is it?	pronouns	language terminology	sound–spelling relationships

16	**WRITING**	A letter of application
18	**COLLOQUIAL ENGLISH**	Family secrets
19	**REVISE & CHECK**	Grammar and Vocabulary

2

20	**A** Once upon a time	the past: narrative tenses, *used to* and *would*	word building: abstract nouns	word stress with suffixes
24	**B** Are there really 31 hours in a day?	distancing	*time*	linking
28	**C** 50 ways to leave your lover	*get*	phrases with *get*	words and phrases of French origin

32	**WRITING**	An article
34	**COLLOQUIAL ENGLISH**	Time and technology
35	**REVISE & CHECK**	Grammar and Vocabulary

3

36	**A** Breaking the silence	speculation and deduction	sounds and the human voice	consonant clusters
40	**B** Lost in translation	adding emphasis (1): inversion	describing books	words with 'silent' syllables
44	**C** Are you suffering from *Affluenza*?	unreal uses of past tenses	money	*ea* and *ear*

48	**WRITING**	A review
50	**COLLOQUIAL ENGLISH**	Women and money
51	**REVISE & CHECK**	Grammar and Vocabulary

4

52	**A** History goes to the movies	discourse markers (2): adverbs and adverbial expressions	history and warfare	stress in word families
56	**B** Help yourself	verb + object + infinitive or gerund	compound adjectives	intonation in polite requests
60	**C** Can't live without it	conditional sentences	phone language; adjectives + prepositions	sounds and spelling /ʃ/, /tʃ/, /ʒ/, /dʒ/

64	**WRITING**	Discursive essay (1): a balanced argument
66	**COLLOQUIAL ENGLISH**	Fact or fiction?
67	**REVISE & CHECK**	Grammar and Vocabulary

		Grammar	Vocabulary	Pronunciation
5				
68	**A** **Who's in control?**	permission, obligation, and necessity	word formation: prefixes	intonation in exclamations
72	**B** **Just any old bed?**	verbs of the senses	place and movement	extra stress on important words
76	**C** **Trick or treatment?**	gerunds and infinitives	health and medicine; similes	word stress
80	**WRITING**	A report		
82	**COLLOQUIAL ENGLISH**	Art and artists		
83	**REVISE & CHECK**	Grammar and Vocabulary		
6				
84	**A** **A moving experience**	expressing future plans and arrangements	travel and tourism	homophones
88	**B** **Pets and pests**	ellipsis and substitution	the natural world	weak and strong pronunciation of auxiliary verbs and *to*
92	**C** **The promised land?**	adding emphasis (2): cleft sentences	words that are often confused	intonation in cleft sentences
96	**WRITING**	Discursive essay (2): taking sides		
98	**COLLOQUIAL ENGLISH**	Encounters with animals		
99	**REVISE & CHECK**	Grammar and Vocabulary		
7				
100	**A** **A recipe for disaster**	nouns: compound and possessive forms	preparing food	-ed adjective endings and linking
104	**B** **Sport on trial**	*so* and *such*	word building: adjectives, nouns, and verbs	homographs
108	**C** **The funniest joke in the world?**	comparison	humour	*augh* and *ough*
112	**WRITING**	A complaint		
114	**COLLOQUIAL ENGLISH**	Cooking round the world		
115	**REVISE & CHECK**	Grammar and Vocabulary		

116	**Communication**
121	**Listening**
136	**Grammar Bank**
157	**Vocabulary Bank**
168	**Sound Bank**

Look out for Study Link

This shows you where to find extra material for more practice and revision.

1A

G discourse markers (1): linkers
V work
P word stress and rhythm

'I owe my success to having listened respectfully to the very best advice, and then going away and doing the exact opposite.'
G. K. Chesterton, English poet and novelist

What motivates you?

1 READING & SPEAKING

a Think of a person you consider to be successful. What makes you think they are successful? What, in your view, are the reasons for their success?

b Read the article and match the headings to each paragraph. There is one heading you don't need.

A **A fierce spirit**
B **Being my own person**
C **Learning from my mistakes**
D **Needing to show them they were wrong**
E **The courage to set out and seek my fortune**

c Read the article again and write the initials (e.g. AP) of the person next to the questions below.
Who…?

1 ☐ found it hard to manage on their own
2 ☐ was motivated by the same desire until they became successful
3 ☐ thinks that a conflict helped them become stronger
4 ☐ was made fun of by a member of their family
5 ☐ is grateful for something their parents did wrong
6 ☐ asked a parent for advice
7 ☐ learnt an important lesson from a parent
8 ☐ was treated in the same way at school and at work

I didn't get where I am today without…
Successful people talk about their inspiration and motivation

1 ☐ **Ann Patchett,**
US novelist

Revenge is a terrific motivating force for young creative people and it certainly kept me going right through to the publication of my first novel. I'd been late to learn to read, and as a result the nuns at my school in Tennessee had me marked down as being somewhere between slow and stupid. They taught me for 12 years and even after I'd caught up and got smarter, I was still thought of as dumb. 'They'll be sorry when they discover I'm a great writer,' I'd say to myself. 'In retirement, the single thing they'll be most proud of will be that they had me as a pupil.' And so it continued right through into the workplace where, in my first teaching job after leaving graduate school, the male head of the department would come to me whenever the secretarial staff were off. 'Type this up for me, will you, Ann?' he'd say habitually. 'One day,' I would think, gritting my teeth, 'One day…'

2 ☐ **John Malkovich,**
US actor, producer, and director

There must have been something unique or, at least, different about me as a boy, because I recall it would sometimes amuse my brother and his friends to throw beer cans at me. Why? Because of the clothes I wore, which they didn't like, or because I wouldn't do whatever it was that they wanted me to, or just because it was fun. But being different is fine. It was my father who encouraged in me the notion that I and I alone am responsible for my own life, for what I do and don't do, for my opinions and beliefs, and it's proved to be a great source of strength. I'm often asked if I read and take notice of critics. Which ones? Those who love the work? Who hate it? Or are indifferent? As a director, as in life, you have to know your own mind and be prepared to stick to your guns.

3 ☐ **Marcus Wareing,**
UK chef

One of my tutors at Southport Catering College knew Anton Edelmann, the chef at the Savoy, and recommended me to him. I was very nervous of leaving my comfort zone and coming to London. I was a loner who'd never made friends because I was always working, and I was happy enough being alone and busy.

But I did come to London, and even though it was a very tough environment, I worked like a trouper and was very quick to learn. The hardest part was being away from my family and having to deal with other people while having no management or interpersonal skills whatsoever. So I called my dad every day, to fill him in on the good and bad, and ask him how he would deal with this or that.

dumb /dʌm/ *adj.* **OPP** smart NAmE stupid
graduate school *noun* NAmE US college for post-graduate studies

Southport a town in north-west England
the Savoy one of London's most prestigious hotels

d Talk in small groups.

1 From reading the text, what impression do you get of the four people's personalities?

2 Which of them do you most identify with? Why?

3 What or who motivates you…?
- in your work or studies
- to improve your English
- to improve other skills, e.g. sport, music, other activities (give examples)

4 ☐ **Paulo Coelho,**
Brazilian writer

The family is a microcosm of society. It's where your spirit and beliefs are first tested. My mother and father wanted only the best for me and my sister, but had very rigid ideas of what that 'best' should be. For me to become a lawyer or even an engineer would have satisfied them, but a writer? Never. I was a determined and rebellious kid, though, and having failed to change my mind by conventional methods, they looked for more dramatic and extreme ones. In a sense, though, I thank them for that. I wouldn't have got where I am without fighting to live the life I wanted for myself. I long since forgave them. We all make mistakes, parents included.

LEXIS IN CONTEXT

e Look at the highlighted phrases and guess the meaning of the ones you don't know from the context. Then match them to the definitions 1–7.

1 _____ to know what you want or like

2 _____ **IDM** (informal) refuse to change your mind about sth even when other people are trying to persuade you that you are wrong

3 _____ in one way

4 _____ (colloquial) the working or living environment in which we feel safe and unthreatened

5 _____ **IDM** be determined to continue to do sth in a difficult or unpleasant situation

6 _____*sb*____ **PHR V** to tell sb about what has happened

7 _____ **PHR V** (with sb) to reach the same level or standard as sb who is better or more advanced

f Choose five more words or phrases from the text that you think are useful for you.

g Read the information about looking up idioms in a dictionary.

> **Looking up idioms in a dictionary**
>
> You will normally find the definition of an idiom under the first 'full' word (noun, verb, adverb or adjective, but NOT prepositions and articles), in a section marked, for example, **IDM**. So the definition of *stick to your guns* will probably be given under *stick*.
>
> ⚠ After some very common verbs, e.g. *be*, *get* and adjectives, e.g. *good*, *bad*, the idioms are at the entries for the next 'full' word.
>
> Phrasal verbs **PHR V** are always after the main verb, e.g. *get off* and *get over* would be under *get*.

h Now look at the following idioms with *mind*. What do you think they mean? Check with a dictionary.

speak your mind   mind your own business
cross your mind   be in two minds about sth

2 GRAMMAR discourse markers (1): linkers

a Without looking back at the text, with a partner try to remember how these sentences continue. Don't worry if you can't remember the exact words.

1 **Ann Patchett:** 'I'd been late to learn to read, and **as a result**…'

2 **John Malkovich:** 'It would sometimes amuse my brother and his friends to throw beer cans at me. Why? **Because of**…'

3 **Marcus Wareing:** 'But I did come to London, and **even though**…, I worked like a trouper and was very quick to learn.'

4 **Marcus Wareing:** 'So I called my dad every day, **to**…'

b Compare your answers with the text.

c Which of the **bold** linkers in **a** introduces…?

1 a result   *as a result*   3 a purpose   _____
2 a reason   _____   4 a contrast   _____

d ⟳ **p.136 Grammar Bank 1A.** Read the rules and do the exercises.

e 🔊 **1.1** Listen to the sentences. When the speakers pause, write down how you think the sentences might continue.

f 🔊 **1.2** Now listen to the whole sentences. Are they similar to what you wrote?

3 SPEAKING & LISTENING

a A recent survey by Chiumento, a British human resources consultancy, established the ten factors that make people happy at work. With a partner, try to agree which are the two <u>most</u> important and the two <u>least</u> important factors.

What makes people happy at work?

- ☐ Being part of a successful team.
- ☐ Doing something rewarding.
- ☐ Doing varied work.
- ☐ Earning a competitive salary.
- ☐ Doing enjoyable work.
- ☐ Feeling that you are making a difference.
- ☐ Having a good boss or manager.
- ☐ Having a good work-life balance.
- ☐ Having friendly, supportive colleagues.
- ☐ Having your achievements recognized.

Source: *Chiumento's Happiness at Work Index*

---

b The survey also established some other factors related to being happy at work. With your partner, discuss whether you think the following were probably true or false according to the research, and say why.

1 Statistically there are more happy people at work than unhappy people.
2 Employees of bigger companies or organizations are happier than those who work for smaller companies.
3 Men are generally happier than women in their work.
4 Full-time workers are happier than part-time workers.
5 People with higher positions in a company are happier than the people below them.
6 The longer you stay in one job, the happier you become.
7 Workers over 55 are the happiest.

c **1.3** Now listen to a radio programme about the survey and check your answers to **a** and **b**. Were you right?

d Look at the photos and read the short article about *innocent drinks*. Does it look like a company you would like to work for? Why (not)?

Working where the grass is always greener

In a *Sunday Times* survey, *innocent drinks* was found to be one of the companies with the happiest employees. This London-based company was set up by three university students in 1999 and started off making smoothies, a drink made with fruit juice and yoghurt. It now employs over 200 people, and has added vegetable pots to its products. The company calls itself 'innocent' because it only uses pure fresh ingredients. Part of its marketing strategy is to use delivery vans which are decorated to look like cows or grassy fields. The company also prides itself on being 'a happy place to work' and 'people-orientated', with a relaxed working environment, which includes having a grass floor in the office!

Why I like working at Innocent

great people (+ free smoothies)

I DONT HAVE TO SHAVE EVERY DAY!

THE GRASS

e **1.4** Now listen to the second part of the programme where Becka Walton, who works for *innocent drinks*, is interviewed. Answer the questions.

1 In general, does she agree that there is a happy and relaxed working atmosphere at *innocent drinks*?
2 Does she mention any downsides?

f Listen again, pausing after each of Becka's answers. Answer questions 1–6 with a partner.

1 What made Becka apply for a job at the company?
2 What example does she give of how the company creates a team environment?
3 What examples does she give of the relaxed atmosphere?
4 What does she say about staff turnover?
5 Does she agree that a competitive salary is *not* an important factor as regards job satisfaction?
6 What does Becka say about the company's product?

g Now listen again with the tapescript on page 121. Is there anything you found difficult to understand? Why?

> **Listening to English in the media**
>
> Try to listen to as much English as you can outside class in a format where you can listen to it again, e.g. a website, a podcast, a video clip, or a DVD. A good way of getting the most out of it is:
> - first listen and try to get used to the speaker(s) and get a general idea of what they are talking about.
> - then listen again, pausing and checking you understand the main points.
> - listen again with a tapescript or English subtitles, if they are available, to help you work out what you didn't understand (perhaps because of the speaker's accent or speed, or use of vocabulary).

h Do Becka's answers confirm that you would / wouldn't like to work for *innocent drinks*? Why (not)?

4 VOCABULARY work

a Match the two halves of the expressions used in the interview.

1 short-term ☐	A balance
2 work-life ☐	B salary
3 working ☐	C turnover
4 line ☐	D contracts
5 staff ☐	E environment
6 competitive ☐	F manager

b **1.5** Listen and check. With a partner, say what you think they mean.

c ➡ p.157 Vocabulary Bank *Work*.

d With a partner, explain the difference between…

a *demanding* job and a *challenging* job
wages and *salary*
a *profession* and a *career*
skills and *qualifications*
being *sacked* and being *made redundant*
getting *a rise* and getting *promoted*
good prospects and *good opportunities*
being *out of work* and being *off work*

5 PRONUNCIATION word stress and rhythm

a Underline the stressed syllable in the **bold** words.

1 I managed to get a **challenging** and **motivating** job.
2 I don't have any **qualifications** or **experience**.
3 There's no **job security** and I might be made **redundant**.
4 I've had a very **rewarding career** in publishing.
5 The job has a **competitive salary** and excellent **benefits**.
6 It's a **stimulating working environment** with good **opportunities** and **prospects**.
7 The **employees** don't enjoy the work, as it's very **monotonous**.
8 After she **retired**, she did **voluntary** work at her local hospital.

b **1.6** Listen and check.

c Listen again and focus on the rhythm of the sentences. Which words are <u>not</u> stressed in the sentences? Practise saying the sentences with good stress and rhythm.

6 SPEAKING

a Think about two jobs you could talk about. Use the questions below to help you. Add any other information that you think would be relevant. Use the words and phrases in **Vocabulary Bank** *Work* to help you.

> **A job you would love to do**
> What do you think the advantages of the job would be?
> What makes you think you might be good at it?
> Do you know anyone who does it?
> Can you think of any drawbacks?

> **A job you would hate to do**
> What do you think the downsides of the job would be?
> Do you know anyone who does it?
> Have you ever done anything similar?
> Can you think of any positive sides of the job?

b **1.7** Listen to two people doing the task. What pros and cons do they mention? What two 'noises' do they use to give themselves time to think?

c Work in groups of three. Take turns to describe the jobs you would love to do.

d Now do the same for the jobs you would hate to do.

e Decide which of the jobs described you think is the most attractive.

1

B

G *have*
V personality; family
P rhythm and intonation

'I've learned that you can tell a lot about a person by the way he / she handles these three things: a rainy day, lost luggage, and tangled Christmas tree lights.'
Maya Angelou, US novelist

Who am I?

1 READING & SPEAKING

a Look at the adjectives of personality below. With a partner, say if you consider them to be positive or negative qualities, and why. Would you use any of them to describe yourself?

cautious conscientious curious easy-going independent logical
loyal mature quiet rebellious self-sufficient   sensitive

b With a partner, read the questionnaire on page 9 and each circle the answer that best describes you. Try to guess the meaning of any unfamiliar words or expressions.

c ⊙ **Communication** *Who am I? p.116.* Find out what personality type you and your partner have and read the descriptions. How accurate do you think the description of your personality is?

LEXIS IN CONTEXT

> **Collocation**
> Collocation is the way words combine to provide natural-sounding speech and writing, e.g. *we say a rough itinerary,* not *an approximate itinerary.* Noticing and recording words that go together will improve the accuracy and fluency of your speaking and writing.

d Complete the questions with a verb from the list in the right form. All these collocations appear in *What's your personality type?*

catch face get go with hurt keep make plan tell

1 Do you usually _____ your holidays a long time **in advance**, or at the last minute?
2 What do you do if you're reading a text in English and you _____ **stuck on** a particular word?
3 Do you always _____ **sure** that you have your mobile with you when you leave the house?
4 When you're shopping for clothes, do you usually buy the first thing that _____ **your eye**, or do you look at a lot of things before you make a decision?
5 When you have to make a decision, do you usually _____ **your gut feeling**, or do you ask other people for advice?
6 Do you tend to _____ problems **head on**, or do you try to avoid conflict?
7 In what situations do you think it's better to _____ **a white lie**, in order not to _____ people's **feelings**?
8 When you reply to a friend's email, do you usually write a lot or _____ it **short**?

e Ask and answer the questions with a partner.

f Choose five more words or phrases from the questionnaire that you think are useful for you.

2 GRAMMAR *have*

a Match sentences 1–8 with A–H.

1 He's not very sociable. ☐
2 My dad's so absent-minded! ☐
3 My brother-in-law's not very ambitious. ☐
4 He's a bit of a hypochondriac. ☐
5 My nephew is a bit egocentric. ☐
6 He's incredibly intolerant. ☐
7 Chris is so rebellious! ☐
8 I think our boss is rather mean. ☐

A I think it's because he **hasn't got** any brothers or sisters.
B He often **has** a drink with us, but he never pays.
C **He's got to** make an effort to be more open-minded.
D He **has** a real tendency to argue with people in authority.
E He **has been working** in the same job for 15 years.
F He **hasn't been** to a party for ages.
G He **has to** write everything down otherwise he forgets it.
H He **has** his blood pressure **checked** every week.

b With a partner, look at sentences A–H and answer the questions.

1 In which sentences is *have*
  a) a main verb   b) an auxiliary verb?
2 What implications does this have for making questions and negatives?

c ⊙ **p.137 Grammar Bank 1B.** Read the rules and do the exercises.

d With a partner, for each of the sentences below say if it's true for you or not and why.

- I can't bear having my photo taken, and I'd hate to have my portrait painted.
- I've got loads of friends online (some of whom I've never met), but I've only got a few close friends who I see regularly face to face.
- I've never ever bought a CD from a shop. I download all my music from the Internet.
- I'm very competitive. Whenever I play a sport or game I always have to win.
- I've got to find a way to do more exercise. I'm seriously unfit.
- I have a few possessions that are really important to me and that I would hate to lose.
- I've been learning English for so long that I now find it difficult to motivate myself.

3 ♪ 1.8 SONG ♫ *The Logical Song*

WHAT'S YOUR PERSONALITY TYPE?

PLANNER OR SPONTANEOUS

1 Are you…?
  a a perfectionist who hates leaving things unfinished
  b someone who hates being under pressure and tends to over-prepare
  c a bit disorganized and forgetful
  d someone who puts things off until the last minute

2 Imagine you have bought a piece of self-assembly furniture (e.g. a wardrobe or a cabinet). Which of these are you more likely to do?
  a Check that you have all the items and the tools you need before you start.
  b Carefully read the instructions and follow them to the letter.
  c Quickly read through the instructions to get the basic idea of what you have to do.
  d Start assembling straight away. Check the instructions only if you get stuck.

3 Before you go on holiday, which of these do you do?
  a Plan every detail of your holiday.
  b Put together a rough itinerary, but make sure you've left plenty of free time.
  c Get an idea of what sort of things you can do, but not make a decision until you get there.
  d Book the holiday at the last minute and plan hardly anything in advance.

HEADS OR HEARTS

7 If an argument starts when you are with friends, do you…?
  a face it head on and say what you think
  b try to find a solution yourself
  c try to keep everyone happy
  d do anything to avoid hurting people's feelings

8 Imagine you had the choice between two flats to rent. Would you…?
  a write down what your ideal flat would be like and then see which one was most similar
  b make a list of the pros and cons of each one
  c just go with your gut feeling
  d consider carefully how each flat would affect other members of your family

9 Imagine a friend of yours started going out with a new partner and they asked you for your opinion. If you really didn't like them, would you…?
  a tell them exactly what you thought
  b be honest, but as tactful as possible
  c try to avoid answering the question directly
  d tell a 'white lie'

FACTS OR IDEAS

4 ⬡ **Communication** *What can you see? p.116*
Which option best describes what you wrote down?
  a It's basically a list of what appears in the picture.
  b It tells the story of what's happening in the picture.
  c It tries to explain what the picture means.
  d It's a lot of ideas that the picture made you think of.

5 You need to give a friend directions to your house. Do you…?
  a write down a list of detailed directions
  b send a link to Google Maps
  c give rough directions
  d draw a simple map showing only the basic directions

6 When you go shopping in the supermarket, do you…?
  a always go down the same aisles in the same order
  b carefully check prices and compare products
  c buy whatever catches your eye
  d go round a different way each time, according to what you want to buy

EXTROVERT OR INTROVERT

10 You are out with a group of friends. Do you…?
  a say hardly anything
  b say a bit less than most people
  c talk quite a lot
  d do nearly all the talking

11 When you meet a new group of people, do you…?
  a try to stay with people you already knew
  b have to think hard about how to keep the conversation going
  c try to get to know as many people as possible
  d just try to enjoy yourself

12 If the phone rings when you are in the middle of something, do you…?
  a ignore it and carry on with what you're doing
  b answer it quickly, but say you'll call back
  c have a conversation, but make sure you keep it short
  d welcome the interruption and enjoy a nice long chat

a Look at the painting *The Family of Carlos IV* by Goya and answer the questions with a partner, giving your reasons.

1 In the painting you can see the king, the queen, and their six children (three sons and three daughters). Who do you think is the eldest son and heir to the throne?

2 Now try to identify the king's sister and brother. Which ones do you think they are?

3 Who do you think the woman (5) is and why might she be looking away?

4 The queen's brother is also in the picture. Who do you think he is?

5 Who do you think is probably the most important person in the family?

6 Who do you think the man (2) in the background on the left might be?

b **1.9** Listen to an audio guide telling you about the painting and check your answers to **a**.

c Listen again. Which of the king's children…?

| **A** Fernando | **B** Maria Isabel | **C** Francisco |
| **D** Carlota | **E** Maria Luisa | |

1 married a relative	☐	☐
2 eventually became a king / queen	☐	☐
3 had a similar personality to their mother	☐	
4 did not look like their father	☐	
5 married several times	☐	

d Imagine that you are going to have a portrait of your family painted. Decide who you want in it and where they are going to stand, and make a rough diagram.

e Show the diagram to your partner and explain who the people are and say something about each of them, including their personality.

5 VOCABULARY family

a Look at the family portrait again. What is the relationship between…?

10 and 7   _brother-in-law and sister-in-law_

6 and 12 _____

8 and 4 _____

13 and 9 _____

b ⟳ **p.158 Vocabulary Bank** *Family.*

c Test your memory. Do the quiz with a partner.

Family quiz

What do you call…?

1 your grandmother's mother
2 all your relatives, including aunts, uncles, cousins, etc.
3 a family where there is only a mother or a father

What's the difference between…?

4 a *stepbrother* and a *half-brother*
5 a *nuclear* family and an *extended* family
6 *take after* your father and *look like* your father

Replace the highlighted phrase with an idiom.

7 My sister and my cousin don't speak to each other.
8 My brother and I don't have the same opinions about politics.
9 Who is the dominant partner in their marriage?
10 They're a strange family. I'm sure they have a few dark secrets.

d Answer the questions below with a partner. Try to use the **bold** words.

- Who do you **take after** in your family? In what way?
- Who are you **closest to** in your family?
- Is there anyone in your family you **don't get on with**?
- Are there any subjects on which you don't **see eye to eye** with other members of your family?
- Are there any people in your family who aren't **on speaking terms**?
- Are there any physical characteristics which **run in your family**?
- How often do you have **family get-togethers**? Do you enjoy them?
- Is there **a black sheep** in your family?

6 PRONUNCIATION & SPEAKING
rhythm and intonation

a Work in groups of three or four. You are going to debate some of the topics below. Each student must choose a different topic and make brief notes about what he or she thinks.

Children are left far too much on their own nowadays. It would be better if one parent didn't work and stayed at home until the children leave school.

Working parents should not use their own parents to look after their children. Grandparents should be allowed to relax and enjoy their retirement.

Your parents brought you up, so it's your responsibility to look after them when they're old.

In the 21st century, friends are the new family.

It's better to be an only child than to have brothers and sisters. You get all your parents' love and attention.

The family is a trap from which it can be difficult to escape.

b **1.10** Listen to the phrases and underline the stressed syllables. Then listen again and repeat them, copying the rhythm and intonation.

agreeing

1 I quite agree.
2 I totally agree.
3 That's what I think, too.
4 Absolutely!

half-agreeing

5 I take your point, but…
6 I see what you mean, but…
7 I agree up to a point, but…

disagreeing

8 I completely disagree.
9 I don't agree at all.

c Have a short debate on the topics you have each chosen. The person who made the notes should give their opinion first, and then the rest of the group say what they think. Try to use language from the box in **b** to agree or disagree with the other people in your group.

1 C

G pronouns
V language terminology
P sound–spelling relationships

'If English is supposed to be the lingua franca, how come there's no word in English for lingua franca?'

anon.

Whose language is it?

1 READING & SPEAKING

a Do you think these statements are probably true or false?

1 40% of the world's population can communicate in English reasonably well.
2 Most conversations in English today are between non-native speakers.
3 In business meetings and international conferences conducted in English, non-native speakers prefer it when there is no native speaker present.

b Read the first part of the article *Whose language?* and check your answers to **a**.

c Before you read the second part of the article, with a partner correct the mistakes in sentences 1–6 below. Do you ever make any of these mistakes? How important do you think they are?

1 'I think the film start at 8.00.'
2 'Is there restaurant in the hotel?'
3 'I think the women normally talk faster than the men.'
4 'My friend gave me some very good advices.'
5 'I phoned to my brother but his mobile was switched off.'
6 'We discussed about global warming in class yesterday.'

d Now read the second part of the article and answer the questions.

1 Which of the mistakes in sentences 1–6 above are mentioned in the text?
2 Does the writer of the article think that grammatical correctness matters
   a) in written English   b) in spoken English?

Whose language?

How many people can speak English? Some experts estimate that 1.5 billion people – around one-quarter of the world's population – can communicate reasonably well in English.

Never in recorded history has a language been as widely spoken as English is today. The reason why millions are learning it is simple: it is the language of international business and therefore the key to prosperity. It is not just that multinational companies such as Microsoft, Google, and Vodafone conduct their business in English; it is the language in which the Chinese speak to Brazilians and Germans to Indonesians.

David Graddol, the author of *English Next*, says it is tempting to view the story of English simply as a triumph for its native speakers in North America, Britain and Ireland, and Australasia – but that would be a mistake. Global English has entered a more complex phase, changing in ways that the English-speaking countries cannot control and might not like.

An important question one might ask is: whose English will it be in the future? Non-native speakers now outnumber native English speakers by three to one. The majority of encounters in English today take place between non-native speakers. According to David Graddol, many business meetings held in English appear to run more smoothly when there are no native English speakers present. This is because native speakers are often poor at ensuring that they are understood in international discussions. They tend to think they need to avoid longer Latin-based words, but in fact comprehension problems are more often caused by their use of colloquial English, especially idioms, metaphors, and phrasal verbs. On one occasion, at an international student conference in Amsterdam, conducted in English, the only British representative was asked to be 'less English' so that the others could understand her.

Professor Barbara Seidlhofer, Professor of English and Applied Linguistics at the University of Vienna, records and transcribes spoken English interactions between speakers of the language around the world. She says her team has noticed that non-native speakers are varying standard English grammar in several ways. Even the most competent speakers sometimes omit the 's' in the third person singular. Many omit definite and indefinite articles where they are required in standard English, or put them in where standard English does not use them. Nouns that are not plural in native-speaker English are used as plurals by non-native speakers (e.g. 'informations', 'knowledges', 'advices'). Other variations include 'make a discussion', 'discuss about something', or 'phone to somebody'.

Many native English speakers will insist that these are not variations, they are mistakes. 'Knowledges' and 'phone to somebody' are simply wrong. Many non-native speakers who teach English around the world would agree. But language changes, and so do notions of grammatical correctness.

Those who insist on standard English grammar remain in a powerful position. Academics who want their work published in international journals have to adhere to the grammatical rules followed by native English-speaking elites.

But spoken English is another matter. Why should non-native speakers bother with what native speakers regard as correct? Their main aim, after all, is to be understood by one another, and in most cases there is no native speaker present.

Professor Seidlhofer says, 'I think that what we are looking at is the emergence of a new international attitude, the recognition and awareness that in many international contexts non-native speakers do not need to speak like native speakers, to compare themselves to them, and thus always feel "less good".'

LEXIS IN CONTEXT

> **Being aware of register**
> When you read a formal text you will find words and phrases which the dictionary will list as *formal*. When you record them, make a note of the neutral / informal alternative, e.g. *ensure* (formal), *make sure* (neutral).

e Look at the highlighted words in both parts of the text. They are all formal register. Match them to their neutral equivalents below.

1 _____ *verb* to be (still)
2 _____ *adj.* bad
3 _____ *verb* to do
4 _____ *verb* to follow
5 _____ *noun* idea
6 _____ *verb* to leave out
7 _____ *verb* to need
8 _____ *verb* to look at
9 _____ *adj.* so
10 _____ *verb* to write down

f Answer the questions in small groups.

1 To what extent do you agree that…?
- when non-native speakers of English talk to each other, they should not worry about making mistakes as long as they can communicate
- non-native speakers do not need to speak like native speakers, nor should they feel inferior to them
- certain grammar mistakes should be considered 'variants' of English, not 'mistakes'

2 How important is it to *you* to be able to…?
- speak English accurately
- write accurately in English
- pass international exams in English
- read academic texts or literature in English
- communicate with native speakers of English
- communicate with non-native speakers of English

2 GRAMMAR pronouns

a Are the **bold** pronouns (✓) right or wrong (✗)? Correct any mistakes. Which of the mistakes (if any) do you think interfere with communication?

1 Can the person who has not switched off **their** phone please do so immediately?
2 **It** used to be a cinema near here, but **it** closed down.
3 We've known **each other** for years, since we were children.
4 I never use an electric razor when I shave **myself**. I prefer the old-fashioned sort.
5 Two men were sitting in the café, talking to **themselves** about the match.
6 David **himself** admitted that he should never have spoken to her like that.
7 They have a terrible relationship. They don't understand **one other** at all.
8 **One** never knows what the future holds.

b ⊙ p.138 **Grammar Bank 1C.** Read the rules and do the exercises.

3 SPEAKING

a 🔊 **1.11** Look at some useful phrases for giving your opinions in English. Underline the word(s) in each phrase that you think has extra stress. Listen and check.

> **Emphasizing that something is your own opinion**
> 1 I'd say that…
> 2 If you ask me,…
> 3 Personally, I think that …
> 4 Personally speaking, …
> 5 In my opinion, …
> 6 In my view…
> 7 I feel that…
> 8 My feeling is that…
> 9 As far as I'm concerned…

b Read some comments from around the world about learning or using English. Compare with a partner and say if you think the situation is the same or different in your country, and how you feel about it. Use the expressions from **a**.

'If you ask me, the one thing that would really improve the level of English here would be if they stopped dubbing all the American programmes on TV and at the cinema, and had them in English with subtitles. But I don't think they'll ever do it. The politicians wouldn't dare.' *Maite, Spain*

'In my opinion, nowadays people in public life really ought to be able to speak good English. I feel really embarrassed when I hear how some of our politicians or sportspeople speak.' *Marc, Grenoble, France*

'Personally I think that pop groups in my country shouldn't sing in English. I mean, I know it's more universal, but they aren't English, and not everybody in Hungary understands English. I think they should sing in Hungarian.' *Ferenc, Hungary*

'In some secondary schools in my country they are now teaching other subjects like maths and science in English, apart from the normal English language classes. In general I think it's a really good idea – so long as the teachers' English is good, of course.' *Karolina, Brno, Czech Republic*

'In Italian they use a lot of English words like *weekend, stress, OK, cool, know-how,* words like that. I personally hate it. I think we ought to use our own words for these things, not just borrow from English. And people even use some words which don't exist, like *footing,* when the English word is *jogging*.' *Paola, Milan, Italy*

4 LISTENING & SPEAKING

a You're going to hear Zoltán from Hungary and Cristina from Argentina, who both live in the UK, talking about their experiences of being non-native speakers of English. Before you listen, check you understand the words in the glossary.

> **Glasgow** a large city in Scotland
>
> **BBC English / Standard English** English as spoken with a 'standard' pronunciation which corresponds to the pronunciation given in a dictionary
>
> **General American** US English as spoken with a 'standard' pronunciation which corresponds to the pronunciation given in a dictionary.
>
> **RP** (received pronunciation) the pronunciation of British English considered to be least regional, being originally that used by educated speakers in southern England
>
> **Scots** a way of speaking English typical in Scotland
>
> **Geordie** a way of speaking English typical from the area in and around Newcastle, in the north-east of England
>
> **University of Michigan** a university in the mid-west of the USA
>
> **The Simpsons** a very well-known US cartoon series

b Answer the following questions with a partner.

1 Do you find it easier to understand native or non-native speakers of English?

2 How do you feel about having your English corrected?

c **1.12** Now listen to Cristina and Zoltán answer the questions. What do they say? Who do you identify with most? Why?

Cristina   Zoltán

d Answer the following questions with a partner.

3 Do you have any funny or embarrassing stories related to misunderstanding someone?

4 Is there anything you still find difficult about English?

e **1.13** Now listen to Cristina and Zoltán answering the questions. What anecdotes do they tell? What do they still find difficult? Do you agree with them about what is difficult?

5 VOCABULARY   language terminology

a Match the words to their definitions.

> collocation   colloquial   an idiom   a metaphor
> a phrasal verb   register   slang   a synonym

1 __idiom__ *noun* a group of words whose meaning is different from the meanings of the individual words, e.g. *to put your foot in it* (= to say something inappropriate and embarrassing)

2 _____ *noun* a frequent combination of words in a language. Often they are the only possible combination to express a concept, e.g. *heavy rain* (not *strong* rain)

3 _____ *noun* the style of written or spoken language that is appropriate to the situation (formal, informal, neutral), e.g. *Can you lend me five quid?* (informal) *Should you require further assistance…* (formal)

4 __a phrasal verb__ *noun* a verb combined with an adverb or preposition, or sometimes both, to give a new meaning, e.g. *throw away, look for, make up for*

5 __slang__ *noun* very informal words and expressions that are more common in spoken language, especially used by a particular group of people, e.g. teenagers. They often go in and out of fashion very quickly. They can sometimes cause offence. *I had to walk home. I didn't have enough dosh (= money) for a taxi.*

6 __colloquial__ *adj.* (of language) words and phrases used in conversation or writing to friends but not in formal speech or writing, e.g. *kids* (= children), *you know what I mean*, etc.

7 __a synonym__ *noun* a word or expression that has the same or nearly the same meaning as another, e.g. *lately / recently*

8 _____ *noun* a word or phrase not used literally, but used to describe sb / sth in a more graphic way and to make the description more powerful, e.g. *When she heard the doorbell ring, she flew to open it.* (= she ran fast, she didn't literally *fly*)

b Do the **Language quiz** on page 15 with a partner. All the words and expressions are from File 1.

Language quiz

1 Idioms

Can you remember what these idioms mean?

1 If you really think you're right, you should *stick to your guns*.
2 When you talk to your boss, I think you ought to *speak your mind*.
3 It started to rain harder, but we *gritted our teeth* and carried on.
4 My husband and I *don't see eye to eye* about our children's education.
5 I don't think there's any doubt about who *wears the trousers* in their marriage!

2 Phrasal verbs

Replace the word or phrase in italics with a phrasal verb which means the same. Use the **bold** verb.

1 I've missed a few classes so I'll need to *get back to the same level as the other students*. **catch** _____
2 We'll have to *postpone* the meeting until next week. **put** _____
3 Your daughter doesn't *look or behave like* you at all! **take** _____
4 After her mother died, she was *cared for until she was older* by her grandmother. **bring** _____
5 My son wants to be a pilot when he *becomes an adult*. **grow** _____

3 Synonyms and register

a Match the words or expressions 1–8 with synonyms A–H.

1 one	☐	A follow
2 so	☐	B perks
3 because of	☐	C but
4 benefits	☐	D consequently
5 omit	☐	E you
6 however	☐	F owing to
7 adhere to	☐	G require
8 need	☐	H leave out

b Which word is more formal in each pair?

4 Collocation

Circle the right word in each pair.

1 I *quite / completely* disagree with you.
2 He really *hurt / damaged* my feelings when he criticized the way I dressed.
3 I'm very *near / close* to my cousin Claudia – we tell each other everything.
4 I've got some *distant / far* relatives in Australia, but I've never met them.
5 The main disadvantage of working here is that there's no job *safety / security*.

6 PRONUNCIATION sound–spelling relationships

According to research, when a non-native speaker is talking to another person in English, the main reason for a breakdown in communication is incorrect pronunciation, often the mispronunciation of individual sounds.

Although many people think that English pronunciation has no rules, especially as regards sounds and spelling, estimates suggest that around 80% of words are pronounced according to a rule or pattern.

a With a partner look at the groups of words and say them aloud. Are the pink letters all pronounced the same, or is one word different? Circle the different word if there is one.

1 /h/ hurt heir adhere hardly himself
2 /əʊ/ throw elbow lower power grow
3 /aɪ/ alike despite river transcribe quite
4 /w/ whenever why whose where which
5 /dʒ/ jealous journalist reject job enjoy
6 /tʃ/ change achieve machine catch charge
7 /s/ salary satisfying spontaneous synonym sure
8 /ɔː/ awful saw flaw drawback law
9 /ɔː/ short corner work ignore reporter
10 /ɜː/ firm dirty third T-shirt require

b 1.14 Listen and check. What's the pronunciation rule? Can you think of any more exceptions?

c Cover the phonetics and definitions, and use your instinct to say the words below. Then uncover and check the pronunciation and meaning.

whirl
/wɜːl/ *verb, noun* ■ *verb* **1** to move, or make sb/sth move around quickly in a circle or in a particular direction **SYN** SPIN

jaw
/dʒɔː/ *verb, noun* ■ *noun* **1** [C] either of the two bones at the bottom of the face that contain the teeth and move when you talk or eat

worship
/'wɜːʃɪp/ *noun, verb* ■ *noun* **1** [U] the practice of showing respect for God, or a god, by saying prayers, singing with others, etc.

hierarchy
/'haɪərɑːki/ *noun* ■ *noun* **1** [C, U] a system, especially in a society or organization, in which people are organized into different levels of importance from highest to lowest

Key success factors

- conveying a positive image of yourself without appearing arrogant
- using appropriate professional-sounding language
- avoiding basic mistakes which will make you look careless

ANALYSING A MODEL TEXT

a You see the following advertisement on a UK world music festival website. Would you be interested in applying for the job? Why (not)?

Stewards required to work at *Festival UK*, a well known world music festival event in the west of England from August 3rd to 7th.

Responsibilities

To ensure the safety and comfort of the public and to assist in the running of a successful festival.

To reduce any crowd-related problems, including maintaining a state of calm to minimize any injury.

To prevent unauthorized access to the site by members of the public.

Requirements

You must be aged 18 or over on the date of the festival and be eligible to work in the UK.

You must be fit and healthy and able to work in a demanding atmosphere.

You should have a high level of English, and some experience of dealing with the public.

How to apply

Email your CV to Emma Richards (E.Richards@festivalmail.co.uk).

b Read the first draft of an email written in response to the advertisement. What information does Kurt give in the three main paragraphs?

To:	E.Richards@festivalmail.co.uk
From:	Kurt Fischer
Subject:	Application

Dear ~~Miss~~ *Ms* Richards,

~~My name is Kurt Fischer.~~ I am writing to apply for the post of steward advertised ~~in~~ the Festival UK website.

I am a final year student at the University of Berlin and I am doing a degree in physical Education. I have a high level of spoken English (C1 on the CEFR), as I lived in the United States during six months as part of an exchange programm between my school and a High school in Utah. I had an American girlfriend during this period but we broke up when I came home.

As you will see from my CV, I have some relevant experience because I have worked for the last three summers helping to organize a tennis tournament in my town, Chemnitz. I was in charge of selling tickets at the entrance gate, so I am used to handing money and, on ocasion, having to refuse people entry. The tournament organizer would be happy to provide a reference. He is in fact distantly related to my mother.

I am very enthusiastic on world music, and would welcome the chance to be part of this event. I believe I would be suitable for the job advertised as, apart of my experience, I am a very cheerful and extrovert person and get on well with people. Friends describe me as being calm and pacient, and I think I would be able to cope if I had to deal with angry or difficult members of the public. I would definitely know how to look after myself if I got into a fight!

I attach a full CV, and if you require any further information, I would be happy to provide it. I would also be grateful if you could send me an information regarding acommodation during the festival.

I look forward to hearing from you.

Yours sincerely,

Kurt Fischer

Improving your first draft

Check your piece of writing for correct paragraphing, mistakes, irrelevant information, over-long sentences, and language which is in an inappropriate register.

c Read the draft again and try to improve it.

1 Cross out three sentences (not including the example) which are irrelevant or inappropriate.

2 Try to find and correct 12 mistakes in spelling (including capital letters), grammar, and vocabulary.

d Do you think the festival organizers would have given him an interview if he had sent his first draft?

USEFUL LANGUAGE

e Look at 1–10 below. Without looking back at the draft, can you remember how Kurt expressed these ideas in a less informal way? Use the **bold** word(s) to help you. Then look at the text again to check your answers.

1 This letter is to ask you to give me the job as a steward. **APPLY**

I am writing to apply for the post of steward.

2 I'm in my last year at uni and I'm doing PE. **FINAL YEAR / DEGREE**

_____

_____

3 I can speak English very well. **HIGH**

_____

_____

4 I've done this sort of job before. **RELEVANT**

_____

_____

5 My job was to sell tickets. **CHARGE**

_____

_____

6 I'd love to work at the festival. **WELCOME**

_____

_____

7 I think I'll be good at this job. **SUITABLE**

_____

_____

8 If you need to know anything else, I'll tell you. **REQUIRE / PROVIDE**

_____

_____

9 Let me have some information about accommodation. **GRATEFUL**

_____

_____

10 Hope to hear from you soon! **FORWARD**

_____

_____

PLANNING WHAT TO WRITE

Brainstorm the content

a Read the job advertisement below and underline the information you will need to respond to. Then make notes about

- what personal information you think you need to include.
- any relevant experience or qualifications you have.
- what aspects of your personality you think would make you suitable for the job, and how you could illustrate them.

Do you want to work for us?
Are you the right person for the job?

We are looking for fun, energetic, experienced people of any age to work as camp monitors at our day and residential summer camps in July and / or August. Children are aged between 7 and 15, and take part in a wide range of sports and activities from swimming and water sports to survival skills and cooking.

Do you enjoy working with children? Are you good at working in a team? Do you have any relevant experience or qualifications? Do you speak English either as a first language or fluently?

You can earn between £200 and £300 per week (food and accommodation provided). Minimum contract: one month.

Interested? Send an email, brief CV, and photo to Richard Cunningham at summercamp@bt.com

---

b Compare notes with a partner, and discuss how relevant you think each other's information is, what you think you should leave out, and what else you might want to include.

TIPS for writing a covering letter / email to apply for a job, grant, etc.
- Make sure you use appropriate sentences to open the letter.
- Organize the main body of the letter into clear paragraphs.
- Make sure you use a suitable style:

Don't use contractions or very informal expressions.

Use formal vocabulary where appropriate, e.g. *require* instead of *need*, *as* instead of *because*.

The use of a conditional can often make a request sound more polite, e.g. *I would be grateful if…, I would welcome the chance to…*
- When you say why you think you are suitable for the job, don't 'over-sell' yourself. Be factual and positive, but not arrogant.
- Make sure you use the appropriate phrases to close the letter.

WRITING

You have decided to apply for the job advertised above. Write a covering letter or email. It should be approximately 250 words.

DRAFT your letter.
- Write an introductory sentence to explain why you are writing.
- Paragraph 1: give relevant personal information.
- Paragraph 2: talk about relevant experience and qualifications you have.
- Paragraph 3: explain why you think you would be suitable for the job.
- Write a closing sentence.

EDIT the letter, cutting any irrelevant information, and making sure it is the right length.

CHECK the letter for mistakes in grammar, spelling, punctuation, and register.

THE INTERVIEW

a You are going to listen to an interview with David Shepherd, an amateur genealogist who, together with his wife, has spent many years researching his family tree. Before you listen, read the glossary and look at how the words are pronounced to help you understand what he says.

> **parish** /ˈpærɪʃ/ *noun* an area that has its own church and that a priest is responsible for
>
> **register** /ˈredʒɪstə/ *noun* a book containing an official record of names and items, e.g. births, marriages, and deaths
>
> **branch** /brɑːntʃ/ *noun* a part of a tree that grows out of the main stem; a group of members of a family that all have the same ancestor
>
> **(the 1911) census** /ˈsensəs/ *noun* the record of all the population (in this case of the UK in 1911), and where they were living, now available on the Internet
>
> **triplet** /ˈtrɪpləts/ *noun* one of three children born at the same time to the same mother
>
> **Dick Shepherd** /dɪk ˈʃepəd/ a famous highwayman (man who used to steal from travellers on public roads) who was executed in the early 18th century

b **1.15** Listen to part 1. Answer the questions with a partner.

1 What made him start researching his family history?
2 According to David, how should you start researching and what should you be careful of?
3 Why are marriage certificates particularly useful?
4 Why did pre-Internet research involve a lot of travelling?
5 How far back can people expect to get when they trace their family tree? What two factors usually make the task easier?
6 How far back has David researched his family? What two factors helped him?

c **1.16** Listen to part 2. Answer the questions with a partner.

What does he say about…?
1 the skeleton in the cupboard that he discovered
2 his emotions when he made the discovery
3 the difficulty of solving the mystery and the only hope of solving it
4 the other unexpected information he found out
5 Dick Shepherd, the highwayman

d **1.17** Listen and complete the phrases with two or three words. What do you think they mean?

COMMON EXPRESSIONS AND IDIOMS

1 …which was fun, but also vastly _____ - _____ , it's so much simpler now.
2 …you can usually get back to the _____ _____ …
3 …there's no, absolutely no way I can find out, so _____ _____ _____ .
4 You hate to give up on it and you _____ _____ _____ and think, 'Is there any way I could find out?'…
5 …there might be some possibility of seeing if they were around somewhere then, but that's a _____ _____ _____ .
6 …but if he is, I haven't got _____ _____ _____ …

e Why do you think David Shepherd's father never told him about his other brothers and sisters? Do you know of any families that have a skeleton in the cupboard?

IN THE STREET

a **1.18** You are going to hear four people talking about their family trees. What three questions do they answer? Who has personally done some research into their family tree? Who seems to know least about it?

| 1 | 2 | 3 | 4 |
| Sheila | Naomi | Tim | Jeremy |

b Listen again. Who…?

1 ☐☐ knows more about their family on their mother's side
2 ☐ thinks that one of their grandparents probably had a difficult life
3 ☐ is of mixed descent
4 ☐ has a parent who has done some research into the family tree
5 ☐ had a grandfather who had a very successful career
6 ☐ would like to know what pastimes one of their ancestors had
7 ☐ has a grandparent who left written records of their early life

c **1.19** Listen and complete the phrases with two or three words. What do you think they mean?

COMMON PHRASES

1 Not _____ _____ _____ actually.
2 Probably my grandfather on my father's side – he died when I was _____ _____ .
3 I think my grandmother on my mother's side also did some research _____ _____ _____ .
4 …we've done some research on my mother's side, less on my father's side, which is _____ _____ _____ a mystery.

d Answer the questions in **a** with a partner.

 **Study Link** MultiROM

Revise & Check

GRAMMAR

a Complete the sentences with one word.

1 Everybody seemed to enjoy the barbecue even _____ the weather wasn't very summery.

2 Will the person who has left one of _____ personal belongings at the security check please go back and collect it?

3 If you've _____ to be at the airport at 7.00, you ought to call the taxi now.

4 This street looks so different from when I was a child. Didn't _____ use to be a sweetshop on the corner?

5 If we lived a bit nearer _____ another, we'd probably spend more time together.

6 The Chinese economy is growing and _____ a result the standard of living in China is rising.

7 I always find Maggie rather reserved – she never talks about _____.

8 She wore a baggy dress _____ people wouldn't notice that she had put on weight.

9 We need to _____ the heating repaired soon, before it starts getting cold.

10 We were very delayed _____ of an accident on the motorway.

b Rewrite the sentences using the **bold** word(s).

1 I've broken my glasses. I need to pay someone to mend them. **HAVE**
I've broken my glasses. I need _____.

2 If you learn a few phrases, the local people will appreciate it. **ONE**
_____ the local people will appreciate it.

3 They managed to get to the meeting on time even though the traffic was heavy. **DESPITE**
They managed to get to the meeting on time _____.

4 It was foggy so the flight was cancelled. **DUE**
The flight _____.

5 Jane sees Martha about twice a month. **EACH**
Jane and Martha _____ about twice a month.

6 The children managed to wrap the present on their own. **BY**
The children managed to wrap the present _____.

7 The last time I saw him was in 1998. **SEEN**
I _____ 1998.

8 She wore dark glasses so that she wouldn't be recognized. **SO AS**
She wore dark glasses _____.

9 If we buy a dishwasher, it won't be necessary to do the washing-up. **HAVE**
If we buy a dishwasher _____.

10 She doesn't have any pictures yet so her flat looks a bit bare. **GOT**
She _____ so her flat looks a bit bare.

VOCABULARY

a Complete the idioms.

1 I know you don't want my mother to come and stay, but you'll just have to grit your _____ and put up with it.

2 Don't worry about what other people think. You need to know your own _____.

3 He's got a terrible temper. In fact it must _____ in the family, because his dad's just the same.

4 Jane definitely wears the _____ in that marriage. Tom lets her walk all over him.

5 I know I'm right and even if everyone in the company disagrees I'm going to stick to my _____!

6 My brothers are always falling out. In fact they're not on speaking _____ at the moment.

b Circle the right word.

1 She'd like to have a *career / profession* in show business.

2 It's a *part-time / temporary* job – I only work mornings.

3 Your sisters are so *like / alike* – they could be twins!

4 My father remarried and had two girls with his second wife, so I've got two *half-sisters / stepsisters*.

5 She doesn't *take after / look like* either of her parents. She's quite reserved, and they're both really outgoing.

6 'Pay' is a *synonym / metaphor* for 'salary', but it's more informal.

c Complete with the right preposition or adverb.

1 Who's in charge _____ the sales conference this year?

2 She's been _____ school for such a long time it will be hard to catch _____ with the others when she goes back.

3 My mother was quite ill when I was a child so I was mainly brought _____ by my grandmother.

4 Can we put the meeting _____ till next week? I've got too much work on at the moment.

5 If you go and talk to Marion, she'll fill you _____ about how the sales campaign has gone.

6 I think we need to deal _____ this situation head _____. It's no good just hoping it will go away.

d Complete the sentences with an adjective formed from the **bold** verb.

1 I'm really excited about my new post. It's _____ but I'm sure that I am going to enjoy it. **CHALLENGE**

2 They're a very _____ family – you don't ever want to play cards with them! **COMPETE**

3 They set up an IT company, but it was _____ and it closed down last year. **SUCCEED**

4 She was a very _____ teenager and was always arguing with her parents. **REBEL**

5 The annual family get-together was actually quite _____ this year. **ENJOY**

6 I do the same thing every day. It's an incredibly _____ job. **REPEAT**

2 A

G the past: narrative tenses, *used to* and *would*
V word building: abstract nouns
P word stress with suffixes

'When you finally go back to your old hometown, you find it wasn't the old home you missed but your childhood.'

Sam Ewing, US writer

Once upon a time

1 READING

a Read some extracts from a book called *When we were young*, where different people recall aspects of their childhood. Choose the heading which best fits each text. There are three headings you don't need.

Christmas   Fears   First love   Food
School holidays   Illness   Nightmares   School
Sundays   Toys and games

When we were young

1

My bad dreams were of two kinds, those about spectres and those about insects. The second were, beyond comparison, the worse: to this day I would rather meet a ghost than a tarantula.

C.S. Lewis British author of *The Chronicles of Narnia*

2

I was one of a group of boys who sat on the floor of our professor's office for a weekly lesson in 'spoken English'. One day the professor put a large sheet of white paper on the wall. The paper had a little black dot on the right-hand corner. When the professor asked, 'Boys, what do you see?' we all shouted together 'A black dot!' The professor stepped back and said, 'So, not a single one of you saw the white sheet of paper. You only saw the black dot. This is the awful thing about human nature. People never see the goodness of things, and the broader picture. Don't go through life with that attitude.'

    Life teaches you lessons in surprising ways and when you least expect it. One of the most important lessons I ever learned came from a sheet of paper and a black dot. They may seem like small things, but they were enough to prompt big changes in my outlook on life.

Kofi Annan Ghanaian ex-Secretary-General of the United Nations

3

As a child my idea of the West was that it was a miasma of poverty and misery, like that of the homeless 'Little Match Girl' in the Hans Christian Andersen story. When I was at boarding school and did not want to finish my food, the teacher would say, 'Think of all the starving children in the capitalist world.'

Jung Chang Chinese author of *Wild Swans*

4

On wet days there was Mathilde. Mathilde was a large American rocking horse which had been given to my sister and brother when they were children in America. Mathilde had a splendid action – much better than that of any English rocking horse I have ever known. She sprang forwards and back, upwards and down, and ridden at full pressure was liable to unseat you. Her springs, which needed oiling, made a terrific groaning, and added to the pleasure and danger. Splendid exercise again. No wonder I was a skinny child.

Agatha Christie British author of detective fiction

---

miasma /miˈæzmə/ a mass of dirty, bad-smelling air (used metaphorically here) (Para 3)
boarding school a school where children live during the year (Para 3)
tea (here) a light meal eaten in the afternoon or early evening (Para 5)
cod liver oil oil from the liver of a cod (a kind of fish) which contains a lot of vitamin A and vitamin D, often given as a medicine (Para 7)

From *When we were young: a compendium of childhood* compiled by John Burningham

LEXIS IN CONTEXT

b Read the texts again carefully. Find a synonym in each paragraph for…

1 _____ (literary) ghosts
2 _____ attitude towards
3 _____ unhappiness
4 _____ (old-fashioned) excellent
_____ likely to
_____ it's not surprising
_____ (informal, usually disapproving) very thin
5 _____ a ceremony
6 _____ (formal) tell off
7 _____ bacteria

> A good dictionary will give information about the register of a word, e.g. *formal, informal, literary, old-fashioned, taboo*, etc. When you record new vocabulary, write down this information too.

5

Tea was always ready for our arrival, and after the long journey we were always made to get that meal over before doing anything else. Then 'May I get down?' and we were free in paradise, sniffing remembered smells as we ran about making sure that familiar things were still in their places. I used first of all to race down to the lake. I had a private rite to perform. Without letting the others know what I was doing, I had to dip my hand in the water, as a greeting to the beloved lake, or as proof to myself that I had indeed come home.

Arthur Ransome British author of *Swallows and Amazons* and other children's books

6

My family still laughs at the story, which I remember well, of when I was five years old in Berlin, and arranged to run away with a little boy because I had been scolded. They watched me pack my clothes and go down the stairs. The little boy, six or seven, was waiting round the corner.

Anaïs Nin French author

7

My mother was always frightened of us catching germs. Every day she used to give us all a good dose of cod liver oil. My brother Jimmy would refuse, but she used to hold his nose until it went down. Afterwards we all got a piece of apple, and then we went to school.

Kathleen Cassidy British tea lady

c Read the extracts again and answer the questions.

1 What was C. S. Lewis most scared of?
2 How do you think the lesson changed Kofi Annan's outlook on life?
3 Where did Jung Chang get her idea that the West was very poor?
4 Why was Agatha Christie's rocking horse better than an English one?
5 What was Arthur Ransome's 'rite', and why did he do it?
6 How did Anaïs Nin's parents react when she tried to run away?
7 Why do you think Kathleen Cassidy's mother used to give the children a piece of apple?

d With a partner cover the extracts and look at the headings. Try to remember what each writer said. Which paragraph reminds you most of your own childhood? Why?

2 GRAMMAR narrative tenses, *used to* and *would*

a Look at the paragraphs again. Which ones are about…?
1 specific incidents in the past
2 repeated or habitual actions in the past

b Look at the verbs in paragraphs 6 and 7 again. What three past tenses are used to describe the incident in paragraph 6? What verb forms are used to show that the actions were habitual or repeated in 7?

c ➔ p.139 **Grammar Bank 2A.** Read the rules and do the exercises.

3 SPEAKING & WRITING

a **2.1** Listen to five people starting to talk about their childhood. What are the different expressions they use to say (approximately) how old they were at the time?

b Look at the headings in exercise **1a**. With a partner, for each heading talk about things you habitually did or felt in your childhood.

> When I was little I used to be terrified of the dark, and I'd always sleep with the light on…

c Now take turns to choose a heading and talk about a specific incident from your childhood.

> I remember the time when we went on our first family holiday abroad…

d Imagine you were asked to contribute to the book *When we were young*. Choose one of the headings and write a paragraph either about a specific incident in your childhood, or about things which happened habitually.

4 LISTENING & SPEAKING

a   **2.2**   Listen to five people talking about their earliest memory. Match the speakers to the emotion they felt at the time.

surprise ☐   sadness ☐   fear ☐   disappointment ☐   happiness ☐

b   Listen again. How old was each person? What was their memory?

c   Now you're going to hear about some research which has been done into first memories. Before you listen, discuss the following questions with a partner.

    1   How far back in our lives can we usually remember?
       a   To when we were a baby (0–2 years old)
       b   To when we were a toddler (2–4 years)
       c   To when we were a small child (5+)
    2   Why can't we remember things before that age?
    3   What kind of a) emotions and b) events might people be more likely to remember?
    4   Are our first memories mostly visual or of sounds and smells?
    5   Why might some people's first memories be unreliable?

d   **2.3**   Listen and check your answers with what the speaker says. Were you surprised by anything?

e   **2.4**   Now listen to the story of Jean Piaget's first memory and write down what you think are the key words. Listen again and try to add more detail. Compare your words with a partner and then together retell the story.

f   Talk to a partner.

Do you have any very early memories of the feelings or incidents below? Do you know approximately how old you were at the time?

feeling surprised
feeling pain
feeling shame or embarrassment
the birth of a brother or sister
a day out
managing to do something for the first time
the death of a pet
a festival or celebration
getting a wonderful or disappointing present

5 VOCABULARY & PRONUNCIATION
word building: abstract nouns; word stress with suffixes

> An abstract noun is one which is used to express an idea, a concept, an experience, or a quality, rather than an object. Thus *embarrassment* or *memory* are abstract nouns, whereas *bed* or *trousers* are not. Some abstract nouns are uncountable in English, but may not be in your language, e.g. *knowledge*.

a Make abstract nouns from the words below and put them in the right columns.

adult	afraid	ashamed	believe	bored	celebrate	child	compete
dead	free	friend	happy	hate	imagine	ill	kind	lose
member	neighbour	partner	poor	relation	sad	wise

+hood	+ship	+dom

+ness	+tion	word changes

b **2.5** Underline the stressed syllable in these words. Listen and check. Which ending(s) cause(s) a change in stress?

1 adult adulthood
2 celebrate celebration
3 compete competition
4 free freedom
5 happy happiness
6 relation relationship

c With a partner, guess which of the abstract nouns in **a** is missing from each quotation.

1 ❛Love, friendship and respect do not unite people as much as a common _____ for something.❜
Anton Chekhov, Russian writer

2 ❛_____ is, of all passions, that which weakens the judgement most.❜
Cardinal de Retz, French churchman and writer

3 ❛To be without some of the things you want is an indispensable part of _____.❜
Bertrand Russell, British philosopher

4 ❛_____ is more important than knowledge.❜
Albert Einstein, physicist

5 ❛Overcoming _____ is not a gesture of charity. It is an act of justice.❜
Nelson Mandela, South African statesman

6 ❛There are only two emotions in a plane: _____ and terror.❜
Orson Welles, US film director

7 ❛I enjoy convalescence. It is the part that makes _____ worthwhile.❜
George Bernard Shaw, Irish dramatist

8 ❛The enemies of _____ do not argue. They shout and they shoot.❜
William Inge, British churchman and writer

d Say in your own words what the quotations mean. Do you agree with them?

'Half our life is spent trying to find something to do with
the time we have rushed through life trying to save.'

Will Rogers, US humorist

Are there really 31 hours in a day?

1 READING & SPEAKING

a Talk to a partner.

1 Which of the following do you do? To what extent do you think doing one thing affects how well you do the other?

- Talk on a hands-free mobile while you are driving.
- Talk on the phone while you are doing housework or cooking.
- Check your emails or chat online while you are working or studying.
- Look at a website while you are having a conversation on the phone.
- Listen to music while you are studying / working.
- Listen to music while you are doing exercise.
- Send a text while talking to a friend.

2 Are there any other activities you do simultaneously?

3 Have you ever made a mistake or had an accident because you were multitasking?

4 Do you think multitasking helps you to use your time better?

b Work in pairs, **A** and **B**. You are going to read different articles about new research into multitasking. Read your texts and be ready to tell your partner about the following:

- what the research has shown
- what sort of multitasking people do
  a) during the day b) during the evening
- Mark Vickery and his wife's experience
- what he thinks the pros and cons are

- a typical teenager's attitude to multitasking
- what the research has shown about multitasking
- what things we can do successfully simultaneously
- what happens when people try to do two or more related tasks simultaneously
- problems that arise from multitasking when you are driving

c Now tell each other the main points in the articles you have just read.

A

Multitasking = 31/7

1 Latest research suggests that typical middle-class city-dwellers now have so many time-saving gadgets that they can fit into 24 hours the same quantity of tasks that a decade ago would have taken 31 hours to complete.

2 For many people, the frenzy starts over breakfast, reading emails on a hand-held BlackBerry® while making toast. It carries on in the car where a driver with a Bluetooth® earpiece holds a conference call while keeping an ear on the radio and checking the satnav.

3 Work is then a blizzard of emails, phone calls, and meetings, often happening simultaneously. However, according to OTX, an American consumer research organization, the most intense period of multitasking appears to be in the evening. 'People will be pressing the television remote control while using a wireless laptop computer balanced on their knee, emailing and texting friends on a mobile phone, and holding a conversation with friends or family members,' said Patrick Moriarty, one of the authors of the report. 'They may be far more mentally engaged than they are in the office.'

4 According to the study, while television remains the main focus of attention in the evening, nearly half the respondents were also using computers and phones to catch up with friends, update their Facebook or other social networks, or download and listen to music.

5 Mark Vickery, 35, from Medway, Kent, agreed that for him and his wife Susan, an NHS doctor, the evening was the peak of multitasking. 'Both of us are out of the house during the day,' said Vickery, a marketing manager. 'When we come back in the evening we tend to have a lot of technology on the go. We'll be using online banking, Facebook, and email, and programming the TV shows we want to watch later.

6 'On the one hand it's good – you get more done. On the other hand, when I left university seven years ago, life was much simpler. There was more talking face-to-face and more time spent over dinner.'

BlackBerry® hand-held device which makes available email, mobile phone, web browsing, etc.

Bluetooth® technology that makes it possible for various devices and peripherals to communicate with each other and with the Internet without the need for cables

satnav a navigation system that receives information via satellite

From *The Times*

The great myth of multitasking

1 You open the door to your teenage daughter's room. 'What are you doing?' you ask.

'Nothing much,' she answers. 'Burning a CD, doing my homework, helping Jade with hers on MSN…'

'All at the same time?'

'Sure, it's easy.'

2 While your daughter may be convinced that she can do all these things at the same time, a number of recently published neuroscience research papers argue that this is not in fact the case. Apparently what is really happening is that our brains juggle these tasks, rapidly switching from one to the other and choosing a sequence in which to do them.

3 This may seem counter-intuitive. Multitasking is a perfectly natural everyday occurrence. We can cook the dinner while engrossed in a soap on TV or we can chat to a friend while walking down the street without bumping into anybody or getting run over. However, research suggests that there is an enormous difference between how the brain can deal with what are referred to as 'highly practised tasks', such as stirring or walking, and how it responds when, for example, you think about adding another ingredient or you decide to change the direction in which you are walking. In this case, our brains will require us to concentrate on the activity at hand.

4 The problem, it seems, occurs when human beings try to carry out two or more tasks that are in some way related. We can see the effect of this if we look at what happens when people use mobile phones while driving (even if they are hands-free). Most people feel they are capable of driving and having a conversation at the same time. This is fine until they need to process language while driving, for example on a road sign. Then the language channel of the brain gets clogged and the brain can no longer cope. A similar thing occurs if the conversation turns to something visual, for example your friend describing what their new flat looks like. In this case, as you try to imagine what they are describing, the visual channel of the brain is overloaded and you can no longer concentrate on the road.

5 David E Meyer, director of the Brain, Cognition, and Action laboratory at the University of Michigan, who is considered to be one of the world's experts in this field, believes that human beings 'will never, ever be able to overcome the inherent limitations in the brain for processing information during multitasking. It just can't be done, any more than the best of all humans will ever be able to run a one-minute mile.'

> **MSN** here refers to *MSN messenger*, an online instant messaging service
>
> **a soap** *informal* a soap opera

LEXIS IN CONTEXT

d Work with the same partner. Find words which mean:

A

1 _____ *noun* a small tool or device that does something useful (Para 1)

2 _____ *noun* a state of great activity (Para 2)

3 _____ *noun* a snowstorm, a large quantity of things that may seem to be attacking you (Para 3)

4 _____ **PHR V** find out what people have been doing, get their latest news (Para 4)

5 _____ *noun* the top of a mountain, the point when sb / sth is best, highest, or strongest (Para 5)

B

6 _____ *verb* to throw a set of three or more objects in the air and catch and throw them again quickly, one at a time, to try to deal with two or more activities at the same time (Para 2)

7 _____ *adj.* so interested in sth that you give it all your attention (Para 3)

8 _____ *verb* to deal successfully with sth difficult (Para 4)

9 _____ *verb* block (Para 4)

10 _____ *verb* to succeed in dealing with a problem that has been preventing you from achieving sth (Para 5)

> **Metaphors**
>
> When you look up a word in the dictionary, the first meaning(s) listed will normally be the literal meaning(s) and metaphorical meanings will be listed later. However, if you know the literal meaning of a word or phrase you can often guess the metaphorical meaning in a text, e.g. if you know the literal meaning of *blizzard* you can easily understand the metaphor *a blizzard of emails*.

e After reading the two articles, do you think that multitasking saves you time, or are you probably wasting time by doing things less effectively? Give examples from your own experience.

2 GRAMMAR distancing

a Look at the highlighted phrases in the two articles. What do they have in common?

b ⊙ **p.140 Grammar Bank 2B.** Read the rules and do the exercises.

c You are a journalist. Your editor has asked you to write a paragraph about one of the news stories whose headlines are below. However, she has asked you to be careful what you say, as the facts haven't been confirmed yet. Choose one story and write a paragraph of approximately 100 words.

EATING CHIPS HELPS YOU STUDY BETTER!

Footballer's wife seeks divorce

POLITICIAN LINKED TO CHARITY SCANDAL

Is jungle plant the key to eternal youth?

a Read the information about a radio phone-in show. Who or what are the 'Time Bandits'?

The Time Bandits

They creep up on us when we least expect it and steal one of the things we value most – our time. They are the time bandits – the people (and situations) that waste our precious minutes and make life even more of a rush.

> **How can we stop the time bandits?**
>
> Call our expert, Richard Anderson, and tell us about your 'time bandits' and find out how to deal with them.

b **2.6** Before you listen to the whole programme, listen and complete some extracts.

1 I think that's a common problem _____ of us.
2 _____ don't complain out loud…
3 _____ I've got this friend of mine and…
4 _____ on time.
5 It's just _____ time.
6 It's been _____ to you…

c Read the information about linking. Then look back at the extracts. Which words are linked? Why? Now practise saying the sentences and phrases trying to link the words.

> **Linking**
>
> When people talk quickly, they usually link words together, i.e. the sound at the end of one word is linked to the sound at the beginning of the next. Being aware of linking will help you understand rapid speech better, and make your own English sound more natural. Some of the rules for linking words are:
>
> 1 A consonant sound at the end of a word is linked to a vowel sound at the beginning of the next, e.g. *I met him a long time ago.*
>
> 2 When a word ending in -r or -re (e.g. are) is followed by a word beginning with a vowel sound, an /r/ sound is added to link the words together, e.g. *We're early.*
>
> 3 When a word ending with a consonant sound is followed by a word beginning with the same consonant sound, one long consonant sound is made, e.g. *I need some more time.*

d **2.7** Now listen to five callers to the radio show. Write a sentence to summarize their problem.

Caller 1 *She wastes a lot of time talking to a friend on the phone.*
Advice ☐

Caller 2 _____
Advice ☐

Caller 3 _____
Advice ☐

Caller 4 _____
Advice ☐

Caller 5 _____
Advice ☐

e With a partner, imagine you are the expert. Discuss and decide what advice you might give the five callers.

f **2.8** Now listen to the expert's advice (A–E), and match them to the problems.

g **2.9** Listen to the whole programme and check your answers to **f**. Was any of the expert's advice similar to yours? What differences were there?

h Do you have any 'time bandits'? What do you do about them? Are there any ideas in the advice the expert gave that you might use?

4 VOCABULARY expressions with *time*

a Can you remember the missing words in these sentences?

1 …w__m_t_l____ my **time** really, waiting for people.
2 I have kids and I work full time, so as you can imagine I don't have much **sp**_____ **time**.
3 My friend swears it **s**_____ her **a lot of time**.
4 Tell them you're a bit **s**_____ **of time** today.
5 Right, I'm afraid **time's u**_____ for now, but thank you all for your calls…

b 2.10 Listen to the extracts and check. What do the expressions mean?

c 🔵 **p.159 Vocabulary Bank** *time*.

5 SPEAKING

Work with a partner and answer the questions in the *Time questionnaire*.

Time questionnaire

About you

🕐 On a typical weekday morning, are you normally pushed for time?

🕐 Do you have any electronic gadgets which you think really save you time?

🕐 What do you usually do to kill time when you're waiting at an airport or at a station?

🕐 When you go shopping, do you like to buy things as quickly as possible or do you prefer to take your time?

🕐 Is there anything or anybody who is taking up a lot of your time at the moment?

🕐 Are you usually on time when you meet friends? Does it bother you when other people aren't on time?

🕐 Do you like to get to the airport or station with time to spare or at the last minute?

🕐 When you were younger, did your parents give you a hard time if you came back home late?

🕐 When you do an exam, do you tend to have time left at the end or do you usually run out of time?

Do you agree?

🕐 Both partners need to take the same amount of time off when they have a baby.

🕐 Retired people have too much time on their hands. They should be encouraged to carry on working longer.

🕐 Everyone would benefit from seeing a psychotherapist from time to time.

🕐 By the time they are 21, all young people should be living independently of their parents.

🕐 It's only a question of time before governments impose a complete ban on alcohol and smoking.

2 C

G *get*
V phrases with *get*
P words and phrases of French origin

'Don't get mad, get everything.'
Ivana, ex-wife of millionaire Donald Trump, giving advice to wronged wives

50 ways to leave your lover

1 READING & SPEAKING

a Read 10 top break-up lines from a website. Which one do you think is the best / worst way of starting a break-up conversation?

> 'We need to talk.'

> 'It's not you; it's me.'

> 'When I said I was working late, I was lying.'

> 'Do you remember when I said that everything was all right…?'

> 'You are like a brother / sister to me.'

> 'I think we'd be better off as friends.'

> 'I don't love you any more.'

> 'I need some time to be on my own.'

> 'You're a fantastic person, but you're too good for me.'

> 'Can I have my keys back, please?'

b Now read three true stories about people getting revenge on a former partner. Answer the questions with a partner. Whose revenge do you think was…?

1 the most ingenious
2 the most satisfying
3 the most embarrassing for the person it was done to
4 the least justifiable
5 the most likely to have a long-lasting effect

LEXIS IN CONTEXT

c Read the stories again and choose the right word or phrase for gaps 1–12.

1	a rejected	b dumped	c broke up
2	a turning	b putting	c creating
3	a praised	b blamed	c ridiculed
4	a replaced	b substituted	c revived
5	a unwillingly	b obviously	c unbearably
6	a stuck	b attached	c posted
7	a invented	b created	c made up
8	a peak	b top	c crowning
9	a get over	b get back	c get rid of
10	a found	b made	c took
11	a set off	b set about	c set up
12	a chopped up	b stamped on	c smashed

Getting your

'Hell hath no fury like a woman scorned' according to the 17th century English playwright and poet William Congreve, and it remains as true today as it was then.

1 What do you do when love has run its course? How do you say 'it's over'? According to singer Paul Simon, 'There must be 50 ways to leave your lover'. Some years ago, fellow singer Phil Collins infamously [1]_____ his second wife by fax. In these more technologically advanced days the Finnish Prime Minister recently broke up with his mistress by SMS. Less cowardly is the face-to-face approach ('We need to talk' / 'This just isn't working' / 'I love you like a friend', etc.).

When Frenchwoman, Sophie Calle received an email on her mobile, she was devastated to discover that it was a message of *adieu* in which her partner claimed that the break-up would 'hurt me more than it will hurt you.' Here is a short extract:

'Whatever happens, you must know that I will never stop loving you in my own way – the way I've loved you ever since I've known you, which will stay part of me, and never die… I wish things had turned out differently. Take care of yourself…'

With hindsight, the man almost certainly wishes that he had followed his first instinct ('It seems to me it would be better to say what I have to say to you face-to-face'), particularly as the woman he was dumping is a conceptual artist who specializes in [2]_____ private pain into art. And that is exactly what she did with her 'Dear Sophie' email.

Too heartbroken to reply, she decided she would 'take care of herself' by sending the man's email to 107 women (including an actress, a poet, a ballet dancer, a singer, a novelist, a psychotherapist, an etiquette consultant, an editor, a policewoman, and even a schoolgirl). She asked all of them to read the email and to analyse it or interpret it according to their job while she filmed or photographed the result. The psychiatrist concluded that the man was a 'twisted manipulator' while the etiquette consultant criticized his manners, and the editor [3]_____ his grammar and syntax.

'The idea came to me very quickly. At first it was therapy, then art took over. After a month, I had got over him. There was no suffering. The project had [4]_____ the man.'

The resulting exhibition *'Prenez soin de vous'* ('Take care of yourself') was put on at the Bibliothèque Nationale in Paris and was later a huge success at the Venice Biennale. And after becoming, [5]_____, the notorious 'star' of an exhibition, it's a sure bet that when Sophie's ex-lover dumps his girlfriends in the future, he will never ever say 'Take care of yourself.'

own back

2 Perhaps, when she embarked on a relationship with a famous composer, actress Jane Slavin was right to wonder if things were too good to be true.

Jane first ⁶_____ a message on his Facebook page last July. It said, 'You are one of my favourite composers'.

He instantly replied, and within minutes he had added her to a list of cyber 'friends'. Later he emailed her asking for a date. 'He invited me to a concert and it went on from there. It was an amazing adventure,' she says. 'It all seemed so magical to be with someone so hugely talented.' However, three months into their relationship, he simply stopped emailing her. 'It went from 30 emails a day to nothing. No phone call, no texts, no emails. I thought he'd died!' So, suddenly and inexplicably rejected, Jane returned to the Internet.

'I put the words "lovely lady" into Google and downloaded a stunning-looking photograph of a woman and I gave her a name, Lucia. I then ⁷_____ a MySpace page for her, and emailed him. The email from 'Lucia' said, 'I don't have any friends on MySpace. I'm a great fan of your music. Will you be my friend?' By the end of the first day, he had sent her more than 100 emails.

The ⁸_____ moment of her revenge came when 'Lucia' agreed to a rendezvous in a little café in London. At the appointed time Jane walked in and said, 'Hi, how are you? I've not heard from you for ages'. He looked horrified.

'He said he was meeting a new PA. I said, "Do you mind if I sit down?" and he said, "Yes, I do, she's going to be here any minute now". I said, "I'll sit down for just a second". I opened my bag and pulled out copies of all his messages to Lucia. When he asked, "Is she a friend of yours?" I leant across the table and whispered to him, "Lucia is all Jane".

'Lucia was my revenge,' says Jane. 'It helped me ⁹_____ him. I have no regrets.'

3 Who can forget the spectacular way in which Sarah Graham-Moon ¹⁰_____ revenge on her ex-husband Sir Peter, the fifth baronet, after seeing his blue BMW parked in the driveway of a 42-year-old blonde?

She promptly poured a can of white paint over the car – but that was only the beginning. Ten days later, she ¹¹_____ 'altering' his clothes. According to Sir Peter's own account, she cut ten centimetres off the left arm of 32 of his Savile Row suits, jackets and overcoats – some of which had cost him £1,000 or more. For good measure, she ¹²_____ a box containing 25 Havana cigars, flattening the lot of them, and threw another six boxes of the Montecristo No 2s out of the window.

But still Lady Graham-Moon hadn't finished. A week later, she went on a bizarre 'milk-round', distributing 24 bottles of his finest vintage wine and port on doorsteps in the village where the woman lived. 'It gave me a hell of a buzz,' she said.

> **Savile Row** a street in London with many shops that sell expensive clothes for men that are often specially made for each person
>
> **milk round** (in Britain) the job of going from house to house regularly, delivering milk

d Without looking back at the stories, try to remember what these numbers refer to.

50	107	30	more than 100
42	32	1,000	25	24

e Look at some famous sayings about revenge. Which saying do you think best fits each of the three stories in **b**? Do you agree with any of them?

'Revenge is sweet.'

'Revenge is a dish best served cold.'

'In revenge, woman is more barbarous than man.'

'An eye for an eye makes the whole world blind.'

2 PRONUNCIATION
words and phrases of French origin

> A number of French words and phrases are used in English. They are usually said in a way that is close to their French pronunciation, and so do not necessarily follow normal English pronunciation patterns, e.g. *ballet* (/ˈbæleɪ/), *rendezvous* (/ˈrɒndeɪvuː/). These words will appear in a good English dictionary.

a Look at the sentences below, and underline a French word or expression in each one. What do you think they mean? Do you use any of them in your language?

1 I made a real faux pas when I mentioned his ex-wife.
2 When we were introduced I had a sense of déjà vu, though I knew we'd never met before.
3 For our first date, he took me to a concert of avant-garde music – there was no second date.
4 She's engaged to a well-known local entrepreneur.
5 I know it's a cliché, but it really was love at first sight.
6 On our anniversary, he always buys a huge bouquet of flowers – he's so predictable!
7 I met Jane's fiancé last night. They told me they're getting married next year.

b **2.11** Listen and focus on how the French expressions are pronounced. Then practise saying the sentences.

3 VOCABULARY   phrases with *get*

a Can you remember expressions with *get* from the texts in **1** which mean…?
a take revenge on someone
b recover from (a broken relationship with someone)

b ⊙ **p.160 Vocabulary Bank** *get*.

4   2.12   SONG ♫ *50 Ways to Leave Your Lover*

5 SPEAKING & LISTENING

a Look at the back cover information of a new book. Then discuss the questions below with a partner. Why is the book called *Love by Numbers*?

b **2.13** Listen to some extracts from *Love by Numbers*, in which the author talks about the research which has been done into the above topics. According to the research what are the correct answers to the questions in **a**?

c Listen again and answer the questions below.

1 What two examples are given to show how friends can strengthen a couple's relationship?

2 What three causes of dispute in a car are mentioned? Which one is becoming less common?

3 What do psychologists say about 'love being blind'?

4 What are the main advantages and disadvantages of online dating? What three pieces of advice are given about posting a profile on a dating site?

5 What percentage of people still thought about their first loves? What percentage of people already in a relationship got involved with their first love again after having got back in touch?

6 According to the Canadian study, what are the most popular ways of taking revenge?

d To what extent did the research back up your discussions in **a**? Were you surprised by any of the statistics?

LOVE BY NUMBERS

Is your relationship unlikely to succeed if your friends dislike your partner?

Where is the most common place for couples to have an argument?

Do opposites really attract?

How successful is Internet dating?

Should you try to get back in touch with an ex?

Does taking revenge on an ex-partner make you feel better?

There is academic research out there that can answer these questions: Dr Luisa Dillner, author of the Guardian column 'Love by Numbers', has sifted through it to give you the facts about flirting, dating, marrying, cheating and much more…

Popular Psychology

LEXIS IN CONTEXT

e **2.14** Listen again to some extracts and complete the expressions with two words. What do you think the expressions mean?

1 When friends tell a couple that they are a _____ _____ and how much they enjoy going out with them…

2 … suggesting that you can _____ _____ anyone, should you get the chance to meet them.

3 Most people also _____ _____ someone as good-looking or as plain as they are.

4 After three months you can 'see' again, and then you usually _____ _____ the person.

5 A study in the US of over 3,000 adults found that 15% knew someone in a _____-_____ relationship that had started online.

6 The biggest _____-_____, apparently, is profiles with poor spelling.

7 80% of these people finished up _____ _____ with their lost love again.

8 Another study by Stephen Hoshimura at the University of Montana asked people what act of revenge they had _____ _____…

6 GRAMMAR *get*

a Look at some sentences from the listening, which all have the verb *get*. Answer the questions with a partner.

  A Online agencies advise **getting** a photo taken where you look friendly, rather than seductive.

  B In another study by Dr Nancy Kalish, California State University **got** randomly selected American adults to agree to be interviewed about their first loves.

  C Also when a couple stays together for a while, their two groups of friends start to make friends with each other, and as a result the couple's relationship **gets** stronger.

In which sentence…?
  1 ☐ does *get* mean *become*
  2 ☐ does *get* mean *make* or *persuade*
  3 ☐ could you replace *get* with *have* with no change in meaning

b ◐ **p.141 Grammar Bank 2C.** Read the rules and do the exercises.

c Read the *get* questionnaire and tick ten questions you'd like to ask someone else in the class. Ask and answer in pairs.

get **questionnaire**

☐ Are you the kind of person who regularly **gets rid of** old clothes or do you tend to keep things for ever?

☐ Did you use to **get into trouble** a lot when you were a child?

☐ Do you consider yourself a person who usually **gets their own way**? Why (not)?

☐ Do you tend to keep up to date with your work or studies or do you often **get behind**?

☐ Do you think young drivers **get stopped** by the police more than older drivers? Do you think this is fair?

☐ Have you ever **got caught** cheating in an exam? Have you ever cheated in an exam and **got away with it**?

☐ Do you think going on holiday together is a good way to <u>really</u> **get to know** people?

☐ Have you ever **got the wrong end of the stick** when you were speaking to someone in English?

☐ How often and where do you normally **get your hair cut**?

☐ If one of your gadgets or electrical appliances breaks down, do you normally try to fix it yourself first or do you immediately phone to **get an expert to fix it**?

☐ If you are meeting someone, do you usually **get there** on time, or are you normally either early or late?

☐ If you were able to **get just one room in your house redecorated**, which would it be and why?

☐ Do you think women are better than men at **getting presents** for people?

☐ If you were invited to a karaoke evening, would you try to **get out of** going?

☐ If you were supposed to **get a flight** the day after there had been a serious air crash, would you cancel it?

☐ Is there anyone in your family or group of friends who really **gets on your nerves**?

☐ What kind of things do/did your parents **get you to do** in the house?

☐ What worries you most about **getting old**?

☐ Where would you go if you really wanted to **get away from** everything and relax?

Key success factors
- getting and keeping the reader's attention
- using rich and precise vocabulary

ANALYSING A MODEL TEXT

a You are going to read an article about childhood covering the areas below. What information would you include if you were writing about your country?

- What are the main differences between a child's life 50 years ago and a child's life now?
- Why have these changes occurred?
- Do you think the changes are positive or negative?

b Now read the article. Did the writer include any of your ideas? With a partner, choose what you think is the best title from the options below and say why you prefer it to the others.

How childhood has changed

Changing childhood

My childhood

Children's lives have changed enormously over the last 50 years. But do they have a happier childhood than you or I did?

It's difficult to look back on one's own childhood without some element of nostalgia. I have four brothers and sisters, and my memories are all about being with them, playing board games on the living room floor, or spending days in the street with the other neighbourhood children, racing up and down on our bikes, or exploring the nearby woods. My parents scarcely appear in these memories, except as providers either of meals or of severe reprimands after some particularly hazardous adventure.

These days, in the UK at least, the nature of childhood has changed dramatically. Firstly, families are smaller, and there are far more only children. It is common for both parents to work outside the home and there is the feeling that there just isn't time to bring up a large family, or that no one could possibly afford to have more than one child. As a result, today's boys and girls spend much of their time alone. Another major change is that youngsters today tend to spend a huge proportion of their free time at home, inside. More than anything this is due to the fact that parents worry far more than they used to about real or imagined dangers, so they wouldn't dream of letting their children play outside by themselves.

Finally, the kind of toys children have and the way they play is totally different. Computer and video games have replaced the board games and more active pastimes of my childhood. The irony is that so many of these devices are called 'interactive'. The fact that you can play electronic games on your own further increases the sense of isolation felt by many young people today.

Do these changes mean that children today have a less idyllic childhood than I had? I personally believe that they do, but perhaps every generation feels exactly the same.

c Answer with a partner.

1 What is the effect of the direct question in the introduction? Where is it answered?

2 What does the first main paragraph (not including the introductory sentence) focus on? What examples are given?

3 What are the changes that the writer has focused on in the third main paragraph, and what reasons have been given for the changes? Do you agree?

4 Underline the discourse markers that have been used to link the points in the second and third main paragraphs, e.g. *Firstly...*

Using synonyms

When you write, try not to repeat the same words and phrases too often. Instead, where possible, use a synonym or similar expression if you can think of one. This will both make the text more varied for the reader and help the article link together. A good monolingual dictionary or thesaurus can help you here.

---

d Find synonyms in the article for...

1 at the present time
_____ / _____ / _____

2 children
_____ / _____ / _____

3 alone, without adults _____ / _____

4 games _____

Using richer vocabulary

You can make your writing more colourful and interesting to read by trying to use a richer range of vocabulary instead of the most obvious words.

---

e Without looking back at the article, try to remember how the words in italics were changed to make the article more enjoyable to read.

1 Children's lives have changed *in a big way*
_____

2 ...being in the street with the other *children who lived near us* _____

3 ...*going* up and down on our bikes... _____

4 ...after some particularly *dangerous* adventure. _____

5 My parents *don't* appear *very often* in these memories... _____

6 ...think that no one *has enough money* to have more than one child. _____

7 ...that children have a less *happy* childhood than I had? _____

PLANNING WHAT TO WRITE

Brainstorm possible content

a Look at the exam question below.

Many aspects of life have changed over the last 30 years. These include:

marriage

dating

the role of women or / and men

Write an article for an online magazine about how <u>one</u> of these areas has changed in your country and say whether you think these changes are positive or negative.

With a partner brainstorm for each topic...

1 what the situation used to be like and what the big changes are.

2 whether the situation has changed a lot in your country.

3 whether you think the changes are positive or negative and why.

Now decide which area you are going to write about and which ideas you want to include.

Remember that this is an article, not an essay. You don't necessarily want to include the most important points, but the ones that you could say something interesting about, or where you can think of any interesting personal examples.

---

b Think of a possible title for your article.

TIPS for writing an article

- Give your article an interesting title.
- There is no fixed structure for an article, but it is important to have clear paragraphs. Use discourse markers to link your points or arguments.
- Make sure you use a suitable style, neither very formal nor informal.
- Make the introduction reasonably short. You could use a question or questions which you then answer in the article.
- Try to engage the reader, e.g. by referring to your personal experience.
- Try to vary your vocabulary using synonyms where possible.

WRITING

You are going to write the article in approximately 250 words.

DRAFT your article, with

- a brief introduction, which refers to the changes and asks a question.
- two or three main paragraphs saying what the situation used to be like, and how it has changed.
- a conclusion, which refers back to the question in the introduction, and says whether you think the changes are positive or negative.

EDIT the article, cutting any irrelevant information and making sure it is the right length.

CHECK the article for mistakes in grammar, spelling, punctuation, and register.

THE INTERVIEW

a You are going to listen to an interview with Tony Hawks, a comedian, author, composer, and charity worker. Before you listen, read the glossary and look at how the words are pronounced to help you understand what he says.

> **bask** /bɑːsk/ *verb* enjoy sitting or lying in the sun as some animals do, e.g. lizards, sharks
>
> **technophile** /ˈteknəfaɪl/ *noun* a person who loves new technology (**OPP** *technophobe*)
>
> **terrestrial** /təˈrestriəl/ *adj.* (of television) operating on earth rather than from a satellite. It is used to refer to the channels that everybody who has a TV can get.
>
> **meltdown** *noun* a serious accident in which the central part of a nuclear reactor melts: (*metaphorical*) *a meltdown on the New York stock exchange*

b **2.15** Listen to part 1. Answer the questions with a partner.

1 What strategy did he use in the past to help him to cope with all his different jobs? Why didn't it work? How well does he think his system works?

2 What strategy does he use now? What metaphor does he use to describe how he deals with his different jobs?

3 Why does he compare himself to a shark?

4 What are the pros and cons for him of email and the Internet?

5 Why does he mention satellite navigation?

c **2.16** Listen to part 2. Answer the questions with a partner.

What does he say about…?

1 the negative effect of remote controls

2 a time he wanted to watch a football match on a friend's TV

3 TV when he was a child

4 TV in Iceland in the 70s and 80s

5 a technological meltdown

6 the new heroes

d **2.17** Listen and complete the phrases with one to three words. What do you think they mean?

COMMON EXPRESSIONS AND IDIOMS

1 But I almost feel, _____, we'd be better off without them…

2 However, if the Internet _____, or the connection _____, I'm like a baby without parents…

3 If you _____ to get up and walk six feet to turn over the channel, …

4 And from then on, I've _____ for remote controls.

5 …we can become nostalgic just for _____ of it.

6 I don't think there'll be a _____ technology…

7 …but I can foresee a time, maybe not in _____…

e To what extent do you agree with what he says about technology?

IN THE STREET 🖵

a **2.18** You are going to hear four people talking about technology. What three questions are they asked? Which technologies do they mention?

| Matt | Brian | Amy | Mark |

b Listen again. Who…?

1 ☐ would control the use of a kind of technology rather than 'disinvent' it

2 ☐ thinks that the problem with some technology is what people do with it

3 ☐☐ values a certain technology because it enables them to keep in touch with other people

4 ☐ wastes time looking for useless information

5 ☐ thinks that a piece of technology makes people mentally lazy

6 ☐ would like to 'disinvent' or control two kinds of technology

7 ☐ spends a large part of their day using a certain piece of technology

c **2.19** Listen and complete the phrases with two or three words. What do you think they mean?

COMMON PHRASES

1 It's easy just _____ and, you know, be told what to do.

2 My family is _____.

3 …and who gets to see _____ on cameras.

4 I think email has actually made people a _____ in the way they communicate with each other.

5 That's _____ really…

d Answer the questions from **a** with a partner.

GRAMMAR

a Right (✓) or wrong (✗)? Correct the mistakes in the highlighted phrases.

1 When I was a child, I would have really long hair – I could even sit on it!

2 The boss appears that he has a new secretary. Did you know anything about it?

3 Did you really used to wear glasses? I can't imagine you in them.

4 It is rumoured that they got married secretly in Hawaii.

5 I need to get renewed my passport urgently.

6 You don't seem to have noticed that I've been to the hairdresser's!

7 When I came into the room, I could sense that they had been talking about me.

8 Marco Polo is thought to have brought pasta back from China.

9 Could you get your brother have a look at my car? It's making a funny noise.

10 When I saw that she wore trousers, I was very surprised as she always wears skirts.

b Rewrite the sentences using the **bold** word.

1 I made a big mistake. I only realized it years later. **HAD**
   I only realized years later _____.

2 It seems that Mr Marshall has disappeared. **HAVE**
   Mr Marshall _____ disappeared.

3 Can you pay someone to fix the tap, please? It keeps dripping. **FIXED**
   Can _____? It keeps dripping.

4 People expect that the team's coach will resign in the coming week. **EXPECTED**
   The team's coach _____ in the coming week.

5 The *Daily Mail* says that the singer has been seen with another woman. **ACCORDING**
   _____ the singer has been seen with another woman.

6 If you leave that glass there, someone will break it. **GET**
   If you leave that glass there, _____.

7 It is said that there are over a million homeless people in this country. **BE**
   _____ over a million homeless people in this country.

8 They don't usually arrive at the airport until the last minute. **GET**
   _____ until the last minute.

9 The dog slept on my bed all night. I noticed it when I woke up. **SLEEPING**
   When I woke up, I noticed that _____.

VOCABULARY

a Complete the sentences with a noun formed from the **bold** word.

1 Please don't let this misunderstanding get in the way of our _____. **FRIEND**

2 _____ of speech is one of the most basic human rights. **FREE**

3 I wish there were a few more good restaurants in our _____. **NEIGHBOUR**

4 There are several courses available to help people who suffer from a _____ of flying. **AFRAID**

5 The _____ of being caught cheating was almost too much for her to bear. **ASHAMED**

6 World leaders must take measures to eradicate child _____. **POOR**

b Collocation: complete with the right verb.

1 It doesn't usually _____ me more than an hour to get to work.

2 We thought we were going to be late, but in the end we got to the airport with plenty of time to _____.

3 I'm trying to _____ hold of Albert. Do you know when would be a good time to call him?

4 I've got so much work to do. I just can't _____ with it all.

5 The match is nearly over – there's only a minute _____.

6 He seems quite reserved at first, but in fact he's incredibly friendly when you get to _____ him.

c Complete the idioms with one word.

1 I lost touch with my closest friend for years and now we are trying to make up for _____ time.

2 Can we meet later instead? I'm a bit _____ for time now.

3 It was an amazing holiday. I had the time of my _____.

4 That music's really getting on my _____. Could you either turn it down or turn it off?

5 I think you'll need to say exactly what you think otherwise he won't get the _____.

6 Only children are often used to getting their own _____.

7 If you don't get _____ of the way, you're going to get hurt.

d Complete with the right preposition or particle.

1 _____ the time we arrived, we were too exhausted to do anything except go to bed.

2 I never really got to know the country because _____ the time I was too busy working.

3 Did you ever see the TV series *Dallas* or was it _____ your time?

4 We're moving house next month so I'm going to have to ask for some time _____.

5 The news on TV has really been getting me _____ lately. It's just one disaster after another.

6 It was a definite foul but the referee didn't see it so the player got _____ with it.

7 Is there any way I can get _____ of going to the wedding? I really don't feel like going.

8 Lilly won't get _____ Mark until she meets a new man.

G speculation and deduction
V sounds and the human voice
P consonant clusters

'Noise is the most impertinent of all forms of interruption.'
Arthur Schopenhauer, German philosopher

Breaking the silence

1 VOCABULARY & WRITING
sounds and the human voice

a How noisy is it where you work / study? What noises can you hear? Do any of the noises affect your concentration?

b Look at a list of the most annoying noises in an office (not in order). Which one do you think was voted the most irritating?

c **3.1** Now listen to the noises, in reverse order (8 = the least annoying). Number the phrases in **b**. Which of these noises do *you* find irritating? Are there any that don't really bother you?

d Make a list of other annoying noises. Then have a class vote on which one is the most annoying.

e → **p.161 Vocabulary Bank** *Sounds and the human voice.*

f **3.3** Listen to the sounds and make a note of what they are. Then write three paragraphs based on the sounds you heard. Begin each paragraph as follows:

1 It was 12.30 at night and Mike had just fallen asleep…
2 Amanda was walking down Oxford Street…
3 It was a cold winter's night in November…

It drives me mad!
Office noises we just can't bear…

According to a nationwide poll, many office workers in the UK are being driven mad by noises made by their colleagues. The problem can be particularly acute where two or three people share a small office and in companies which have 'open plan' offices. Amplifon, the organization which conducted the online opinion poll, said 'People are easily offended by sounds in the office but very few do anything about it. Most people just suffer in silence.'
The most irritating noises (not in order) were:

- ☐ Other people's mobile ring tones
- ☐ People making personal phone calls
- ☐ People slurping tea and coffee
- ☐ People tapping the keyboard of their computer
- ☐ The boss's voice
- ☐ The crunch of people eating crisps
- ☐ The 'hold' music on the telephone
- ☐ The hum of the air conditioning

2 PRONUNCIATION
consonant clusters

Consonant clusters (combinations of two or three consonant sounds, e.g. *clothes*, *spring*) can be difficult to pronounce, especially if it is a combination that is not common in your language.

Three-consonant clusters at the beginning of words always begin with *s*, e.g. *scream*.

Three-consonant clusters at the end of words are often either plurals (*months*), third person singular verbs (*wants*), or regular past tenses (*asked*).

a **3.4** Read the information box and listen to the words below. Then practise saying them.

At the beginning of a word:

two sounds:	three sounds:
click	screech
slam	scream
crash	splash
slurp	
drip	
snore	
stammer	

At the end of a word:

two sounds:	three sounds:
shouts	crunched
sniffs	mumbled
yelled	crisps
hummed	rattled

b **3.5** Listen and repeat the sentences.

1 She **scream**ed when her **fr**iend **spl**ashed her in the **sw**imming pool.
2 The **br**akes **scr**eeched and then there was a **tr**emen**d**ous **cr**ash.
3 I hate the **cr**unching of someone eating **crisps**.

c Write three sentences of your own, each using two of the words from **a**. Give them to your partner to say.

3 LISTENING & SPEAKING

a When you go for a coffee, do you prefer a quiet coffee bar or somewhere more lively?

b **3.6** Listen to Julian Treasure, an acoustician, talking on the BBC Radio 4 *Today* programme about noise pollution. Tick the best summary of what he says.

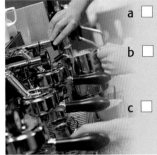

a ☐ Companies need to pay attention not only to how they look, but also to how they sound.

b ☐ Businesses and organizations should stop playing background music. Silence is much more relaxing.

c ☐ It's more important for restaurants and shops to have the right background noise than it is for offices.

c Look at the glossary and listen to the programme again. Then with a partner try to answer the questions.

> **barista** /bəˈrɪstə/ *noun* person who works in a coffee bar
> **chiller cabinet** /ˈtʃɪlə ˌkæbɪnət/ *noun* large fridge where cold drinks are kept
> **knowledge worker** /ˈnɒlɪdʒ ˌwɜːkə/ *noun* a person whose job involves handling or using information

1 What does the book *Sound Business* claim?
2 What are some of the noises he complains about…?
  a in the mobile phone shop b in the coffee shop
3 According to the reporter, what are the three most annoying noises?
4 What effect does
  a appropriate sound b inappropriate sound
  have on sales in a shop?
5 How many of the people he stopped seemed positive about background music?
6 When Julian visits the BBC office, what does he call 'the most distracting sound in the whole world'?
7 What is the problem with the way businesses are using sound at the moment?
8 What do experts think is the right kind of sound to have in a public place?
9 Where was it used and why? What effect did it have?

d Do you agree with Julian Treasure that businesses should think more carefully about how they use sound?

e Talk to a partner.

What kind of sounds or music (if any) do you think you should have…?

- in bars and restaurants
- in class at a language school
- in an office
- in a hotel reception
- at the hairdresser's
- in a supermarket
- in a clothes shop

- on public transport
- in the weights room of a gym
- while you're having a massage
- at the dentist's while you're being treated
- when a plane is taking off and landing
- when you're put on hold on the phone

4 GRAMMAR speculation and deduction

a With a partner, circle the right form. Try to say why the other one is wrong.

1 **A** That sounds like the neighbours' dog.
  B It *can't be / mustn't be*. They've gone away for the weekend and they've taken the dog with them.

2 There's no sound coming from his room. He *probably hasn't / hasn't probably* woken up yet.

3 **A** Didn't you hear that bang in the middle of the night? It woke me up.
  B Yes, I did. It *must be / must have been* the wind.

4 Can you turn the music down? If we make too much noise, the woman upstairs *will likely call / is likely to call* the police.

5 **A** Can I speak to Raymond, please?
  B Sorry, he's not back yet. He *must work / must be working* late.

b ⊙ p.142 **Grammar Bank 3A.** Read the rules and do the exercises.

5 READING & SPEAKING

a Read the introduction to the article and look at the photos. What do you think the article is going to be about?

b Read the rest of the article. What is Susie Rea's project? What paradox of modern life does her project highlight?

c Look at the photos of people Susie sees every day in London. With a partner, speculate about…
  what they might do.
  how old they must be.
  where they might be from.
  what kind of person they might be.

Breaking the silence

Have you ever wondered who the people are you see every day on the way to work? You've never spoken to them, but you see them every single morning. You know what clothes they wear, the paper they read, the way they always stand at the same place at the bus stop or on the railway platform. They also see you there every day. But they're still strangers…

A community is now a non-geographical concept. Friends and family are scattered widely, with contacts kept by mobile phone and email. Our real-life neighbourhood becomes an unknown zone. We can look at the television or the Internet to find out about what's happening thousands of miles away, day and night. But the streets outside? It can be a no-man's land which we navigate, but never really know.

Photographer Susie Rea lives in London and her latest project, entitled *Intimate Strangers*, aims to discover more about the strangers she passes every day. She says, 'In London you don't talk to strangers or ask who they are and what they do. Day to day, I find myself inventing the answers; creating snapshots of lives in my head that are entirely imagined.'

So what would happen if you stopped that stranger and introduced yourself? Would they shake your hand and become an acquaintance? Susie decided to find out.

Susie's starting point was seeing a man in a Panama hat each day. He was always wearing it and it intrigued her to think about who he might be. 'I thought he must be a writer or a teacher wearing a hat like that'. But approaching him was difficult. 'It's not easy to suddenly talk to someone you recognize, but have never spoken to…it was a very weird experience.'

d **3.7** Listen to Susie talk about the people. What did you find out about them? Were you surprised by anything?

e What kind of person do you think Susie is? What do you think of her experiment? Can you imagine someone doing the same project where you live?

f Read some readers' responses to Susie Rea's experiment. Complete them with one of the phrases below. There are two phrases you don't need.

A We exchanged a 'good morning' and a smile
B But in all this time I never actually found out what her name was
C It is a joy to be able to walk among strangers.
D It just goes to show how far a friendly gesture might lead.
E Maybe if we got to know the people who share our community
F Maybe soon we'll be brave enough to say hello to some of our 'intimate strangers'.
G My partner commutes to London every day for work.
H Now I really regret not speaking to her
I Then in 1987 a hurricane hit the country

LEXIS IN CONTEXT

g Look at the highlighted words and phrases and work out the meaning of any that you don't know. Check with your dictionary.

h Have you had any similar experiences to the people who wrote to the website? How well do you know *your* neighbours and people you pass every day? Would you like to get to know them better?

Add comments on this story.

For about 18 months I saw the same woman when I was on the way to work and I nicknamed her 'The Irish lady'. ¹ ☐ and finding out if she really was from Ireland.
Jerry, South London

This sounds like a fascinating project! You could say the same thing about your next-door neighbours. You see the same people day in day out, but you never find out what they're really like. ² ☐ , the world would be a safer place.
Simone, Brussels

I catch a bus to work once a week and it's always the same people. For the last six months, I've been chatting to a woman from our street, and we talk about all sorts of things, from the weather to childcare problems. ³ ☐ until last week – and that's only because she told my little girl.
Sarah, High Wycombe

Love the article! And this definitely applies to where my parents live. My parents and I had been living in the same street for more than 10 years and had never really got to know our neighbours. ⁴ ☐ and an enormous tree blew down and crashed through our roof. The neighbours all came round and offered us food and any help we needed. But then everything went back to normal. My parents still live in the same house and they've never spoken to the neighbours since.
S Taylor, Weybridge, Surrey

I used to pass the same woman every day as I walked to work and never said hello or even acknowledged her. I decided this was ridiculous, so one morning I went up to her and said 'hello'. ⁵ ☐ for the next couple of weeks. But then she changed her route to work. Even though it was only a greeting and a smile, it seems some people just prefer to be left undisturbed.
Nigel, Birmingham

The reason why I choose to live in London is that I love the fact that I don't have to get to know my neighbours and pretend to be interested in their small talk. ⁶ ☐ If you want to be overly friendly with your neighbours, go and live in the north of England! London is fine as it is, thank you very much!
Carl, North London

I commute into central Leeds every day and I used to see the same gentleman on the station platform every morning. We would exchange nods and smiles and eventually he came up to me and we started chatting. Then we met for a drink and got to know each other better. We are now engaged and are getting married next July. ⁷ ☐
Cyndi, West Yorkshire

6 WRITING
Write your own 50–70 word response to Susie's article.

3 B

G adding emphasis (1): inversion
V describing books
P words with 'silent' syllables

'A room without books is like a body without a soul.'
Cicero, Roman orator and philosopher

Lost in translation

1 READING

a In teams of four or five, do the quiz.

First and last lines quiz

Look at some famous first and last lines from novels. Which do you think are first lines and which last lines? Write F or L.

1 ☐ All children, except one, grow up.

2 ☐ It is a truth universally acknowledged that a single man in possession of a good fortune must be in want of a wife.

3 ☐ 'Oh, my girls, however long you may live, I never can wish you a greater happiness than this!'

4 ☐ James Bond, with two double bourbons inside him, sat in the final departure lounge of Miami Airport and thought about life and death.

5 ☐ Mr and Mrs Dursley, of number four, Privet Drive, were proud to say that they were perfectly normal, thank you very much.

6 ☐ 'Tomorrow, I'll think of some way to get him back. After all, tomorrow is another day.'

7 ☐ Happy families are all alike; every unhappy family is unhappy in its own way.

8 ☐ Two gin-scented tears trickled down the sides of his nose. But it was all right, everything was all right, the struggle was finished. He had won the victory over himself. He loved Big Brother.

9 ☐ Many years later, as he faced the firing squad, Colonel Aureliano Buendía was to remember that distant afternoon when his father took him to discover ice.

10 ☐ Renowned curator Jacques Saunière staggered through the vaulted archway of the museum's grand gallery.

Match the first and last lines to the novels they are from.

A ☐ *1984* by George Orwell, 1949

B ☐ *Goldfinger* by Ian Fleming, 1959

C ☐ *Gone With The Wind* by Margaret Mitchell, 1936

D ☐ *Anna Karenina* by Leo Tolstoy, 1877

E ☐ *One Hundred Years Of Solitude* by Gabriel García Márquez, 1967

F ☐ *Harry Potter and the Philosopher's Stone* by JK Rowling, 1997

G ☐ *Little Women* by Louisa May Alcott, 1868

H ☐ *The Da Vinci Code* by Dan Brown, 2003

I ☐ *Peter Pan* by JM Barrie, 1911

J ☐ *Pride and Prejudice* by Jane Austen, 1813

b Which do you think is the best first line? Does it make you want to read the book?
Which (if any) of these books have you already read? What did you think of it / them?

2 VOCABULARY & SPEAKING describing books

a Complete some readers' comments about books with an adjective from the list.

depressing entertaining fast-moving gripping haunting
heavy-going implausible intriguing moving thought-provoking

1 A wonderful book. So _____ it brought tears to my eyes! ☆☆☆☆☆

2 A _____ novel that raised many interesting questions. ☆☆☆

3 Rather _____. I had to make a real effort to finish it. ☆☆

4 A _____ story. I was hooked from the very first page. ☆☆☆☆☆

5 A light but _____ novel, perfect for beach reading! ☆☆☆

6 The plot was _____. It was impossible to predict how it would end. ☆☆☆☆

7 The characters were totally _____. I couldn't take any of them seriously. ☆

8 A _____ story which jumps from past to present and back again at breakneck speed. ☆☆☆☆

9 A well-written novel, but so _____ it made me feel almost suicidal! ☆☆☆

10 A _____ tale which stayed with me long after I'd finished reading it. ☆☆☆☆

b Take turns with a partner to choose an adjective from the list and say a book or a film that you could use the adjective to describe.

c **3.8** Listen to a man talking to a friend about a book he couldn't put down. Write down four positive adjectives he uses to describe the book.

d Now talk to a partner about your reading tastes. Try to use a variety of adjectives to describe the books.

3 GRAMMAR adding emphasis (1): inversion

a Match the halves to make sentences from novels.

1 ☐ His voice was low, but I was able to hear what he said, though **only later** did I understand…

2 ☐ **Never** had he been so unnatural and artificial, even with an outsider or when making a formal call,…

3 ☐ **Not only** was Venus Maria an adored and controversial superstar,…

4 ☐ **Not until now** have I been ready to confess…

5 ☐ **No sooner** had one campaign come to an end…

A as he was that day.
(*Anna Karenina* by Leo Tolstoy, translated by Constance Garnett)

B what he meant.
(*Girl with a Pearl Earring* by Tracy Chevalier)

C that I am a writer.
(*Tough Guys Don't Dance* by Norman Mailer)

D she was also Lucky's best girlfriend.
(*Dangerous Kiss* by Jackie Collins)

E than the candidates began anticipating the next.
(*Imperium* by Robert Harris)

b Look at the verbs after the **bold** adverbial expressions. What is unusual about the word order? What is the effect of putting the adverbial expression at the beginning of the sentence?

c ⟶ p.143 Grammar Bank 3B. Read the rules and do the exercise.

d Imagine you are a novelist. Complete the sentences in your own words using inversion to make them as dramatic as possible.

1 Not until the last moment…
2 Never in my life…
3 Not only… but…
4 Only after the wedding…
5 No sooner… than I realized…

Tell your partner about a book…

that you were made to read at school and hated.

that you feel you should have read, but you haven't.

that you have read but that you can't remember anything about.

that you decided to read after seeing the film.

that you think would make a good film.

that you couldn't put down.

that you started but couldn't finish.

that you have bought, but have never opened.

4 PRONUNCIATION   words with 'silent' syllables

a **3.9** You are going to hear ten sentences. For each one, write down the last word you hear.

b Read the information box below. Then cross out the vowels that are not pronounced in the words you wrote down in **a**.

> Some common multi-syllable words in English have vowels which are often not pronounced, e.g. the middle *e* in *vegetable* and the second *o* in *chocolate*. When this happens, the word loses an unstressed syllable. If you pronounce these vowels, you will still be understood, but leaving them out will make your speech sound more natural, and being aware of them will help you to understand these words in rapid speech.

c **3.10** Listen and check. Practise saying the words.

5 READING

a If you read an English novel, would you prefer to read it in the original version or translated into your language? Why?

b You are going to read an article about translation. Before you read the article, look at the two extracts, which are different translations from the Japanese of the first lines of a novel by Haruki Murakami. Answer the questions with a partner.
   1 What details do you find out in the first translation that you don't in the second, and vice versa?
   2 What differences do you notice
       a) in tenses and vocabulary   b) in the length of sentences?
   3 Which translation do you prefer? Why?

c Now read the whole article and answer the questions.
   1 What is the author's attitude towards translators?
   2 Whose translation made many readers fall in love with Murakami? Why?
   3 In what way were Constance Garnett's translations controversial?
   4 What metaphor does Kornei Chukovsky use to describe her translations? What do you think he means by it?
   5 Why do you think Andrew Bromfield chose to translate *War and Peace* in such a different way?

LEXIS IN CONTEXT

d Look at the highlighted adjectives and adverbs, and guess the meaning of the ones you don't know. Then match them to meanings 1–12.

   1 _____ *adv.* hardly
   2 _____ *adv.* deeply
   3 _____ *adv.* it could be argued
   4 _____ *adj.* enormous
   5 _____ *adj.* with little colour or excitement
   6 _____ *adj.* difficult to deal with
   7 _____ *adj.* original, strange
   8 _____ *adj.* humble, low in status
   9 _____ *adj.* with short sharp sounds
   10 _____ *adv.* tidily
   11 _____ *adj.* flat and even
   12 _____ *adj.* true and accurate

e Which translation of *War and Peace* do you think you would prefer to read? Why?

LOST IN TRANSLATION

THE IMPORTANCE of the lowly translator to our understanding of foreign literature cannot be underestimated. Like ghosts hovering over the text, these rarely mentioned linguists can profoundly alter the tone and style of a book. The difference a translator can make to the style and flow of a novel can be vast. Here are two interpretations of the opening lines to *The Wind-Up Bird Chronicle* (1997) by the Japanese novelist Haruki Murakami.

Extract 1
'When the phone rang I was in the kitchen, boiling a potful of spaghetti and whistling along with an FM broadcast of the overture to Rossini's *The Thieving Magpie*, which has to be the perfect music for cooking pasta.'

Extract 2
I'm in the kitchen cooking spaghetti when the woman calls. Another moment until the spaghetti is done; there I am, whistling the prelude to Rossini's *La Gazza Ladra* along with the FM radio. Perfect spaghetti-cooking music.

The first is written by Murakami's officially sanctioned translator, Jay Rubin, and flows neatly and cleanly.

Jay Rubin   Haruki Murakami

The second, written by Alfred Birnbaum, is much more staccato, even neurotic. The former gained Murakami a wider English-speaking audience; however countless fans are besotted with Birnbaum's quirky style – to them he has become the voice of Murakami.

Constance Garnett with Tolstoy and Dostoevsky

TRANSLATING can also be a controversial business. Constance Garnett (1861–1946) was arguably the first to bring the Russian literary giants to British readers, and churned out 70 English translations of major works throughout her lifetime. She worked incredibly quickly, making mistakes and skipping awkward passages and phrases. Yet one of Garnett's greatest crimes, according to Russian critics, was that she applied Victorian sensibilities to works by the likes of Tolstoy and Dostoevsky. Kornei Chukovsky, commenting on Dostoevsky's *Notes from Underground*, wrote 'With Constance Garnett it becomes a safe, bland script: not a volcano, but a smooth lawn mowed in the English manner – which is to say a complete distortion of the original.' Russian-born American poet Joseph Brodsky remarked: 'The reason English-speaking readers can barely tell the difference between Tolstoy and Dostoevsky is that they aren't reading the prose of either one. They're reading Constance Garnett.'

Translators continued to use Garnett's texts as a guide for decades, until the acclaimed Richard Pevear and Larissa Volokhonsky set out to finally produce faithful versions of the Russian masterworks in the nineties. Yet in October 2007 British translator Andrew Bromfield's edition of *War and Peace* blew the debate wide open. Shortening the novel from 1,267 pages to just 886, and giving it a happy ending, his publisher Ecco boasted that the Bromfield edition was 'twice as short, four times as interesting…More peace and less war.'

From The Observer

6 LISTENING

a You are going to listen to an interview with Beverley Johnson, a professional translator working in Spain. Before you listen, think of three questions you might ask her about translating.

b **3.11** Listen to the interview. Did she answer any of the questions you or other students came up with?

c Listen again. Choose a, b, or c.

1 One of the reasons why Beverley decided to become a translator was because…
  a she thought teaching English was boring.
  b she really enjoyed the postgraduate course that she did.
  c she wanted to be self-employed.

2 Most people who translate novels into English…
  a don't do any other kind of translation work.
  b prefer translating authors who are no longer alive.
  c often only ever translate one particular writer.

3 She mentions the advertising slogan for Coke™ as an example of…
  a how difficult it is to convey humour in another language.
  b how you cannot always translate something word for word.
  c how different cultures may not have the same attitude to advertising.

4 *The Sound of Music* was translated into German as…
  a 'All dreaming together'
  b 'Tears and dreams'
  c 'My songs, my dreams'

5 Which of these is <u>not</u> mentioned as a problem when translating film scripts?
  a Having enough room on the screen.
  b Conveying the personality of the speaker.
  c Misunderstanding the actors' words.

6 The problem with translating swear words in a film script is that…
  a they may not have the same strength in both languages.
  b they may not be translatable.
  c you can't use taboo words in some countries.

7 Which of these is mentioned as one of the downsides of being a freelance translator?
  a A low salary.
  b No paid holidays.
  c Time pressure.

8 Beverley's advice to would-be translators is to…
  a specialize.
  b study abroad.
  c do a translation course.

d Does being a translator appeal to <u>you</u> as a career? Why (not)?

7 WRITING

a Choose a famous novel in your own language, preferably one that has a dramatic beginning or ending. Translate either the first few sentences or the last few into English.

b Read some other students' translations and see if you can identify the novels.

3C

G unreal uses of past tenses
V money
P ea and ear

'You can be young without money, but you can't be old without it.'
Tennessee Williams, US dramatist

Are you suffering from *Affluenza*?

1 READING & SPEAKING

a Look at the lesson title. 'Affluenza' is an invented word, made from putting two words together, *affluent* and *influenza*. Look at the dictionary definitions, and decide what you think it means.

> **affluent**
> /ˈæfluənt/ *adj.* ■ having a lot of money and a good standard of living

> **influenza**
> /ˌɪnfluˈenzə/ *noun* ■ (formal) flu, an infectious illness

b Read the product description from an online book retailer and a review of Oliver James' book *Affluenza*.

1 Check your answer to **a**.
2 Is the journalist's review positive or negative? Underline the parts of the text which tell you.

Affluenza: How to Be Successful and Stay Sane

by Oliver James

Product description

There is currently an epidemic of 'affluenza' throughout the world – an obsessive, envious, keeping-up-with-the-Joneses – that has resulted in huge increases in depression and anxiety among millions. Over a nine-month period, bestselling author and psychologist Oliver James travelled around the world to try and find out why. He discovered how, despite very different cultures and levels of wealth, 'affluenza' is spreading. Cities he visited include Sydney, Singapore, Moscow, Copenhagen, New York, and Shanghai, and in each place he interviewed several groups of people in the hope of finding out not only why this is happening, but also how one can increase the strength of one's emotional immune system. He asks: why do so many more people want what they haven't got and want to be someone they're not, despite being richer and freer from traditional restraints?

REVIEW

The sick society

Affluenza by Oliver James

In his earlier book *Britain on the Couch*, Oliver James asserted that 'advanced capitalism makes money out of misery and dissatisfaction, as if it were encouraging us to fill up our emotional emptiness with material goods'. In this book, he explores the idea further, and it's terrific. A lot of readers, wanting to put their finger on why the affluent world they live in makes them so uneasy, will want to cheer. Here he is saying, loud and clear, that capitalism is bad for your mental health. And then he tells us why this is the case, and what we can do about it.

'My focus,' explains James, 'is on why we are so messed up, not with giving a false promise of the possibility of happiness.' So why are we so messed up? It's because of what James calls 'selfish capitalism', or, more catchily, *Affluenza*, a virus-like condition that spreads through affluent countries. In these countries, notably English-speaking ones, people define themselves by how much money they make. They are also ruled by superficial values – how attractive they look, how famous they are, how much they are able to show off.

It's a wonderfully clear and cogent thesis. *Affluenza*, as defined by Oliver James, is clearly recognizable as our way of life. It spreads because it feeds on itself; when you try to make yourself feel better by buying a car, or building muscles in the gym, or spraying on a fake tan, or having a facelift, you actually make yourself feel worse, which makes you want to buy more things.

The author's antidote for *Affluenza* is simple: look inward, not outward. Don't be a sheep. Try to be 'beautiful' rather than 'attractive'. Embrace the family. Don't see life as a competition. Don't watch too much TV. Simple, perhaps. But will it be enough?

From The Guardian

c Read both texts again and answer the questions with a partner.

1 How did Oliver James do his research for this book?
2 What did he want to find out?
3 According to Oliver James, why do we feel the need to buy material goods?
4 What four things do sufferers from 'affluenza' value most?
5 Explain what the reviewer means by 'it feeds on itself'.
6 What do you think the advice 'be beautiful rather than attractive' means?

d Would you like to read this book? Why (not)?

e Do the questionnaire below, which comes from the book *Affluenza*.

HAVE YOU CONTRACTED THE 'AFFLUENZA' VIRUS?

Put a tick or cross next to the following statements:

- ☐ I would like to be a wealthy person.
- ☐ I would like to have my name known by many people.
- ☐ I would like to successfully hide the signs of ageing.
- ☐ I would like to be admired by many people.
- ☐ I would like to have people comment often about how attractive I look.
- ☐ I like to keep up with fashions in hair and clothing.
- ☐ I often compare what I own with what others own.
- ☐ Possessions can be just as important as people.
- ☐ Shopping or thinking about what to buy greatly preoccupies me.
- ☐ I'm less concerned with what work I do than with what I get paid for it.
- ☐ I admire people who own expensive homes, cars, and clothes.
- ☐ My life would be better if I owned certain things I don't have now.
- ☐ The things I will own will say a lot about how well I've done in life.
- ☐ I want a lot of luxury in life.

f ⊙ **Communication** *Have you got 'affluenza'? p.117.* According to your answers, are you suffering from 'affluenza'? Do you think the questionnaire is fair?

g Talk to a partner. Do you agree with the author of *Affluenza* that…?

- in our society people are defined by how much money they earn
- nowadays people are ruled by superficial values
- people today have an unhealthy interest in the lives of celebrities
- people buy things to make themselves feel happier
- being affluent makes people unhappy

2 VOCABULARY money

a Can you remember words from the text which mean…?
1 rich: **a**_____, **w**_____
2 to have something that belongs to you: **o**_____
3 (the enjoyment of) special and expensive things, e.g. food, clothes, surroundings: **l**_____

b ⊙ **p.162 Vocabulary Bank** *Money.*

c Choose the right word from each pair according to meaning, collocation, or register.
1 Mum, can you lend me some money? I'm *broke / penniless*.
2 I'm trying to get a *loan / mortgage* from the bank to buy a car.
3 We're going to have to be a bit careful this month if we don't want to end up in the *red / black*.
4 The company has been *in / on* debt for the last six months and may have to close down.
5 One of my cousins is absolutely *affluent / loaded* – she inherited a fortune from her parents.
6 When you're abroad, you get a better *currency / exchange rate* if you take money out at a cash machine.
7 We like living here because we have a much better *cost / standard* of living.
8 I need to get a better job. We can't *make / get* ends meet.

d Take turns to tell your partner about a person you know who…

is rather tight-fisted.	buys and sells shares.
lives beyond their means.	charges high fees for what they do.
has more money than sense.	has difficulty making ends meet.
was given a grant to study abroad.	has spent a fortune on cosmetic surgery.

3 PRONUNCIATION *ea* and *ear*

a Say the sentences below. Do the pink letters make the same or different sounds in each sentence?
1 My great-grandfather was very wealthy, but incredibly mean.
2 I've just had a really good idea!
3 Even though I left home early, I nearly missed the flight.
4 I've heard that he doesn't earn much.

b **3.12** Listen and check.

c Put the words from the list in the right columns.

appear	bear	beat	break	creak	deal	death	earring	earth
fear	hear	heart	jealous	learn	neatly	nuclear	pear	please
pleasure	scream	spread	steak	unhealthy	wear			

d **3.13** Listen and check. What are the most common pronunciations of *ea* and *ear*?

⚠ When you come across a new word with *ea* or *ear*, it's best to check the pronunciation in a dictionary.

4 READING

a Do you know of any couples where you think one of them married for money? Are / Were the marriages successful, as far as you know?

b You are going to read one of a series of articles from *The Times* called *Family Secrets*, which are unsigned and use fictitious names, and in which readers of the newspaper confess a secret. Read the article once. What is your initial reaction to what the woman says?

I wish I had married for money, not love

WHEN BILL AND I GOT MARRIED, his relaxed attitude to money amused me. He's a teacher and enjoys his job. I work in medical sales: more stressful, but it pays well. I have, however, become secretly, overwhelmingly, envious of my friends, who can rely on their
5 husbands as the breadwinners.

Our first home was a tiny flat in a lovely area, which was fine even when our first daughter was born. Our second daughter's arrival two years later put a strain on space and finances, so we had to move – and I had to learn to bite my tongue so as not to seem ungrateful.
10 It was then that I noticed that my best friend Carol's standard of living was better than ours: her husband is a consultant surgeon and their first home was a five-bedroom detached house. We bought a three-bedroom house in a nice street, but I couldn't help comparing it with friends' houses. I've had promotions, but Bill has no plans to apply for
15 anything beyond head of department, his current position; I think he should go for a deputy head post.

Bill is a brilliant dad, and with the girls now reaching their teens, I appreciate how well he gets on with them and puts so much effort into their homework and hobbies. But although I'd never admit this to
20 friends, I believe that there's more to life than being good parents. Carol is having a champagne party for her 40th, as well as a week in Paris with her husband and a weekend in New York with their 14-year-old daughter. I pretended to be thrilled, but was sick with envy. I know many people can't take a holiday at all, but we mix with people who
25 have no mortgages, work part-time or not at all, can afford private education and have three or four holidays a year.

I feel resentful, especially as it's the men who bring in the money; and even if Bill were a head teacher, he wouldn't come close. When I go out with my girlfriends I hear Susan moan about John's business
30 trips and I have to stop myself from shouting that his £250,000 salary must make up for some of his absences. Or Trisha: she inherited a house from her parents, which means that though her husband is on a normal salary, she needn't work, and spends her time at the gym. Bill tells our girls that they can achieve anything and I agree, but when
35 they start dating, I'll try to guide them (behind his back) towards men who can give them the sort of life I've never had.

Feminism's fine, but there's a lot to be said for having your bills paid.

---

deputy head /ˌdepjuti ˈhed/ the assistant to the director of a school
consultant surgeon /kənˌsʌltənt ˈsɜːdʒən/ a surgeon of the highest rank in a hospital

c Read the text again and then discuss the following with a partner:

1 how and why the woman's opinion of her husband's attitude to money changed over the years.
2 what is it about her friends that makes her feel so envious.
3 how she plans to 'guide' her own daughters.

LEXIS IN CONTEXT

d With a partner, say in your own words what the woman means by these idioms and phrases.

1 rely on their husbands as the breadwinners (l.4)
2 put a strain on space and finances (l.8)
3 **IDM** bite my tongue (l.9)
4 **PHR V** go for a deputy head post (l.16)
5 reaching their teens (l.17)
6 **IDM** sick with envy (l.23)
7 he wouldn't come close (l.28)
8 moan about (l.29)
9 **PHR V** make up for some of his absences (l.31)
10 **IDM** behind his back (l.35)
11 there's a lot to be said for (l.37)

e Which of these sentences best sums up your reaction to the woman's confession?

'She's refreshingly honest!'

'I'd hate to be married to her. I pity her poor husband (and her daughters).'

'It's depressing that a woman can think like this in the 21st century.'

'She's only saying what a lot of women think but don't dare say.'

'It's a bit over the top, but she has got a point.'

'She's unbelievably materialistic.'

5 GRAMMAR
unreal uses of past tenses

a Look at the highlighted verbs in these sentences. Which ones are really about the past? What time do the others refer to?

1 When Bill and I got married, his attitude to money amused me.
2 If Bill got promoted, our standard of living would go up.
3 I wish we were better off.
4 I was so jealous when I heard about Carol's weekend in New York.
5 I think it's time we thought about moving to a bigger house.
6 I'd rather my daughters married a man with money.
7 I wish I'd married my first boyfriend!
8 If I'd married Sean, I would have a much better standard of living.

b ○ **p.144 Grammar Bank 3C.** Read the rules and do the exercises.

c Make questions to ask a partner.

Would you rather…?
Do you ever wish…?

* your children married for money or for love
* you had been born in another decade or century
* you could have a year off to travel
* you could learn a new skill
* you had a boring but well-paid job or a stimulating but badly-paid job
* you had chosen to study different subjects at school / university
* you had more free time for your hobbies
* you lived in another town or city
* you had bitten your tongue and not said something
* you were self-employed or you worked for someone else

6 LISTENING

a You are going to listen to a lecture given by Michael Norton, Assistant Professor in the Marketing unit at Harvard Business School, who has recently been researching the relationship between money and happiness. Before you listen, which do you think his conclusion will be? Choose from a–c.

Having more money than they had before…
a never makes people happier, regardless of what they do with it.
b can make people happier if they spend some of it on other people.
c always makes people happier even if the amount of extra money is small.

b 3.14 Read the glossary. Then listen to the first part of the lecture. Did you predict correctly?

c Listen again and answer the questions.
1 What is the paradox that puzzled Norton?
2 What did he and his colleagues think the reason for this was?
3 What did the research show?

> **the University of British Columbia** one of the top Canadian universities
> **domain** /dəˈmeɪn/ area, field
> **field study** research or study that is done in the real world rather than in a library or laboratory
> **Boston** a university city on the east coast of the USA
> **profit-sharing bonus** an extra payment made to workers when the company has made a profit

d 3.15 Now listen to the rest of the lecture and choose the correct answer.

1 The research into prosocial spending done with employees in Boston showed that the important factor was…
a the size of the bonus they received.
b the percentage of the bonus that they spent on others.
c the total amount of money that they spent on others.
2 The second study showed that _____ will affect your happiness.
a even spending a small amount on others
b only spending a large amount on others
c only regularly spending money on others
3 Previous research showed that people become happier when they…
a get at least a ten percent rise in their salary.
b are rich and then become extremely rich.
c have very little money and then become reasonably well off.
4 Norton and his researchers also wanted to test whether knowing in advance about prosocial spending _____ the effect on people's happiness.
a would minimize
b would eliminate
c would increase
5 The research showed that this knowledge _____ the positive effect of prosocial spending.
a did not reduce
b greatly reduced
c slightly reduced

e Are you convinced by the results of Norton's research? Why (not)?

7 3.16 SONG ♫ *A Lady of a Certain Age*

Key success factors
- being able to express a reasonably sophisticated opinion
- using a range of vocabulary to describe what you are reviewing (plot, dialogue, characters, etc.)
- being able to summarize

ANALYSING A MODEL TEXT

a Which of the following would normally influence you to read a certain book?
- A friend of yours has recommended it.
- It's a best-seller – everybody is reading it.
- You've seen and enjoyed a film based on it.
- You were told to read it at school or university.
- You have read a good review of it.

b Read this newspaper book review. In which paragraph do you find the following information? Write 1–4 in the boxes, or DS if the review doesn't say. Does the review make you want to read the book?

☐ The strong points of the book
☐ The basic outline of the plot
☐ What happens in the end
☐ Where and when the story is set
☐ The weaknesses of the book
☐ Whether the reviewer recommends the book or not
☐ How good the English translation is
☐ Who the author is
☐ Who the main characters are
☐ How much the book costs
☐ Who the book is suitable for

When writing a book or film review, give your reader a <u>brief</u> idea of the plot (without giving away the whole story!). Try to make your description as concise as possible to leave you space to give your own opinion.

The Girl Who Played with Fire

The Girl Who Played with Fire is the second novel in the Millennium trilogy by Swedish writer Stieg Larsson. A thriller, set in modern-day Sweden, it immediately became an international best-seller.

In this book the same main characters from the first book reappear, journalist Mikael Blomkvist and the extraordinary girl Lisbeth Salander, a freelance investigator. This time Lisbeth herself becomes the suspect of a triple murder. Three people are shot on the same day, and her fingerprints are found on the murder weapon. She goes quickly into hiding, and Mikael, whose life she saved in the previous book, is determined to prove her innocence. Devastated by the fact that two of the murder victims were colleagues of his, but convinced that Lisbeth cannot possibly have been involved, he works first on his own, and then with the police, to discover what really happened. Meanwhile Lisbeth, carefully keeping out of everyone's sight, is making her own investigations…

The great strength of this book, and what makes Larsson's books so different from other recent detective fiction and thrillers, is the character of Lisbeth. Most famous fictional detectives or investigators tend to be either middle-aged policemen with marital problems, female forensic scientists, or middle-aged male intellectuals. Lisbeth, however, is a young slightly autistic girl from a broken home, who is also a computer genius. She is an intriguing character, and in this book we find out a lot more about her, among other things who her father is, and why she spent her teenage years in a psychiatric hospital. My only criticism of the novel would be that the early sub-plot about Grenada is not very relevant and could have been cut.

Not only is this a complex and absolutely gripping novel, but it also tackles real problems in society, and most unusually I think for a sequel, is even better than its predecessor. For all lovers of crime novels and thrillers the Millennium trilogy is a must.

c Look at these extracts from the second paragraph. Which words did the author leave out to make it more concise? Then read the rules for **Participle clauses** to check.

> **Because he is devastated by the fact** that two of the murder victims were colleagues of his, but **he is convinced that** Lisbeth cannot possibly have been involved, he works first on his own, and then with the police, to discover what really happened.
>
> Meanwhile Lisbeth, **who is carefully keeping out of everyone's sight**, is making her own investigations…

Participle clauses

The writer uses participles (*devastated, convinced, keeping*) instead of a subject + verb. Past participles replace verbs in the passive, and present participles (*-ing* forms) replace verbs in the active. The subject of the clause is usually the same as the subject of the main clause.

Participle clauses can be used:

- instead of a conjunction (*after, as, when, because, although*, etc.) + subject + verb, e.g. *Devastated by the fact*… instead of *Because he is devastated*…
- instead of a relative clause, e.g. *carefully keeping* instead of *who is carefully keeping*.

d Rewrite the highlighted phrases to make them more concise using participle clauses.

1 As she believes him to be the murderer, Anya is absolutely terrified.
_____

2 Armelle, who has been forced to marry a man she does not love, decides to throw herself into her work.
_____

3 Simon, who realizes that the police are after him, tries to get out of the country.
_____

4 It was first published in 1903 and it has been reprinted many times.
_____

5 Because he is deeply ashamed of how he has behaved, Luke cannot face his family and friends.
_____

6 It is set during the First World War and, it tells the story of a young soldier.
_____

7 When he hears the shot, Mark rushes into the house.
_____

e Underline the adverbs of degree in these phrases from the review. What effect do they have on the adjectives?

> Lisbeth, however, is a young, slightly autistic girl from a broken home…
> Not only is this a complex and absolutely gripping novel…

f Use your instinct. Cross out any adverbs which don't fit in these sentences. Tick if all are possible.

1 My only criticism is that the plot is **a bit / slightly / a little** implausible.
2 The last chapter is **really / very / absolutely** fascinating.
3 The end of the novel is **rather / pretty / quite** disappointing.
4 The denouement is **rather / incredibly / extremely** thrilling.

g Where all the adverbs are possible, is there any difference in meaning or register?

PLANNING WHAT TO WRITE

Brainstorm the content

a Think of a book or film that you have read or seen recently. Write a paragraph of approximately 100 words explaining who the main characters are and summarizing the plot, but without giving away the ending. Use the present tense, and try to include at least one participle clause.

b Swap your paragraph with other students to see if they can identify the book or film.

TIPS for writing a book / film review

- Choose a book or film that you know well.
- Organize the review into clear paragraphs.
- Make sure you use a suitable style, neither very formal nor informal.
- Use the present tense when you describe the plot. Using participle clauses will help to keep it concise.
- Try to use a range of adjectives that describe as precisely as possible how the book or film made you feel, e.g. *gripping, moving*, etc. (see page 41). Use adverbs of degree to modify them, e.g. *absolutely gripping*.
- Remember that even a good review will usually include some criticism as well as praise.

WRITING

A student magazine has asked for reviews of recent books and films. You are going to write a complete review.

DRAFT your review, using the same paragraph structure as the model. It should be approximately 250 words.

- Paragraph 1: The title of the book or film, and the author or director. Where and when it is set.
- Paragraph 2: The plot, including information about the main characters.
- Paragraph 3: What you liked about the book / film, and any criticisms you may have.
- Paragraph 4: A summary of your opinion and a recommendation.

EDIT the review, making sure you've covered all the main points and making sure it is the right length.

CHECK the review for mistakes in grammar, spelling, punctuation, and register.

THE INTERVIEW

a You are going to listen to an interview with Sarita Gupta, vice president of Women's World Banking (WWB). Before you listen, read the glossary and look at how the words are pronounced to help you understand what she says.

microfinance /ˌmaɪkrəʊˈfaɪnæns/ *noun* the provision of financial services to low-income clients, to help poor people out of poverty

Muhammad Yunus Bangladeshi developer of the microcredit movement, and winner of the 2006 Nobel Peace prize

collateral /kəˈlætərəl/ *noun* property or sth valuable that you promise to give to sb if you cannot pay back money that you borrow

peer /pɪə/ *noun* a person who has the same social status as you

the DR the Dominican Republic

cantina /kænˈtiːnə/ *noun* Spanish for a canteen or kitchen

embroider /ɪmˈbrɔɪdə/ *verb* to decorate cloth with a pattern of stitches usually using coloured thread

middle man *noun* a person or a company that buys goods from the company that makes them and sells them to sb else

b **3.17** Listen to part 1. Answer the questions with a partner.

1 What issues were discussed in the 1975 International Year of Women, and what issue did they decide to work on?
2 What did Muhammad Yunus see that the poor needed, and why couldn't they get it?
3 What three innovations did he come up with?

c **3.18** Listen to part 2. Make notes for each case study about:

The country the woman lived in
The situation she was in
The business she set up

d **3.19** Listen and complete the phrases with two or three words. What do you think they mean?

COMMON EXPRESSIONS AND IDIOMS

1 So if we could only discuss one issue, sort of _____ one issue…
2 There had been, by that time, several decades of what we call 'the Western World' giving _____ of aid to the developing world.
3 There are really three innovations that he came up with that are brilliant _____.
4 So that _____ food, she was selling cigarettes, beer, candy, etc.
5 …while he took care of _____ over her head, she had absolutely no means of earning more money for herself or her kids…
6 The son had _____ school to join his father to push a similar cart…

e To what extent do you think microfinance would be useful in your country?

IN THE STREET 🖥

a **3.20** You are going to hear five people talking about money. What three questions are they asked? Do the majority of speakers consider themselves good or bad with money?

| 1 | 2 | 3 | 4 | 5 |
| Ian | Sheila | Jerry | Kate | Jason |

b Listen again. Who…?

1 ☐ thinks that having more money would enable them to have a better lifestyle
2 ☐ gives a specific example of how men and women spend money in different ways
3 ☐☐ definitely considers that women are better than men at managing money
4 ☐ confesses to being extravagant in one area
5 ☐ thinks that how much money you need to make you happier depends on where you live

c **3.21** Listen and complete the phrases with one to three words. What do you think they mean?

COMMON PHRASES

1 It makes me anxious.
It _____.
2 So I think that's pretty _____ seeing as I'm quite old now.
3 I'm just kind of an organized person, _____.
4 I'm very lazy looking for _____…
5 I'm not very good at making budgets and _____.

d Answer the questions from **a** with a partner.

Study Link MultiROM

Revise & Check

GRAMMAR

a Right (✓) or wrong (✗)? Correct the mistakes in the highlighted phrases.

1 Not only we saw the sights in New York, we also managed to do some shopping as well.
2 Dave is incredibly late, isn't he? I think he might get lost.
3 Only when the main character dies does her husband realize how much he loved her.
4 The waiter didn't probably notice that they had left without paying.
5 Children, it's time you go to bed.
6 I think it's unlikely that I will be given a work permit.
7 If only they weren't coming! I'd really like to have an early night.
8 What a wonderful smell! Somebody must bake some bread.
9 You definitely won't pass your driving test if you drive that fast!
10 I'd rather you come tomorrow, not today, if that's OK with you.

b Complete with the verb in brackets in the right form.

1 She's unlikely _____ before 7.00. (arrive)
2 Not until all the guests had gone _____ able to sit down and rest. (we / be)
3 Maria is bound _____ the news – everybody was talking about it yesterday. (hear)
4 No sooner _____ married than James lost his job. (they / get)
5 I really wish we _____ that sofa – it gets dirty far too easily. (not buy)
6 I can hear a really strange noise downstairs. Do you think someone might _____ to break in? (try)
7 It will soon be time Marta _____ going to nursery school. She's nearly four, isn't she? (start)
8 Never _____ such a wonderful view. It completely took my breath away. (I / see)
9 My neighbour can't _____ very long hours. He's always home by early afternoon. (work)
10 I'd rather _____ there, if you don't mind. You're blocking my garage. (you / not park)

VOCABULARY

a Correct the mistakes in the highlighted idioms.

1 I really wanted to tell him what I thought of him. I had to bite my lip.
2 She shouldn't really be in debt, but I think she lives above her means.
3 I really hate it when people criticize me behind my shoulders. I think they ought to say things to my face.
4 That's an amazing dress. It looks as if it cost a mortgage. Did it?
5 She's incredibly extravagant – she wastes money like water.
6 I'm finding it impossible to pay my rent and my bills on the salary that I'm on. I just can't make ends match.

b Complete the verbs in the past simple.

1 Mabel **sl**_____ the door and walked off angrily.
2 'Thanks darling,' she **wh**_____ softly in his ear.
3 He **wh**_____ a happy tune as he walked along the road.
4 'I'm afraid it's too late,' she **si**_____. 'Maybe another time.'
5 The wind was so strong that the windows **ra**_____.
6 The brakes **sc**_____ and the car stopped just in time.

c Write the words for the definitions.

1 _____ (*noun and verb*) to make a continuous low sound
2 _____ (*noun and verb*) (of liquid) to fall in small drops
3 _____ _____ (*noun*) polite conversation about ordinary or unimportant subjects
4 _____ - _____ (*adj.*) something that makes you think
5 _____ (*adj.*) with little colour, excitement, or interest
6 _____ (*noun*) the money you pay to travel by bus, plane, etc.
7 _____ (*noun*) the units of equal value into which a company is divided, and which people buy and sell
8 _____ (*noun*) money that is available to a person or organization and a plan of how it will be spent over a period of time
9 _____ (*noun*) money that you pay for professional advice or services
10 _____ (*adj.*) very interesting because of being unusual or not having an obvious answer or ending

d Write synonyms for the following words or phrases.

1 rich   **w**_____
2 unlikely to be true   **i**_____
3 mean   **t**_____-**f**_____ (*informal*)
4 broke (*informal*)   **p**_____ (*formal, literary*)
5 huge   **v**_____
6 follow (rules)   **a**_____ to (*formal*)
7 deeply   **pr**_____
8 enormous   **v**_____

4A

G discourse markers 2: adverbs and adverbial expressions
V history and warfare
P stress in word families

'You come out of *Gone with the Wind* feeling that history isn't so disturbing after all. One can always make a dress out of a curtain.' *Dilys Powell, British film critic*

History goes to the movies

1 VOCABULARY history and warfare

a Which of the films below do you consider to be historical films? Why (not)?

Apocalypse Now   *Che Part 1 and Part 2*   *Dances With Wolves*   *Gladiator*   *Schindler's List*
The Queen   *The Reader*   *Shakespeare in Love*   *Titanic*   *The Untouchables*

b Read the descriptions of three famous scenes from films. Complete each text with words from the list.

The scenes you'll never forget
– our film critics choose their favourite moments.

1 'They will never take our freedom!'

2 'As God is my witness...'

Braveheart Mel Gibson, 1995

arrows   outnumbered   overthrow   ~~rebel~~   troops   victorious

The film is set in 13th-century Scotland. Mel Gibson plays the Scottish ¹*rebel* William Wallace, who tries to ²_____ the English who ruled Scotland at that time. One of the most memorable scenes is the Battle of Stirling, when Wallace's army, hopelessly ³_____, wait in an open field for the English to attack. The English fire thousands of ⁴_____ into the air but the Scots defend themselves with shields. Then the English knights on horseback charge at full speed, but at the last moment the Scottish ⁵_____ raise their spears and the English knights are thrown from their horses and slaughtered. A fierce battle then takes place and Wallace's army are ⁶_____. The scene is not a model of historical accuracy, but with its spectacular special effects and stunts, it's tremendous fun. 'They may take our lives, but they will never take our freedom!'

Gone with the Wind Victor Fleming, 1939

besieged   Civil War   looted   side

Gone with the Wind is based on the best-selling book by Margaret Mitchell. It tells the story of a manipulative woman, Scarlett O'Hara (played by Vivien Leigh), and an unscrupulous man, Rhett Butler (Clark Gable), who carry on a turbulent love affair in the American South during the ¹_____. The Confederates, the ²_____ Scarlett's family supports, are losing, and Scarlett is living in Atlanta, which is ³_____ by the Union army. She escapes, and goes home only to find her mother dead, her father disoriented, and her family home ⁴_____. She asks for food and is told the soldiers have taken everything. In this dramatic scene, Scarlett, starving and desperate, suddenly sees a turnip in the ground. She falls on it, pulls it from the ground and eats it. She is nearly sick, then rises from the ground, looks round the ruined land and vows 'As God is my witness, I'll never be hungry again'.

52

c **4.1** Listen and check.

d ⊃ **p.163 Vocabulary Bank** *History and warfare.*

e With a partner, say what the difference is between…
- *an arrow* and *a spear*
- *survivors* and *refugees*
- *a coup* and *a revolution*
- *a ceasefire* and *a treaty*
- *withdraw* and *retreat*
- *defeat* and *overthrow*

f Re-read the texts and try to memorize the information. Then in groups of three, cover the texts and take turns to describe what happens in each of the scenes.

3 'I'm Spartacus!'

Spartacus Stanley Kubrick, 1960

| capture | casualties | defeat | forces | rebellion | weapons |

This epic film tells the story of the rise and fall of a slave in the Roman Empire. Spartacus (Kirk Douglas) is trained as a gladiator, but he rebels against his Roman owner and escapes. He forms an army of slaves and becomes their leader. Although they have fewer ¹_____ and are less well organized, they win several victories against the Roman ²_____ which are sent to put down the ³_____. But a final climactic battle just outside Rome results in the total ⁴_____ of the rebel army, with heavy ⁵_____ on both sides, and the ⁶_____ of many of the survivors, including Spartacus. Crassus (Laurence Olivier), the Roman general, promises the captives that they will not be punished if they will identify Spartacus. In this powerful scene, one by one, each surviving soldier stands and shouts out 'I'm Spartacus!' Crassus finally condemns them all to be executed in a mass crucifixion along the Appian Way.

2 PRONUNCIATION stress in word families

> It is often useful to learn words in 'families', e.g. *to rebel, a rebel, rebellion,* etc. However, you should check whether the stressed syllable changes within the 'family'.

a Complete the chart.

noun	person	adjective	verb
capture	/ captor	captive	
		civil / civilized	
execution			
history	historian	/ historic	
looting	looter		
rebellion		rebellious	
siege			
		surviving	
			withdraw
	victorious		

b **4.2** Underline the stressed syllable in all the words. Listen and check. Then test a partner on the words in the chart.

3 SPEAKING & WRITING

> In this dramatic scene, Scarlett, starving and desperate, suddenly sees a turnip in the ground. She falls on it, pulls it from the ground and eats it.
>
> We normally use the present simple ('the dramatic present') when we describe a scene from a film, or the plot.

a Work in groups of three or four. Each think of a film you really enjoyed that was set in a historical period or based on a real event. Make notes under the following headings to help you to talk about it.
- Where and when is the film set?
- Who are the main characters and who are they played by?
- What is it about?
- What is the most memorable scene?
- What makes it so powerful / moving / dramatic, etc.?

b Describe the film and the scene to others in the group, and see if they can name the title of the film.

c Now write a paragraph describing the film and the scene using the three texts in **1b** as models.

4 READING

a How important do you think it is that a historical film should get all the facts right? Why?

b Quickly read part of the preface of the book *History Goes to the Movies* by US author Joseph Roquemore. What kind of book is it?

a It compares historical films to what really happened.

b It is a guide to the best ever historical films.

c It analyses the effect historical films have on young people.

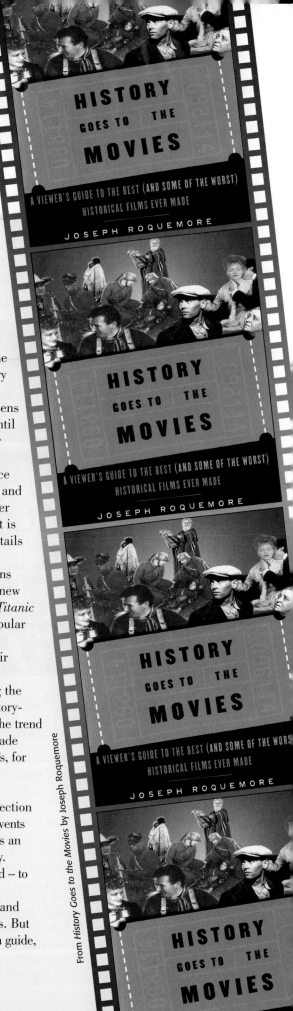

From *History Goes to the Movies* by Joseph Roquemore

History Goes to the Movies

When asked in 1993 to comment on accusations that the movie *In the Name of the Father* grossly distorts contemporary British and Irish history, female lead Emma Thompson famously responded 'I don't give a damn'. Ever since the premiere in 1915 of *The Birth of a Nation*, film-makers have rewritten history to create top-dollar entertainment. The films are very persuasive: well-made movies hold your interest continuously, riveting your attention on 'what happens next', and pulling you forward with no time to reflect on individual scenes until the final credits roll. The result: you don't remember much about a film after watching it for the first time. Very few people can recall even half the plot in reasonable sequence, and still fewer can remember facial expressions or voice intonation associated with specific dialogue sequences (including politically and morally loaded conversations). For this reason, films have extraordinary power – unmatched by any other medium – to leave you with a strong sense of what is right and what is wrong, who is bad and who is good, even though critical details presented in the movies may be biased or false.

Well, so what? They're just movies. In fact they're not just movies. Millions of Americans are fanatical history lovers, and they pack theaters every time new films on historical figures or events come to town. *Saving Private Ryan* and *Titanic* raked in viewers and cash for months. One of the History Channel's most popular programs, ***Movies in Time***, is shown twice daily. Many high school teachers screen movies in the classroom. Clearly countless Americans get most of their history from television and the big screen.

Some of the industry's finest historical and period films premiered during the past decades. But the 1960s also triggered a flurry of politically charged history-based movies full of factual distortions and, occasionally, outright lies. Today the trend continues on a larger scale: many films released in the 1990s and the first decade of the 21st century reflect blatant disdain, at least as intense as Ms Thompson's, for solid reliable history.

History Goes to the Movies is a source of information and, it is hoped, entertainment for everyone interested in the actual history behind a wide selection of movies grouped into twelve sections – 11 covering historical periods and events and a twelfth containing biographies and period films. Each film review includes an essay on the history covered in one or more movies, and a brief plot summary. Star ratings (five stars: don't miss it) reflect each movie's historical accuracy and – to a far lesser degree – its power to amuse.

Obviously expecting textbook accuracy from films would be ridiculous – and producers have delivered a remarkable number of historically faithful movies. But some of them get too much of their history wrong. *History Goes to the Movies* is a guide, however imperfect, for readers and viewers aiming to get it right.

c Now read the text again carefully and choose a, b, or c. Compare with a partner and explain why you think the answer you have chosen is right.

1 Emma Thompson said that ___ that the film *In the Name of the Father* was historically inaccurate.
   a she was upset
   b she didn't care
   c she wasn't aware

2 When people see a film they tend to remember ___.
   a quite a lot of what people said
   b what happened in chronological order
   c who the heroes and villains were

3 According to the author, what most Americans know about history comes from ___.
   a what they learned at high school
   b documentaries on the History Channel
   c films they have seen in the cinema and on TV

4 Films made in recent years have been historically inaccurate because film makers ___.
   a don't check the facts
   b are not concerned about historical accuracy
   c want to make politically correct films

5 The star system Joseph Roquemore uses refers ___.
   a equally to historical accuracy and entertainment value
   b more to entertainment value than historical accuracy
   c more to historical accuracy than entertainment value

LEXIS IN CONTEXT

d Look at the highlighted words and expressions related to cinema. With a partner say what they mean. Check any you're not sure of in a dictionary.

e Complete the sentences with a word or expression from **d**.

1 The latest James Bond movie is expected to be _____ early next summer.

2 After years as a respected theatre actress, she has finally been given her chance to appear on the _____.

3 I can't stand it when people get up and leave the cinema as soon as the film ends when I'm trying to watch the _____.

4 The special effects were fantastic but the _____ was a bit implausible.

5 Many of the biggest names were there at last night's _____.

5 LISTENING & SPEAKING

a Two of the films mentioned in *History Goes to the Movies* are *Titanic* and *Braveheart*. Have you seen either of them? How historically accurate did you think they were?

b **4.3** Listen to a film critic talking about them. How many stars did the author Joseph Roquemore give the films? Does the film critic agree?

c Listen again and make notes about what was inaccurate about the two films. Compare your notes with a partner. How serious do you think the inaccuracies were?

> *Titanic* 1997 Director James Cameron
> Inaccuracies:

> *Braveheart* 1995 Director Mel Gibson
> Inaccuracies:

d Can you think of any films you have seen which you think were very inaccurate? Did this spoil your enjoyment of the film?

6 GRAMMAR
discourse markers (2): adverbs and adverbial expressions

a **4.4** Listen to some extracts from what the film critic said and complete the phrases below with one to three words. What do they tell you about what the speaker is going to say next?

1 _____, these characters and their story are fictitious…
2 _____, I think his assessment is about right.
3 William Wallace is portrayed as a kind of poor primitive tribesman living in a village. _____, he was the son of a rich landowner.
4 _____, the Scots stopped wearing woad hundreds of years earlier.
5 _____, the reason why the Scots won the battle is because the English soldiers got trapped on the narrow bridge.

b ⊙ p.145 Grammar Bank 4A. Read the rules and do the exercises.

c ⊙ **Communication** *Guess the sentence A p.117 B p.119.*

4 B

G verb + object + infinitive or gerund
V compound adjectives
P intonation in polite requests

Help yourself

'A kleptomaniac is a person who helps himself because he can't help himself.'

Henry Morgan, broadcaster

1 READING & SPEAKING

a What do you understand by the term 'self-help book'? Can you think of any which have been best-sellers in your country?

b Look at the cover of a recent self-help book, and read the review below. Answer the questions with a partner.

1 What is the situation described at the beginning of the article?
2 Why is it relevant?
3 Does the journalist think it is worth reading?

c Work in pairs **A** and **B**. Each read a different extract from the book to find the following information.

What is the technique suggested?
What experiment(s) were done to prove that it worked?

d Tell your partner in your own words about the technique and the research.

The persuaders

How can I jump a queue? A new book on the secret psychology of persuasion has the answer.

I was sitting in a car outside Marks & Spencer in Camden when I realized that Professor Robert Cialdini had completely changed my way of looking at the world.

There I was, waiting for my wife to emerge from the exit with some shopping. All the while I was watching a man selling copies of *The Big Issue* to people going into the shop's entrance. Or at least, trying to sell copies. He wasn't having much luck. People were sweeping past him.

Now the thing about the doors at M&S is that you can't go out of the 'in' doors. But then one lady shopper tried to do exactly that. And the *Big Issue* man was kind enough to push the door open from his side.

At that moment I knew what would happen next. Absolutely knew it. And it did. The lady shopper bought a copy of *The Big Issue*.

I'm sure that she didn't connect the door-opening and the magazine-buying, but connected they were. For reciprocity – our almost automatic instinct to return even quite small favours – is one of the main forms of social influence identified by the leading social psychologist, Robert Cialdini.

His idea – and it's not a bit of pop psychology, it's real academic work based on published papers and careful experimentation – is that we react almost unconsciously, in fairly predictable but sometimes fairly odd ways, to a range of social situations.

> **Marks & Spencer** a British chain of department stores, often just called M&S
>
> **The Big Issue** a magazine published on behalf of and sold by homeless people in the UK
>
> **pop psychology** the use by ordinary people of simple or fashionable ideas from psychology in order to understand or explain people's feelings and emotional problems

From *The Times*

A single word will help your persuasion.

Let's think about queuing. Whether you're at a bank, a supermarket, or an amusement park, queuing is probably not your idea of fun. Under what circumstances would you be willing to let another person jump the queue and move in front of you? Is it possible that just a single word from a requester could drastically increase the likelihood that you'd say, 'Yes, go ahead'?

Yes, and the word is *because*. Behavioural scientist Ellen Langer and her colleagues decided to put the persuasive power of this word to the test. In one study she arranged for a stranger to approach someone waiting to use a photocopier and ask, 'Excuse me. I just have five pages. May I use the machine?' In this situation, 60% of the people agreed to allow the stranger to go ahead of them. However, when the stranger followed the request with a reason ('because I'm in a rush') almost everyone (94% of the people) complied. Then Langer repeated the experiment. This time the stranger also used the word *because*, but followed it with a completely meaningless reason ('because I have to make copies'). Even with this meaningless reason, 93% agreed to let the stranger go first.

This study demonstrates the unique motivational influence of the word *because*.

Of course like most things, the power of *because* has its limits. In the previous study the request was small – five copies. Langer repeated the experiment, but told the person to ask to make 20 copies. This time, when the stranger did <u>not</u> use the word *because*, only 24% agreed, and when the meaningless reason was added, this produced no increase in compliance at all. However, when the request was made with a good reason, 50% of the people asked agreed.

These findings serve as a reminder to always be sure to accompany your request with a rationale, even when you think the reasons might be fairly clear. Too often we mistakenly assume that other people understand the reasons behind our requests. Rather than telling your children to 'come to the table for dinner now' or 'go to bed immediately', a more effective strategy would be to provide a reason why you are asking them to take that action – and not just 'because I said so'.

e Discuss with a partner:
- What did you think of the two strategies? Do you think they would work on you?
- Do you think they would help you in situations where you need to persuade someone to do something?

B

Asking for a little can go a long way.

Throughout this book we've attempted to provide evidence to support our claims that we can successfully and ethically move people to say yes. But in certain situations and environments it's also important to understand why people say no to reasonable requests, such as a request to donate to a legitimate charity.

Along with several colleagues, one of us set out to do just that. We thought that, when asked to make a donation, even those who would like to support the charity in some way say no, because they can't afford to donate very much, and they assume that the small amount that they can afford wouldn't do much to help the cause. Based on this reasoning, we thought that one way to urge people to donate in such a situation would be to inform them that even an extremely small sum would be helpful.

To test this hypothesis our research assistants went door to door to request donations for the American Cancer Society. After introducing themselves, they asked the residents, 'Would you be willing to help by giving a donation?' For half the residents the request ended there. For the other half, however, the research assistant added 'Even a penny will help'.

When we analysed the results we found that, consistent with our hypothesis, people in the 'even a penny will help' half of the sample were almost twice as likely to donate to the cause. And the amount the individuals gave was also found to be more or less the same in both halves, so the people in the 'even a penny' half did not donate less.

The study suggests that if you want somebody to do something for you, simply pointing out that even a small offering on their part would be acceptable is likely to be an effective strategy. Applications in the workplace might be, to a colleague regarding a joint project, 'Just an hour of your time would really help'; to a colleague whose handwriting is illegible, 'Just a little more clarity would help'. The chances are that this little step in the right direction won't prove so little after all.

From *Yes! 50 secrets from the science of persuasion* by Noah J Goldstein, Steve J Martin, and Robert B Cialdini

2 GRAMMAR
verb + object + infinitive or gerund

a Right (✓) or wrong (✗)? With a partner, correct any mistakes in the highlighted phrases.

1 The man with *The Big Issue* was trying to persuade people to buy his magazine.
2 When I was a child I was often made do the washing up.
3 I want that you finish these exercises in five minutes.
4 I'll meet you there at 7.00 – and please don't keep me waiting!
5 Do you think you could let me have the reports before the end of the week?
6 I don't mind you not finish everything, but at least eat your vegetables!
7 I suggest you taking the 7.30 train – it'll be less stressful than trying to catch the earlier one.
8 We'd love you to come – please say you can!
9 My father recommended that we should go to the museum before lunch, when it's less crowded.
10 The job involves me to travel abroad at least twice a month.

b ⭕ **p.146 Grammar Bank 4B.** Read the rules and do the exercise.

3 PRONUNCIATION
intonation in polite requests

a **4.5** Listen and write down six requests.
1 _____? It's a bit stuffy in here.
2 To Victoria Station. _____?
3 _____? I need someone to help me with this report.
4 If you're going to the canteen, _____?
5 _____, and not this one?
6 _____? My car's being serviced.

b **4.6** Now listen to the same requests said twice. Which of the two do you think sounds the most polite? Why? How does the other one sound?

1 a b   2 a b   3 a b
4 a b   5 a b   6 a b

c **4.7** Listen to the polite requests again and repeat, copying the intonation.

d Think of something you would really like someone to do for you, e.g. give you a lift home, look after a pet for the weekend, lend you some money, go somewhere with you, etc. Ask other students, and see if you can find three people who are prepared to help you. Try to be as persuasive as possible. Remember the advice you read in the extract from *Yes!* and use polite intonation.

4 LISTENING & SPEAKING

a Look at the covers of four more self-help books. Which of the four, if any, might you be tempted to buy? Which one would you definitely not buy?

b Now read an extract from each book. Was it more or less what you expected from the cover? Why (not)?

A Whenever there is an obvious flaw in your argument that is apparent to everyone around you, don't be phased. You must say with great self-assurance that this is not a flaw at all but the operation of another important psychological process of which you were already fully aware. In fact you have been researching it. Here is when your powers of imagination come into play. Make up a phrase to label it, which will always begin with 'The' and end with 'Effect'. The middle is up to you, and the more obscure and ponderous, the better. 'The Indirect McCollough Effect' is a real example, and 'The Coaxial Reverse Bunion Effect' isn't. But no-one will know the difference.

B We can be massively depressed or microscopically annoyed by something completely trivial, but if we associate food with comfort, we'll eat. We both ate if our children were unwell, and we both ate if the plumber had failed to turn up. We ate because it was raining. We ate because we'd had a tiny argument with our partners. We ate because we'd stubbed our toe, or because somebody was sick in hospital. The gravity or otherwise of the situation had nothing to do with it. We ate because, for whatever reason, we felt sad.

C We believe once you get engaged a wedding date should be set – no endless engagements. When a man proposes, it should be with a ring and a wedding date within one year, not longer, unless you are young (under twenty-five years old) in which case a two-year engagement is fine. If your fiancé is stalling on a wedding date, you may have to give him back the ring and move on.

D

1 Imagine that it's five years from today, and your life is filled with the most wonderful things imaginable. Your life is truly rich in every way! Write a paragraph or two about what has happened in each of the following areas:
   Health   Career / Finances   Relationships   Spirituality   Lifestyle

2 Go back to each paragraph you've written and circle, underline, or highlight each key goal or milestone that emerged.

3 Now, for each of the major goals or milestones, ask yourself 'What do I want this for? What will having this give me?' Your answers should be just a few words long – things like 'a feeling of joy', 'a sense of achievement', 'freedom', or 'making a contribution'.

c **4.8** Now listen to a radio programme where people discuss these self-help books. How many of the books did they find helpful?

d Listen again and match the books (A–D) to the statements.

1 It is packaged with supplementary material. ☐
2 It was not the first book of this kind that the reviewer had read. ☐
3 It will help the reviewer socially. ☐
4 The reviewer may try out things recommended by the book. ☐
5 The reviewer chose it because of a recent event in their personal life. ☐
6 The reviewer intends to read more about the subject. ☐
7 The book is very one-sided. ☐
8 The book promises to help you by changing the way you think. ☐

BOOKSHOP

'No, I *won't* show you where the self-help books are.'

www.CartoonStock.com

e 4.9 Look at some extracts from the listening which all include modifiers. Listen and complete the phrases with between two and four words. What do they mean?

1 Well, I have _____ friends who are into psychology.

2 I see myself as _____ expert on diet books.

3 According to this book, making a marriage work is _____ the wife.

4 …the husband doesn't have to _____.

5 The wife just has to try to be exactly what her husband wants her to be, and then everything will be _____.

f Does what the speakers said change your mind about reading one of the books?

g Look at a list of some typical self-help topics. Have you used any books, DVDs, magazines, and websites related to any of these areas? Did you find them helpful?

childcare

health, nutrition, and diets

fitness

personality and relationships

men and women

astrology

business, money, and economics

DIY and home improvements

food and cooking

improving your appearance

improving memory

study tips

UNDERSTANDING YOUR PARENTS' BEHAVIOUR

www.CartoonStock.com

5 VOCABULARY   compound adjectives

> A compound adjective is an adjective made of two parts. It is usually written with a hyphen, e.g. *a self-help book, a bad-tempered person, a well-off person, a one-sided article.*
>
> The second word in compound adjectives is often a past participle.

a Combine words from each circle to make ten compound adjectives to complete questions 1–10.

second
last   long
duty
worn
air   home
narrow   part
well

made
conditioned   time
minute   free
out
hand
behaved   minded
term

1 Have you ever bought a _____ car or motorbike? Did you have any problems with it?

2 Do you think it's possible for people to carry on a _____ relationship if they are living in different towns or countries?

3 Do you usually do a lot of _____ revision the night before an exam?

4 Do you often buy things in the _____ shop when you travel by plane? What kind of things do you buy?

5 Do you have any old clothes that you still like wearing even though they are a bit _____?

6 Do you prefer _____ food to restaurant meals? Why (not)?

7 In the summer do you spend much time in _____ buildings or cars? Do you consider it a necessity or a luxury?

8 Would you like to have a _____ job, i.e. only work a few hours a day? Why (not)?

9 Do you think as people get older they tend to get more _____ and intolerant?

10 Do you think children should be asked to leave restaurants if they are not reasonably _____?

b Ask and answer the questions with a partner.

c Now combine words to make ten more compound adjectives. Write three questions to ask a partner using some of the adjectives.

mass
short   high
kind
blue   first
hands
easy   left
absent

class
heeled   minded
free
sighted   going
produced   handed
hearted
eyed

4 C

G conditional sentences
V phone language; adjectives + prepositions
P sounds and spelling: /ʃ/, /tʃ/, /ʒ/, /dʒ/

'Every form of addiction is bad, no matter whether the narcotic be alcohol, morphine or idealism.'
Carl Jung, Swiss psychologist

Can't live without it

1 VOCABULARY & LISTENING

a How good is your 'phone vocabulary'? Do the quiz with a partner.

Phone quiz

1 What three verbs are most commonly used to mean 'to telephone' somebody?

2 What are the missing verbs in these phrases?
 a Can you _____ me a **ring** this afternoon?
 b I need to _____ a few **calls** now. I'll get back to you later.

3 What's the missing word in these phrasal verbs?
 a Sorry, I've got to **hang** _____ now. I'm in a hurry.
 b I'm going to have to _____ my phone **off** now – my flight's boarding.
 c We were suddenly **cut** _____ in the middle of a conversation.
 d My mobile is pay-as-you-go, so I have to remember to **top** _____ my credit from time to time.
 e I'm **running** _____ of credit on my mobile, so I don't know how long we can keep on talking.
 f I tried calling her office all day but I couldn't **get** _____. The lines were permanently busy.
 g Sorry, I can't hear you very well. Could you _____ **up** a bit?
 h If you hold the line, I'll _____ you **through** to the accounts department.

4 Complete the missing words.
 a I need to **c**_____ my phone – the battery's very low.
 b Do you want my mobile number or my **l**_____?
 c I've been calling Tom on his mobile, but it's **e**_____ all the time.
 d I know he's been trying to ring me all day because I've got three **m**_____ calls from him.
 e If you don't know the number, call **d**_____ enquiries.
 f You have reached the **v**_____ service for 35364890. Please leave a message when you hear the tone.
 g There are usually **p**_____ **p**_____ in public places such as airports and stations for people who don't have or can't use their mobile phones.

b How would not having a mobile affect your life? Read the beginning of an article. What is the journalist's experiment? What is a 'nomophobe'?

My life is out of my hands

We are so addicted to our mobile phones that we suffer acute anxiety when we are without them. Or do we? Francesca Steele finds out.

It is 10 p.m. on a cold Friday and I am standing in a smelly phone box speaking to a barman, trying to persuade him to find my friends. 'Can you shout out?' I ask, 'or maybe look for them?'

The friends I'm supposed to meet later are in a bar somewhere in Central London, and we haven't yet made any definite arrangements about where to meet. 'They're about 26,' I yell over the music. 'And, er, they're probably wearing suits.' The barman disappears for a few minutes. Then he comes back to the phone. 'Hey, I think I've found them.' Another voice comes on the line. 'Er, hi. This is Richard. Who's that?' Wrong person. I hang up, thanking God that the experiment will be over tomorrow.

Welcome to life in the 21st century without a mobile phone. A recent study has discovered that we are so dependent on our phones that when we find ourselves without them, discover that the battery isn't charged, or are forced to switch them off, 53% of us feel extremely anxious and stressed, a 'condition' so prevalent that it has even been given a name, nomophobia.

But perhaps our condition is misguided. Sure, mobiles seem practical, but back in the old days we just planned better, didn't we? People were late less often and didn't expect you to always be contactable. A life without a mobile might even be better, more organized and relaxing. But could a nomophobe survive, let alone enjoy, a week without one? My newspaper asked me to try…

From The Times

2 PRONUNCIATION sounds and spelling: /ʃ/, /tʃ/, /ʒ/, /dʒ/

a Look at the words below from **Vocabulary & Listening**. Decide what sounds the pink letters make, and write the words in the right column.

addiction	anxious	arrangement	attachment	century
conclusion	condition	crucial	decision	engaged	future
journalist	message	obsession	occasion	officially
pleasure	pressure	surgery	switched	technician

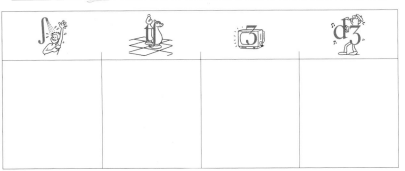

b **4.12** Listen and check. Practise saying the words.

c Now practise saying these sentences.

1 Addictions and obsessions can make you anxious.
2 We need to take some crucial decisions in the near future.
3 It's a pleasure to attend this social occasion.
4 The doctor's surgery was engaged so I left a message.

3 GRAMMAR conditional sentences

a Match the halves of the conditional sentences.

1 If I'd had my mobile, ☐
2 If I wasn't a journalist, ☐
3 If I called my mother more on the landline, ☐
4 If I'd known exactly where my friend lived, ☐
5 If I lost my phone, ☐
6 If I were asked to repeat this experiment, ☐

A I wouldn't know what to do.
B I'd enjoy our conversations more.
C I wouldn't do it.
D I'd have sent her a text.
E I wouldn't have got lost.
F I would never have done the experiment.

b Which sentences refer to present or future situations and which ones refer to the past? What is different about sentence 2?

c ➡ **p.147 Grammar Bank 4C.** Read the rules and do the exercises.

d In groups of three or four, discuss the questions.

- What gadgets do you use that you wouldn't be able to live without?
- Supposing the Internet hadn't been invented, to what extent would this affect the way you work / study / use your free time?
- If you could go back in time, is there anything you would change about your career / studies?
- Would you be prepared to go and work or study in another country even if you didn't speak the language at all?
- What language would you have chosen to study if you hadn't had to learn English?
- Would you be prepared to lend your car / motorbike to somebody provided that they were insured to drive it?

---

c **4.10** Listen to Francesca describing her week. Look at sentences 1–6 below and write the day of the week (M to F) each thing happened on.

1 She was late because she had to make a call from her landline. ☐
2 She wasn't able to warn a friend that she was going to be late. ☐
3 She wasted a lot of money calling from a pay-phone. ☐
4 She discovered an advantage of not having a mobile. ☐
5 She arrived late because she couldn't call and ask for directions. ☐
6 She felt an overwhelming desire to check her text messages. ☐

d Listen again for more detail about what happened on each day. Compare with a partner and retell the main events in Francesca's week.

e **4.11** Now listen to what happened on Saturday. What does she conclude is the result of not having a mobile? What decision did she take?

f If you had done the same experiment as the journalist, do you think you would have come to the same conclusion?

4 READING

a Apart from mobile phones, what other gadgets or activities do you think people are addicted to or obsessed with in the 21st century?

b Read the article once. What exactly are 'behavioural addictions'? In what way are they different from what most people think of as addictions? How can they be treated?

Are we hooked on addiction?

The word 'addict' for most people conjures up images of drug users or alcoholics. But today there is a new breed of addicts...

Dr MARK COLLINS is the head of the addictions unit at the Priory, an expensive clinic in Roehampton. 'Over the last 18 months we have noticed a big rise in the number of behavioural addictions, so-called to distinguish them from substance dependencies,' he says. 'People are looking down on smokers, alcoholics, and cocaine addicts, but then go and spend five hours in an Internet chat room,' says Collins. Behavioural addictions include compulsive attachments to plastic surgery, the Internet, mobile phones, and even sun beds.

It seems that in our fast-paced pressurized modern life, we are increasingly turning to comfort behaviour, activities which temporarily make us feel happier, less stressed and lonely. And experts warn that these are the very things that can lead us into dependency no matter how harmless they may seem at first. And while behavioural addictions may sound less serious than being hooked on drink or drugs, according to experts, their potential for wrecking lives may actually be quite similar. They can lead to obsession, debt, and the breakdown of relationships.

Internet addiction

Caroline Harrison, 37, a full time mother of three, admits to compulsively using the Internet. 'I was surfing to discover something about my youngest child's skin problem when I found this amazing parenting website with lively message boards,' she says. 'Soon I found I couldn't go a day without logging on. I started spending all evening 'chatting' to my new online friends instead of spending time with my husband. It never crossed my mind that it could be addictive. But now I feel edgy and tense if I can't access my computer. It's as if I can't help myself. The people there seem more real and supportive than my own family and friends. I often feel depressed and lonely in real life because my husband works long hours, so being on the site makes me feel good. Well, temporarily good.'

Tanning obsession

Even more worrying is the behaviour of 14-year-old Tracey Barlow, who is now seeking treatment for her addiction to tanning. The teenager has been visiting tanning parlours three times a week, and at one stage was having treatments five days a week. Her skin is already prematurely aged, and she has been warned that she risks getting skin cancer, but despite being warned of the risks she says she feels overwhelmingly anxious if she perceives her tan to be fading. 'It's like an illness with her,' says her despairing mother. 'She hates being pale.'

Shopaholic

For 26-year-old sales manager Emily Lane, it was her love of shopping that got dangerously out of hand. Her compulsive spending on designer clothes, shoes, and handbags left her with £30,000-worth of debt and destroyed her relationship with her boyfriend, James. She admits that many of the items she bought remain unused, but that she found it impossible to stop spending. 'Coming home with armfuls of bags gave me an enormous high, and I needed to keep on buying more clothes, shoes, and accessories to keep getting it. I would shop in my lunch hour, after work, and at weekends, but I couldn't see that I had a problem until James split up with me over it.'

Dr ROBERT LEFEVER, of the Promis Recovery Centre, who has himself overcome addictions to gambling and work, explains, 'Deep down sufferers are usually depressed. In that state you can become hooked on anything that changes the way you feel and even if you try to stop the behaviour, you will find it extremely hard, at least without becoming bad-tempered or anxious.'

Dr Lefever believes that compulsive behaviour often manifests itself in clusters. There is, for example, the 'eating disorder cluster', which also includes shopping and spending, work, cosmetic surgery, and exercise, the 'hedonistic cluster' which includes alcohol, drugs, caffeine, sex, and gambling, and the 'relationship cluster' which includes compulsive helping of others, and addiction to love and being in love. 'If you are addicted to one thing in the cluster, you are at risk of becoming addicted to the others,' he says.

Whatever your age, Lefever believes that if you have a serious compulsive problem that is interfering with your life, then the most effective treatment is a stay in a clinic, or therapy with a psychologist who understands addiction. 'Addiction is treatable,' he says. 'And I see this every day, in myself and in other people.'

From the Daily Mail

c Read the article again. Then choose a, b, or c from the options below.

1 According to experts, behavioural addictions ____.
   a are not as serious as being addicted to drink or drugs
   b are more serious than being addicted to drink or drugs
   c can be just as serious as being addicted to drink or drugs

2 Caroline Harrison says that she feels the need ____.
   a to do something about her addiction
   b to chat online every day
   c to spend more time with her husband

3 Tracey Barlow ____.
   a is slightly less addicted than she used to be
   b can no longer afford to pay for so many tanning sessions
   c has an illness as a result of her addiction

4 Emily Lane thinks that ____.
   a if she hadn't been a shopaholic, her boyfriend wouldn't have left her
   b her boyfriend should have helped her overcome her addiction
   c the money she owed caused the break-up with her boyfriend

5 Dr Lefever thinks that ____.
   a if you are addicted to coffee, you might also become addicted to shopping
   b if you have an eating disorder, you will probably become addicted to smoking
   c if you are addicted to going to the gym, you may also become addicted to having cosmetic surgery

LEXIS IN CONTEXT

d Look at the highlighted words and phrases related to addictions. With a partner, decide what you think they mean.

e Do you think the addictions referred to in the article are a problem in your country?

5 VOCABULARY adjectives + prepositions

a Complete the prepositions column with one from the list.

for   of   on   to   with

	prepositions
1 A lot of people are **obsessed** ☐ celebrities and their lifestyles.	____
2 Some young people are becoming **addicted** ☐ social networking websites.	____
3 People are normally very kind and **helpful** ☐ foreign tourists.	____
4 Most young people are **dependent** ☐ their parents until their mid-twenties.	____
5 People are totally **fed up** ☐ the number of commercials on TV.	____
6 Older people aren't as **open** ☐ new ideas and fashions as younger people are.	____
7 People are **sick** ☐ being bombarded with depressing news by the media.	____
8 Our country is **famous** worldwide ☐ its cuisine.	____
9 A lot of people are **hooked** ☐ Latin-American soap operas.	____
10 As a nation we are very **proud** ☐ our achievements on the football pitch.	____
11 Couples are not as **keen** ☐ having children as they used to be.	____

b Cover the prepositions column and say the sentence with the correct preposition.

c With a partner, say to what extent the sentences are true for your country, and give examples.

6 LISTENING & SPEAKING

a **4.13** Listen to five people talking about obsessions. What are they or the people they mention obsessed with or addicted to?

b Listen again and answer with the number(s) of the speaker. Who…?
   ☐ A says that their obsession started as a result of a family incident
   ☐ B doesn't really think that they are obsessive
   ☐ C thinks that the obsession makes the person bad company
   ☐ D says that the obsession started because of a family member
   ☐ E doesn't think that the obsession serves any purpose

c Talk in small groups. Try to think of someone for as many categories as possible.

Do you know anyone who is

'addicted' to…?
- a machine or gadget
- a particular TV series
- work
- shopping
- chatting online
- electronic games
- anything else

obsessed with…?
- tidying / cleaning
- their appearance
- keeping fit
- healthy eating
- anything else

How long has it been going on for?

Does it interfere with his / her life?

Does it affect the people around him / her?

Does he / she talk about it?

How serious do you think it is?

Do you think they should do something about it?

7 **4.14** **SONG** ♫ *Addicted to Love*

Key success factors
- being able to construct an argument
- being able to link points together in a logical sequence
- using appropriate discourse markers to connect, contrast, and balance points

ANALYSING A MODEL TEXT

a You have been asked to write the following essay:

Text-messaging is an important advance in communication – or is it?

With a partner, discuss three reasons you think text messaging represents an important advance in communication and three reasons why it does not. Order them 1–3 according to their importance.

b Read the model essay and see if the writer has mentioned some or all of your arguments. Does the writer put her main argument first in both paragraphs?

c Look at the three introductory paragraphs below and choose which one you think is best for the essay. Compare with a partner, and discuss why you think it is the best, and why the other two are less suitable. Then do the same with the concluding paragraphs.

Introductory paragraphs

1 Since the first SMS was sent in 1992, text messaging has become one of the most popular forms of communication, especially among the younger generation, with billions of messages being sent every year. But has this technology really improved interpersonal communication?

2 Text messaging clearly has important advantages and disadvantages. In this essay, I am first going to analyse the advantages of SMS technology and then I will outline some important disadvantages before finally drawing my conclusions.

3 Can you imagine life without sending and receiving SMSs? Almost certainly not, as this cheap and convenient technology has become such a vital tool for organizing our social lives and communicating instantly with our friends and family. How did we manage before it was invented?

Concluding paragraphs

1 In conclusion, text messaging has important advantages and disadvantages, but on the whole, I believe that it has improved our lives in a significant way.

2 In my view, text messaging has improved communication considerably and it is highly useful, for example, if you are trying to contact someone in a very noisy place, such as a club, where it would be impossible to hear a phone call. In conclusion, it is a very vital piece of technology.

3 To sum up, although text messages are a cheap and useful way of communicating, they have arguably led to young people being less able to express themselves correctly in writing. On balance, I believe that text messaging does not represent an advance in communication.

Text-messaging is an important advance in communication – or is it?

'Just think of it as if you're reading a long text-message.'

Introduction

_____

Arguments in favour

Being able to send short, written messages via mobile phone has clearly advanced communication in certain respects.

The greatest benefit of texting is that it allows us to communicate instantly with other people wherever they are, but without interrupting them in the way that a phone call would, and allowing them to reply whenever it is convenient for them to do so. In addition, sending a text, for example to arrange where to meet someone, is a quick, concise, and efficient way of communicating, as people normally only include the vital information. Finally, text messaging is a very cheap form of communication, which is a particular advantage for young people or for people who are travelling, when mobile phone conversations can be prohibitively expensive.

Arguments against

On the other hand, however, there are strong arguments to suggest that text messaging has had a negative effect on how we communicate. One downside is that there is a tendency for people to use texts as an excuse to get out of conversations which might be uncomfortable to have either face-to-face or on the phone. Another drawback is that people increasingly text while they are in company, suddenly switching off from a conversation and focusing on their phone screens. However, perhaps the most important and worrying downside of texting is the effect it is having on written communication. Teachers worldwide complain that the idiosyncratic language of text messages, such as abbreviated words and the use of letters and numbers to convey meaning has led to a generation of young people being unable to spell or form correct sentences.

Conclusion

_____

Introductions and conclusions

In an essay it is important that the introduction engages the reader's attention. It should introduce the topic, but should not include the specific points that you are going to mention in the body of the text.

A good introductory paragraph describes the present situation and gives supporting evidence. It should refer to the statement or question you have been asked to discuss. This can often be done in the form of a question to the reader which the subsequent paragraphs should answer.

The conclusion should briefly sum up the arguments you have made, and can include your personal opinion. The opinion you express should follow logically from the arguments you have presented.

USEFUL LANGUAGE

d Complete the missing words. Some (but not all) are in the model essay.

Expressing the main points in an argument	
+	
1 The greatest **b**_____ is that	texting allows us to communicate instantly with other people.
2 **First and most im**_____	
−	
3 One **d**_____ of texting is that	people use texts as an excuse to get out of conversations.
4 Another **dr**_____ to text messaging is that	

Adding supporting information to a main argument, or introducing other related arguments	
5 In a_____,	
6 **What is m**_____,	sending a text is a quick, concise, and efficient way of communicating.
7 **Not o**_____ that, but	
8 **Another point in f**_____ **of** this technology is that	

Describing cause and effect	
9 Text messaging can **r**_____ **in** / can **l**_____ **to**	an inability to write correctly.
10 Other problems can arise **because of / d**_____ **to**	text messaging.

Weighing up arguments	
11 **On b**_____,	I believe that it does not represent an advance in communication.
12 **On the wh**_____,	
13 **A**_____ **in a**_____,	

PLANNING WHAT TO WRITE

Brainstorm the content

Low-cost airlines have revolutionized travel – but at what price?
The growth of online shopping has greatly improved life for the consumer.

a Look at the essay titles above, and with a partner choose one of them. Brainstorm the pros and cons of either low-cost airlines or online shopping. Then decide the three main arguments on each side which are relevant to the title.

b Write an introduction for the essay. Follow this pattern:
1 Write an introductory sentence about how low-cost airlines or online shopping affect our lives nowadays.
2 Write a second sentence supporting the first one, or describing the result of it.
3 Ask a question that you intend to answer in the essay.

c Compare your introduction with a partner. Together, make a final version.

TIPS for writing a discursive essay where you put both sides of an argument
- Brainstorm points for and against and decide which two or three you think are the most important.
- Use a neutral or formal style.
- Write a clear introduction, which engages the reader. You could end with a question you are going to answer.
- Link your ideas together with varied discourse markers and linking phrases, e.g. *due to*, *this can lead to*, etc. because an essay should show the development of a logical argument; it is not just a list of random ideas and opinions.
- Make sure your conclusion is a summary of what you have previously said and refers back to what you were asked to write about. It is important that this is not just a repetition of your arguments. It is a summary of what you believe your arguments have proved.

WRITING

Write the essay in approximately 250 words.

DRAFT your essay in four paragraphs:
- introduction
- arguments in favour of low-cost airlines or online shopping
- arguments against low-cost airlines or online shopping
- conclusion, saying whether you think the advantages outweigh the disadvantages or vice versa

EDIT the essay, cutting any irrelevant information and making sure it is the right length.

CHECK the essay for mistakes in grammar, spelling, punctuation, and register.

THE INTERVIEW

a You are going to listen to an interview with Adrian Hodges, who has written screenplays for both films and TV series. Before you listen, read the glossary and look at how the words are pronounced to help you understand what he says.

> **Caligula** /kə'lɪɡjulə/ the third Roman emperor, reigning from 37 to 41 AD.
>
> **period films** /'pɪəriəd fɪlmz/ films which are set during the life of a particular person or in the history of a particular country.
>
> **a glaring anachronism** /'gleərɪŋ ə'nækrənɪzəm/ something in a book or a film that is very obviously placed in the wrong period of history
>
> **the Senate** /'senət/ a political institution in ancient Rome
>
> **toga** /'təuɡə/ clothing worn by the citizens of ancient Rome
>
> **Macbeth** /mək'beθ/ a play by Shakespeare about a King of Scotland
>
> **William the Conqueror, Charles II, Victoria** English monarchs from the 11th, 17th, and 19th century
>
> **to play fast and loose with** IDM (*old fashioned*) to treat sth in a way that shows you feel no responsibility or respect for it
>
> **the received version** /rɪ'siːvd 'vɜːʃən/ the version accepted by most people as being correct

b **4.15** Listen to part 1. Answer the questions with a partner.

1 What are the main reasons he gives to explain the popularity of historical films and dramas?

2 What does he mean by saying 'you get a double hit' when you base a film on a story from history?

3 What reasons does he give to explain why period films are so much more expensive to make?

c **4.16** Listen to part 2. Answer the questions with a partner.

What does he say about…?

1 the importance of accuracy in historical drama

2 the extent to which you *can* change details when you are writing a historical drama

3 the difference between writing a drama based on ancient history and one based on recent history

4 the writer's responsibility to be truthful to history

5 the danger of a film becoming the 'received version of the truth'

6 why *Spartacus* is a good example of this

7 the film *Braveheart*

d **4.17** Listen and complete the phrases with two or three words. What do you think they mean?

COMMON EXPRESSIONS AND IDIOMS

1 You know that part of your audience at _____ will already have some knowledge of that story.

2 …every shot has to be _____ to make sure that there's nothing in it which, which betrays the period.

3 *Rome* was a _____. We needed big crowds…

4 …all of them have to be dressed in, you know, in togas _____.

5 So I tend to take the view that in a way accuracy isn't the issue when _____ the drama.

6 So, it's all _____ perspective in some ways.

7 You can't say this is true when you know _____ it isn't.

e To what extent do you agree with what he says about the importance of accuracy in historical films? Can you think of any other historical films apart from *Spartacus* where the film is the only version of the truth that people know?

IN THE STREET 📺

a **4.18** You are going to hear five people talking about history. What two questions are they asked? Who chooses a) the most recent b) the most distant period in answer to the first question?

| Tim | Edmund | Mark | Amy | Jerry |

b Listen again. Who do they admire and why?

c **4.19** Listen and complete the phrases with one to three words. What do you think they mean?

COMMON PHRASES

1 …you know, you had the Beatles _____ to America.

2 And I quite _____ of living in Italy, so…

3 Sort of _____ in a toga doing lots of thinking…

4 I think his writing's _____ and very much ahead of its time.

5 I think to _____ an idea so simple and so brilliant…

d Answer the questions from **a** with a partner.

GRAMMAR

a Choose the best answer, a, b, or c.

1 I must make sure I'm home by midnight. _____, my parents won't let me go out tomorrow night.
   a As a matter of fact   b Otherwise   c After all

2 Naomi seems depressed. _____, I think she still hasn't got over the break-up of her marriage.
   a Basically   b Incidentally   c At least

3 We have interviewed all three candidates and _____ we think that Joe is the most suitable person for the post.
   a all in all   b in conclusion   c by the way

4 I'm too tired to go out tonight. _____, I'm rather short of money this month.
   a That's to say   b Besides   c On the other hand

5 _____ discipline is concerned, I think it is a very good school.
   a As long as   b As for   c As far as

6 It poured with rain all week and the hotel was awful. _____, our holiday was a complete disaster.
   a In other words   b As I was saying   c Anyway

7 I'd like _____ at about 6.00, if that's possible.
   a that they come   b them coming   c them to come

8 If we hadn't had to work late tonight, _____ the match right now.
   a I'd be watching   b I'd have watched   c I'll watch

9 You can't stop people _____ big cars unless you raise the tax on them.
   a buy   b to buy   c buying

10 I'll pay for the classes _____ you promise not to miss any.
   a supposing   b unless   c providing

b Put the verb in brackets in the right form.

1 My parents always encouraged me _____ foreign languages. (learn)

2 If I hadn't read the book before I saw the film, I think I _____ the film more. (enjoy)

3 My new job involves me _____ to North America two or three times a year. (travel)

4 They are incredibly generous people and they wouldn't let me _____ for anything. (pay)

5 Daniel can stay the night as long as he _____ sleeping on the sofa. (not mind)

6 Supposing Manchester United drew their last match, who _____ the league in that case? (win)

7 Marcus might have hurt his head badly if he _____ a helmet when he fell off his bike. (not wear)

8 We would like you _____ our annual conference this year. (attend)

9 _____ you _____ me earlier that you were coming, I would have taken the day off. (tell)

10 The children are staying indoors today. I don't want to risk them _____ a cold just before our holiday. (catch)

11 If my husband hadn't inherited a lot of money, we definitely _____ in a house like this now. (not live)

12 It's impossible to imagine how beautiful the Taj Mahal is unless you _____ it with your own eyes. (see)

VOCABULARY

a Complete the missing words.

1 I'll be at home this evening, so call me on the **l**_____, not on my mobile.

2 It was a fierce battle and **c**_____ were heavy on both sides.

3 After two days of fighting both sides agreed to a **c**_____.

4 She wasn't answering her mobile so I left a message on her **v**_____.

5 My father-in-law is rather intolerant and narrow-**m**_____.

6 We can call directory **e**_____ and get the number of the restaurant.

7 I'm getting a bit short-**s**_____. I think I need glasses.

8 After a **s**_____ of three months, the city finally surrendered to the enemy.

9 You'd better throw those trousers away. They're completely **w**_____ out.

10 The English troops used their bows to fire thousands of **a**_____ into the air.

11 When the general saw that his soldiers were totally outnumbered, he gave the order to **r**_____.

12 During the civil war thousand of **r**_____ fled and lived in camps in neighbouring countries.

b Complete the phrasal verbs.

1 War has just _____ **out** between the two countries.

2 I tried to call Bill at the office, but I couldn't _____ **through**. All the lines were busy.

3 You'll have to **speak** _____ a bit. My grandmother is very deaf.

4 The rebels tried to _____ **up** the railway station, but the bomb didn't explode.

5 I've **run** _____ **of** credit on my mobile phone.

6 Gina got so angry with me on the phone last night that she **hung** _____ in the middle of the conversation.

c Complete with a preposition.

1 I'm so proud _____ you. I never thought you would pass.

2 Luke is nearly 30 but he's still dependent _____ his parents.

3 I'm completely fed up _____ my job. I dread going to work every morning.

4 My sister is totally hooked _____ that new reality show on TV.

5 We're going to drive to Spain, as my wife isn't very keen _____ flying.

5A

G permission, obligation, and necessity
V word formation: prefixes
P intonation in exclamations

'Bad laws are the worst sort of tyranny.'
Edmund Burke, Irish writer and philosopher

Who's in control?

1 READING & SPEAKING

a Read the *Wikipedia* entry for the expression 'nanny state'. With a partner, summarize in one sentence what the expression means.

Nanny state

In general this expression is used in reference to policies where the state is characterized as being excessive in its desire to protect ('nanny'), govern, or control particular aspects of society or groups of people. Policies such as mandatory helmet laws and bans on smoking in public places, high taxes on junk food, bans on recreational drug use, gun control, a legal drinking age or legal smoking age that is higher than the age of majority, political correctness, and censorship, are often criticized as 'nanny state' actions. Such actions result from the belief that the state (or, more often, one of its local authorities) has a duty to protect citizens from their own harmful behaviour, and assumes that the state knows best what constitutes harmful behaviour.

From Wikipedia

b Then look at the title of the article below. What do you think it will be about?

c Discuss whether you think the following are true or false about some areas in California. Tick (✓) the ones that you think are probably true.

1   It's against the law to smoke in the street.
2   Speed cameras control how fast people drive.
3   Teachers are not allowed to use the words 'Mom' and 'Dad' when they talk to children.
4   You can't get plastic bags for your shopping at supermarkets.
5   Restaurants have to display the number of calories in each dish they serve.
6   Shops are not allowed to open on Sundays.
7   It's illegal to drive 4x4 vehicles in urban areas.
8   Restaurants have to serve tap water, not bottled mineral water.
9   There are cameras in most shopping malls and other public areas to control criminal behaviour.
10 Scouts are not allowed to make campfires.
11 There is a ban on opening new fast-food restaurants.
12 Toy shops must not sell any kind of toy weapons, e.g. guns or swords.

d Read the article and check. Mark the sentences T, F, or DS (doesn't say).

Welcome to ~~California~~ Nanny

It was one o'clock in the morning. John Lutz had just left the Grand Palace Stadium cinema complex in the wealthy LA suburb of Calabasas and was standing next to his Mini, smoking a cigarette. As he did so, a massive SUV pulled up alongside him. The driver wound down his window, leant out, and said: 'Hey, buddy, you can't smoke here. Put it out.'

John, a staff writer for a popular American TV show, paused for a second, unable to believe that his decision to smoke in an empty car park in the small hours of the morning was of so much interest to a complete stranger. He exhaled slowly. And then he told the driver, using language not suitable for publication, that no, actually, he wouldn't put it out.

He was unaware that an hour earlier, at midnight, the Calabasas Comprehensive Secondhand Smoke Control Ordinance, the most restrictive anti-smoking policy anywhere in the world, had come into force.

The outdoor smoking ban of which John Lutz ran foul is just one example of a frenzy of puritanical edicts from California's politicians that in the past few weeks has outlawed trans fat in all restaurant food, prevented LA supermarkets from handing out plastic bags, and stopped new fast-food restaurants opening in one of the suburbs. Other recent bans have challenged such monumental threats to human wellbeing as helium balloons, camp fires, the use of wild animals in circuses, swearing, texting while stopped at traffic lights, dogs sitting on drivers' laps, and the use of the terms 'Mom' and 'Dad' in school classrooms (in case they offend children from single-parent families).

Of course, some of these things deserve to be discouraged. But criminalized? Until recently, with Arnold Schwarzenegger serving as the Republican governor, California seemed to have avoided many of the worst examples of nanny-stateism inflicted on, say, Britain and remains more laid back. Tax on petrol isn't designed to punish you for not wanting to get on a bus, speed cameras remain unheard of, and CCTV is rare. But things began to change a couple of years ago. This week, for example, a new law will be brought in that intends to force restaurants in LA to display the number of calories of each item on their menus.

John Lutz, the cigarette smoker, says the real problem with bans is that they tend to be selective, and they usually focus, conveniently, on the vices of other people. 'The people who think they have the right to tell you what to do are usually the exact same people who drive around in SUVs and drink bottled water every day,' Lutz says. 'I'm pretty sure both of those things are the very worst things you can do to the environment. Yet they'll go crazy if they see me stubbing out a cigarette butt in my own backyard.'

SUV (NAmE) Sports Utility Vehicle = a 4x4 car, e.g. a Land Rover™
buddy (NAmE informal) friend
trans fat a kind of fat which encourages the development of cholesterol
CCTV closed circuit TV, e.g. used to control shopping centres, car parks, etc.
backyard (NAmE) back garden

From The Times

LEXIS IN CONTEXT

e Look at the following phrasal verbs and prepositional verbs in context. With a partner say what you think they mean.

pull up (l.4)
wind sth down (l.4)
lean out (l.5)
put sth out (l.5)
hand sth out (l.17)
bring sth in (l.30)
stub sth out (l.38)

f Read the article again. Underline words and phrases which show the author's attitude towards the laws in California. What is his point of view?

g Which of the Californian laws mentioned in the text would you like to see passed in the area where you live? Why? Are there laws or regulations where you live which you consider to be 'nanny state'?

2 GRAMMAR   permission, obligation, and necessity

a Look at the pairs of sentences. With a partner, say if they are the same or different in meaning. In which pair of sentences is there a difference in register?

1 **It is not permitted to** take food or drink into the library.
  You're not allowed to take food or drink into the library.
2 **You'd better** turn your mobile off.
  You ought to turn your mobile off.
3 **We're supposed to** speak English all the time in class.
  We have to speak English all the time in class.
4 **You needn't** wear a suit – the party's going to be quite informal.
  You don't need to wear a suit – the party's going to be quite informal.
5 **I should have** bought my mother a present.
  I had to buy my mother a present.

b ⟶ **p.148 Grammar Bank 5A.** Read the rules and do the exercises.

3 SPEAKING

a Talk in small groups. Imagine the following laws have been proposed for the area where you live. Would you be in favour of them or do you think they are too 'nanny state'? Try to use the **bold** expressions in your answers.

On the road
⊘ Cyclists **should have to** pass a test to get a cycling licence before they are allowed on the road.
⊘ Car drivers **should not be allowed to** eat or drink while driving.
⊘ **It should be an offence for** pedestrians to cross roads while wearing earphones.

At home
⊘ **It should be compulsory for** people to turn off electrical appliances at night and not leave them on standby.
⊘ **It should be illegal to** leave children under 12 alone in the house.
⊘ **It should be against the law for** parents to give fast food to seriously overweight children.

Public health
⊘ Smoking in the street **should be banned**.
⊘ Restaurants and bars **should not be allowed to** serve more than two units of alcohol per person.
⊘ People who abuse their health **should be made to** contribute to expensive medical treatment.

Society
⊘ **It should be against the law not to** vote in elections.
⊘ All advertising aimed at children under the age of 12 **should be banned**.
⊘ Couples **should be obliged to** attend three months of marriage counselling before they are allowed to get divorced.

Education
⊘ Teachers **should not be allowed to** use red pens to correct exercises as this is psychologically harmful to students.
⊘ Schoolchildren **should not be given** marks in exams, only general indications, so that they can't compare themselves with other children.
⊘ Competitive sport **should be banned** in the school system, so that children's self-esteem is not affected by losing.

b In your groups, agree on a new law or regulation which you would like to see introduced for two of the categories. Then try to convince other groups to vote in favour of passing your law.

4 VOCABULARY word formation: prefixes

> The most restrictive **anti**-smoking policy anywhere in the world had come into force…
>
> California's politicians have **out**lawed trans fat in all restaurant food…

a Look at the two highlighted words from *Welcome to Nannyfornia*, which both have prefixes. What do the prefixes add to the meaning of the base word?

b Look at some more highlighted words with prefixes from previous lessons and with a partner say what the prefix means.

1 Non-native speakers of English now **out**number native speakers by three to one.

2 I think this film is very **over**rated. Personally, I thought it was rather mediocre.

3 **Re**awakening a romance can be an incendiary experience.

4 The character of Captain Smith was **mis**represented in the film *Titanic*.

5 The importance of the lowly translator to our understanding of foreign literature should not be **under**estimated.

6 When people spend that money **pro**socially on others (giving gifts to friends, donating to charities) they are happier than when they spend it on themselves.

7 Her skin is already **pre**maturely aged.

8 The pound has been **de**valued so you now get more euros to the pound.

c Add a prefix from **a** or **b** above to the **bold** word and make any other necessary changes to complete the sentences.

1 I completely _____ Alan. I thought he was a really weak character, but he isn't at all. **judge**

2 This paragraph in your essay is totally unclear. You're going to have to _____ it. **write**

3 I'm going to install new _____ software that's just come out. **virus**

4 My wife and I have a _____ signal for when we want to leave a dinner or a party. **arrange**

5 Our product _____ its main competitor by 20% and is now the market leader. **sell**

6 _____ forces are now controlling the area previously held by the rebels. **government**

7 The team seem rather _____ since the coach was fired. **motivate**

8 I'd hardly studied at all for the exam, so I felt very _____. **prepare**

9 We're not going back to that restaurant – they _____ us last time we went. **charge**

10 The hotel has an _____ swimming pool, which is open from June to September. **door**

5 LISTENING & SPEAKING

a Divide into teams. Try to agree on answers to the questions below, which come from a quiz book based on a British TV programme.

b ⊙ **Communication** *QI quiz*. A p.117 B p.119.

QI Quiz

1 What was Tutankhamun's curse?

2 What do chameleons do, and why?

3 What man-made artefacts can be seen from the moon?

4 What do kilts and whisky have in common?

5 Which metal is the best conductor?

6 Which African mammal kills more humans than any other?

From *The Book of General Ignorance*

c **5.1** Listen to someone talking about the TV quiz show and books which the questions below came from. Answer the questions with a partner.

1 Why did they call the show *QI*?
2 What is the basic principle behind the show and its books?
3 What examples does he give from the books?
4 Why is it so popular?
5 What are the two reasons Lloyd and Mitchinson give for why children often do badly at school?

7 What would probably have killed you in an 18th-century sea battle?

8 What did the American Thomas Edison invent, which English speakers use every day?

9 How does television damage your health?

10 Why is a marathon 42.195 km long?

d **5.2** Now listen to the speaker explaining how the *QI* principles could change education. Tick the seven suggestions mentioned.

- Children should not start school before they are seven years old.
- Learning should never feel like hard work.
- Children should be able to decide on their own curriculum.
- The same importance should be given to arts as to science and mathematics.
- Children shouldn't be expected to learn to read until they actually want to.
- Children shouldn't be made to go to school every day if they don't want to.
- There should be no evaluation or assessment of children by teachers.
- Children should make their own class rules and should be responsible for enforcing them.
- Children should teach each other skills that they have mastered, e.g. how to ride a bike or play a musical instrument.
- Children should learn theories through practical activities.
- Children should spend at least half their time outdoors, interacting with nature.
- There should be no official school-leaving age.

e What do you think of Lloyd and Mitchinson's suggestions? Do you think any of the other suggestions in **d** would improve the learning environment?

6 PRONUNCIATION intonation in exclamations

a **5.3** Listen to the dialogues, and complete the exclamations.

A Did you know that in California schools they're not allowed to say Mom and Dad any more in case they offend someone from a one-parent family?
B _____!

A Did you know that America was named after a British merchant called Richard Ameryk?
B _____! I'd always wondered where the name came from.

b Listen again and focus on the intonation in the exclamations. Answer the questions with a partner.

1 Does the intonation on the adjectives in the exclamations go _____?
   a up
   b down
   c up and down
   d down and up
2 What consonant sound is added between *How* and the adjective? Why?

c Practise saying some more common exclamations with *What* and *How*.

What a great idea!   What an amazing coincidence!
What a terrible experience!   How annoying!
How embarrassing!   How weird!

d ⊙ **Communication** *What a ridiculous idea! A p.117 B p.120.* Respond to what your partner says with an exclamation.

G verbs of the senses
V place and movement
P extra stress on important words

'There are painters who transform the sun into a yellow spot, but there are others who with the help of their art and their intelligence, transform a yellow spot into the sun.'

Pablo Picasso

Just any old bed?

1 LISTENING & SPEAKING

a Look at the photos. Four of the objects are famous and expensive works of art. The other four are ordinary objects. With a partner, decide which are the works of art.

b ➲ **Communication** *Four works of art p.118.* Did you guess right? What do you think the artists were trying to communicate?

c 5.4 Listen to an art expert talking about two of the works of art and answer the questions.

1 What are…?
 a installations
 b modern sculptures
2 What basic similarity is there between installations and other more traditional forms of art?
3 Why might artists today choose to create an installation rather than a painting?
4 Why are some people sceptical when they see an installation?
5 What special skills did Damien Hirst need to create *Away from the Flock*?
6 What does it communicate?
7 How is Tracey Emin's *My Bed* different from her real bed?
8 What does it communicate?
9 Why might it communicate more than a traditional self-portrait?

d Listen again and check your answers.

e Talk in small groups.

1 Does what the expert said change the way you see the two works of art? What did you agree / disagree with?
2 Would you pay to go and see any of the four works of art? Why (not)?
3 Have you seen any installation art? What did you think of it?
4 If you were going to make an installation to represent your life, what objects would you include?
5 Do you have a favourite…?
 • portrait
 • landscape painting • self-portrait
 • still-life • abstract painting
 Do you have any other favourite works of art?

2 GRAMMAR verbs of the senses

a 5.5 Complete three sentences from the listening with the right form of one of the following verbs. Listen again and check.

look as if	look at	look like	see

1 When people _____ some installations, they think 'Well, I could do that', they don't _____ that there's any expertise involved at all.
2 And then of course, he had to arrange it in a particular way, this animal is in a particular pose, so that it _____ it's quite alive, although of course we all know that it isn't.
3 I mean the bed is something that you _____ and you think 'Yeah, that _____ my bed in the morning'.

b Answer the questions with a partner.

1 What's the grammatical difference between *look as if* and *look like*, and the difference in meaning between *look at* and *see*?

2 Apart from *sight*, what are the other four senses?

3 What verbs do you associate with them?

c ⭕ **p.149 Grammar Bank 5B.** Read the rules and do the exercises.

d Ask and answer with a partner.

- Are there any paintings or images that you like or dislike looking at because of how they make you feel?
- If you were offered plastic surgery to make you look like a celebrity, which celebrity would you choose, and why?
- What makes a voice sound attractive / unattractive to you?
- Are there any sounds or kinds of music that you don't like hearing because they make you feel uncomfortable?
- Do you think people tend to dislike foods more because of their smell, their taste, or their texture?
- What kind of perfumes do you really like or dislike on yourself or on other people? Why?
- Are there any medicines you hate (or enjoy) taking because of their taste?
- Would you be prepared to touch these creatures in a zoo? Why (not)?

  a snake   a tarantula   a lion   a lizard   a rat   a budgerigar
- Are there certain materials you never wear or love to wear because of the way they feel?

3 PRONUNCIATION   extra stress on important words

a 5.6 Read and listen to the poem and answer the questions.

1 Where does the conversation take place?

2 Who are 'they'?

3 What does the speaker do, and why?

4 What do you think the poet is trying to communicate?

b Listen to the poem again. Why do you think some of the words are in *italics*? In pairs, practise reading it aloud.

c 5.7 Read the information box below. Then listen to the sentence *I wanted to buy a flat in London* pronounced in five different ways. Listen again and match each version to the continuations below.

> **Extra stress on important words**
>
> Sometimes we give extra emphasis to a word in a sentence to convey meaning. These may even be words which are not usually stressed, e.g. articles or pronouns.
>
> This is not just *any* cold fried egg on *any* chipped plate. (= they are special)
>
> I don't want *this* bag. (= I want another one)
>
> Excuse me. I ordered a *chicken* sandwich. (= not the one you've brought me)

A ☐ ____, but my wife didn't.

B ☐ ____, but my wife wanted a house.

C ☐ ____, but we couldn't afford one.

D ☐ ____, not in Liverpool.

E ☐ ____, not rent one.

d 5.8 Listen and check. Then practise saying the five complete sentences, stressing a different word each time.

e ⭕ **Communication** *Stressing the right word.* A p.118 B p.120.

One of a series

'My word,'
I said,
'That really is
a remarkable likeness
of a cold fried egg
on a chipped plate.
How much is it?'

'Actually,'
they said
'It *is* a cold fried egg
on a chipped plate.
It is one of a series
created
by Laura Carambo.
£150,000.'

And I said
'?????'

And they said
'This is not just
any cold fried egg
on *any* chipped plate.
It is *this* cold fried egg
on *this* chipped plate.

Carambo's work celebrates
the *thisness* of things.

She shows us how *this* and the *other*
move in a perpetual dance,
mediating between
and uniting
the amphimetropic opposites
of our Janus-faced universe.'

Well
I could see that it all made sense
And between you and me,
I've looked at the reviews
and the auction catalogues,
and I reckon
I got a real bargain.
Come and look.

by Michael Swan

amphimetropic = an invented word

4 READING

Read and listen to the story and answer the questions, section by section.

In a Season of Calm Weather

BY RAY BRADBURY

GEORGE AND ALICE SMITH detrained at Biarritz one summer noon and in an hour had run through their hotel onto the beach into the ocean and back out to bake upon the sand. To see George Smith sprawled burning there, you'd think him only
5 a tourist flown to Europe and soon to be transported home. But here was a man who loved art more than life itself.

"George?" His wife loomed over him. "I know what you've been thinking. I can read your lips."

He lay perfectly still, waiting.

10 "And?"

"Picasso," she said.

He winced. Some day she would learn to pronounce that name.

"Please," she said. "Relax. I know you heard the rumour this morning, but you should see your eyes – your tic is back.
15 All right, Picasso's here, down the coast a few miles away, visiting friends in some small fishing town. But you must forget it or our vacation's ruined."

"I wish I'd never heard the rumour," he said honestly.

"If only," she said, "you liked other painters."

20 Others? Yes, there were others. He could breakfast most congenially on Caravaggio still-lifes of autumn pears and midnight plums. For lunch: those fire-squirting, thick-wormed Van Gogh sunflowers. But the great feast? The paintings he saved his palate for? Who else but the creator of *Girl Before*
25 *a Mirror* and *Guernica*?

> **5.9**
>
> 1 What do you find out about the characters George and Alice Smith from this first section?
> 2 Guess roughly what these verbs mean from the context: *detrained* (1.1), *sprawled* (1.4), *loomed* (1.7), and *winced* (1.12).

"I keep thinking," he said aloud, "if we saved our money..."

"We'll never have five thousand dollars."

"I know," he said quietly. "But it's nice thinking we might bring it off some day. Wouldn't it be great to just step up to
30 him, and say 'Pablo, here's five thousand! Give us the sea, the sand, that sky, or any old thing you want, we'll be happy...' "

After a moment, his wife touched his arm.

"I think you'd better go in the water now," she said.

"Yes," he said. "I'd better do just that."

35 During the afternoon George Smith came out and went into the ocean with the vast spilling motions of now warm, now cool people who at last, with the sun's decline, their bodies all lobster colours, trudged for their wedding-cake hotels.

The beach lay deserted for endless mile on mile save for two
40 people. One was George Smith, towel over shoulder. Far along the shore another shorter, square-cut man walked alone in the tranquil weather. He was deeper tanned, his close-shaven

head dyed almost mahogany by the sun, and his eyes were clear and bright as water in his face. So the shoreline stage
45 was set, and in a few minutes the two men would meet.

> **5.10**
>
> 3 What is George's dream?
> 4 What do you understand by the metaphors...?
> 'their bodies all lobster colours' 'their wedding-cake hotels'
> 'the shoreline stage was set'
> 5 What impression do you get of what the other man on the beach looks like?

The stranger stood alone. Glancing about, he saw his aloneness, saw the waters of the lovely bay, saw the sun sliding down the late colours of the day, and then half-turning spied a small wooden object on the sand. It was no more than the
50 slender stick from a lime ice-cream delicacy long since melted away. Smiling he picked the stick up. With another glance around to re-insure his solitude, the man stooped again and holding the stick gently with light sweeps of his hand began to do the one thing in all the world he knew best how to do.

55 He began to draw incredible figures along the sand. He sketched one figure and then moved over and still looking down, completely focused on his work now, drew a second and a third figure, and after that a fourth and a fifth and a sixth.

George Smith, printing the shoreline with his feet, gazed here,
60 gazed there, and then saw the man ahead. George Smith, drawing nearer, saw that the man, deeply tanned, was bending down. Nearer yet, and it was obvious what the man was up to. George Smith chuckled. Of course, of course... along on the beach this man – how old? Sixty-five? Seventy? – was scribbling
65 and doodling away. How the sand flew! How the wild portraits flung themselves out there on the shore! How...

George Smith took one more step and stopped, very still.

The stranger was drawing and drawing and did not seem to sense that anyone stood immediately behind him and the
70 world of his drawings in the sand.

> **5.11**
>
> 6 What does the stranger start doing, and how does George react?
> 7 Look at the two groups of three words. What's the connection between the three?
> a *glance* (1.46)   *spied* (1.48)   *gazed* (1.60)
> b *sketched* (1.56)   *scribbling* (1.64)   *doodling* (1.65)

George Smith looked down at the sand. And, after a long while, looking, he began to tremble.

For there on the flat shore were pictures of Grecian lions and Mediterranean goats and maidens and children dancing. And
75 the sand, in the dying light, was the colour of copper on which was now slashed a message that any man in any time might read and savour down the years.

The artist stopped.

George Smith drew back and stood away.

The artist glanced up, surprised to find someone so near. Then he simply stood there, looking from George Smith to his own creations flung like idle footprints down the way. He smiled at last and shrugged as if to say. Look what I've done; see what a child? You will forgive me, won't you? One day or another we are all fools... you, too, perhaps? So allow an old fool this, eh? Good! Good!

But George Smith could only look at the little man with the sun-dark skin and the clear sharp eyes, and say the man's name once, in a whisper, to himself.

They stood thus for perhaps another five seconds, George Smith staring at the sand-frieze, and the artist watching George Smith with amused curiosity.

George Smith opened his mouth, closed it, put out his hand, took it back. He stepped towards the picture, stepped away. Then he moved along the line of figures, like a man viewing a precious series of marbles cast up from some ancient ruin on the shore. His eyes did not blink, his hand wanted to touch but did not dare to touch. He wanted to run but did not run.

5.12

8   What is the artist's attitude to George, and George's to the artist?

9   Look at these verbs in the text: *tremble* (1.72), *slash* (1.76), *draw back* (1.79), *shrug* (1.83), *stare* (1.90), *blink* (1.96). What kind of actions do you think they are?

10   Why might George have 'wanted to run'?

He looked suddenly at the hotel. Run, yes! Run! What? Grab a shovel, dig, excavate, save a chunk of this all too crumbling sand? Find a repair-man, race him back here with plaster-of-Paris to cast a mould of some small fragile part of these? No, no. Silly, silly. Or...? His eyes flicked to his hotel window. The camera! Run, get it, get back, and hurry along the shore, clicking, changing film, clicking until...

George Smith whirled to face the sun. It burned faintly on his face, his eyes were two small fires from it. The sun was half underwater and, as he watched, it sank the rest of the way in a matter of seconds.

The artist had drawn nearer and now was gazing into George Smith's face with great friendliness as if he were guessing every thought. Now he was nodding his head in a little bow. Now the ice-cream stick had fallen casually from his fingers. Now he was saying good night, good night. Now he was gone, walking back down the beach towards the south.

George Smith stood looking after him. After a full minute, he did the only thing he could possibly do. He started at the beginning of the fantastic frieze and he walked slowly along the shore.

And when he came to the end of the animals and men he turned round and started back in the other direction, just staring down as if he had lost something and did not quite know where to find it. He kept on doing this until there was no more light in the sky, or on the sand, to see by.

5.13

11   What is George's dilemma? What options does he consider? What does he decide to do in the end? Why?

12   Look at these verbs in the text: *grab* (1.98), *flick* (1.102), *whirl* (1.105), *nod* (1.111). What kind of movements do you think they are?

He sat down at the supper table.

"You're late," said his wife. "I just had to come down alone. I'm ravenous."

"That's all right," he said.

"Anything interesting happen on your walk?" she asked.

"No," he said.

"You look funny; George, you didn't swim out too far, did you, and almost drown? I can tell by your face. You did swim out too far, didn't you?"

"Yes," he said.

"Well," she said, watching him closely. "Don't ever do that again. Now – what'll you have?"

He picked up the menu and started to read it and stopped suddenly.

"What's wrong?" asked his wife.

He turned his head and shut his eyes for a moment.

"Listen."

She listened.

"I don't hear anything," she said.

"Don't you?"

"No. What is it?"

"Just the tide," he said, after a while, sitting there, his eyes still shut. "Just the tide, coming in."

5.14

13   Why do you think George didn't tell his wife about his experience?

14   How do you think he is feeling as he listens to the tide come in?

5 VOCABULARY   place and movement

a   Look at six sentences from the story. Without looking back at the story, complete the gaps with a word from the list. Then check with the story.

along	away	back (x3)	into	onto
round	~~through~~	towards (x2)	upon	

1   George and Alice...in an hour had run *through* their hotel _____ the beach _____ the ocean and _____ out to bake _____ the sand (1.2).

2   He stepped _____ the picture, stepped _____. Then he moved _____ the line of figures, like a man viewing a precious series of marbles... (1.93).

3   Now he was saying good night, good night. Now he was gone, walking _____ down the beach _____ the south (1.113).

4   And when he came to the end of the animals and men he turned _____ and started _____ in the other direction (1.118).

b   ⊃ **p.164 Vocabulary Bank** *Place and movement.*

6   5.15   SONG ♫ *Vincent*

5
C

G gerunds and infinitives
V health and medicine; similes
P word stress

'The art of medicine consists in amusing the patient while nature cures the disease.'
Voltaire, French author and philosopher

Trick or treatment?

1 SPEAKING & LISTENING

a How much medical vocabulary do you know? Do the quiz with a partner.

Medical Quiz

1 When might you get…?
a a bruise
b a blister
c a rash

2 Why might you be given…?
a a plaster
b a bandage
c antibiotics
d stitches
e an X-ray
f a scan

3 When might you need to see…?
a your GP
b a specialist
c a surgeon

4 What are the symptoms of…?
a a cold
b flu
c food poisoning
d a heart attack
e asthma

5 What might happen to you if you…?
a had to stand for a long time in a hot crowded room
b drank too much champagne
c were stung on your hand by a wasp
d switched on a light with wet hands

b Look at some commonly-held beliefs related to health and medicine. With a partner, discuss each one and decide if you think it is true or a myth.

c **5.16** Now listen to a doctor talking about these beliefs. Were you right?

d Listen again. Why is each belief true or a myth? Make notes and then compare with a partner.

LEXIS IN CONTEXT

e **5.17** Complete the extracts from the listening with the missing word. Listen and check.

1 If you're **w**_____ your weight, what matters is what you eat, not when you eat it.
2 Colds, we know, are caused by **v**_____, which you catch from an infected person…
3 But recent research has found that being exposed to cold temperatures does, in fact, lower our body's **d**_____.
4 As a matter of fact there is a medical condition called 'night-eating **s**_____', which affects 2% of the population.
5 Reading in the dark or in bad light can cause a temporary **s**_____ on the eyes, but it rapidly goes away once you return to bright light.
6 …our body heat, and certain chemicals in our **s**_____.

f Did any of this information surprise you? Will it affect the way you behave? Are there any other strongly-held beliefs about health and medicine in your country which you think are probably myths?

Never shower in a thunderstorm.
Surprising facts and misleading myths about our health and the world we live in…

Truth or myth?

1 Avoid eating late at night if you don't want to put on weight.
2 If you stay out in the cold and wind, you are more likely to catch a cold.
3 Never have a shower during a thunderstorm – you might get electrocuted.
4 Reading in dim light will ruin your eyesight.
5 Some people attract mosquitoes more than others.
6 Bottled water is safer than tap water.

2 VOCABULARY similes

a Read the information about similes. Then complete sentences 1–10 with a word from the list.

> A simile is a fixed informal / colloquial expression of comparison using *as* or *like*. Similes add emphasis to an adjective, adverb, or verb, e.g. *I think Jane's a bit underweight for her age – she's **as light as a feather**.* (=very light).

bat   dream   fish
flash   gold   horse   log
mule   post   sheet

1 My husband's **as stubborn as a** _____. He refuses to go to the doctor about his bad back.

2 She's **as white as a** _____. I think she's going to faint.

3 He **drinks like a** _____. He ought to cut down or he'll have problems with his liver.

4 He's **as deaf as a** _____. You'll have to speak up a bit.

5 She **sleeps like a** _____. I don't think she's ever had problems with insomnia.

6 Your mother's **as blind as a** _____. I think she ought to get her eyes tested.

7 She's been **as good as** _____. She took all her medicine without making any fuss.

8 My new medication **works like a** _____. I feel a hundred times better.

9 When I pressed the button the nurse came **as quick as a** _____, and immediately changed my drip, which was running out.

10 My son **eats like a** _____. I sometimes think he's got worms.

b Try to think of three people or things you could describe with these similes. Compare with a partner.

3 GRAMMAR gerunds and infinitives

a **5.18** Listen and write the verbs or phrases in the right box.

+ *to* + infinitive

+ gerund

+ infinitive without *to*

b Use your instinct. Cross out the wrong form. Tick (✓) if both are possible.

1 I regret *not going / not having gone* to the doctor earlier.

2 I hate *telling / being told* that I've put on weight.

3 I would like *to have brought / to bring* you some flowers, but I didn't have time.

4 I was stupid *not to take / not to have taken* all the antibiotics.

5 Is there anywhere *to park / park* near the hospital?

6 I've got enough tablets *to last / for lasting* until the end of the month.

7 It's no use *worrying / to worry* until you know what's wrong with you.

8 She was the first woman *to become / becoming* a professor of cardiac surgery.

c ⏺ **p.150 Grammar Bank 5C.** Read the rules and do the exercises.

d ⏺ **Communication** *Guess the sentence. A p.118 B p.120.*

4 VOCABULARY & PRONUNCIATION

a Look at some words which describe types of alternative medicine. Do you know what any of them are, and what they're used for?

- ☐ homeopathy
- ☐ osteopathy
- ☐ aromatherapy
- ☐ herbal medicine
- ☐ chiropractic
- ☐ reflexology
- ☐ hypnotherapy
- ☐ acupuncture

b **5.19** Now listen to eight definitions and match them with the words.

c **5.20** Listen and check. Then underline the main stressed syllable.

d **5.21** Listen and underline the main stressed syllable in the following words. In which word families does the stress change?

an acupuncturist	a chiropractor	a homeopath	homeopathic medicine
hypnosis	a hypnotherapist	an osteopath	a reflexologist

5 LISTENING & SPEAKING

a What forms of alternative medicine are popular in your country? Why do you think some people are sceptical about them?

b **5.22** Listen to four people talking about their experience of alternative medicine. Complete the chart.

	What did they use?	What for?	Was it successful?
Speaker A			
Speaker B			
Speaker C			
Speaker D			

c Listen again. Write the number of the speaker.

Who...?

1 took more than the recommended dose ☐
2 had a physical side effect ☐
3 felt slightly better immediately after the treatment ☐
4 had been unwell for some time before trying alternative medicine ☐
5 has been using alternative medicine for a very long time ☐
6 thought that the dose they had to take was very high ☐
7 tried alternative medicine because of a previous bad experience ☐
8 never gave their children conventional medicine ☐

d Have *you* ever used any alternative medicine, or do you know anyone who has? Was your / their experience positive or negative?

6 READING & SPEAKING

a Read a review from *The Sunday Times* about a new book on alternative medicine and answer the questions with a partner.

1 Do the authors of the book believe that alternative medicine is a trick or a valid form of treatment?
2 Do they think there are any exceptions?
3 Does the reviewer agree?

Trick or treatment?
Alternative Medicine on Trial

'For 2,400 years,' wrote the historian of medicine, David Wootton, 'patients believed doctors were doing them good; for 2,300 years they were wrong.' Only in the past 100 years have treatments in mainstream
5 medicine been consistently subject to clinical trial, to discover what works and what doesn't. Much medicine, though, still stands defiantly outside this mainstream. Can these alternative therapies really claim to be medically effective judged by today's
10 standards, or are they no better than the blood-letting and snake oil of darker centuries?

Simon Singh, a science writer, and Edzard Ernst, a doctor, have set out to reveal the truth about 'the potions, lotions, pills, needles, pummelling, and
15 energizing that lie beyond the realms of conventional medicine.' Their conclusions are damning. 'Most forms of alternative medicine,' say the authors, 'for most conditions remain either unproven or are demonstrably ineffective, and several alternative
20 therapies put patients at risk of harm.'

One by one, they go through the most influential alternative therapies (acupuncture, homeopathy, chiropractic, and herbal medicines) and subject them to scientific scrutiny. In each case, they
25 ask what the evidence is for saying that a given therapy 'works'. Acupuncture, homeopathy, and chiropractic all come out badly. Singh and Ernst build a compelling case that these therapies are at worst positively dangerous – chiropractic neck
30 manipulation can result in injury or death – and at best, are more or less useless. For example, tests done in Germany have shown that 'real' acupuncture works no better in easing migraines than sham acupuncture, a random application of
35 wrongly positioned needles, working as a placebo.

Singh and Ernst do not deny that placebos are powerful things. This being so, does it matter if homeopathy really 'works' in scientific terms? If it makes me feel better to rub arnica cream into a
40 bruise, what harm is done? The authors argue that it does matter, for three reasons.

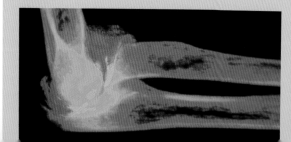

First, if, as the evidence indicates, homeopathy is
merely a placebo, then the price tag is a rip-off.
A second problem lies in the ethics of the doctor-
45 patient relationship. In order to make the placebo
effect work, doctors would have to suppress their
knowledge that homeopathy was bogus. 'In
fact, the best way to exploit the placebo effect
is to lie excessively to make the pill seem extra-
50 special, by using statements such as 'this remedy
has been imported from Timbuktu, etc.'. Third,
and most worrying, by putting his or her faith in
homeopathy, a patient may fail to seek out more
effective conventional treatment. In the case of a
55 minor bruise, this doesn't matter. It's altogether more
serious when it comes to asthma, say, or cancer.

Does this mean that all alternative therapies are to be
dismissed? In the case of herbal medicines, Singh and
Ernst admit that some are effective, but even here
60 they argue that, once an alternative treatment passes
proper tests, it is accepted into the mainstream and
ceases to be alternative. The examples they give are
St John's Wort for the treatment of mild depression
and fish oils for preventing heart disease, as well
65 as osteopathy (a gentler alternative to chiropractic).
They would like to see all alternative medicines jump
through the same expensive hoops as mainstream
drugs. Until they have passed such tests, they should
come with cautions ('Warning: this product is a
70 placebo'), though of course any such warning would
work against the placebo effect.

The authors admit that, in the 19th century, patients
were sometimes better off with homeopathy (i.e. no
treatment at all) than with the mainstream practices
75 of 'blood-letting, vomiting, sweating, and blistering,
which generally stressed an already weakened
body', but point out that today's medicine is, of
course, infinitely more effective in the treatment
of disease. However, in my opinion, mainstream
80 medicine is hopelessly primitive when it comes to
preventing illness. The 'evidence-based' medicine
that Singh and Ernst are so fond of does not look
so great when we consider the profiteering of big
pharmaceutical companies, which would rather sell
85 us drugs to manage our illnesses than help us stay
well. Alternative medicine flourishes in the space
that conventional medicine, which, focusing on cure
rather than prevention, neglects. Is it any wonder
that some people – against all the evidence – prefer
90 the warm lies of the alternative practitioners to the
cold drugs of the men in white coats?

From *The Sunday Times*

b Read the article again and choose the right answers.
1 'Mainstream medicine' (1.4) refers to…
  a medicine which is considered normal and used by most doctors.
  b all kinds of medicine, including alternative medicine.
  c medicine which has been given to patients for thousands of years.
2 'Damning' (1.16) means…
  a rather unclear.   b extremely negative.   c ambiguous.
3 In paragraph 3, the German tests are cited to show that…
  a acupuncture is the least effective of the three therapies mentioned.
  b any benefits from acupuncture are due to the placebo effect.
  c some alternative therapies can be dangerous.
4 What most concerns the authors about alternative medicine is that…
  a seriously ill patients may choose to use it and not get effective mainstream treatment.
  b it is ridiculously expensive considering that it does no real good.
  c doctors would have to be dishonest in order for the placebo effect to work.
5 St John's Wort is given as an example of a medicine which…
  a doesn't really work.
  b has not passed proper tests.
  c should no longer be considered alternative.
6 The reviewer believes that some people use alternative medicine because…
  a the practitioners pay them more attention than mainstream doctors.
  b it is cheaper than having to pay the high prices charged by big pharmaceutical companies.
  c they believe all the evidence about alternative medicine.

LEXIS IN CONTEXT

c Find the opposite of the **bold** word or expression in the text.

1 **alternative medicine**   *conventional* or _____ medicine
2 a **proven** theory   an _____ theory
3 **effective** treatment   _____ treatment
4 a **useful** remedy   a _____ remedy
5 **real** acupuncture   _____ (or *bogus*) acupuncture
6 **a bargain**   a _____
7 **severe** depression   _____ depression

d Do you agree with the following points made in the article?
- Alternative medicine only works because of the placebo effect.
- Mainstream medicine is far more effective in treating serious illnesses.
- Some alternative medicine can actually be harmful.
- All alternative medicines should be tested in the same way that conventional medicines are.
- Drug companies have no interest in preventing or eradicating illnesses, only in controlling them.
- Alternative medicine does more than mainstream medicine to prevent illness.

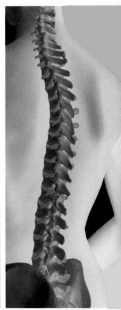

blood-letting medical treatment used in the past in which some of a patient's blood was removed

pummel to keep hitting hard with your hand or fist

placebo a substance that has no physical effects, given to patients who do not need medicine but think that they do, or when testing new drugs

St John's Wort a plant with yellow flowers (*hypericum perforatum*) which has been used for centuries to treat mental disorders and nerve pain

Key success factors
- being clear and concise
- making sensible recommendations based on your observations

ANALYSING A MODEL TEXT

a The owners of a language school are doing some research into student satisfaction, and have asked several students to interview all the students at the school and write a report. Read their report and then from memory tell a partner what the school's main strengths and weaknesses are in each area.

b Without looking back at the model text, try to remember how some of the highlighted phrases below were expressed in a less informal way. Check back with the text for those you can't remember.

1 What this report is for is…
The _____ is…

2 …is to find out how happy students are with the classes and facilities.
…is to _____ with the classes and facilities.

3 In general, students thought the teachers were very good.
In general, students _____.

4 About class sizes, most students think that there should no more than twelve students in a class.
_____, most students think that there should no more than twelve students in a class.

5 As for how long the classes last, they officially last an hour.
As for _____, they officially last an hour.

6 We suggest buying more computers…
We suggest _____ more computers…

7 Most students feel
_____ feel…

8 …that if you make the changes we suggest, it will be an even better place to study.
…that if _____, it will be an even better place to study.

King James's Language School:
A report

Introduction
The aim of this report is to assess student satisfaction with the classes and facilities at King James's Language School, and to make suggestions for improvements.

Testing and registration of new students
Most students were satisfied with the testing process for new students. However, they complained about the long queues at registration. We believe it would be preferable either to have more staff available to deal with registrations, or to give students a specific day and time to register.

The classes
In general students rated the teachers very highly. Their main criticisms were of class sizes and the length of classes. As regards class sizes, most students think there should be no more than 12 students in a class. As for the duration of classes, they officially last an hour, but in practice they are usually only 45 minutes because of latecomers. We propose that all students who arrive more than five minutes late should have to wait until the break for admittance.

The self-study centre
It is generally thought that the self-study centre, while useful, has two major drawbacks. There are not enough computers, and at peak times they are always occupied. Also the centre closes at 7 p.m., so students who come to the later classes cannot use the centre at all. We suggest purchasing more computers and extending the opening times until 9 p.m.

The cafeteria
The cafeteria was replaced last year by vending machines for drinks and snacks. Although it is true that people often had to wait to be served, most students vastly preferred the cafeteria and would like it to be re-opened.

Conclusion
Overall, the majority of students are extremely positive about the school, and feel that if the suggested changes are implemented, it will be an even better place to study.

USEFUL LANGUAGE

c Complete the missing words.

Some common expressions for generalizing

1 Generally **sp**_____, people think…

2 In **g**_____, people think…

3 The general **v**_____ is that certain improvements need to be made.

4 It is generally **co**_____ / **thought** …

5 **Ov**_____, the majority of students think…

d Rewrite the following sentences.

Making suggestions

1 Please buy new computers
   We suggest _____
   _____.

2 You ought to improve the registration process.
   It would be advisable _____
   _____.

3 Why don't you make the classes smaller?
   We propose _____
   _____.

4 You really should change the opening hours.
   I strongly recommend _____
   _____.

5 It would be much better if classes lasted an hour.
   It would be far preferable for classes _____
   _____.

PLANNING WHAT TO WRITE

Brainstorm the content

a Read the following task and all the relevant information. Then with a partner decide

1 how many headings you will need and what they should be.
2 how to express the relevant information in your own words.
3 what suggestions for improvements could be made under each heading.

> Your language school has just started four-week study trips to the UK. You have been asked by the principal of the school to get feedback from all the students who participated and write a report detailing what students were positive about, what problems they had, and making suggestions for improving future study trips.
>
> You have made notes covering the views of the majority of participants:
>
> *People with families much happier than ones who stayed in the halls of residence, because they were able to speak to the families a bit.*
>
> *School OK and classes good but almost everyone complained about the lunch (just a sandwich). Some thought six hours a day too much.*
>
> *People not very keen on some weekend cultural programmes. Trips to London and Oxford great, Bath and Stratford boring.*
>
> *On all trips too much sightseeing and not enough time for shopping!*

b Together, suggest improvements to the study trips beginning with a different expression each time.

TIPS for writing a report

- Look carefully at who the report is for and what they need to know. This will help you choose what information you have to include.
- In the introduction state what the aim of the report is.
- Decide what the subdivisions are going to be within the areas of the report and think of headings for them.
- For each paragraph state the situation (strengths and weaknesses) and then make a recommendation.
- If in an exam you are given information on which to base your report, try not to use exactly the same words.
- Try to use a variety of expressions for generalizing and making suggestions.
- Use an appropriate professional style, avoiding very informal expressions.

WRITING

You are going to write the report. It should be approximately 250 words.

DRAFT your report, using the headings and suggestions you worked on in the planning stage.

EDIT the report, deciding if there is any information that should be left out and making sure the report is the right length.

CHECK the report for mistakes in grammar, spelling, punctuation, and register.

THE INTERVIEW

a You are going to listen to an interview with Patricia Melvin, an American painter. Before you listen, read the glossary and look at how the words are pronounced to help you understand what she says.

> **in situ** /ɪn ˈsɪtjuː/ (from Latin) in the original or correct place
>
> **sketch** /sketʃ/ *noun* a simple picture that is drawn quickly and doesn't have many details
>
> **pose** /pəʊz/ *noun* a particular position in which sb stands, sits, etc. especially in order to be painted
>
> **canvas** /ˈkænvəs/ *noun* a piece of strong heavy material used for painting on
>
> **the Hudson** /ˈhʌdsən/ one of the rivers which flow through New York City

b **5.23** Listen to part 1. Answer the questions with a partner.

1 What is it about New York that attracts and inspires creative people?
2 Why does she prefer working in situ to working from photos?
3 Why does working in situ mean she has to work fast?
4 Does she normally take a long time to finish a painting?
5 What does she say is the main difference between painting a cityscape and a landscape?
6 What is the advantage of painting in the countryside?
7 What problem does she have with painting portraits?

c **5.24** Listen to part 2. Answer the questions with a partner.

What does she say about…?
1 the Hudson River; her parents
2 sunrise
3 the advantages of painting just before and during the spring
4 the places where she'd like to paint
5 what an artist has to sacrifice and why

d **5.25** Listen and complete the phrases with two or three words. What do you think they mean?

COMMON EXPRESSIONS AND IDIOMS

1 I _____ a little in the studio sometimes or finish things.
2 …as opposed to down a street, where it's so clear and easy, kind of, to _____ .
3 I love it because I'm usually alone, _____ alone there, and I'm not distracted by passers-by.
4 And that's a real big sacrifice _____ your social life…
5 They contradict one another _____ .

e If you were an artist, what would you choose to paint and why?

IN THE STREET

a **5.26** You are going to hear four people talking about art. What three questions are they all asked? Which speaker(s) go to art galleries most / least often?

| 1 Jason | 2 Jerry | 3 Amy | 4 Ian |

b Listen again. Match the speakers to the statements.

1 ☐ They don't like paintings of people.
2 ☐☐ Their favourite paintings are based on photos.
3 ☐ They don't have a favourite style of painting.
4 ☐ They like paintings which show nature, and especially the sea.
5 ☐ They like their favourite paintings mainly because of the colour.

c **5.27** Listen and complete the phrases with one to three words. What do you think they mean?

COMMON PHRASES

1 I have a Kandinsky that I'm _____ .
2 … you know, a photograph of Florence, _____ , and he'll take out some buildings and invent some replacements…
3 A lot of my friends go _____ and I never seem to find the time.
4 … sort of large blocks of _____ magenta and grey.

d Answer the same questions with a partner.

GRAMMAR

a Put the verb in brackets in the right form.

1 Do you think I ought _____ to Mario? (apologize)

2 Rick hates _____ that he doesn't dance very well. (tell)

3 I would love _____ the exhibition, but it finished the day before we arrived. (see)

4 Alex seems _____ a lot recently. Do you think he's studying enough? (go out)

5 Isn't there anywhere _____ here? (sit down)

6 You'd better _____ to the doctor about that cough. (go)

7 There's no point _____ him. He always has his mobile switched off when he's driving. (phone)

8 It's important for celebrities _____ at all the right parties. (see)

9 You're not supposed _____ your mobile at work but everyone does. (use)

10 You needn't _____ any food or drink to the barbecue. We've already got plenty. (bring)

b Circle the right phrases. Tick if both are possible.

1 *I'm supposed to take / I have to take* the medicine every day.

2 *I can hear / I am hearing* voices in the flat next door. I thought the neighbours were away.

3 It looks *as if / as though* there's going to be a storm tonight.

4 *You should have listened / You should listen* to my advice, but it's too late now.

5 It *is not allowed / is not permitted* to feed any of the animals.

6 *You look / You seem* a bit down today. Is everything OK?

7 This coffee *tastes like / tastes of* tea. It's undrinkable!

8 *You don't need to / You needn't* be especially tall to join the police force nowadays.

9 *I needn't have taken / I didn't need to take* any summer clothes. In the end it was too cold to wear them.

10 It smells *as if / like if* someone has burnt the toast.

VOCABULARY

a Circle the right word.

1 We drove *under / below* the bridge and into the town centre.

2 It's only a tiny cut on your finger. Just put a *bandage / plaster* on it.

3 I was so tired I slept like a *bat / log* last night.

4 I've been walking all day and my new shoes have given me a *blister / bruise* on my toe.

5 The actor *scribbled / sketched* his autograph on the piece of paper.

6 My husband is as stubborn as a *horse / mule*.

7 If you've got a problem with your back, you should see a(n) *osteopath / homeopath*.

8 Shall we go for a walk *along / through* the river bank?

9 I only *glanced / gazed* at the woman but I would say she was Spanish or Italian.

10 He never hears the door bell. He's as deaf as a *wall / post*.

b Write words for the definitions.

1 _____-_____ *noun* a painting or drawing that you do of yourself

2 _____ *verb* to open and shut your eyes quickly

3 _____ *noun* a piece of modern sculpture made using objects, sound, etc.

4 _____ *noun* a Chinese method of treating pain and illness using needles

5 _____ *verb* to shake because you are nervous, frightened, excited, etc.

6 _____ *noun* a kind of treatment which uses hypnosis to treat physical or emotional problems

7 _____ *verb* to draw lines or shapes, especially when you are bored or thinking about something else

c Complete the sentences using the **bold** word and a prefix.

1 The man didn't speak clearly and I totally _____ what he said. **UNDERSTAND**

2 I get very _____ when I feel that I'm not making any progress. **MOTIVATE**

3 Even though the Scottish soldiers were completely _____ by the English, they won the battle. **NUMBER**

4 The film isn't as good as everyone says it is. I think it is very _____. **RATE**

5 There was a huge _____ demonstration in the main square last night. **WAR**

6 Look, I think they have _____ us. The bill should be 80 euros, not 60. **CHARGE**

7 When I am travelling, I usually use _____ phone cards to make calls. **PAY**

8 The meeting has been postponed and will be _____ for a later date. **ARRANGE**

d Complete the phrasal verbs.

1 **Put** that cigarette _____! Can't you see the 'No smoking signs?

2 A car **pulled** _____ outside our house and a man got out.

3 The teacher **handed** _____ the exam papers to the students.

4 You should never **lean** _____ the window on a train. It's very dangerous.

5 The driver **wound** _____ his window and asked me the way to the town centre.

6 The government want to **bring** _____ a new law to reduce the speed limit.

G expressing future plans and arrangements
V travel and tourism
P homophones

'I have found out there ain't no surer way to find out whether you like people or hate them than to travel with them.'

Mark Twain, US writer

A moving experience

1 READING & SPEAKING

a The guidebook series *The Rough Guide* has published a book called *25 Wonders of the World*. Think of five places, sights, or monuments that you would put in it. Compare your list with a partner.

b Read the article once. Why is it called 'My 25,000 Wonders of the World'?

My 25,000 Wonders of the World

The coaches at the Uluru Sunset Viewing Area were parked three deep. Guides were putting up tables and setting out wine and snacks. Ten minutes to go. Are we ready? Five minutes, folks. Got your cameras? OK, here it comes...

5 Whether an American backpacker or a wealthy traveller, Danish, British, or French, we all saw that sunset over Uluru, or Ayers Rock, in what seems to be the prescribed tourist manner: mouth full of corn chips, glass full of Château Somewhere, and a loved one posing in a photo's foreground, as the all-time No 1 Australian icon behind us
10 glowed briefly red.

Back on the coach, our guide declared our sunset to be 'pretty good', although not the best she'd witnessed in her six years. Behind me, Adam, a student from Manchester, reinserted his iPod earphones: 'Well, that's enough of that rock'. Indeed. Shattered from getting up
15 at five in order to see Uluru at dawn, I felt empty and bored. What was the point? What made this rock the definitive sunset rock event? Why had we come here? Well, I suppose my sons would remember it always. Except they'd missed the magical moment while they checked out a rival tour group's snack table, which had better crisps.

20 So now I've visited four of the '25 Wonders of the World', as decreed by Rough Guides. And I think this will be the last. While in my heart I can see myself wandering enchanted through China's Forbidden City, in my head I know I would be standing grumpily at the back of a group listening to some Imperial Palace Tour Guide. At the Grand Canyon I
25 would be getting angry with tourists watching it through their cameras – eyes are not good enough, since they lack a recording facility.

As we become richer and consumer goods are more widely affordable, and satisfy us only briefly before becoming obsolete, we turn to travel to provide us with 'experiences'. These will endure,
30 set us apart from stay-at-home people and, maybe, fill our lives with happiness and meaning. Books with helpful titles like *1,000 Places to See Before You Die* are best-sellers. I'd bet many backpacks

> **And yet viewing the main sight of any destination is rarely the highlight of a trip. Mostly it sits there on your itinerary like a duty visit to a dull relative.**

on the Machu Picchu Inca Trail are filled with copies, with little ticks pencilled in the margins after each must-see sight has been
35 visited. Travel is now the biggest industry on the planet, bigger than armaments or pharmaceuticals. And yet viewing the main sight of any destination is rarely the highlight of a trip. Mostly it sits there on your itinerary like a duty visit to a dull relative. The guilt of not visiting the Sistine Chapel, because we preferred to stay in a bar
40 drinking limoncello, almost spoilt a weekend in Rome.

In Queensland, the Great Barrier Reef reproached us. How could we travel 15,000 miles without seeing it? How would we explain back home that we were too lazy, and preferred to stay playing a ball game in our hotel pool? In the end we went to the reef and it was fine.
45 But it won't rank highly in the things I'll never forget about Australia. Like the fact that the banknotes are made of waterproof plastic: how gloriously Australian is that? Even after a day's surfing, the $50 note you left in your surfing shorts is still OK to buy you beer! And the news item that during a recent tsunami warning, the surfers at
50 Bondi Beach refused to leave the sea: what, and miss the ride of their lives? Or the stern warning at the hand luggage X-ray machine at Alice Springs airport: 'No jokes must be made whilst being processed by this facility' – to forestall, no doubt, disrespectful Aussie comments: 'You won't find the bomb, mate. It's in my suitcase.'

55 The more I travel, the clearer it seems that the truth of a place is in the tiny details of everyday life, not in its most glorious statues or scenery. Put down your camera, throw away your list, the real wonders of the world number infinitely more than 25.

From The Times by Janice Turner

c Read the article again. Then answer the questions with a partner.

1 What do you think the author means by 'the prescribed tourist manner' in l.7? Does she think it's a good thing?

2 What were her main emotions after seeing the sunset?

3 Why does she think that Uluru is probably the last 'wonder of the world' she will see?

4 What kind of tourists is she criticizing when she says 'eyes are not good enough…' in l.26?

5 What does she say that a lot of backpackers carry with them nowadays? Why?

6 What does she compare visiting the main tourist sights to? Why?

7 What does she mean by 'the Great Barrier Reef reproached us'?

8 What three aspects of Australia did she find really memorable? Why?

d Talk to a partner.

Do you agree with the author's view about famous tourist sights?

1 Have you ever…?
- been to see a famous sight and thought it was overrated
- been to see a famous sight which lived up to your expectations
- felt guilty about not seeing a sight when you were on holiday somewhere
- been disappointed at not being able to see a famous sight

2 Think of the last place you visited as a tourist. Can you think of a 'tiny detail of everyday life' that made the place or the moment special?

3 What 'real wonders of the world' would you recommend to people visiting your country / town?

2 VOCABULARY & SPEAKING
travel and tourism

a Find words from the text in 1 which mean…

1 _____ a person who travels cheaply carrying their equipment and clothes in a bag they carry on their back.

2 _____ an interesting place in a town or city often visited by tourists.

3 _____ the place where you are going to.

4 _____ a plan of a journey including the route and the places that you visit.

5 _____ the natural features of an area, e.g. mountains, valleys, rivers, or forests.

b ⊙ **p.165 Vocabulary Bank** *Travel and tourism.*

c Do the questionnaire with a partner. Which alternative would you choose in each case, and why? Try to use the expressions below.

> **Expressing preferences**
>
> I'd prefer to…   I (definitely) wouldn't…
> I'd (much) rather… (than…)   Given the choice, I'd…
> I'd go for option b, because…   If it was up to me, I'd…

What kind of a traveller are you?

1 You are in Naples, Italy, for work, and you have one free day. You can either…
a go on a day trip to Pompeii, which is about an hour away.
b spend the day shopping, walking, and getting to know the city.
c stay in your hotel, go to the pool, and have a great meal.

2 Your family are planning a holiday. Which would you try and persuade them to choose?
a Going on a safari in Botswana, with accommodation in tents.
b Renting a villa on a lively but rather touristy Greek island.
c A package holiday to the United Kingdom, with several excursions to the main sights included.

3 You and three friends want to go away for a short holiday together. The possibilities are…
a a three-day city break in a foreign city, staying at a cheap hotel.
b three days in a luxury spa hotel in your country.
c a week camping somewhere off the beaten track with beautiful scenery.

4 You have to go on a business trip from London to San Francisco which involves a long-haul flight. There are two possible itineraries:
a an economy-class flight which leaves very early in the morning, with a 24-hour stopover in New York.
(Flying time: London–New York 7.5 hours; New York–San Francisco 6.5 hours)
b a business-class flight which leaves at midday, but with no stopover. (Flying time: 13 hours)

5 You and a friend really want to visit Vietnam, which you have heard is very beautiful. You can either…
a book a package holiday through a travel agent, including guided tours of famous sights.
b go backpacking, organizing your flight beforehand, but finding accommodation as you go.
c buy a good guidebook and organize the trip yourself, booking hotels and transport on the internet.

6 You are booking a flight with a low-cost airline to a major city, where you are going to spend the weekend with some friends. Apart from the flight, would you also…?
a take out insurance
b pay extra to offset your carbon footprint
c pay extra to check in a suitcase

d Look at your partner's answers again. What kind of traveller do you think he / she is?

3   6.1   SONG ♫ *I Wish I Could Go Travelling Again*

4 PRONUNCIATION homophones

> 'We visited the **site** of the Battle of Gettysburg.'
>
> 'I didn't have time to see many of the tourist **sights** in New York.'
>
> *site* and *sight* are homophones. They are words which are spelled differently and have different meanings, but are pronounced exactly the same.

a With a partner, think of homophones for the **bold** words:

1 We're going to have to **wait** until two hours before the flight to check in. /weɪt/
  What's the maximum _____ for hand luggage on this flight?

2 We're **bored**! We don't want to visit any more museums! /bɔːd/
  Can you check on the departures _____ to see what time the train leaves?

3 We went on a city-**break** to Prague. /breɪk/
  The airport bus had to _____ suddenly when a lorry pulled out in front of us.

4 It's not **fair**! Jane's family's going to Spain and we're just going to Brighton. /feə/
  How much is the air _____ to Australia?

5 Can you find the **piece** of paper with our flight details? /piːs/
  We want to go somewhere off the beaten track for a bit of _____ and quiet.

6 It's a four-star hotel, and it's even got a tennis **court**. /kɔːt/
  We only just _____ the train – it left seconds after we'd got on it.

7 We went on a day trip to Lake Victoria, which they say is the **source** of the Nile. /sɔːs/
  I quite like the meat, but the _____ tastes really strange.

8 I can take you to the beach on my bike, but you'll have to hold on to my **waist** really tight. /weɪst/
  Don't bother going to see the castle. It's a _____ of time. It's just a ruin.

9 We're staying at a beautiful hotel for our honeymoon – we've booked the bridal **suite**. /swiːt/
  I don't really like the local liqueur, it's too _____ for me.

10 We walked along the **quay**, watching the fishing boats returning with their catch. /kiː/
  I'm terribly sorry but I can't find my _____. Could you give me another one?

11 If you're taking out travel insurance, make sure you give them the **serial** numbers of your laptop and mobile. /ˈsɪəriəl/
  There wasn't much choice for breakfast – just toast and _____.

12 **Would** you mind filling in this form, please? /wʊd/
  We walked through the _____ until we came to the lake.

b Test a partner. **A** say one of the homophones, **B** say what the two spellings and meanings are. Then swap roles.

5 GRAMMAR
expressing future plans and arrangements

a How do you normally get to the place where you work or study? How long does it take you? Do you know any people who travel for more than an hour each way every day?

b Read an article about 'extreme commuting'. What are the pros and cons for Nick Thorner?

'Extreme commuting' – would *you* do it?

Job recruiters say that it is getting more and more difficult today to convince candidates to relocate. Instead people are increasingly open to 'extreme commuting' as an alternative to relocation. Extreme commuting is the term used to describe a daily journey to work by car or train that takes more than 90 minutes each way, or a plane journey to work and back each week. Family ties are the leading reason for resistance to relocating, according to half the recruiters surveyed, while lifestyle preferences (25%) and housing market costs (10%) are also contributing factors.

Nick Thorner works in publishing in the UK. He commutes every day to get from his home in south-east London to his office in Oxford, and then back again. 'My journey to work and back usually eats up about 6 hours of my day. The morning trip involves getting up at the crack of dawn. Going home is marginally more tiring because I have to contend with rush-hour traffic. If I leave the office by 5.15 p.m. I'll normally struggle through my front door by around 8.30 p.m. I'll then have an hour to eat, read a story to my daughter, and iron clothes for the next day before I go to bed.

I do it because my wife and daughter are quite settled where we are and they'd prefer not to move. For my part, I enjoy my job so feel it's worth the commute. The long journey does have its advantages, too. It gives me some precious 'me time' when I can listen to music or radio programmes that my family don't like listening to at home.'

c **6.2** Listen to Nick on a typical morning and answer the questions.

1 What time does he leave home?
2 What four different ways does he travel?
3 What time does he get to work?

d **6.3** Now listen and complete some of Nick's sentences. What do they have in common?

1 I _____ home very shortly.
2 I'm _____ get on my bike to cycle to the tube station.
3 My bus _____ at 6.40.
4 It's _____ arrive at 8.20, but it depends a bit on the traffic.
5 I need to be on time today – I _____ a client at nine o'clock.

e ○ p.151 Grammar Bank 6A. Read the rules and do the exercises.

A journey to remember

Famous people recount travel experiences they remember and sometimes would rather forget...

a **6.4** You are going to listen to an edition of the radio programme *A journey to remember* where an orchestral conductor describes a journey he made by air taxi. Listen to part 1 and answer the questions.

1 Where was he going to / from, and why?
2 Why did he choose to use an air taxi?
3 What problem did he find when he got to the airport?
4 What problem did he notice when he got into the plane?
5 If you had been in that situation, what would you have done?

b **6.5** Listen to part 2 and make notes about the problems that arose during the flight.

c **6.6** Listen to part 3 and answer the questions.

1 What happened next? Did he make it in time for his rehearsal?
2 After that experience, would you have made the return journey with the same company?
3 What did he do? What happened on the way back?

LEXIS IN CONTEXT

d Look at the highlighted expressions. What do you think they mean? Can you remember how the sentences continued?

1 …when I arrived at the airport, my heart sank because…
2 …I was still hoping to make it in time for…
3 Then to my horror I realized that…
4 By this point the co-pilot himself had realized that…
5 but presumably because of the pressure or the cold I don't know,…
6 To my relief we landed…
7 Then on the way back the pilots were…
8 …nothing was going particularly wrong, but I noticed that…

e If you were asked to speak on the programme *A journey to remember*, which travel experience would you talk about? (It could be an exotic journey when you were travelling somewhere, or just something unexpected that happened on your way to work or school.) Work in groups of three or four and tell each other about your experience.

6

B

G ellipsis and substitution
V the natural world
P weak and strong pronunciation of auxiliary verbs and *to*

'I loathe people who keep dogs. They are cowards who haven't got the guts to bite people themselves.'
August Strindberg, Swedish dramatist

Pets and pests

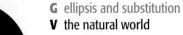

1 READING

a Look at the photos of animals. What kind of people do you think would choose them as pets?

b Read an article about pets and their owners. Which of the owners do you think has most in common with their pet(s)?

Pets and owners 'become more alike over time'

Pets and their owners are just like married couples and they get more alike over time, according to recent research. In a study carried out by a British university 2,500 pet owners were asked to complete an online questionnaire about their personalities and those of their pets. The study showed that many dog lovers, cat owners, and even reptile keepers shared many of the same traits such as happiness, intelligence, and sense of humour as their pets.

The dog owner

Paul Keevil, a photographer and artist, believes he and his pet dog Crosby are growing more grumpy together as they get older. Mr Keevil bred Crosby, a rare Dandie Dinmont terrier, and has kept him as a pet for the past eight years. Not only does he think they look alike, he says they have increasingly developed the same personality over the years. 'I'm becoming a bit more bad-tempered as I get older,' Mr Keevil said, 'and so is he. We like our own space, and we are not as tolerant as we used to be. I certainly enjoy my food as much as he does, although I'm a bit fussier. Other than that, I think I am a little bit more intelligent.' He added 'I think quite possibly pets and owners do grow alike as they get older. It also may be that there is something subliminal when it comes to us choosing our pets. If someone is happy and cheerful, then they tend to choose a dog that is always wagging its tail.'

The cat owner

Laila El Baradei said that she and her cat shared one behaviour trait: they both enjoy harassing her husband. The 30-year-old London lawyer has owned Philphil (Arabic for Papa) for four years. 'She bites my husband's toes and attacks him on my behalf, constantly harassing him when he's trying to do something,' Mrs El Baradei said. 'In that sense she is like me – and shares my sense of humour. We both like to snuggle up at night. I get very cold, and warm myself up, and Philphil sleeps on the radiator.' While Mrs El Baradei admitted to numerous similarities, she hoped there were differences. 'While she is smart, I'd like to think I am more intelligent than my cat.'

The reptile owner

Graham Martin, who keeps lizards, said their personalities change to become more like his. 'I've had bearded dragons calmly sitting and watching the telly when I do. If you've got lots of energy, they pick up on that, and if you are afraid, they are too. They tend to reflect whoever has brought them up. If they've had a stressed owner, then they can be very stressed, they can behave like absolute lunatics. But generally, because I'm calm, they tend to calm down themselves.'

The fish owner

Sarah Ogilvie believes she is far more serene since acquiring a similarly relaxed goldfish, called Garfield. A marketing consultant, who works in a stressful environment, Ms Ogilvie says she looks forward to coming home from work to see him swimming lazily in his tank. 'I just sit in my armchair with a glass of wine and watch him swirl around,' she said. 'It's better than watching TV by far. I'm sure he recognizes me – he always comes up to the glass when I walk towards him, but maybe that's because I feed him. He's more friendly than a lot of those aquarium fish you see in big offices. He's quite a character. Am I happier because of Garfield? I think I probably am. They say that being near water is calming in itself, so maybe that has something to do with it.'

The bird owner

Friends tell Juliet Eberle that she is eccentric, just like her five birds. 'It's not so much me who thinks that, but I think some of my friends do,' she conceded, 'and if enough people say it, then it might be true.' Ms Eberle said that she had undoubtedly picked up some of her birds' traits. 'The way I talk sometimes and bob my head has become more parrot-like,' she admitted. Her parrots include a huge Mealy Amazon called Molly, two Eclectus parrots, and a pair of African greys. They all have individual traits she sees in herself. 'Molly loves people,' said Ms Eberle. 'At times she's a bit of a show-off, like me. And the greys have got a great sense of humour.'

From *The Daily Telegraph*

c Now read the article again and find answers to the questions below. Answer with D (the dog owner), F (the fish owner), C (the cat owner), R (the reptile owner), or B (the bird owner).

Who…?

1 finds that their pet creates a different atmosphere from the atmosphere at work ☐
2 enjoys the same pastimes as their pet ☐
3 thinks that having a pet has changed them ☐
4 says that other people think that they and their pet have similar personalities ☐
5 thinks that people unconsciously buy pets which are like them ☐
6 thinks that pets' personalities change according to the owners they have had ☐
7 thinks that they and their pet have developed in the same way simultaneously ☐
8 thinks that their pets are changing to become more like them ☐
9 thinks that they now have gestures which they have picked up from their pets ☐
10 sleeps in the same way as their pet ☐

LEXIS IN CONTEXT

d Find the following words in the text related to personality.

Introduction

| 1 | _____ | (*adj.*) | similar to sb / sth |
| 2 | _____ | (*noun*) | a particular quality in your personality |

The dog owner

3	_____	(*adj.*)	bad-tempered
4	_____	(*adj.*)	able to accept what other people do and think
5	_____	(*adj.*)	concerned about unimportant details

The fish owner

| 6 | _____ | (*adj.*) | calm |

The cat owner

| 7 | _____ | (*adj.* NAmE) | clever |

The reptile owner

| 8 | _____ | (*noun*) | crazy people |

The bird owner:

| 9 | _____ | (*adj.*) | strange or unusual |
| 10 | _____ | (*noun*) | a person who tries to impress other people by showing how good he or she is at doing sth |

e Think of pets you have or have had, or people you know who have pets. Do you agree with the article that pets and their owners become more alike over time?

2 GRAMMAR   ellipsis and substitution

a Complete the sentences from the text with an auxiliary verb. What is their function in the sentences?

• 'I'm becoming a bit more bad-tempered as I get older, and so _____ he.'
• 'I certainly enjoy my food as much as he _____.'
• 'Am I happier because of Garfield? I think I probably _____.'
• 'I've had bearded dragons calmly sitting and watching the telly when I _____.'
• 'It's not so much me who thinks that, but I think some of my friends _____.'

b ⊙ **p.152 Grammar Bank 6B.** Read the rules and do the exercises.

3 PRONUNCIATION
weak and strong pronuncation of auxiliary verbs and *to*

a   **6.7**   Read the dialogues and underline the auxiliaries or *to* when you think they are stressed. Listen and check. Then practise saying the dialogue.

A Do you like dogs?
B No, I don't, but my husband does.
A So does mine. We have three Alsatians.

A I went to Iceland last summer.
B Lucky you. I'd love to go there. Did you see any whales?
A No. I wanted to, but I get seasick, and you have to go on a boat.

A Allie doesn't have any pets, does she?
B She does have a pet. She has a hamster.
A Ugh. I don't like hamsters.
B Neither do I. They're too much like mice.

b Answer the questions with a partner.

1 Are auxiliary verbs stressed (S) or unstressed (U) in the following?
   • in question tags
   • in short answers
   • in *wh-* questions
   • in negative sentences
   • when they are used for emphasis
   • with *so* and *neither*
   • when they come as the last word in a sentence
2 What vowel sound do unstressed auxiliaries usually have?
3 How is *to* pronounced
   a) when it's unstressed   b) when it's stressed?
4 When is *to* stressed?

c ⊙ **Communication** *Match the sentences A p.118 B p.120.* Match the sentence halves.

4 VOCABULARY the natural world

a Work with a partner. How many of the quiz questions can you answer?

Animals, birds, and insects

1 What do you call a young…?
  a dog _____
  b cat _____
  c horse _____
  d cow _____

2 Which creatures live in…?
  a a nest _____
  b a hive _____
  c a stable _____
  d a kennel _____
  e a tank _____
  f a cage _____

3 What animals make the following noises?
  a squeak _____
  b bark _____
  c neigh /neɪ/ _____
  d miaow _____
  e roar _____
  f grunt _____

b ⊙ p.166 Vocabulary Bank *The natural world.*

c Choose five circles. Tell your partner something about a person you know who…

- hunts regularly
- has an unusual pet
- doesn't eat meat or fish because of their principles
- is allergic to bee or wasp stings
- has a dog which barks incessantly
- is often in the doghouse with their partner
- has been bitten by a snake
- is an animal activist
- is a bit of a dark horse
- is a member of an organization which protects the environment
- doesn't believe in wearing fur
- has been attacked by a wild animal
- can't eat shellfish
- breeds animals
- has a bark that is worse than their bite

5 LISTENING

a What animals are considered pests in your country? Why?

b **6.8** **6.9** Listen to two extracts from different news broadcasts, one about wolves and dogs, and one about foxes. What do the stories have in common?

c Read summaries of the two stories. Can you remember any of the missing words? Listen again and complete the summaries with one or two words in each gap.

1 When Jean Luc Renaud was walking in the Alps, he met a man who was covered in [1]_____.

The man had been attacked by a breed of dog called the [2]_____ dog.

These dogs can weigh as much as [3]_____. They have been brought into the French Alps to defend [4]_____ from [5]_____.

There are now about [6]_____ wolves in the Alps. The [7]_____ has spent money on helping farmers to protect the flocks with [8]_____ and [9]_____.

However, the dogs are now attacking [10]_____, some of whom have taken the shepherds to [11]_____. There are also reports that a number of dogs have been [12]_____.

2 In London, the fox population is around [1]_____.

The noise they make is stopping residents in areas like Hampstead from [2]_____.

One Hampstead resident found a large fox in her garden, which seemed to be [3]_____.

She phoned Camden Council and asked for the [4]_____ department, but was put through to the [5]_____ department.

They told her to check whether the fox was [6]_____, and offered to give her [7]_____.

She refused, and said that she wanted the council to [8]_____ the fox.

The fox project then offered to send [9]_____ for the fox. At this point the fox left the garden.

d Who do you sympathize with the most in each story? Are any species of wild animal being protected where you live? Do you think it is a good thing or is it creating problems?

6 SPEAKING

a **6.10** Listen to some short extracts of people discussing the issues below and complete the phrases with an adverb.

> **Common adverb collocations**
> 1 Now this is something I feel _____ _____ about…
> 2 Well, I don't feel _____ _____ about it either way.
> 3 I have to say I am _____ against zoos nowadays…
> 4 Oh no, I _____ disagree with you there…
> 5 Well, I couldn't disagree with you _____.
> 6 Well, I don't _____ agree with you…
> 7 Well, I'm _____ convinced that the animal does not want to be there…
> 8 Well, I'm _____ sure that kids could get the same amount of pleasure from seeing animals in the wild.

b Work in groups of three or four. You are going to debate some of the issues below. Each choose a different issue, for which you will open a debate. Plan what you are going to say, making a few notes to help you.

Animal debates

People should not be allowed to keep very aggressive breeds of dog such as Rottweilers as pets.

In a civilized society there is no place for entertainment which involves cruelty to animals.

Animal activists are right when they object to animals being used in experiments.

Zoos nowadays serve no useful purpose and should be banned.

It is hypocritical for people who call themselves animal lovers to eat meat and fish.

People who live in flats should not be allowed to have pets which require exercise.

Hunting as a sport should be banned.

Animals bred for food should be kept in humane conditions.

c Hold your debates. On which topic, as a group, do you most strongly a) agree b) disagree? Try to incorporate language from **a**.

G adding emphasis (2): cleft sentences
V words that are often confused
P intonation in cleft sentences

'We can have no "50–50" allegiance in this country. Either a man
is an American and nothing else, or he is not an American at all.'
Theodore Roosevelt, US President

The promised land?

Poland

Renata

Spain

1 LISTENING & SPEAKING

a Can you think of some reasons why people decide to go and live
in another country, or in another city in their country? Can you
imagine doing it yourself?

b Talk to a partner. What do you think are the pros and cons of...?
- living in a country which is not your own
- living in a city in your country which is not your own

c **6.11** **6.12** You are going to listen to two people who emigrated
to another country. Make brief notes in the chart.

d Compare the information in the chart. Who do you think feels
most positive about their adopted country?

	Renata, from Poland, who lives in Spain	Andrew from the UK, who lives in Italy
1 Why did they go there in the first place?		
2 How long have they been living there?		
3 What is the positive side of living there?		
4 What is the downside?		
5 What do they miss most about their home country?		
6 Do they think they'll ever go back to their country? Why (not)?		

LEXIS IN CONTEXT

e Look at some expressions that Renata and Andrew used. In what
context did they use them? What do you think they mean?

Renata
1 It was **a bit of a fluke**, really.
2 ...**the paperwork**, which would have been very complicated.
3 ...But **bit by bit** we managed to find jobs and somewhere to live.
4 Of course – **loads of** things!

Andrew
5 I'm still **living the dream**...
6 ...too **politically biased**...
7 ...Italy still **hasn't gone too far down that road**.

f Talk to a partner.
1 Do you have any friends who have emigrated to another country or
who are foreigners who have come to live in your county? Where
have they gone to or come from?
2 How do you think they would answer the questions that Renata
and Andrew answer in **d**?

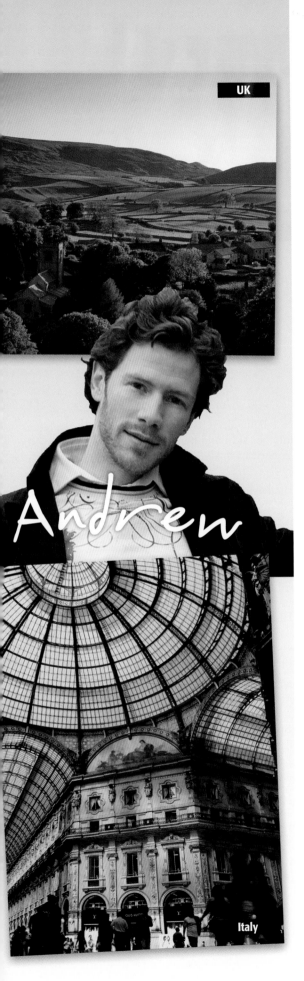
UK

Andrew

Italy

2 GRAMMAR adding emphasis (2): cleft sentences

a Sentences 1–4 below convey ideas which the speakers expressed, but they phrased them in a slightly different way. Can you remember what they actually said?

1 In fact, my husband first came up with the idea of moving here.
'In fact, it _____.'

2 If you're prepared to work hard you can get what you want, and that's what I like best.
'What _____.'

3 I first came here because I'd always wanted to go and live abroad...
'The reason _____.'

4 The countryside and the BBC are the things I miss most about the UK.
'The _____.'

b **6.13** Listen and check. Now look at the pairs of sentences. What's the difference between them?

c ➡ **p.153 Grammar Bank 6C.** Read the rules and do the exercises.

3 PRONUNCIATION & SPEAKING intonation in cleft sentences

Cleft sentences beginning with *What...* or *The person / place*, etc. typically have a fall-rising tone at the end of the *what...* clause.

What I hate about my job is having to get up early.

The reason why I went to France was because I wanted to learn the language.

Cleft sentences beginning with *It...* typically have a falling tone in the clause beginning with *It*.

It was her mother who really broke up our marriage.

It's the commuting that I find so tiring.

a **6.14** Read the information in the box and listen to each example sentence twice.

b **6.15** Listen and repeat the sentences below, copying the intonation patterns.

1 What I don't understand is why she didn't call me.
2 The thing that impresses me most about Jack is his enthusiasm.
3 The reason why I left early was because I had an important meeting.
4 The place where I would most like to live is Ireland.
5 It was the neighbours that made our lives so difficult.
6 It was then that I realized I'd left my keys behind.

c Complete the sentences in your own words. Then use them to start conversations with your partner.

What I would find most difficult about living abroad is...
What I love about the summer is...
What I least like about this town is...
The person I most admire in my family is...
The place where I would most like to live is...
The reason why I decided to come to this school was...
What I love about...
What I hate about...
The reason why I...

4 READING & SPEAKING

a You are going to read an extract from *The Joy Luck Club*, a best-selling book by Amy Tan about first and second generation immigrants, which has also been made into a film. Before you read, answer the questions below with a partner.

1 Do you know any second generation immigrants to your country?

What country did their parents originally come from?

Do the parents in the family still keep up their language and culture? What about the children?

2 Do you think some children of immigrants might have a conflict of identity? Why (not)?

b Now read an extract from the book. To what extent do you think Waverly has an identity crisis? What does her mother feel about it?

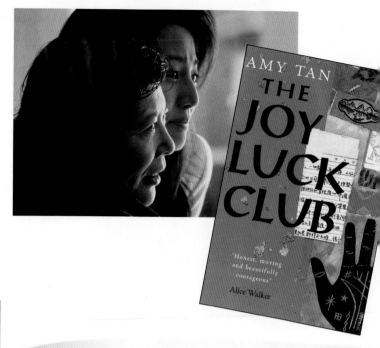

> *The Joy Luck Club* is the story of four Chinese mothers and their first generation Chinese-American daughters; two generations of women struggling to come to terms with their cultural identity. Here Lindo Jong, one of the mothers, talks about her daughter, Waverly.

LINDO JONG

Double Face

1 My daughter wanted to go to China for her second honeymoon, but now she is afraid.

'What if I blend in so well they think I'm one of them?' Waverly asked me. 'What if they don't let me come back
5 to the United States?'

'When you go to China,' I told her, 'you don't even need to open your mouth. They already know you are an outsider'.

'What are you talking about?' she asked. My daughter likes to speak back. She likes to question what I say.

10 'Aii-ya', I said. 'Even if you put on their clothes, even if you take off your makeup and hide your fancy jewelry, they know. They know just watching you walk, the way you carry your face. They know you do not belong.'

My daughter did not look pleased when I told her this,
15 that she didn't look Chinese. She had a sour American look on her face. Oh, maybe ten years ago, she would have clapped her hands – hurray! – as if this were good news. But now she wants to be Chinese, it is so fashionable. And I know it is too late. All those years I tried to teach her!
20 She followed my Chinese ways only until she learned how to walk out the door by herself and go to school. So now the only Chinese words she can say are *sh-sh*, *houche*, *chr fan* and *gwan deng shweijyau*. How can she talk to people in China with those words only? Pee-pee, choo-choo train,

25 eat, close light, sleep. How can she think she can blend in? Only her skin and her hair are Chinese. Inside – she is all American-made.

It's my fault she is this way. I wanted my children to have the best combination: American circumstances and
30 Chinese character. How could I know these two things do not mix?

I taught her how American circumstances work. If you are born poor here, it's no lasting shame. You are first in line for a scholarship. If the roof crashes on your head,
35 no need to cry over this bad luck. You can sue anybody, make the landlord fix it. You do not have to sit like a Buddha under a tree letting pigeons drop their dirty business on your head. You can buy an umbrella. Or go inside a Catholic church. In America, nobody says you
40 have to keep the circumstances somebody else gives you.

She learned these things, but I couldn't teach her about Chinese character. How to obey parents and listen to your mother's mind. How not to show your own thoughts, to put your feelings behind your face, so you
45 can take advantage of hidden opportunities. Why easy things are not worth pursuing. How to know your own worth and polish it, never flashing it around like a cheap ring. Why Chinese thinking is best.

No, this kind of thinking didn't stick to her. She was
50 too busy chewing gum, blowing bubbles bigger than her cheeks. Only that kind of thinking stuck.

'Finish your coffee,' I told her yesterday. 'Don't throw your blessings away.'

'Don't be so old-fashioned, Ma,' she told me, finishing
55 her coffee down the sink. 'I'm my own person.'

And I think, How can she be her own person? When did I give her up?

c Read the extract again. Then with a partner choose a, b, or c.

1 Lindo thinks her daughter will not be mistaken for a native-born Chinese mainly because of the way she _____.
   a speaks
   b looks
   c moves
   d dresses

2 Lindo's daughter _____.
   a wishes she had learned to speak Chinese
   b never behaved like a Chinese person
   c has forgotten all the Chinese she ever knew
   d became less Chinese as she grew older

3 What Lindo most likes about the American way of life is that _____.
   a you don't have to accept your fate
   b education is free for everybody
   c you can choose your religion
   d other people always help you

4 Which of these is *not* an aspect of Chinese character, according to Lindo?
   a hiding your real feelings
   b doing what your parents tell you to do
   c showing off
   d being aware of your strengths

5 Lindo gives the example of the chewing gum to show that _____.
   a her daughter was stupid as a child
   b American habits were very easily acquired by her daughter
   c the American way of life is inferior to the Chinese
   d young people don't pay attention to adults

LEXIS IN CONTEXT

d Look at the following verbs in the text and guess their meaning.

blend in (l.25)
sue (l.35)
obey (l.42)
pursue (l.46)
polish (l.47)
flash around (l.47)
stick to (l.49)

e Whose problems do you identify with most, the mother's or the daughter's? Why?

5 VOCABULARY words that are often confused

a The words *foreigner*, *outsider*, and *stranger* are often confused. What is the difference in meaning?

b Look at some more words which are often confused. For each pair, complete the sentences with the right word. (You may need to change the form.)

1 **suit** /suːt/ / **suite** /swiːt/
   a The hotel upgraded us and gave us a _____ instead of a double room.
   b You should definitely wear a _____ to the interview – you'll make a better impression.

2 **beside / besides**
   a Don't let's go out tonight. I'm tired, and _____ there's a programme I want to watch on TV.
   b They live in that new block of flats _____ the school.

3 **lay / lie**
   a Please _____ down and relax. This will only take a minute.
   b If you _____ her on the sofa gently, I'm sure she won't wake up.

4 **actually / currently**
   a The inflation rate is _____ 2%.
   b I thought I wouldn't enjoy the film, but _____ it was very funny.

5 **announce / advertise**
   a It is rumoured that the Royal Family will _____ the prince's engagement this weekend.
   b The company are planning to _____ their new product both on TV and on billboards.

6 **affect / effect**
   a How does the crisis _____ you?
   b What are the main _____ of the crisis?

7 **ashamed / embarrassed**
   a As soon as the man from the garage arrived, the car started! I was so _____.
   b When the manager of the shop told my father I had stolen some sweets, I felt so _____.

8 **deny / refuse**
   a The accused does not _____ being in the house, but he insists that he did not touch anything.
   b The man _____ to put out his cigarette.

9 **compromise / commitment**
   a I know we will never agree about what to do, but we should try to reach a _____.
   b The company's _____ to providing quality at a reasonable price has been vital to its success.

10 **economic / economical**
   a I think we should buy the Toyota. It's nicer looking, and it's much more _____ on petrol.
   b I don't agree with this government's _____ policy.

c Complete the sentences with words from **b**. Then with a partner say if you think they are more true of men or women, or equally true of both.

1 They let personal problems _____ them at work.
2 They feel _____ when they have to talk about feelings.
3 They are afraid of making a long-term _____ in a relationship.
4 They tend to buy things because they are _____ on TV.
5 They often say they can do something well when _____ they can't.
6 They _____ to admit they are wrong in an argument.

Key success factors
- constructing an argument
- sustaining your case with examples
- showing that you have considered the opposing viewpoint

ANALYSING A MODEL TEXT

a   You have been asked to write the following essay:

Tourism always brings a place more harm than good.

Discuss the question with a partner. Do you think that the effect of tourism on a country, city, or region is in general more positive or more negative? Why?

Topic sentences
In a well-written essay, the first sentence of a paragraph establishes what the paragraph is going to be about. This is sometimes called the 'topic sentence'.

b   Read the topic sentences below one by one and, in pairs, imagine how the paragraph will continue. Do you think the essay will be in favour of or against tourism?

   A   The infrastructure of an area is also often improved as a result of tourism.
   B   It is often claimed that popular tourist destinations are spoilt as a result of overdevelopment.
   C   Tourism remains one of the world's great growth industries.
   D   Badly behaved tourists can often be a source of annoyance for the local population.
   E   Another point in favour of tourism is that governments are becoming aware of the need to protect tourist areas in order to attract visitors.
   F   The main positive effect of tourism is on local economies and employment.

c   Now read the model essay and fill the gaps with a topic sentence. There is one sentence you don't need.

Tourism always brings a place more harm than good

1 _____ People today are travelling further and further, no longer just in the summer but throughout the year. Although some people argue that mass tourism has a negative effect on destinations, in my view its influences are generally positive.

2 _____ Tourists need places to stay and things to do and this creates a wide range of skilled and unskilled jobs for local people. Holidaymakers also spend a great deal of money, which stimulates the economy of the region as well as benefiting the country as a whole.

3 _____ For example, when tourists start visiting an area, roads and public transport tend to improve, or an airport may be built, all of which benefit local people as well as tourists.

4 _____ Not only is this leading to better conservation of historic buildings and monuments in towns and cities, but also of areas of natural beauty and endangered habitats in country areas.

5 _____ For instance, many people argue that tourist development just leads to a proliferation of ugly hotels and apartment blocks. This may have been true in the past, but nowadays there are far more restrictions placed on both planners and builders to ensure that the character and architectural harmony of the place is maintained.

To sum up, I believe that tourism has, on the whole, a positive influence provided its development is properly planned and controlled. In my opinion, it is possible for both tourists and local people to benefit, and for popular tourist destinations to have a sustainable future.

Study Link MultiROM

d Read each paragraph again, including the correct topic sentence. Answer the questions with a partner.

1 Where does the writer state his opinion about tourism?

2 How many arguments are given to support his view?

3 What is the purpose of paragraph 5?

Using synonyms and richer vocabulary

When you are writing an essay, remember to vary and enrich your vocabulary by using synonyms where appropriate.

---

e Find synonyms in the essay for the following words and expressions:

1 tourists _____ _____

2 effects _____

3 for example _____

4 to profit from _____

USEFUL LANGUAGE

f Complete the missing words in the expressions. Some (but not all) are in the model essay.

Giving personal opinions

1 I **f**_____ that…

2 I **b**_____ that…

3 In my **v**_____ the influences of tourism are generally positive.

4 In my **o**_____…

5 **P**_____, I think that…

Expressing opposite arguments

6 Some people **ar**_____…

7 It is often **cl**_____ that popular destinations are spoilt by tourism.

8 There are **th**_____ who say…

Refuting them

9 This **m**_____ **h**_____ been true in the past, but nowadays…

10 There are a number of **fl**_____ in this argument.

11 This is simply not the **c**_____.

PLANNING WHAT TO WRITE

Brainstorm the content

a Read the essay titles below. For each one, decide which side of the argument you are going to take, and think of three or four reasons.

Drivers should be charged for using motorways and roads linking major towns and cities.

Marrying someone from a different country will always be more problematic than marrying someone from your own country.

b Compare with a partner. Decide which you think are the three most important reasons. Decide if there are any typical opposing arguments which you could refute.

c Choose which of the essays you are going to write. Write topic sentences for the main paragraphs. Show your topic sentences to a partner and see if you can improve each other's sentences.

TIPS for writing a discursive essay where you take one side of an argument

- Organize your essay into paragraphs, with a clear introduction and conclusion (see page 64).
- Begin each paragraph with a clear topic sentence and then develop the idea.
- Use synonyms to avoid repeating yourself.
- Use a variety of phrases for giving your opinion, or introducing an opposing argument and refuting it.

WRITING

You are going to write one of the essays above. It should be approximately 250 words.

DRAFT your essay in four paragraphs:

- an introductory paragraph where you introduce the topic and state your opinion.
- three or four paragraphs giving your reasons.
- if relevant, a paragraph stating a common counter argument(s), and refuting it (them).
- a conclusion, stating what your arguments have shown.

EDIT the essay, making sure your arguments link together and making sure it is the right length.

CHECK the essay for mistakes in grammar, spelling, punctuation, and register.

THE INTERVIEW

a You are going to listen to an interview with Peter Jinman, a vet in Herefordshire. Before you listen, read the glossary and look at how the words are pronounced to help you understand what he says.

> **zoologist** /zuˈɒlədʒɪst/ *noun* a scientist who studies animals and their behaviour
> **surgery** /ˈsɜːdʒəri/ *noun* the place where a doctor or a vet treats their patients
> **cameloids** /ˈkæmələɪdz/ *noun* the group of animals that includes camels and llamas
> **cattle** /ˈkætl/ *noun* cows and bulls that are kept as farm animals
> **sow** /saʊ/ *noun* a female pig
> **piglet** /ˈpɪɡlət/ *noun* a baby pig
> **vivarium** /vɪˈveəriəm/ *noun* a container for keeping wild animals in, e.g. reptiles

ferret   guinea pig

llama   collie

b **6.16** Listen to part 1. Answer the questions with a partner.

1 Why did he decide not to become a zoologist and to become a vet?
2 What particular advantage does he see in treating farm animals rather than pets?
3 Why are cameloids difficult animals to treat?
4 Why does he mention 'the dreaded cardboard box'?
5 What evidence does he give that collies are intelligent?
6 In what way are the good and bad sides of his job opposites?

c **6.17** Listen to part 2. Answer the questions with a partner.

What does he say about…?
1 using animals to test cosmetics
2 dangerous dogs
3 assessing the danger of the animals he treats
4 his son's pet
5 the particular challenge of being a vet in the Internet age

d **6.18** Listen and complete the phrases with two or three words. What do you think they mean?

COMMON EXPRESSIONS AND IDIOMS

1 It's surprising what people _____ in the surgery.
2 But I _____ that when somebody brought a tarantula spider in one day…
3 I suppose the worst is always having to _____ an animal _____, put it to sleep.
4 And the principle of leaving children with dogs is one that should not on any occasion occur, _____ good anybody believes a particular dog is.
5 So you're constantly having to be kept _____ by reading, attending lectures…
6 'We think our dog has got _____'.

e How attractive does he make his job sound? To what extent do you think his job has influenced his lifestyle, and his opinions on animal testing and dangerous dogs?

IN THE STREET

a **6.19** You are going to hear three people talking about animals. What two questions are they all asked?

Priti   Sheila   Jerry

b Listen again. Who…?

1 ☐ had close contact with an animal despite being very afraid of it
2 ☐ doesn't react as badly as he / she used to when faced with a creature they are afraid of
3 ☐ was in a vehicle at the time of the frightening experience
4 ☐ almost behaved in completely the wrong way when faced with a dangerous animal
5 ☐ is afraid of a creature because of a medical condition
6 ☐ missed out on a meal because an animal ate it

c **6.20** Listen and complete the phrases with two or three words. What do you think they mean?

COMMON PHRASES

1 …when we _____ a tiger in the middle of the path coming up towards us…
2 So he said, 'I'll just _____ and get my battery for the camera,'…
3 … and _____ he _____.
4 So _____ in the restaurant said, 'Just be careful, don't get too close.'
5 So there was _____, but it was quite frightening.

d Answer the questions from **a** with a partner.

GRAMMAR

a Cross out the pronoun where possible.

1 I was talking on the phone while I was cooking the dinner.
2 She saw him at the party but she didn't speak to him.
3 After lunch, I either have a nap or I go for a short walk.
4 Julian left school and then he immediately went to university.
5 You can watch TV after you finish your homework.
6 My wife is very stressed because she's working too hard.
7 I always try clothes on before I buy them.

b Complete the sentences with one word.

1 I'll be _____ in the office this afternoon so you can call me there.
2 Both sides are on the _____ of signing a ceasefire agreement.
3 What happened _____ that we got completely lost.
4 I've never been to Patagonia, but my sister _____.
5 **A** Will you be able to come?
   B I don't think _____. We'll probably be away.
6 She hasn't gone back to work yet, but she hopes _____ next month.
7 I would like to move to the country, but my wife doesn't want _____.
8 I haven't told Karen yet what happened, but I think that I _____.
9 **A** Do you think Miriam will be promoted?
   B I hope _____. She deserves it.
10 **A** Did you manage to get tickets?
   B I'm afraid _____. They were sold out.

c Rewrite the sentences using the **bold** word.

1 I didn't bring any sunscreen because the weather forecast said rain. **REASON**
   The _____ because the weather forecast said rain.
2 The meeting should begin in half an hour. **DUE**
   The meeting _____ in half an hour.
3 I spoke to the head of customer service. **PERSON**
   _____ the head of customer service.
4 The train is going to leave any minute now. You'd better get on it. **ABOUT**
   The train is _____. You'd better get on it.
5 I don't like the way my boss always blames other people. **WHAT**
   _____ he always blames other people.
6 I'll have a white suit on so you'll easily recognize me at the airport. **WEARING**
   I _____ so you'll easily recognize me at the airport.
7 I only said that I thought she was making a big mistake. **ALL**
   _____ I thought she was making a big mistake.
8 A boy from my school was chosen to carry the Olympic torch. **IT**
   _____ was chosen to carry the Olympic torch.

VOCABULARY

a Circle the right word.

1 The airline *refused / denied* to give me my money back.
2 The cat scratched me with his *paws / claws*.
3 It was a very exhausting *travel / trip* to Buenos Aires.
4 I love just *laying / lying* on the sofa and doing nothing.
5 A wasp *stung / bit* me while I was gardening.
6 Michael looked a bit *embarrassed / ashamed* when he was awarded the prize for best student of the year.
7 It's a very quiet place completely off the beaten *road / track*.
8 We're going to have to put *off / away* our holiday until next month.
9 Our company has been bought by a multinational but it won't *affect / effect* my job.
10 It will be cheaper if we fly with a *low-cost / low-price* airline.

b Complete the words.

1 A tortoise has a very hard **sh**_____.
2 From our hotel we had an absolutely **br**_____-_____ view of the mountains.
3 The tiger is an endangered **sp**_____ in many countries.
4 We're going on a **p**_____ holiday to Thailand with everything included.
5 We only realized there were sharks around when we saw their **f**_____ sticking out of the water.
6 If we want to miss the traffic, we'll have to set **o**_____ early in the morning.
7 Long-**h**_____ flights are much more tiring than short ones.
8 Animal **ac**_____ are trying to get a worldwide ban on experiments involving animals.
9 The guide told us that the nearby field was the **s**_____ of a famous battle.

c Correct the animal idioms.

1 You need to take the bull by the legs and ask your boss to give you a rise.
2 I made a real dog of myself last night. I ate far too much.
3 Don't worry about my dad. His tail is far worse than his bite.
4 We don't know anything about Jake's private life. He's a bit of a white horse.
5 The interview for the job went really well but I don't want to count my ducks.
6 Let's order the new curtains when we buy the bed. That way we can kill two birds with one bullet.

7A

G nouns: compound and possessive forms
V preparing food
P -ed adjective endings and linking

'There is one thing more exasperating than a wife who can cook and won't, and that's a wife who can't cook and will.'

Robert Frost, US poet

A recipe for disaster

1 VOCABULARY preparing food

a Imagine you are in a restaurant, and are given the English menu below. Study it for a couple of minutes, and choose what to have. Compare with a partner.

Ben's Brasserie

starters

cobb salad	**£4.95**
grilled chicken, avocado, blue cheese, and rocket with raspberry vinaigrette	
steamed mussels	**£6.95**
with coconut and chilli	
grilled sardines	**£5.50**
with parsley, lemon, and garlic	

main courses

thai chicken curry	**£14.95**
stir-fried chicken, Thai spices, peppers, onions, cashew nuts, and coconut cream with jasmine rice or egg noodles	
pork sausages	**£12.95**
with garlic mashed potatoes and onion gravy	
herb crusted lamb chops	**£13.50**
with potatoes, steamed French beans, and gravy	
smoked haddock	**£12.95**
with mashed potatoes, poached egg, and Hollandaise sauce	
baked aubergines	**£13.95**
stuffed with basmati rice, pecorino cheese, and pistachios	

desserts

plum and almond tart	**£5.95**
with amaretto custard	
apple and blackberry pie	**£6.50**
with vanilla ice cream	

please note that the menu is subject to change
a discretionary service charge of 10% will be added to your bill

b Complete the chart with words from the menu. Try to find at least three for each column.

Ways of preparing food	Vegetables	Fruit	Sauces and dressings	Fish and seafood

c What fruits, vegetables, and fish / seafood are really popular in your region / country? Do you know how to say them in English?

d ⊙ **p.167 Vocabulary Bank** *Preparing food.*

2 PRONUNCIATION
-ed adjective endings and linking

a Write the words in the chart according to how the *-ed* ending is pronounced.

baked   boiled   chopped   grated   grilled   mashed
melted   minced   peeled   scrambled   sliced   steamed
stir-fried   stuffed   toasted   whipped

-ed = /t/	-ed = /d/	-ed = /ɪd/

b 🔊 **7.1** Listen and check.

c 🔊 **7.2** Practise saying the phrases below, linking the two words together. Listen and check. Why are the words linked?

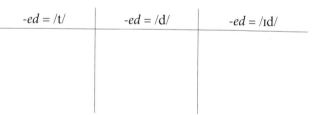

baked apples   scrambled eggs   stuffed aubergines
boiled eggs   sliced onions   toasted almonds
peeled oranges   steamed asparagus

d 🔊 **7.3** How do you think you say these phrases? Listen and check.

chopped tomatoes   stir-fried tofu   grilled tuna

e What adjectives can you put in front of these items to describe the way they are cooked, for example *fried eggs*?

eggs   meat   chicken   vegetables

3 LISTENING

a **7.4** Listen to three people describing cooking disasters and complete the information in the chart.

	Who were they cooking for?	What ingredients do they mention?	What went wrong?	What happened in the end?
Speaker 1				
Speaker 2				
Speaker 3				

LEXIS IN CONTEXT

b **7.5** Listen to some extracts from the listening. What do you think the missing words are? How do you think they are spelt and what do you think they mean?

1 …and Jeff, the friend who'd come, took one _____ of the spaghetti bolognese before either of us did…
2 …so that the top of the meat was completely _____ and underneath it was completely _____.
3 You're supposed to _____ the garlic on the bread.
4 And I put the tomato sauce on and handed it to my family and they all _____ it out. It was _____.

c Have you ever had a cooking disaster, or experienced somebody else's? What was the dish being made? What went wrong?

4 SPEAKING

a Work in groups of three. Imagine you have friends coming round in the evening, and there is nowhere near where you can eat out or get a takeaway. All you have in the house (apart from oil, salt, flour, sugar, etc.) are the ingredients below. Decide what you're going to serve and how you're going to cook it.

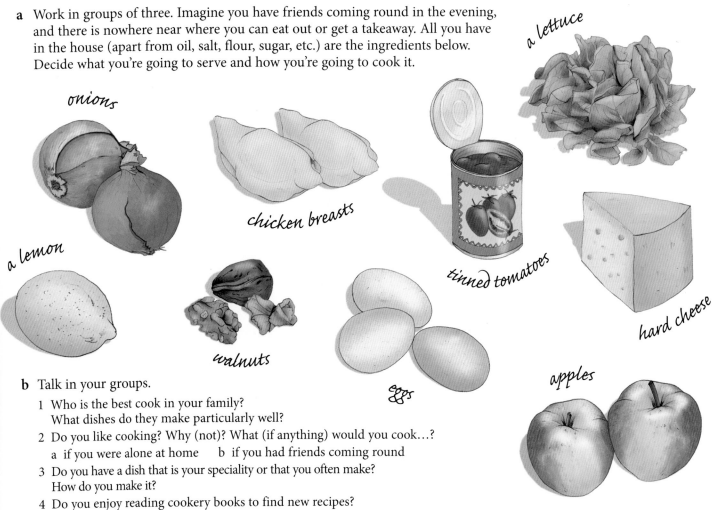

onions

a lettuce

chicken breasts

a lemon

walnuts

tinned tomatoes

hard cheese

eggs

apples

b Talk in your groups.

1 Who is the best cook in your family? What dishes do they make particularly well?
2 Do you like cooking? Why (not)? What (if anything) would you cook…?
   a if you were alone at home   b if you had friends coming round
3 Do you have a dish that is your speciality or that you often make? How do you make it?
4 Do you enjoy reading cookery books to find new recipes?

5 GRAMMAR
nouns: compound and possessive forms

a Circle the right phrase in each pair. If you think both are possible, explain what the difference between them is.

1 a recipe book / a recipe's book
2 a tuna salad / a salad of tuna
3 children's portions / children portions
4 a coffee cup / a cup of coffee
5 a chef hat / a chef's hat
6 a tin-opener / a tins opener
7 James' kitchen / James's kitchen
8 a John's friend / a friend of John's

b ➲ **p.154 Grammar Bank 7A.** Read the rules and do the exercises.

6 READING

a Read the introduction to a book called *My Last Supper* and find the answers to the questions.

1 What is the 'My last supper' game?
2 Who plays the game in the book?
3 What does the book contain, apart from their answers?

b Read the introduction again and answer the questions with a partner.

1 Why does Anthony Bourdain think chefs are good at the 'My last supper' game?
2 Why does he think their answers are surprising? Do you agree?
3 What impression does he give of a typical chef's character? Do you think this is accurate?
4 What, according to Anthony Bourdain, is the difference between cooking and eating? Do you agree?

MY LAST SUPPER

INTRODUCTION
BY CHEF ANTHONY BOURDAIN

CHEFS have been playing the 'My last supper' game, in one version or another, since humans first gathered round the flames to cook. Whether late at night, after their kitchens had closed, sitting at a wobbly table on the periphery of Les Halles in nineteenth century Paris and drinking *vin ordinaire*, or while nibbling bits of chicken from skewers in after-hours izakayas in Tokyo, or perched at the darkened bar of a closed New York City restaurant, enjoying vintages they couldn't otherwise afford, someone always piped up, 'If you were to die tomorrow, what single dish, what mouthful of food from anywhere in the world or any time in your life would you choose as your last?'

I've played the game myself, hundreds of times, with my crew in Manhattan, line cooks in San Francisco and Portland, chefs from Sydney to Kuala Lumpur to São Paulo – and with many of the subjects in this book. It's remarkable how simple, rustic, and unpretentious most of their selections are. These are people who, more often than not, have dined widely and well. They know what a fresh white truffle tastes like. The finest beluga for them holds no mysteries. With chefs travelling so much these days, many have enjoyed every variety of edible exotica. Which is to say, chefs know good stuff. And they get a lot of it.

And yet, when we ask ourselves and each other the question, what would we want as that last taste of life, we seem to crave reminders of simpler, harder times. A crust of bread and butter. Poor-people food. When we think of what we would eat last, we revert from the loud obsessive dominating control freaks we have become to the children we once were. Not that all of us were happy children, but we were children just the same. If cooking professionally is about control – about manipulating the people, the ingredients, and the strange physical forces of the kitchen universe to do our bidding, always anticipating, always preparing, always dominating one's environment – then eating well is about submission. About letting go.

Melanie Dunea managed to convince a number of the world's best and best-known chefs to behave for a few moments like children, and then to allow those moments to be photographed…

Les Halles	the traditional central market of Paris, which was demolished in 1971
izakaya	a type of Japanese drinking establishment which also serves food to accompany the drinks

LIDIA BASTIANICH

Melanie Dunea/CPi-syndication.com

c Now look at the questions and some of the answers. Whose choices do you most agree with?

THE QUESTIONS

1 What would your last meal on earth be?
2 What would the setting for the meal be?
3 Would there be music?
4 Who would your dining companions be?

d Read the answers again and complete the sentences in your own words.

1 Ferran Adrià and Guillaume Brahini differ from the others in their choice of food because…
2 The most commonly chosen setting is…
3 Jamie Oliver is the only chef who wouldn't…
4 Raymond Blanc would particularly like to have his partner Natalia with him because…

LEXIS IN CONTEXT

e Read the article again and underline any words for items of food or drink which you did not know. Compare with a partner, and check their meaning with a dictionary. Are any of these words ones that you wouldn't consider to be English?

f Now find words in the text to match the definitions below. They are all connected with food or eating.

Introduction	1	_____	*verb* take small bites of sth, especially food
	2	_____	*noun* a long thin piece of metal that is pushed through pieces of meat or vegetables to hold them together while they are cooking
	3	_____	*adj.* that can be eaten
	4	_____	*verb* have a very strong desire for sth, especially food
	5	_____	*noun* the hard outer surface of bread
Lidia Bastianich	6	_____	*adj.* fully grown and ready to be eaten
Jamie Oliver	7	_____	*noun* a deep round container used for cooking things in
Ferran Adrià	8	_____	*noun* a lot of different dishes served in small quantities
Raymond Blanc	9	_____	*verb* (*formal*) have dinner

g With a partner, answer the four questions, and explain your choices.

THE ANSWERS

LIDIA BASTIANICH ITALIAN

1 My last meal would consist of a plate of sliced San Daniele prosciutto with some ripe black figs; linguine with white clam sauce; a plate of Gran Padano; and perfectly ripe juicy peaches.
2 The setting would be in my house overlooking the Adriatic, while the waves crashed against the rocky shore.
3 *Scheherazade* would be playing in surround sound.
4 I would like my family and closest friends with me.

JAMIE OLIVER BRITISH

1 I would have a big pot of spaghetti all'arrabbiata made with three types of chillies – my perfect comfort food. If I were going to have dessert, it would be home-made rice pudding with roasted peaches. The rice pudding would be served very cold and topped with the hot caramelized peaches.
2 I would be in my house in Essex, cuddled up on the sofa with my wife. There would be some rubbish on television and a fire going. The window would be open just a crack, with the fresh air cooling the back of my neck after all those chillies.
3 Just the telly playing in the background.
4 My wife Jools would be sitting beside me.

FERRAN ADRIÀ SPANISH

1 I love seafood, so my last meal would be a tasting menu that featured a variety of seafood, prepared in many different ways, and inspired by the cuisine at *Kiccho Restaurant* in Kyoto, Japan. I would finish the meal with fruit from the Amazon that I had never tasted before.
2 I wouldn't like to have my last meal on earth, but if there were no alternative I would have it at *Kiccho*. The restaurant is a Japanese house with a beautiful Zen garden.
3 I would like to listen to fusion music, and the same Berber music that they have in *Yahout* restaurant in Marrakesh. To see Berber musicians performing transports you to ancestral times and places, while at the same time it sounds so progressive and modern.
4 My companions would be my wife, my family, and my friends.

GUILLAUME BRAHINI FRENCH

1 Definitely a multicourse feast, starting with oysters and caviar, followed by some foie gras, then a nice piece of rib eye steak, and lastly some cheese.
2 At home. As a chef, I'm home too little, so it is always a great luxury to be in my house, seated in my favourite chair, with my children bouncing and playing around me.
3 I love opera. I'd like to hear my favourite of all time, Verdi's *La Traviata*.
4 My family. I have three daughters aged one, four, and seven, and am very close to my family in France. We're a very Latin bunch, so it would involve lots of talking, hugging, tears, and laughter.

GIORGIO LOCATELLI ITALIAN

1 My last meal on earth would be something simple and fresh – grilled mackerel and broccoli with chilli and garlic.
2 A beach in Sicily, at sunset with a bonfire.
3 My wife Plaxy and her friend Antonia would sing for the night.
4 Lots of friends and family. I'd have a big party on the beach under the stars. What could be a better send-off?

RAYMOND BLANC FRENCH

1 I imagine the food would be something humble and simple, something very casual with comfortable flavours like a big fat local saucisse de Morteau with some Gruyère to accompany it, and a crusty traditional baguette. That would be just fine.
2 We would definitely be in France, somewhere near where my parents live in Besançon.
3 The Rolling Stones come to mind. Afterwards I am likely to need peace and quiet, so Arvo Pärt, the Estonian composer, would perform his *Spiegel im Spiegel*. That would be perfect.
4 I would dine with my friend René, who has been my best friend since I was two. My two sons would have to be there, since they are not only my sons but my best friends as well. My partner Natalia would bring a little humour to the whole process. Being Russian, she has a great knowledge of the grieving process. The Russians love their dead, and mourn them openly for years. Their cemeteries are in the woods, and they plant trees there to shadow the graves. Once a year they go to them with vodka and bread and let their grieving out. It's a very different approach to the English way.

7 B

G *so* and *such*
V word building: adjectives, nouns, and verbs
P homographs

'Sports do not build character. They reveal it.'
Heywood Broun, US journalist

Sport on trial

1 READING & SPEAKING

a Look at the photos. Do you do any of the activities, or have you ever done them? Is / Was your experience positive or negative?

b Read an article from *The Guardian* newspaper where these activities are compared. Answer the questions as quickly as possible with one (or more) of the activities.

According to the text, with which sport(s)…?
1 are there two different varieties
2 can you easily get addicted
3 can you easily get bored if you don't vary what you do enough
4 do some specific muscles become stronger
5 do you work on the lower body more than the upper body
6 does it take the longest time to show any benefits
7 does having the right teacher strongly influence your enjoyment
8 is it difficult to actually improve
9 can you aggravate an existing injury if you don't do it properly
10 may you not actually improve your fitness
11 will you learn to stand better
12 will you lose weight the most quickly

c Read the text again. In each pair of activities which do you think, according to the article, was the winner?

LEXIS IN CONTEXT

d Look at the definitions below. Can you remember what any of the words are? Find the ones you can't remember in the text.

1 _____ *noun* one long step (also vb *to walk with long steps*)
2 _____ *noun* the row of small bones that are connected together down the middle of the back
3 _____ *noun* a period of physical exercise that you do to keep fit
4 _____ (to) *adj.* likely to suffer from
5 _____ a place where two bones are joined together in the body
6 _____ *verb* the act of putting your arms or legs out straight and contracting your muscles
7 _____ *noun* an exercise in which you lie on your stomach and raise your body off the ground with your hands until your arms are straight
8 _____ *noun* an exercise for making your stomach muscles strong, in which you lie on the floor on your back and raise the top part of your body
9 _____ *noun* the main part of the body apart from the head, arms, and legs

BATTLE OF THE WORKOUTS

Running or aerobics? Yoga or Pilates? Making the decision to get fit is the easy part – choosing how to go about it is the difficult bit. Peta Bee offers some advice.

RUNNING v AEROBICS

RUNNING

How quickly will it make a difference? After two to three weeks if running three or more times a week.

How many calories does it burn? Around 612 per hour if you run ten kilometres per hour. You will burn more calories running off-road as your legs have to work harder on soft ground.

Will it keep me motivated? Treadmill running, hamster fashion, can be tedious: run outside, changing your route and terrain whenever you can. As you get fitter, challenge yourself more by entering fun runs.

What are the specific benefits? The basic running action strengthens the hamstring, quadriceps, iliopsoas muscles at the front of the hips, calf, and the gluteus maximus muscles each time you take a stride forward. The pumping action of your arms will strengthen the upper body to some extent. And it's among the best forms of aerobic exercise.

What are the risk factors? Your feet absorb three to four times your body weight every time they strike the ground and a shock reverberates up through your legs and into your spine. Good shoes help to cushion the blow and reduce the risk of injury to the knees and other joints.

AEROBICS

How quickly will it make a difference? After four to five weeks of twice-weekly classes.

How many calories does it burn? 374 per hour.

Will it keep me motivated? It depends on your instructor. Classes that stick to exactly the same format every week can become too predictable for both muscles and mind. As with all class-based workouts, there is little scope for progress, so there will come a time when you will want to try something different.

What are the specific benefits? Aerobics classes incorporate an element of dance that will improve coordination and spatial awareness.

What are the risk factors? Low-impact aerobics – at least one foot remains in contact with the floor at all times – are preferable to high-impact classes for anyone prone to back and joint problems.

WINNER

YOGA v PILICATES

YOGA v PILATES

YOGA

How quickly will it make a difference? After eight weeks of thrice-weekly sessions.

How many calories does it burn? 102 per hour for a general, stretch-based class. Power yoga burns 245 per hour.

Will it keep me motivated? Yoga is all about attaining a sense of unity between body and mind rather than setting and achieving personal targets. However, you will feel a sense of accomplishment as you master the postures and there are many different types to try.

What are the specific benefits? In a study for the American Council on Exercise (ACE), Professor John Porcari found that women who did three yoga classes a week for eight weeks experienced a 13% improvement in flexibility, with significant gains in shoulder and trunk flexibility. They were able to perform six more press-ups and 14 more sit-ups at the end of the study compared to the beginning.

What are the risk factors? Don't fall for the line that celebrities get fit on yoga alone. According to ACE, even power yoga constitutes only a 'light aerobic workout'.

PILATES

How quickly will it make a difference? After five to six weeks of thrice-weekly sessions.

How many calories does it burn? 170–237 per hour.

Will it keep me motivated? Once you start noticing positive changes in the way you move and hold your body, Pilates is hard to give up.

What are the specific benefits? Widely used by dancers and top athletes, it improves postural awareness and strength. Studies at Queensland University in Australia have shown that Pilates exercises can develop the deeply embedded traversus abdominal muscles, which support the trunk.

What are the risk factors? Another study by ACE last year found the cardiovascular benefits of Pilates to be limited. Even an advanced 55-minute session raised participants' heart rates to a maximum of only 62% (below the recommended 64–94% said to constitute an aerobic workout) and was deemed the energy equivalent of walking 3.5 miles an hour. If you have back pain, make sure you see a teacher who is also a physiotherapist, as poor technique can make matters worse.

WINNER

From The Guardian

---

e Match the verbs on the left with their collocates in the text. Which two verbs are similar in meaning?

master	a sense of unity
challenge	the postures
attain	calories
perform	personal targets
set / achieve	six press-ups
burn	yourself more by entering fun runs

f Think of a sport or activity which you have done or know something about. What is it good for? What is it not so good for? Tell your partner about it, answering the questions in the text.

2 VOCABULARY
word building: adjectives, nouns, and verbs

a Without looking back at the text, complete sentences 1 and 2 with a word made from *strong*.

1 The pumping action of your arms will _____ the upper body to some extent.

2 Widely used by dancers and top athletes, it improves postural awareness and _____.

b Complete the chart.

Adjective	Noun	Verb
strong		
long		
deep		
short		
wide		
high		
weak		
thick		
flat		

c Complete the sentences with words from **b** in the right form.

1 I often have to _____ new trousers because they're usually too long for me.

2 Can you measure the _____ and _____ of the living room? I want to order a new carpet.

3 I'm more or less the same _____ as my sister, but my brother's much taller than us.

4 People's joints tend to _____ as they get older.

5 **A** What's the _____ of the water here?
   B About ten metres, I think.

6 If you want to _____ the sauce, add butter and flour.

7 People do sit-ups to try to _____ their stomach.

8 He's almost unbeatable. He doesn't have any real _____.

9 This road needs _____. It's far too narrow.

10 My grandfather suffers from _____ of breath. He used to be a heavy smoker.

3 SPEAKING & LISTENING

a Look at the information about the book *Foul Play*. Tick (✓) the points you agree with and cross (✗) the ones you disagree with. Try to think of at least one good reason why you agree / disagree.

b In groups of three or four, discuss each point, explaining why you agree or disagree and giving examples where possible. Try to decide whether as a group you agree or disagree with the statements.

c **7.6** Now listen to Mike Brearley, psychoanalyst and former captain of the England cricket team talking about the topics in **a**. Mark the statements A if he agrees, PA if he partially agrees, and D if he disagrees. Do his opinions coincide with what you said in your groups?

d Listen again and note down the reasons he gives.

FOUL PLAY
What's wrong with sport?

In his book, *Foul play*, sports journalist Joe Humphreys challenges the idea that sport is a positive influence on athletes, spectators, and the world as a whole.

According to Humphreys:

1 Sport brings out the worst in people, both fans and athletes. It does not improve character or help to develop virtues such as fair play and respect for opponents. ☐ ☐

2 Sport doesn't make you happy. Spectators as well as athletes have higher than normal levels of stress, anxiety, and hopelessness because of their engagement with professional sport. ☐ ☐

3 Sport is like a religion in its ability to 'move the masses'. ☐ ☐

4 Doping is no worse than any other kind of cheating and really no different from using other kinds of technology to gain an advantage, e.g. high-tech running shoes. ☐ ☐

5 It's ridiculous to expect professional athletes to be role models. ☐ ☐

6 Sport occupies a disproportionately high place in the media, often making the headlines in papers and on TV. ☐ ☐

4 GRAMMAR so and such

a Complete the sentences with *so, so much, such,* or *such a / an.*

1 Sport is _____ big business nowadays that winning has become a matter of life or death.

2 Professional footballers are _____ well paid that most of them can live off their earnings when they stop playing.

3 It was _____ close match that it wasn't decided until the last minute.

4 He was _____ disappointed to have come second! He'd been _____ sure that he was going to win.

5 There's _____ sports news on TV that you'd think it was more important than anything else.

6 That commentator talks in _____ excited way that you can't understand a word he says.

b ▶ **p.155 Grammar Bank 7B.** Read the rules and do the exercises.

5 PRONUNCIATION homographs

a Read the information box about homographs.

> Homographs are words which are spelled the same but have different meanings and which can be pronounced differently, e.g.
>
> **bow** /baʊ/ = move your head or the top half of your body forwards and downwards, as a sign of respect or to say goodbye
>
> **bow** /bəʊ/ = 1 a weapon used for shooting arrows 2 a hair decoration made of ribbon
>
> There are not very many words like this, but the common ones are sometimes mispronounced, and learning the correct pronunciation will avoid misunderstandings.

b Look at the sentences which contain homographs. Match them with pronunciation **a** or **b**.

   close   a /kləʊz/ or b /kləʊs/?

1 ☐ It was a really close finish, and they had to use a video replay to see who won the race.

2 ☐ What time does the ticket office close? We need to get our tickets for the match on Saturday.

   row   a /rəʊ/ or b /raʊ/?

3 ☐ The coach had a row with one of his players, and threw a boot at him.

4 ☐ We were sitting in the front row so we could almost touch the players.

5 ☐ People who row tend to have very well-developed biceps.

   minute   a /ˈmɪnɪt/ or b /maɪˈnjuːt/?

6 ☐ He was disqualified because they found a minute quantity of a banned substance in his blood sample.

7 ☐ He scored a goal just one minute before the referee blew the final whistle.

   tear   a /teə/ or b /tɪə/?

8 ☐ If you tear a muscle or a ligament, you may not be able to train for six months.

9 ☐ As she listened to the national anthem play, a tear rolled down her cheek.

   content   a /ˈkɒntent/ or b /ˈkənˈtent/?

10 ☐ Football players never seem content with their contracts. They're always trying to negotiate better conditions.

11 ☐ The content of the programme was a two-hour analysis of the match.

   wound   a /wuːnd/ or b /waʊnd/?

12 ☐ He wound the tape tightly round his ankle to prevent a sprain.

13 ☐ You could see his head wound bleeding as he was taken off the pitch.

   use   a /juːz/ or b /juːs/?

14 ☐ If you use a high-tech swimsuit, you will be able to swim much faster.

15 ☐ It's no use complaining; the umpire's decision is final.

c **7.7** Listen and check. Practise saying the sentences.

6 **7.8** SONG ♫ *Eye of the Tiger*

7 C

G comparison
V humour
P *augh* and *ough*

'What do you mean, funny? Funny peculiar or funny ha-ha?'
Ian Hay, Scottish writer

The funniest joke in the world?

1 LISTENING

a **7.9** Listen and read the five jokes. Then score them 1–5 (1 = not funny at all, 5 = very funny). Compare with a partner.

Is one of these jokes 'the funniest joke in the world'?

A worldwide Internet survey devised by psychologist, Professor Richard Wiseman, set out to find a joke which was universally thought to be funny. 40,000 jokes were sent in to a website from all over the world and two million people from 70 countries scored the jokes from 1–5. Which joke was the winner?

1 Did you hear about the man who was so proud when he completed a jigsaw in half an hour? It said 'five to six years' on the box.

2 What kind of murderer has fibre? A cereal killer.

3 Sherlock Holmes and Doctor Watson went camping. They pitched their tent under the stars and went to sleep. Some time in the middle of the night, Holmes woke Watson and said: 'Watson, look up at the sky and tell me what you see.'

Watson said: 'I can see millions and millions of stars.'

Holmes said: 'And what do you deduce from that, Watson?'

Watson replied: 'Well, if there are millions of stars, and even if a few of those stars have planets, then it's quite likely there are some planets like ours out there. And if there are planets like earth out there, there might also be life.'

And Holmes said: 'Watson, you idiot, it means that someone has stolen our tent.'

4 A man goes to a hospital for a check-up. After weeks of tests the doctor tells the man he has some good news and some bad news.

'What's the bad news?' asks the man.

'You have a rare and incurable disease,' says the doctor.

'And what's the good news?' asks the man.

And the doctor says: 'We're going to name it after you.'

5 Two hunters are out in the woods when one of them collapses. He doesn't seem to be breathing and his eyes are glazed. The other guy takes out his phone and calls the emergency services. He gasps 'I think my friend is dead! What can I do?' The operator says, 'Calm down. I can help. First, let's make sure he's dead.' There is silence, and then a shot is heard. Back on the phone, the guy says 'OK. Now what?'

b **7.10** You are going to listen to a journalist talking about the research. Listen to part 1 and answer the questions.

1 What does the journalist say that the funniest jokes have in common?
2 Why do we enjoy hearing jokes about people in authority?
3 Who do the English, the Mexicans, and the French tell jokes about? Why?
4 What was Sigmund Freud's theory about humour?
5 What kind of jokes do old people find especially funny?
6 What is a pun? Which joke is an example of a pun?
7 What differences were found between men and women's sense of humour?
8 Do different nationalities enjoy the same kind of jokes? Give examples.

c **7.11** Listen to part 2 and answer the questions.

1 Which joke (1–5) was voted the funniest?
2 Who submitted it? Why does he sometimes tell it?
3 Does Professor Wiseman believe it is the 'funniest joke in the world'? Why (not)?

2 VOCABULARY & SPEAKING humour

a Look at the questions and with a partner, check that you know what the **bold** words or phrases mean.

Your country

- Do people in your country **make fun of** another nationality in jokes? Which?
- Who is probably the most popular **comedian** in your country nowadays? What is the most popular **comedy series** on TV? Do you personally like them?
- Oscar Wilde was famous for being **witty**. Is there a public figure in your country who is considered witty?
- Do newspapers in your country have **political cartoons**? Do you have a favourite **cartoonist**? Why do you find him / her **amusing**?
- Do you think that people in your country are good at **laughing at themselves**, or do they tend to **take themselves** quite **seriously**?

You

- Are you good at **telling jokes**?
- Would you ever **laugh at** a joke even if you didn't **get it**?
- Which of these kinds of humour do you tend to find funny, **black humour**, **surreal humour**, **puns** and **wordplay**, **slapstick**, or **irony**?
- Can you think of a book or a film that was so **hilarious** that it made you **laugh out loud**?
- Have you ever **burst out laughing** at an embarrassing moment?
- How important is it for you that your friends or colleagues have **a good sense of humour**?

b Ask and answer the questions with a partner.

3 PRONUNCIATION augh and ough

a How are *augh* and *ough* pronounced in irregular past tenses, e.g. *brought*, *caught*, and *taught*?

> The combination *augh* and *ough* can be pronounced in several different ways. You need to learn the pronunciation of the common words which have these letters, and to check the pronunciation of new words in the dictionary.

b Look at the definitions and phonetics for other common words with *augh* or *ough*. Write the words.

1 *laugh* /lɑːf/ *verb* to make the sounds that show that you think something is funny
2 _____ /ɪˈnʌf/ *adj.* sufficient
3 _____ /drɑːft/ *noun* a flow of cool air in a room
4 _____ /draʊt/ *noun* a long period of time where there is little or no rain
5 _____ /θruː/ *prep.* from one end or side of sth to the other
6 _____ /ɔːlˈðəʊ/ *conj.* despite the fact that
7 _____ /rʌf/ *adj.* 1 not smooth; 2 not exact; 3 violent
8 _____ /tʌf/ *adj.* 1 difficult; 2 strict / firm; 3 strong
9 _____ /ˈdəʊnʌt/ *noun* a small cake made of fried dough, usually in the shape of a ring, and filled with jam
10 _____ /kɒf/ *noun, verb* to force out air suddenly and noisily through your throat, for example when you have a cold
11 _____ /plaʊ/ *noun, verb* a piece of farming equipment pulled by a tractor used for digging and turning over soil
12 _____ /ˈθʌrə/ *adj.* with great attention to detail

c **7.12** Look at the phonetics again. How do you pronounce the words? Listen and check.

d Test your partner's pronunciation using the definitions in **a**.

e **7.13** Listen and write the sentences.

'I can resist everything except temptation.'

Oscar Wilde

4 GRAMMAR comparison

a Right (✓) or wrong (✗)? Correct the mistakes in the highlighted phrases.

1 The more superior a joke makes us feel, we laugh more.
2 Women find jokes about men being stupid far funnier than jokes about women being stupid.
3 This joke got a little more votes than that joke.
4 Americans don't enjoy wordplay so much as the British.
5 There are much more jokes about men and women than about animals.
6 The shorter the joke, the best.
7 The research took twice as long as the psychologist expected.

b ➲ p.156 Grammar Bank 7C. Read the rules and do the exercises.

c In groups of three, discuss each of the topics below for at least two minutes.

- The nicer the food is, the worse it is for you.
- The more expensive clothes are, the longer they last.
- The older you get, the less tolerant you become.
- The more interesting a job, the less well paid it is.
- The smaller the country, the more patriotic the people are.
- The bigger the family, the more fun the children have.
- 'Whatever women do, they must do twice as well as men to be thought half as good. Luckily, this is not difficult.'

Winston Churchill

5 READING

You are going to read some examples of British humour. Read each text carefully. Which one did you enjoy most / least? Why?

Famous put-downs

One of the people most famous for his witty and often cruel put-downs was British Prime Minister, Winston Churchill.

If you were my husband, I'd put poison in your coffee.
Lady Astor, politician

If you were my wife, I'd drink it.
Winston Churchill, in reply

Winston, you're drunk!
Bessie Braddock, politician

Bessie, you're ugly. And tomorrow morning I shall be sober.
Winston Churchill, in reply

Am reserving two tickets for you for my premiere.
    Come and bring a friend – if you have one.
**Telegram from dramatist George Bernard Shaw
    (also famous for his put-downs)**

Impossible to be present for the first performance.
    Will attend second – if there is one.
Churchill's telegram in reply

'put-down *noun* (*informal*) a remark or a criticism that is intended to make sb look or feel stupid

Lady Astor

George Bernard Shaw

Bessie Braddock

BRITISH

Yes, Minister

This is an extract from a famous BBC TV comedy programme, *Yes Minister*. Jim Hacker is a slightly unintelligent government minister who always allows himself to be controlled by his civil servants. Here, Hacker is complaining to his private secretary about all the paperwork he has to deal with.

Jim Hacker   When am I going to get through all this correspondence?

Bernard Woolley   You do realize, Minister, that you don't actually have to?

Jim Hacker   Don't I?

Bernard Woolley   Not if you don't want to, we can draft an official reply.

Jim Hacker   What's an official reply?

Bernard Woolley   It just says, 'The Minister has asked me to thank you for your letter' and we say something like 'The matter is under consideration', or, even if we feel so inclined, 'under active consideration'.

Jim Hacker   What's the difference?

Bernard Woolley   Well, 'under consideration' means we've lost the file, 'under active consideration' means we're trying to find it.

Script by Jonathan Lynn and Antony Jay

> ,private 'secretary *noun* **1** a secretary whose job it is to deal with the more important and personal affairs of a business person **2** a civil servant who acts as an assistant to a senior government official

FIRST DATE
She

I said I liked classical music.
It wasn't exactly a lie.
I hoped he would get the impression
That my brow was acceptably high.

I said I liked classical music.
I mentioned Vivaldi and Bach.
And he asked me along to this concert
And here we are sitting in the half-dark.

I was thrilled to be asked to the concert.
I couldn't decide what to wear.
I hope I look tastefully sexy.
I've done what I can with my hair.

Yes, I'm thrilled to be here at this concert.
I couldn't care less what they play
But I'm trying my hardest to listen
So I'll have something clever to say.

When I glance at his face it's a picture
Of rapt concentration. I see
He is totally into this music
And quite undistracted by me.

FIRST DATE
He

She said she liked classical music.
I implied I was keen on it too.
Though I don't often go to a concert
It wasn't entirely untrue.

I looked for a suitable concert
And here we are, on our first date.
The traffic was dreadful this evening
And I arrived ten minutes late.

So we haven't had much time for talking
And I'm a bit nervous. I see
She is totally lost in the music
And quite undistracted by me.

In that dress she is very attractive –
The neckline can't fail to intrigue.
I mustn't appear too besotted.
Perhaps she is out of my league.

Where are we? I glance at my programme
But I've put my glasses away.
I'd better start paying attention
Or else I'll have nothing to say.

by Wendy Cope

Wendy Cope

> 'highbrow *adj.* **1** (sometimes *disapproving*) concerned with or interested in serious artistic or cultural ideas **SYN** INTELLECTUAL *highbrow newspapers* **OPP** LOWBROW

HUMOUR

Key success factors

- being able to summarize the issue clearly
- maintaining an assertive but respectful tone
- being clear and reasonable about what you expect to be done

ANALYSING A MODEL TEXT

a Have you ever had a very bad experience at a restaurant or a hotel? What happened? Did you make a complaint either in person or in writing? What response did you get?

b Read the model letter. What exactly is the complaint about?

c With a partner discuss which phrase is better for each gap and why.

1. a I'm sorry to say
   b I am afraid to say
2. a did not live up to our expectations
   b was a complete disaster
3. a was supposed to provide
   b was going to give us
4. a it didn't happen
   b this was not the case
5. a fed up
   b dissatisfied
6. a we were told
   b they told us
7. a to our great disappointment
   b really irritatingly
8. a a pack of lies
   b totally inaccurate and misleading
9. a we are owed an apology
   b you ought to say sorry
10. a some form of compensation
    b a lot of money back

Dear Sir / Madam,

I am writing to complain about a three-night holiday to Scotland we booked through your company. ¹_____ that the *Highland Dreams* (booking reference LG61367) ²_____ and did not reflect the description on your website.

According to your website, the hotel where we stayed ³_____ an evening entertainment programme, which was described as being 'varied and fun packed'. Unfortunately, ⁴_____ and it left us and the other guests feeling extremely ⁵_____.

On the first evening, there was a comedian. However, not only was he not funny at all, but he also told racist jokes, and many guests left during his performance. When we complained to the hotel management ⁶_____ that 'we did not have a sense of humour'. On the second day, according to the programme, we were going to be taught some traditional Scottish dances, which sounded more promising, but ⁷_____, the event was cancelled at the last minute without any explanation being given. The final night's entertainment was a 'Karaoke Evening', which was a complete failure as most of the guests were elderly people who were too embarrassed to sing in public.

I feel strongly that the description of the entertainment programme on your website should be changed as it is ⁸_____. We were extremely disappointed by this aspect of our holiday and in the circumstances we believe that ⁹_____ and we should receive ¹⁰_____.

I look forward to hearing your views on this matter.

Yours faithfully,

USEFUL LANGUAGE

d Without looking back at the letter, try to remember how the writer expressed the following in a more formal way.

1 In this letter I want to complain…

_____

2 It said on your website…

_____

3 The comedian was not funny at all and told racist jokes.

_____

4 I really think that you should change the description on your website…

_____

5 I'd like to know what you think about this.

_____

PLANNING WHAT TO WRITE

Brainstorm the content

a Read part of an email to Hannah from a friend. What exactly is the 'Board first' service? What problem did she have?

New Message

Send | Chat | Attach | Address | Fonts | Colors | Save As Draft

Hi Hannah,

Just got back from Rome. That's the last time I fly with GreenAir!

It says on their website that there's this 'Board first' service meaning that if you pay €20 extra per person you can get on the plane first. As I was with the kids I thought it'd be worth the extra money so we could all sit together. Anyway when it was time to board we went through the gate first, but instead of going straight on to the plane it turned out that the plane was miles away from the gate and there was a bus to take us there. So what happened? All the people who hadn't paid the extra money got onto the same bus, and then got off the bus before us! So we paid €60 for nothing – we were almost the last ones on the plane and couldn't sit together!

I'm going to email GreenAir and make a fuss. It's a complete rip-off! And if they don't do anything about it, I'll write to the Air Transport Users Council.

Apart from that, the holiday was great. Rome was a dream…

---

b You are going to write the email to GreenAir. With a partner…

- underline the relevant information in the email.
- summarize exactly what it is that you are dissatisfied with.
- think of reasons why your complaint is justified.
- discuss what would be reasonable for GreenAir to do to compensate you for the inconvenience.
- decide what other details you think might be important to include in the email, e.g. the date and the flight number, and invent them.

TIPS for writing an email or letter of complaint

- Make a note of all the relevant details you want to include before you start drafting your email.
- Decide what action you want the person you are writing to to take.
- Use appropriate expressions for opening and closing the email.
- Use a formal style, and be clear and assertive but not aggressive.
- Try to use a variety of expressions for generalizing and making suggestions.
- Use the passive, e.g. *we were told*, *we are owed an apology*, etc. to make it more impersonal or to make it clear that you are not accusing individuals.

WRITING

You are going to write an email to the airline. It should be approximately 250 words.

DRAFT your email, explaining why you are writing, what the complaint relates to, giving the details, and asking for some action from the airline.

EDIT the email, making sure you are happy with the content and tone throughout, and making sure it is the right length.

CHECK the email for mistakes in grammar, spelling, punctuation, and register.

THE INTERVIEW

a You are going to listen to an interview with Chantelle Nicholson, a New Zealand chef who works as sous-chef at the Marcus Wareing restaurant in London. Before you listen, read the glossary and look at how the words are pronounced to help you understand what she says.

> **foodie** *informal* a person who is very interested in food and cooking
>
> **the Gordon Ramsay scholarship** a scholarship for young chefs set up by the celebrity chef Gordon Ramsay, where the winner gets work experience and a cash prize
>
> **Josh Emmet** the head chef at the Savoy Grill (at the Savoy Hotel in London)
>
> **Marcus Wareing** well-respected British chef who runs the Savoy Grill and several other restaurants
>
> **beetroot** a dark red root vegetable
>
> **delicacy** a type of food considered to be very special
>
> **scallops** a kind of shellfish
>
> **tarte Tatin** a French tart usually made with apples or pears

b **7.14** Listen to part 1. Answer the questions with a partner.

1 Who taught her to cook?
2 What did she have to do when she applied for the scholarship?
3 What happened as a result of her meeting Josh Emmet?
4 What does she think Marcus Wareing's positive qualities are?
5 How does she describe the style of cooking at the restaurant?

c **7.15** Listen to part 2. What does she say about…?

1 the difference between a sous-chef and a head chef
2 the hours she works
3 things that cause stress in the kitchen
4 why she doesn't cook at home very much
5 her last meal on earth

d **7.16** Listen and complete the phrases with two words. What do you think they mean?

COMMON EXPRESSIONS AND IDIOMS

1 …so I thought, 'Well, why not _____ that a _____ ?'
2 …and it was just too good an opportunity to _____ _____ .
3 …as opposed to making a carrot taste like a beetroot, which, in a sense, I think some people get a little _____ _____ with.
4 It makes a big difference, kind of the way diners come in as well, if they all come in _____ _____ …
5 …the guests that have ordered that particular dish, they have to wait a long time, but also it creates _____ in a sense…
6 …and if you're organized and kind of a bit forward-thinking and always _____ _____ ahead…

e What impression do you get of Chantelle's attitude to her job? Is it a job that would appeal to you?

IN THE STREET

a **7.17** You are going to hear three people talking about food. What three questions are they asked? Who is most / least positive about the cuisine in their country? Which is the most popular foreign cuisine?

Sheila (UK)

Liz (USA)

Naomi (NZ)

b Listen again and answer the questions.

The UK: Sheila

1 What examples does she give to show that people in the UK are more interested in cooking nowadays?
2 What does she mean by 'the balance tips towards junk food rather than healthy food'?
3 What does she say is the difference between Indian food and Thai food?

The USA: Liz

4 What specific things does she think are unhealthy about US cuisine?
5 In what way is Liz different from the other speakers? How does this affect her favourite cuisines?

New Zealand: Naomi

6 In what way has the cooking changed?
7 What do her favourite cuisines have in common?

c **7.18** Listen and complete the phrases with one to four words. What do you think they mean?

COMMON PHRASES

1 …still there's a _____ before we can say, in general people in the UK are good cooks.
2 …there are also an _____ really awful fast food outlets encouraging you to eat junk.
3 …and full of fat and salt, and all that _____ .
4 So yeah, I think _____ , it's a pretty healthy place.

d Now answer the same questions with a partner.

GRAMMAR

a Right (✓) or wrong (✗)? Correct the mistakes in the highlighted phrases.

1 He's my brother's friend.
2 Have you got a tins opener?
3 It was such an awful weather that we decided not to go.
4 She has far more money than I do.
5 What's the name of the shop where you bought that skirt?
6 It was a so good film that we saw it twice.
7 He's not nearly as stupid as he looks.
8 **A** I'd love a wine glass.
   B Sure. Red or white?
9 The sky got more and more dark, until it seemed as if it was night.
10 Birmingham is the second-largest city of the UK.

b Circle the right phrases. Tick if both are possible.

1 *The capital city of Japan / Japan's capital city* is Tokyo.
2 I found an old *photo album / album of photos* in the attic.
3 Come around 9.00. We'll be *at Tom's / at Tom's house*.
4 The best place to hide valuables is in the *children bedroom / children's bedroom*.
5 I've got *so many / such a lot of* books that I'm running out of shelf space.
6 You don't need to hurry. We've still got *a few / a bit* more time.
7 She's *far more / much more* intelligent than her brother.
8 They're *such / so* lovely people. I'm sure you'll like them.
9 Why do you want to buy this bag? It's twice *so / as* expensive as the other one.
10 I think her latest novel is *by much / by far* the best book she's written.
11 It's only *a few / a little* more weeks before we go back to the UK.
12 *The book's end / The end of the book* was very disappointing.

VOCABULARY

a Write the words for the definitions.

1 _____ _____ *noun* a thing you use to cut vegetables on
2 _____ *verb* to cook at a very low heat
3 _____ *verb* to move sth round, e.g. a sauce using a spoon
4 _____ *verb* to fill, e.g. a vegetable with another type of food
5 _____ *verb* make liquid as a result of heating
6 _____ *noun* a flow of cool air
7 _____ *noun* the row of small bones that are connected together down the middle of your back
8 _____ *adj.* extremely funny
9 _____ *adj.* (of fruit and crops) fully grown and ready to be eaten

b Complete the sentences with a verb.

1 If you're hungry, there's some pasta left over from yesterday. You could _____ it in the microwave.
2 To make an omelette, first break two eggs into a bowl and then _____ them lightly with a fork.
3 When she saw the surprised look on his face she _____ out laughing.
4 Relax! Don't _____ it so seriously – it's not the end of the world.
5 We thought that the painting my grandmother left me was worthless, but it _____ out to be a very valuable work by a well-known German painter.
6 It's cruel to _____ fun of people who stammer.
7 You'd _____ more calories if you did power yoga instead of normal yoga.
8 _____ yourself a realistic goal, and then gradually work towards it.

c Complete the sentence with a word formed from the **bold** word.

1 He's a great _____. He's in the *Sunday Times* every week. **CARTOON**
2 The real _____ of the film is the witty dialogue. **STRONG**
3 I need to get someone to _____ my new jeans. I'm useless at sewing. **SHORT**
4 The pole-vaulter Sergei Bubka was the first man to clear the _____ of six metres. **HIGH**
5 I swam 20 _____ of the swimming pool this morning. **LONG**
6 Nowadays there are far more female _____ than there used to be. **COMEDY**
7 Cover the mousse with _____ cream and then decorate with grated chocolate. **WHIP**

Communication

1B What can you see? **Students A + B**

Look at the picture below. Write down on a piece of paper what you see. Allow yourself about 30 seconds for this.

◑ **p.8** and continue choosing your answers.

1B Who am I? **Students A + B**

a For each section, find out which personality type you are.

1 more a and b = **planner**
   more c and d = **spontaneous**
2 more a and b = **facts**
   more c and d = **ideas**
3 more a and b = **head**
   more c and d = **heart**
4 more a and b = **introvert**
   more c and d = **extrovert**

b With your four types, find out which of the categories below you fit into. Then read the description of your personality type.

c Now find out what your partner's personality type is, and read the description.

BIG THINKER = Spontaneous + Ideas + Heart + Extrovert
How they see themselves talkative, curious, logical, self-sufficient
What they are like ingenious, bored by routine, can be rude, rebellious, critical of others

COUNSELLOR = Planner + Ideas + Heart + Introvert
How they see themselves gentle, peaceful, cautious
What they are like relaxed and creative, deeply private, can be difficult to get to know

GO-GETTER = Spontaneous + Facts + Head + Extrovert
How they see themselves inventive, enthusiastic, determined, alert
What they are like resourceful, tough-minded, may become frustrated by routines and constraints

IDEALIST = Spontaneous + Ideas + Heart + Introvert
How they see themselves bright, forgiving, curious
What they are like generally easy-going, flexible, can be stubborn, may refuse to compromise

INNOVATOR = Spontaneous + Ideas + Heart + Extrovert
How they see themselves imaginative, sociable, sympathetic
What they are like energetic, sensitive, creative, sometimes illogical, rebellious, unfocused

LEADER = Planner + Ideas + Head + Extrovert
How they see themselves bright, independent, logical
What they are like organized, good at solving large-scale problems, can be critical and aggressive

MASTERMIND = Planner + Ideas + Head + Introvert
How they see themselves logical, thorough, bright
What they are like efficient, independent, rarely change their minds, critical of those who don't understand them

MENTOR = Planner + Ideas + Heart + Extrovert
How they see themselves intelligent, outgoing, sensitive
What they are like articulate, warm, lively, extremely sensitive to people's needs, may become overbearing

NURTURER = Planner + Facts + Heart + Introvert
How they see themselves gentle, conscientious, mature
What they are like quiet and caring, may have trouble making decisions that could hurt others, tend to avoid conflict, others may take advantage of them

PEACEMAKER = Spontaneous + Facts + Heart + Introvert
How they see themselves steady, gentle, sympathetic,
What they are like sensitive to the feelings of others and the world around them, often animal lovers, can be self-critical, often difficult to get to know

PERFORMER = Spontaneous + Facts + Heart + Extrovert
How they see themselves enthusiastic, sociable, sensitive
What they are like fun-loving, outgoing, often good motivators, can be unreliable

PROVIDER = Planner + Facts + Heart + Extrovert
How they see themselves sympathetic, easy-going, steady
What they are like warm, caring, traditional, tend to avoid conflict, not afraid to express their beliefs

REALIST = Planner + Facts + Head + Introvert
How they see themselves mature, stable, conscientious
What they are like loyal, straightforward with others, good at meeting deadlines, respect facts and rules, can be obsessed with schedules, critical of others, may not have faith in other people's abilities

RESOLVER = Spontaneous + Facts + Head + Introvert
How they see themselves understanding, stable, easy-going
What they are like independent, rational, good at finding solutions, natural risk-takers, they enjoy an adrenaline rush, often focus on short-term results, sometimes lose sight of the bigger picture

STRATEGIST = Spontaneous + Ideas + Head + Introvert
How they see themselves bright, logical, individualistic
What they are like quiet, easy-going, intellectually curious, logical, may forget practical issues, e.g. paying bills or buying groceries, may be critical or sarcastic, can be insensitive to the emotional needs of others

SUPERVISOR = Planner + Facts + Head + Extrovert
How they see themselves stable, practical, sociable
What they are like natural organizers and administrators, irritated when people don't follow procedures, other people find them bossy

3C Have you got 'affluenza'?
Students A + B

If you answered 'yes' to **any** of the questions, then you have the virus. The more 'yes' answers, the worse you have it.

4A Guess the sentence   Student A

a Look at sentences 1–6 and imagine what the missing phrase could be. Remember ⊞ = positive verb and ⊟ = negative verb.

1 A lot of people say the book is better than the film, but actually I _____. ⊞

2 He's supposed to be really mean. Apparently, he never _____ on her birthday. ⊞

3 It wasn't a particularly nice day for the garden party but at least _____. ⊟

4 The sea was blue, the sun shone, and the picnic was marvellous. All in all, it _____. ⊞

5 On the one hand, dogs are far better company than any other pets, but on the other hand you _____ at least twice a day. ⊞

6 Make sure your suitcase weighs less than 20 kilos, otherwise you _____. ⊞

b Read your sentences to **B**. Keep trying different possibilities until you get each sentence exactly right.

c Listen to your partner's sentences. Tell them to keep guessing until they get it exactly the same as yours.

7 I'm not sure you would enjoy the play and in any case it will be very difficult **to get tickets**.

8 Some of the teachers aren't very stimulating, but on the whole I think **it's a good school**.

9 Laura's husband only thinks of himself and he always gets his own way. In other words, **he's totally selfish**.

10 I have my own import-export company. Basically, **I buy and sell** fruit and vegetables.

11 I don't feel like going to Miranda's birthday party and besides, I haven't **got anything to wear**.

12 It's no big surprise that Leo didn't do very well in his exams. After all, he **didn't study at all**.

5A QI quiz   Student A

a Read the answers to questions 1–5 and remember the information.

b Explain the answers to **B** in your own words. **B** will tell you the answers to 6–10.

1 What was Tutankhamun's curse?

There wasn't one. The story of the curse was made up by a journalist. When the British archaeologist Howard Carter discovered the tomb of King Tutankhamun in Cairo in 1922, a journalist who was writing for the British newspaper the Daily Express reported that there was an inscription above the door of the tomb which said, 'They who enter this sacred tomb shall swiftly be visited by wings of death'. In fact, there is no such inscription, but the story of the curse spread round the world and after this every time a member of the expedition died, people said it was because of the curse.

2 What do chameleons do and why?

We all learn at school that chameleons change colour as a form of camouflage, for example they change to grey so that they can hide on a rock, but in fact this is a total myth. Chameleons do change colour, but not to match the background. They change colour when they are frightened or after a fight and they sometimes change colour due to changes in light or temperature.

3 What man-made artefacts can be seen from the moon?

No points if you said The Great Wall of China! In fact <u>no</u> man-made structures can be seen from the moon – even continents are barely visible. You <u>can</u> see the Great Wall of China from <u>space</u> (which starts about 100 kilometres from the earth's surface), as well as seas, railways, cities, and even some buildings, but not from the moon.

4 What do kilts and whisky have in common?

The answer is that neither of them is Scottish in origin! Kilts were invented by the Irish and whisky by the Chinese.

5 Which metal is the best conductor?

Many people think that the answer is copper, but actually this is the second-best conductor. The best conductor is silver, but copper is more commonly used in electrical equipment simply because it is much cheaper.

5A What a ridiculous idea!   Student A

a Read your sentences to **B**. He / She will respond with an exclamation.

- Did you know that you're not supposed to call a female actor an actress because it's considered sexist?
- I was fined by a policeman yesterday for talking on my mobile when I was parked.
- My parents were burgled last night. They took all my mum's jewellery.
- I thought we could go to the cinema and then have dinner at the new Italian place down the road.
- Did you know my parents were both born on exactly the same day?
- I really put my foot in it at the party. I called Tom's partner 'Anna', but in fact that's his ex-wife's name!
- You won't believe it, but my sister's just won €200,000 in the lottery!

b Respond to **B**'s sentences with an exclamation beginning with either *How...!* or *What (a)...!* Make sure you use expressive intonation, and link the words where appropriate.

Communication

5B Four works of art **Students A + B**

My Bed (1999) Tracey Emin

Away from the flock (1994) Damien Hirst

Balloon dog (yellow) (1994–2000) Jeff Koons

Felt suit (1970)
Joseph Bueys

5B Stressing the right word **Student A**

a Read your sentence 1 to **B**. He / She will respond, giving one word extra stress. Continue with 2–6.

1 That girl really looks like your sister.
2 Did you say she was American?
3 Is the shoe shop the one after the traffic lights?
4 Shall we get her this bag then?
5 I thought you said you'd read the book?
6 I left your case on your bed.

b Now respond to **B** with your number 7 below, giving extra stress to one of the words. Continue with 8–12.

7 He's not my dog. He's my partner's dog.
8 Sorry, I asked for a tuna salad.
9 I gave him the money. He'd never be able to pay me back.
10 It looks expensive, but actually it was really cheap.
11 I am going out. I haven't been out for ages.
12 They lost 2–1 you mean.

5C Guess the sentence **Student A**

a Look at sentences 1–7 and imagine what the missing phrase could be.

1 I would love _____ the boss's face when you told him you were leaving. +
2 There's no point _____. He never goes to parties. +
3 It's no good _____ pay you back. She's completely broke. +
4 We would rather _____ holiday in July, but in the end we had to go in August. +
5 I absolutely hate _____ I should do. I prefer to make my own mistakes. −
6 You'd better _____. There are speed cameras on this road. −
7 Jack completely denied _____ his ex-girlfriend again, but I don't believe him. +

b Read your sentences to **B**. Keep trying different possibilities until you get each sentence exactly right.

c Now listen to your partner's sentences. Tell them to keep guessing until they get it exactly the same as yours.

8 It's a very rewarding job which involves **working in a** team.
9 Lucy seems **to be seeing** Danny a lot recently. Do you think they're going out together?
10 We hope **to have found** a new flat by the end of the year.
11 Our plan is **to rent** a house in the north of Italy for two weeks in September.
12 There's absolutely **nothing to do** in this town. There isn't even a cinema.
13 My father was the first person in my village **to go to** university.
14 I really regret **not having known** my grandfather. He died before I was born.

6B Match the sentences **Student A**

a Read your sentences to **B**. Make sure you stress auxiliaries and *to* where appropriate. **B** will choose a response.

1 Have you ever been to Canada?
2 I absolutely hate getting up early.
3 Is Lina coming swimming this afternoon?
4 Your brother lives in Liverpool, doesn't he?
5 Your aunt doesn't smoke, does she?
6 You do like cabbage, don't you?

b Now **B** will read you his / her sentences. Choose a response from below. Make sure you stress auxiliaries and *to* where appropriate.

☐ He is! He won the under-18s cup this year.
☐ I don't, but my partner does. I'm too lazy!
☐ No, and neither does her brother. Maybe they were adopted.
☐ No, there weren't. Where were you, by the way?
☐ She said she wanted to, but she wasn't sure if she'd be able to.
☐ We'd like to, but we're not sure if we can afford to.

c Practise all 12 mini-dialogues again, making sure you get the stress right

4A Guess the sentence **Student B**

a Look at sentences 7–12 and imagine what the missing phrase could be. Remember ⊞ = positive verb and ⊟ = negative verb.

7 I'm not sure you would enjoy the play and in any case it will be very difficult _____. ⊞

8 Some of the teachers aren't very stimulating, but on the whole I think _____. ⊞

9 Laura's husband only thinks of himself and he always gets his own way. In other words, _____. ⊞

10 I have my own import-export company. Basically, _____ fruit and vegetables. ⊞

11 I don't feel like going to Miranda's birthday party and besides, I haven't _____. ⊟

12 It's no big surprise that Leo didn't do very well in his exams. After all, he _____. ⊟

b Listen to your partner's sentences. Tell them to keep guessing until they get it exactly the same as yours.

1 A lot of people say the book is better than the film, but actually I **preferred the film**.

2 He's supposed to be really mean. Apparently, he never **buys his wife a present** on her birthday.

3 It wasn't a particularly nice day for the garden party but at least **it didn't rain**.

4 The sea was blue, the sun shone, and the picnic was marvellous. All in all, it **was a great day**.

5 On the one hand, dogs are far better company than any other pets, but on the other hand you **have to take them for a walk** at least twice a day.

6 Make sure your suitcase weighs less than 20 kilos, otherwise you **may have to pay extra**.

c Now read your sentences to **A**. Keep trying different possibilities until you get each sentence exactly right.

5A QI quiz **Student B**

a Read the answers to questions 6–10 and try to remember the information.

b **A** will tell you the answers to 1–5. Then explain the answers to 6–10 to **A** in your own words.

6 Which African mammal kills more humans than any other?

The hippopotamus. Most attacks occur because somebody in a rowing boat accidentally hits a hippopotamus on the head and it decides to overturn the boat, or because a hippo leaves the water and tramples on people who are walking by the side of a river.

7 What would probably have killed you in an 18th-century sea battle?

A splinter. In spite of what you see in Hollywood films, cannon balls didn't actually explode, they just tore through the side of the ship, and made huge splinters of wood fly around the decks, and these splinters killed anyone they came into contact with.

8 What did the American Thomas Edison invent, which English speakers use every day?

Of course Edison is famous for inventing the electric light bulb, but English speakers also have to thank him for suggesting the word 'hello' as the best way to answer the telephone. Before 'hello' was used telephone operators used to say 'Are you there?' or 'Who are you?' when they answered the phone. And the man who invented the telephone, Alexander Bell, actually preferred 'Ahoy! Ahoy!', which is what sailors use to attract attention.

9 How does television damage your health?

Not by sitting too close to it! Until the 1960s televisions used to emit low levels of radiation, which made it dangerous to sit too near, but this is not the case any more. The real damage caused to our health by TV is obesity, because of the lazy lifestyle it creates.

10 Why is a marathon 42.195 km long?

Many people think that it is because this was the exact distance a Greek messenger ran from Marathon to Athens to announce that the Persians had been defeated by the Greeks. This distance was approximately 40 kilometres, and this is the reason why at the first three modern Olympic Games the marathons were roughly that length. However, the reason why the modern day marathon is exactly 42.195 kilometres is because of the British royal family. In 1908 when the Games were held in London, the starting line was put outside Windsor Castle so that half of the royal family could see it from their windows, and the finish was in front of the royal box in White City, London, where the rest of the royal family was waiting. The distance was exactly 42.195 kilometres, and this became the standard length of the marathon.

Communication

5A What a ridiculous idea! Student B

a Respond to **A**'s sentences with an exclamation beginning with either *How…!* or *What a…!* Make sure you use expressive intonation, and link the words where appropriate.

b Read your sentences to **A**. He / She will respond with an exclamation.

- I was at home all morning waiting for the electrician to come and he didn't turn up.
- We're going for a long weekend to New York on Friday.
- Jack's going to take Sue to the theatre and then have a candlelit dinner at the new Italian restaurant.
- My sister got married on Saturday and it rained all day.
- Even though I got 70% in the exam the teacher refused to pass me.
- My daughter's goldfish died this morning.
- Maria's husband collects photos of Angelina Jolie. He's got hundreds.

5B Stressing the right word Student B

a **A** is going to read you a sentence. Respond with your number 1 below, giving extra stress to one of the words. Continue with 2–6.

1 She is my sister.
2 No, I said she was Canadian.
3 No, it's the one before the traffic lights.
4 Personally, I still think she'd prefer that one.
5 I've bought it, but I haven't read it yet.
6 Could you put it under my bed, please?

b Read your sentence 7 to **A**. He / She will respond, giving one word extra stress. Continue with 8–12.

7 Is that your dog?
8 Here you are. A tuna sandwich and a Coke.
9 Did you lend John the money he needed to buy the car?
10 That coat looks really expensive.
11 You're not going out tonight, are you?
12 Manchester United won 2–1 on Saturday.

5C Guess the sentence Student B

a Look at sentences 8–14 and imagine what the missing phrase could be.

8 It's a very rewarding job which involves _____ team. +
9 Lucy seems _____ Danny a lot recently. Do you think they're going out together? +
10 We hope _____ a new flat by the end of the year. +
11 Our plan is _____ a house in the north of Italy for two weeks in September. +
12 There's absolutely _____ in this town. There isn't even a cinema. −
13 My father was the first person in my village _____ university. +
14 I really regret _____ my grandfather. He died before I was born. −

b Listen to your partner's sentences. Tell them to keep guessing until they get it exactly the same as yours.

1 I would love **to have seen** the boss's face when you told him you were leaving.
2 There's no point **inviting him**. He never goes to parties.
3 It's no good **expecting her to** pay you back. She's completely broke.
4 We would rather **have gone on** holiday in July, but in the end we had to go in August.
5 I absolutely hate **being told what** I should do. I prefer to make my own mistakes.
6 You'd better **not drive so fast**. There are speed cameras on this road.
7 Jack completely denied **having seen** his ex-girlfriend again, but I don't believe him.

c Now read your sentences to **A**. Keep trying different possibilities until you get each sentence exactly right.

6B Match the sentences Student B

a **A** will read you his / her sentences. Choose a response from below. Make sure you stress auxiliaries and *to* where appropriate.

☐ I love it. It's cauliflower I can't stand.
☐ No she doesn't, but she drinks like a fish.
☐ No, but I'd love to if I ever got the chance.
☐ She isn't but her children are. She didn't want to.
☐ So do I. Luckily I don't often have to.
☐ Yes, and so does my sister.

b Read your sentences to **A**. Make sure you stress auxiliaries and *to* where appropriate. **B** will choose a response.

7 Are you going to go skiing at Christmas?
8 Katie doesn't look at all like her parents, does she?
9 Were there many people in class yesterday?
10 Do you do a lot of gardening?
11 Erica did say she was coming, didn't she?
12 Adam isn't particularly good at tennis, is he?

c Practise all 12 mini-dialogues again, making sure you get the stress right.

Listening

1.3 **Presenter 1** Welcome to *Workplace* and in today's programme we're looking at the results of two recently published surveys, which both deal with the same topic – happiness at work. John, tell us about the first survey.

Presenter 2 Well, this was done by a human resources consultancy, who interviewed more than 1,000 workers, and established a top ten of the factors which make people happy at work. The most important factor for the majority of the people interviewed was having friendly, supportive colleagues. In fact, 73% of people interviewed put their relationship with colleagues as being the key factor contributing to happiness at work, which is a very high percentage. The second most important factor was having work that is enjoyable per se, that is people actually liking what they do. The two least important factors were having your achievements recognized, and, rather surprisingly, earning a competitive salary.

Presenter 1 So we're not mainly motivated by money?

Presenter 2 Apparently not.

Presenter 1 Any other interesting information in the survey?

Presenter 2 Yes, for example 25% of the working people interviewed described themselves as 'very happy' at work. However, 20% of employees described themselves as being 'unhappy'.

Presenter 1 That's quite a lot of unhappy people at work every day.

Presenter 2 It is, isn't it? And there were several more interesting conclusions revealed by the survey. First of all, small is beautiful: people definitely prefer working for smaller organizations or companies with less than 100 staff. We also find out that, generally speaking, women were happier in their work than men.

Presenter 1 Yes, we're a miserable bunch, aren't we?

Presenter 2 And workers on part-time contracts, who only work four or five hours a day, are happier than those who work full-time. The researchers concluded that this is probably due to a better work–life balance.

Presenter 1 Are bosses happier than their employees?

Presenter 2 Yes, perhaps not surprisingly, the higher people go in a company, the happier they are. So senior managers enjoy their jobs more than people working under them.

Presenter 1 Does the period of time you spend with the same company affect how happy you are?

Presenter 2 Well, according to the survey, happiness declines the longer people stay with the same company or organization. The most contented people were those who'd been with a company for less than two years, and the least contented were those who'd been in the same place of work for more than ten years.

Presenter 1 So you can stay too long in the same place.

Presenter 2 So it seems. And lastly, according to the survey, apparently the happiest workers of all are those who are 55 years old or older, probably because they feel they're working at the peak of their powers.

Presenter 1 Presumably, though they haven't spent more than ten years in the same job.

Presenter 2 Exactly. So how long have you been here then, Michael?

Presenter 1 Eight years! Maybe I should start thinking about looking for a new job…

1.4 **Presenter 1** The second survey we're looking at in today's programme is a *Sunday Times* survey which was all about the best UK companies to work for. Apparently, one of the best small companies to work for is *innocent drinks*. Well, I have with me in the studio Becka Walton, who works for *innocent drinks*. Becka, tell us what made you apply for the job at *innocent*.

Becka Well, I've always really liked them as a company, I'd always followed their website and their weekly newsletter, I'd always thought that they would be people that I would like to work for, so it was a case of just keeping my eyes on the job page and waiting for something that I thought I could do to come along.

Presenter In a recent survey about what makes people happy at work, *innocent* was listed as one of the top companies to work for. You obviously think it is a happy company. Now why do you think that?

Becka Well, I can see how we would have scored quite highly on that scale, I think there's quite a big emphasis on a team environment at work, we're all mixed up so nobody sits according to the group of people that they work with, which means that you get to make friends in different areas of the business. Everybody's aware of the projects that people are working on, the pressures that they're under so it, it makes for a really good team environment. I think that's important.

Presenter And how does that compare with other companies that you've worked for?

Becka I've not really worked for any big corporations before – *innocent* is the biggest company that I've worked for. I know friends of mine complain about really dry working environments, we're really quite informal in our outlook, things are quite relaxed and a lot of my friends are quite surprised that we don't have to dress up to come to work, often people don't even wear shoes, and we have a grassy floor in our office, and it's just kind of, it's a relaxed place to work.

Presenter What would you change about the company if there was something that you could change?

Becka Oh, I, I'm not really sure how to answer that question, I think that, a thing that does come up when we survey people is perhaps the work–life balance, I think people are quite passionate about their jobs, and that's a good thing, but it can lead to people working very long hours.

Presenter So you are overworked?

Becka I wouldn't have gone quite that far but it would be easy to be overworked, yes.

Presenter You're obviously very happy in your work, but is there a high staff turnover? Do people generally stay for a long time?

Becka I know that Daisy, my line manager, was the first girl employed by the company and we're coming up for our tenth birthday. She's only leaving now, so I think that she's quite happy. Obviously we have people on short-term contracts, but as a general rule I would say that people, people are happy and people do tend to stay at *innocent* for quite long lengths of time.

Presenter OK, in the other survey, the one about the ten things that make people happy at work, the issue of a competitive salary was the last in the list. What's your view on that?

Becka Well, I've thought about this and I hope it doesn't make me sound terribly shallow, but I struggled to think of ten things that might be more important, of course, it's important to, you know, for a good work–life balance and to, I suppose, have fun at work and to enjoy the people you work with, but I think it probably is quite important to feel like you're adequately financially rewarded for what you do.

Presenter OK. And finally, I should ask you, do you drink smoothies yourself and if you do, are they always *innocent?*

Becka I really love, I really love smoothies and if I didn't it would be the wrong place for me to work, and, and of course they're always *innocent* smoothies. I think that the working environment reflects in the passion that we all have and I think that's because we know we've got a really good product.

Presenter Thank you very much, Becka Walton.

1.9 In the spring of 1800, the court painter, Francisco de Goya was commissioned by the Spanish King Carlos IV, direct ancestor of King Juan Carlos, to paint a portrait of the royal family. At the time, the royal family were all staying at the summer palace of Aranjuez, near Madrid. First on the left is Prince Carlos, the King's second son, and next to him is his older brother Prince Fernando, who was the heir to the throne. Fernando grew up hating his parents, especially his mother, but in fact, he took after his mother in that he was very vain and authoritarian, and when he eventually became king he was extremely unpopular. The old woman just behind Prince Fernando is Maria Josefa, the King's sister. Single and childless, she died shortly after the painting was finished. Next to Maria Josefa is a young woman whose face we cannot see because she is looking away, and she is the 'mystery person' in this painting. There are two theories about her identity. One theory is that she is Princess Maria Amalia, one of the King's daughters, who'd died in childbirth three years before the picture was painted. The fact that she's looking away would be to show that she was, in fact, dead. However, the other more popular theory is that she represents the woman that Crown prince Fernando would one day marry. It would have been important to put her in the picture to show that the prince would marry one day, and have a son to carry on the dynasty. If this theory is true, the woman would be looking away because she didn't actually exist at that time. In fact, Fernando did marry, not once but four times. The young girl next to the mystery woman is Princess Maria Isabel, the King's youngest daughter. She went on to marry her cousin, and had twelve children. Next to her is the Queen, Maria Luisa. Goya made her the central figure in the painting because she had a very strong personality, and she completely dominated her husband the King. As a young woman she had been very beautiful and was rumoured to have had numerous lovers. In middle age, as she is here, she was still very vain. She tried to compensate for the fact that her beauty was fading by wearing exquisite dresses and jewellery, as we can see in the picture. The little boy with the Queen is her youngest son, Prince Francisco. He was a very sensitive boy and he suffered all his life due to the fact that he looked incredibly like one of his mother's lovers. As a result, people assumed that he was not in fact the King's son. The King, who is standing next to him, was a weak man. Although he came to the throne full of ideas and dreams, his wife and his advisors made sure that he never managed to achieve any of them and he died frustrated and disappointed. The King's brother is standing behind him, and on his right, although you can only actually see part of her head, is the King's eldest daughter Carlota. Her parents arranged a marriage for her when she was only ten years old. She was an ambitious girl and eventually became Queen of Portugal. The final group of three figures shows the Queen's brother, Don Luis de Parma, his wife, Maria Luisa and their first child, a baby boy. In fact, Maria Luisa was not only Don Luis's wife, she was also his niece, as she was the King's second daughter. In fact, Don Luis was supposed to have married the King's eldest daughter, Carlota, but he fell in love with Princess Maria Luisa, who was lively and intelligent, and he insisted on marrying her. The royal family didn't all pose together for the painting – it would have taken too long.

Instead Goya made individual studies of each family member and later used them to create this work. The painting took him two years to complete, and it was the last royal portrait he ever painted. Incidentally, he included himself in the painting – he is standing in the background on the left, behind the two princes. Carlos IV called this painting 'the family all together picture', and it was originally hung in the Royal Palace in Madrid.

1.12 **Interviewer** Do you find it easier to understand native or non-native speakers of English?

Cristina Well, it all depends where they come from. I suppose it's more or less the same. Some non-natives are more difficult than others if you're not used to the accent. For instance, I used to find some Japanese and Chinese speakers difficult to understand, but then because of work I went to the Far East lots of times, and then it became OK. Natives, again it all depends. I was taught RP, and one assumes that everybody speaks that. And of course I had friends from lots of parts of Britain who did not speak RP, in fact, it is pretty rare thing these days. So we have a good friend from Glasgow and it was always embarrassing for me because I could not understand most of what he was saying – I still don't.

Interviewer How do you feel about having your English corrected?

Cristina I don't mind. My children used to love correcting me – they still say I speak very funny English. But usually adults in this country do not correct you. I would like to be corrected.

Interviewer Do you find it easier to understand native or non-native speakers of English?

Zoltán It depends what you mean. As far as pronunciation goes, it's a lot easier to understand native speakers with a 'standard' accent like BBC English or General American and for me some of the regional dialects are quite easy to understand as well. Other dialects are a lot harder to decipher like Scots, or Geordie, or New Zealand, are really hard to understand. As far as content is concerned, it's a lot easier to understand non-native speakers, because they don't use idiomatic expressions or obscure cultural references, they don't use regional slang. They also use the Latin verb instead of a phrasal verb, for example like 'continue' rather than 'carry on' which is less easy to confuse. And the other thing about non-native speakers is that they are a lot more direct, when they speak in English, they say what they mean, there are no allusions and metaphors, and references to other things.

Interviewer How do you feel about having your English corrected?

Zoltán I don't mind. I'm sometimes annoyed with myself for making a recurring mistake again like mixing up *he* and *she*. And I find it a bit weird when a non-native speaker who's less fluent than me corrects my English. I also think that non-native speakers, good non-native speakers, are often better at spelling than native speakers because we learn words with their spelling, whereas native speakers learn the word first and learn the spelling years later. Just recently an English friend of mine corrected my spelling of 'accommodation', which I'd spelt with double *c* and double *m*, and he insisted that it was spelt with a single *m*. In fact, *I* was right!

1.13 **Interviewer** Do you have any funny or embarrassing stories related to misunderstanding someone?

Cristina Yes, misunderstanding and being misunderstood, several. Some I don't think I would like to tell you about. But I'll tell you one. I was a student at the University of Michigan, in the United States, and my phonetics professor was *very* handsome, and therefore I did extremely well, not in all subjects, but it was worth studying that one. But I remember my first tutorial when he said, 'See you later.' And I thought, 'Mmm, interesting. Where?' And in class he'd said, I'd asked a question and he'd said 'Interesting question', so I thought 'Great! He thinks I'm clever, and maybe he thinks I'm interesting to meet somewhere else.' But I couldn't understand how I was going to find out where or when. I luckily didn't ask. It would have been very embarrassing.

Interviewer Is there anything you still find difficult about English?

Cristina Yes, I think that there are things that have especially to do with cultural aspects. I used to find when my children were little that I didn't know the same nursery rhymes that you know here, I didn't know the actions. And I still don't know lots of things. It's, I don't know, to give you an example, say I had learned American English but I still didn't know who the Simpsons were.

Interviewer Do you have any funny or embarrassing stories related to misunderstanding someone?

Zoltán Hungarians aren't generally interested in birdwatching – and most Hungarians I know can't tell one bird from another. And recently a friend of mine told me about seeing some kites over the fields near their house the previous weekend, and I said that flying kites is really popular in Budapest, too, meaning that people go into the hills at the weekend to fly their home-made paper kites. It never occurred to me for a second that she may be talking about a bird. I don't think a Hungarian would ever tell someone else about seeing some birds several days before.

Interviewer Is there anything you still find difficult about English?

Zoltán Not really. I've been learning English for 26 years. If I had to say anything, I would say counting, numbers. If I have to count anything, I have to switch back to Hungarian, even if the person I'm speaking to will need the English sum.

1.15 **Interviewer** Why did you start researching your family history?

David Well, it was mainly, I think, because in 1995 we were given a present by a friend of ours of a computer program, that was a family tree programme and we'd been talking about it from time to time, but this was the incentive, if you will, to start typing in what we knew and then we realized how much we didn't know, so that's where we started.

Interviewer When you start researching, what's the first step, the first thing you do?

David Well, the first thing you do is to ask living people about what they know, but that can be very dangerous because family myths grow up and you can often find that what you're told isn't accurate, so then you start with birth certificates and marriage certificates and you keep going back because the marriage certificate will give you the name of the parent of the bride, the parent of the bridegroom, and then you go back to birth certificates, so you work back using those two.

Interviewer In practical terms, what difference has the Internet made to researching family history?

David Oh, it's made an absolutely massive difference. There is no comparison. In the days before the Internet, it involved going to London, initially, to two different places, one to look at births, marriages, and deaths and the other a completely different building to look at census records, and then, of course, once you've got back as far as you could, then it involved travelling perhaps over, around the country to visit a church, to get parish records. It was fun, but also vastly time consuming. It's so much simpler now.

Interviewer How far could most people expect to be able to trace back their families?

David It's fairly easy to get back to 1837 when the birth, marriage, and death registers were compiled and started, most people can get back there. With a little bit more work involving parish registers, you can usually get back to the late 1700s and it gets progressively more difficult after that. It's easier if you have an unusual name and it's easier if they come from a small village, as opposed to London.

Interviewer How far back have you managed to trace your family?

David Well, one particular branch, thanks to the very helpful material from a lady in Oxfordshire, I've got back to 1490, but this is only because that particular branch were somewhat better off than the others, so there were wills left and records of business deals and things like that, but that's an awful lot of hard work, and this lady must have spent years and years researching it and very generously shares it with me and other people.

1.16 **Interviewer** Was there anything in particular that you hoped to find out when you began researching?

David Yes, I really didn't know anything about beyond my grandparents because it wasn't something that was ever discussed in the family, so I was curious to find out where they came from, things like that.

Interviewer Have you found out anything surprising, any skeleton in the cupboard?

David Yes indeed, in fact it was this year when the 1911 census was released, it was released two years early, I discovered that instead of just having two aunts and my father there were another seven children, which I had no knowledge of at all, including triplets who were one month old, so, and they were never spoken about and there's no way of finding out what happened to them or where they went.

Interviewer And how did you feel when you found this out?

David I think it made me angry, to be honest, because my father had never ever mentioned anything like that, and they were a lot of kids, there were triplets, there were two more brothers and it may just have been as though they hadn't lived at all, because there was no mention ever in the family about it. And frustratingly, of course, there's no, absolutely no way I can find out, so that's a shame.

Interviewer Why is there no way you can find this out?

David Well, there's no record of their birth, there's no record of their death, if they were given away, which I don't think is impossible, because they were a poor family, then the surname would have changed and there would have been no record of that, so, and there's no living relatives that I can talk to.

Interviewer So have you just given up on it?

David You hate to give up on it and you rack your brains and think, 'Is there any way I could find out?' and of course, the only possibility with the Shepherd family I mentioned in the 1911 census is when the next one comes out in another ten years, there might be some possibility of seeing if they were around somewhere then, but that's a long way away.

Interviewer Did you find out anything else surprising?

David I did in fact find some births that were quite close to the marriage dates, and that was a little unexpected, but my secret wish, I suppose, was to hope that Dick Shepherd, the highwayman, might have been somewhere in the family tree, but if he is, I haven't got that far back, but I wouldn't mind at all. It would be quite exciting to have that sort of ancestor, I think.

Interviewer Do you think that research into family histories is addictive?

David Oh yes, yes I think any hobby can become so, but this is a fascinating hobby. Perhaps fortunately both my wife and I work and we're still working, so time available is dictated by work schedules, but yes it can be, it's a fascinating, fascinating hobby.

1.18 **Interviewer** How much do you know about your family tree?

Sheila Not a great deal actually.

Interviewer Have you ever researched it?

Sheila I haven't, but my cousin has and she's looked into the family history of my mother's side of the family. And it would be really interesting to find out what she's learned really.

Interviewer Is there someone in your family that you'd like to know more about?

Sheila Both my grandfathers. So my grandfather on my mother's side, he was a musician, professional musician, and travelled a lot during the war and I think he made quite a lot of money because I've got lots of photographs of him with racing cars and motorbikes. I think he was a bit of a boy racer, so it would be quite interesting to find out more about him. And my other grandfather on my father's side, I think he was a code breaker in the war, so he's got a bit of a secretive side that it would be interesting to research.

Interviewer How much do you know about your family tree?

Naomi I have to admit that I personally don't know all that much about my own family tree, really. A little bit, I probably can go back a couple of generations, maybe.

Interviewer Have you ever researched it?

Naomi I haven't researched it personally but my dad has. He's done some research on it, and I think my grandmother on my mother's side also did some research a while back.

Interviewer Is there someone in your family that you'd like to know more about?

Naomi Yeah, probably my dad's mother. She was a single mum basically and she raised my dad on her own and I think if she were alive now, I'd probably like to ask her a few more questions about what that was like and how she felt and what it was like growing up as well, because I think it would have been different for her.

Interviewer How much do you know about your family tree?

Tim I wouldn't say I know too much extensively about my family tree. I know I'm Polish and French-Indian. But I only know up to my grandparents. I've never really researched into the history of my family or my family tree that much.

Interviewer Is there someone in your family that you'd like to know more about?

Tim Probably my grandfather on my father's side – he died when I was pretty young. And I know he had a lot of hobbies that I'd be interested in. But I didn't really get a chance to spend a lot of time with him.

Interviewer How much do you know about your family tree?

Jeremy I know a little bit about my family tree. We've done some research on my mother's side, less on my father's side, which is a bit of a mystery. My grandfather, in fact, he wrote his sort of memoirs of his childhood and his parents and grandparents, which I've kind of helped my mum type up. So I know about them. He was a chauffeur, his father worked as, I think, a footman in some country house and his grandfather was, I think, something, I don't know what he did, but something like that.

Interviewer Are there any other people in your family you'd like to know more about?

Jeremy I'd like to know more about my father's side, because I take after my dad, everyone says I look like him and I don't really know much about his parents or his grandparents, so that would be interesting to find out about them.

2.2 **Interviewer** What is your earliest memory?

Speaker 1 I was born on the Atlantic coast of New England and my earliest memory is swimming between my mother and my father in the Atlantic Ocean.

Interviewer Oh, wow.

Speaker 1 Because I swam before I could walk. And it was wonderful.

Interviewer How amazing! How old were you then?

Speaker 1 I think I was like, actually, I must have been really really young, maybe, maybe I'd already walked by that point, I must have been one and a half when I had that memory. Really young, it was really, it was a beautiful experience then, I'm sure and remembering it makes me very happy.

Speaker 2 My earliest memory is of being completely by myself, lost in what seemed to be a great big forest, it probably wasn't. I was about 18 months old and we were living in Cornwall, which is where I was born, and I was on a sort of path in the middle of a really really dark forest and I remember looking behind me and it was just darkness and, and big dark trees and the same ahead of me, and just having this feeling of being completely on my own, and calling out for my sister, Lynn, who was seven years older than me, who was supposed to be minding me and not being able to find her.

Speaker 3 I guess I was about three or maybe four, and I remember sitting on my father's shoulders and we were going to the zoo and there was an elephant, and the elephant took my ice cream…

Speaker 4 I remember it was 1966 and I was sitting on a bus with my grandmother, and I'd been given a brand new one penny coin, it was brand new, it was sparkling, and it was beautiful, and I remembered deciding then and there that this was going to be my earliest memory, I was going to remember this day in 1966 when I was sitting there with this brand new penny. And then I remember the bus conductor came along and wanted the fares and my granny was a penny short, so that was the end of my penny.

Speaker 5 One of my very earliest memories is pulling away in a car looking out of the window seeing our dog Sam, sort of pining for us through a window, and we were basically having to say goodbye to Sam because we were moving to a flat where they didn't allow dogs. So we were having to say goodbye to him, and it was very sad, he was sort of pining in his new home and we were pulling away. It was horrible.

2.3 **Presenter** Are our first memories reliable, or are they always based on something people have told us? What age do most people's first memories come from? John Fisher has been reading a fascinating new book about memory by Professor Draaisma called *How Memory Shapes our Past,* and he's going to answer these questions for us and more. Hello John.

John Hello.

Presenter Let's start at the beginning then. At what age do first memories generally occur?

John Well, according to both past and present research, 80% of our first memories are of things which happened to us between the ages of two and four. It's very unusual to remember anything that happened before that age.

Presenter Why is that?

John There seem to be two main reasons, according to Professor Draaisma. The first reason is that before the age of two, children don't have a clear sense of themselves as individuals – they can't usually identify themselves in a photo. And you know how a very small child enjoys seeing himself in a mirror, but he doesn't actually realize that the person he can see is him. Children of this age also have problems with the pronouns *I* and *you*. And a memory without *I* is impossible. That's to say, we can't begin to have memories until we have an awareness of self.

Presenter And the second reason?

John The second reason is related to language. According to the research, first memories coincide with the development of linguistic skills, with a child learning to talk. And as far as autobiographical memory is concerned, it's essential for a child to be able to use the past tense, so that he or she can talk about something that happened in the past, and then remember it.

Presenter I see. What are first memories normally about? I mean, is it possible to generalize at all?

John Early memories seem to be related to strong emotions, such as happiness, unhappiness, pain, and surprise. Recent research suggests that three quarters of first memories are related to fear, to frightening experiences like being left alone, or a large dog, or having an accident – things like falling off a swing in a park. And of course this makes sense, and bears out the evolutionary theory that the human memory is linked to self-preservation. You remember these things in order to be prepared if they happen again, so that you can protect yourself.

Presenter Are first memories only related to emotions or are there any specific events that tend to become first memories?

John The events that are most often remembered, and these are always related to one of the emotions I mentioned before, are the birth of a baby brother or sister, a death, or a family visit. Festive celebrations with bright lights were also mentioned quite frequently, much more frequently than events we might have expected to be significant, like a child's first day at school. Another interesting aspect is that first memories tend to be very visual. They're almost invariably described as pictures, not smells or sounds.

Presenter First memories are often considered unreliable, in that perhaps sometimes they're not real memories, just things other people have told us about ourselves or that we have seen in photos. Is that true, according to Professor Draaisma?

John Absolutely! He cites the famous case of the Swiss psychologist, Jean Piaget…

2.9 **Host** And now it's time for our weekly dose of *Time Bandits*, the section of the show where we try to deal with your time issues. And we're going to be talking to our time management guru, Richard. And now we're going to line 1, which is Jade from North London. Hi Jade.

Caller 1 Hello, hi, right I have this friend who's always phoning me and, well, she just won't let me get off the phone – I waste so much time just listening to her telling me every single thing she's been doing and every little problem that she has.

Host Yeah, I think that's a common problem for all of us – so Richard, what advice have you got?

Expert Well, look, say you'd love to chat, but you can't right now and you'll ring back another time. How about that? Or say you've only got five minutes and mean it, I mean say goodbye when the five minutes are up. Use a finishing up expression like, 'Oh, it's been great talking to you, but I really must go now.'

Caller 1 Yeah, OK, thank you.

Expert Not at all.

Host That's great advice Richard. Must remember to use that with the mother-in-law. Right, we're going to line 2 now. We're talking to Nigel from Bury. Hi Nigel.

Caller 2 Hiya, it's Bury, actually. What I wanted to say was I am a very punctual person, you know, it's something I pride myself on, and I do spend a lot of my time, wasting my time really waiting for people. Like, for example I've got this friend of mine, and

we'll often have like an informal lunch together or something, and I will always arrive on time, I will arrive at the restaurant on time, but I have to wait for him, well, it's at least ten minutes, sometimes more, for him to arrive.

Host OK Nigel, so, over to you, Richard.

Richard Well, look Nigel I do know what you mean, because I've got friends like that too! I think the best thing to do, and I'm speaking from experience, is send your friend a text or email on the morning of your get-together, and tell them you're a bit short of time today so you don't want to hang around too much. And ask him or her to let you know if they're going to be late! That should make them get the message.

Host That's great advice, Richard. Right moving punctually on to line 3 which is Judy from Horndean. Hello Judy.

Caller 3 Oh hello. Oh dear. Well, it's my husband. He always expects me to help him find whatever he can't find, you know, usually his car keys or a particular shirt he wants to wear. Even when I'm busy, and I spend too much time helping him, and not getting on with doing what I'm supposed to be doing.

Host Right I see. OK, Richard, what do you make of that?

Richard Rule number one, Judy. Look, never, ever, drop what you're doing to go and help. Now, if he shouts at you from another room, just tell him you can't hear him properly. Let him come to you. Pretend you're really busy even if you aren't.

Caller 3 Oh, I'll try.

Host That's fantastic, Richard. Thank you. Now, moving on to caller 4, who's Wendy from Leeds. Wendy, what's your problem?

Caller 4 Hi. Every morning when I get up, I spend ages just standing in front of the wardrobe and try and decide what to wear. It's just such a waste of time, especially as I end up then wearing the same thing again and again.

Host I know how you feel, Wendy. Richard, what's your advice?

Richard OK. Straight up, Wendy. I got this advice from a friend of mine who works in fashion. She recommends you completely reorganize your wardrobe. Set aside ten minutes one day, make a list of your five favourite outfits, and hang them all together.

Caller 4 Right.

Richard Then stick the list inside the door of the wardrobe. And when you can't think of what to wear, just look at the list and wear one of the outfits. Well, I tell you, my friend swears it saves her a lot of time.

Caller 4 Wow! Thank you.

Host That's great advice, Richard. I should remember that myself. Now, time's ticking swiftly on so we need to take our last caller and that is Sue from Staines. Hello Sue.

Caller 5 Oh, hi. Am I on?

Host Yes, you are. What's your problem?

Caller 5 I have kids and I work full time, so as you can imagine I don't have much spare time, and I'm often in a hurry when I go to the supermarket. And somehow I always manage to have someone in front of me in the queue who seems to have all the time in the world, you know, who's really slow and, even more annoying, gets into a conversation with the cashier. Do you have any tips?

Host Any tips, any tips for Sue, there Richard?

Richard Of course, of course, well, first of all, don't complain out loud, because that might easily annoy the other person and make them take even longer. No, the thing to do is just politely interrupt and ask the cashier a question. Now this should bring the person ahead of you back to reality, and that will remind the cashier that there are other people waiting to be served.

Caller 5 All right.

Richard All right?

Host That's great advice, Richard. I think a lot of people could use that. Right, I'm afraid time's up for now, but thank you all for your calls…

2.13

1 No relationship is an island; it's surrounded by friends and family, all of whom have something to say about it. In a study undertaken by Illinois University, researchers found that both men and women felt happier and were more committed to each other when their friends approved of their relationship. When friends tell a couple that they are a good match, and how much they enjoy going out with them, that couple start believing that they really are a couple. Also when a couple stays together for a while, their two groups of friends start to make friends with each other, and as a result the couple's relationship gets stronger.

2 Cars are small confined spaces, which makes them ideal to fight in. A survey conducted for a driving magazine found that one driver in ten will be arguing with a partner within 15 minutes of starting the journey. About 40% of the arguments are caused by men criticizing their partner's driving, and another 10% by the man taking control of the car stereo. At least disputes about map reading can now be solved by satellite navigation!

3 Relationship research would say that it's conclusively proven that like attracts like, in other words that we are generally attracted to people who are similar to us. This research shows that couples usually share religious and political beliefs and are about the same age. They are fairly similar in education, intelligence, and what they think matters in life. Most people also go for someone as good-looking or as plain as they are. You may, however, be familiar with the phrase 'love is blind', suggesting that you can fall for anyone, should you get the chance to meet them. But psychologists argue that such 'blindness' is temporary: after three months you can 'see' again, and then you usually go off the person.

4 Today the Internet is one of the most popular ways for people to get dates. On the one hand, the opportunity to remain anonymous for a while is an advantage. People feel that they can express their emotions more readily online and get to know each other more quickly. On the other hand, people can lie more easily, the most common lies being about weight, age, and of course about already being married. But if you have reasonable expectations, online dating is a good way to start looking for dates. Increase your success by posting a photo and a truthful profile. Online agencies advise getting a photo taken where you look friendly, rather than seductive. Best of all, use a dictionary when composing your profile. The biggest turn-off, apparently, is profiles with poor spelling. But once you've found a date, will the relationship last? A study in the US of over 3,000 adults found that 15% knew someone in a long-term relationship that had started online and according to research the success rates of these relationships are very similar to offline methods of meeting people, such as meeting people at work or in a bar.

5 Early loves are incredibly powerful and, with the Internet, increasingly accessible. A survey in *Time* magazine found out that nearly 60% of people interviewed still thought about their first loves. In another study by Dr Nancy Kalish, California State University got randomly selected American adults to agree to be interviewed about their first loves. One third said they would reunite with their first loves if they could. Then, by advertising in the media, Dr Kalish got data on 2,500 first love couples who got back in contact with each other. With the ones who were single when they found their lost loves, things moved quickly with 40% of them together again within three weeks, and most of them then getting married (and still together several years later). But there was a different story with the couples who were already in committed, usually happy relationships. Most of these people had casually Googled their old love in a speculative fashion with no plan for what to do if they found that person. 80% of these people finished up getting involved with their lost love again, and generally they became unhappy as a result. Dr Kalish strongly warns people who aren't single not to Google lost loves because of the destruction it can cause families and relationships.

6 You've just been dumped by your partner and you want revenge. But will it make you feel better? In a Canadian study, the most popular methods of revenge were flirting with friends or enemies of their ex, damaging their car, or breaking something they own, and writing nasty letters or emails. The question is, what will the revenge achieve? Another study by Stephen Hoshimura at the University of Montana asked people what act of revenge they had carried out, and what they had wanted to achieve, and how they felt afterwards. The research showed that most people felt anxious and sorry afterwards rather than feeling any happier. But most of all, they still felt angry. It seems that unfortunately, for most people, revenge is *not* sweet.

2.15 **Interviewer** You're a comedian, a writer, a musician, a composer, you raise money for charity, how do you fit it all in?

Tony Well, some days I don't fit it in very well at all, I feel that it's all closing in on me. I sometimes open up my emails, sort of ten emails all on a different thing, and so you do have to try and get organized and I've tried in the past to delegate and it didn't go terribly well because I got somebody in to help, but then you end up, sort of, just having to chase them and find out where they are with everything, so I usually, what I usually do is try to say right for the next hour I'm working on this, I've got this hat on for the next hour I've got that on, that hat on, and some days you just realize that you've just neglected something hopelessly and someone phones you up and chases you, or tells you off, but, I wouldn't say I'm the best person in the world at doing it. I could be much better.

Interviewer How do you switch off?

Tony I play the piano, I actually go, I quite like a bit of physical exercise, I'll go for a run or a swim, I'll play tennis if I can arrange a game with someone like that. If the sun's out, I just love sitting in the sun and just bask, I'm a good basker, I'd be a good shark. I've picked a ridiculous country to live in obviously for basking in the sun, but things like that. I also have started to do five minutes or so of meditation if I can, so I try to concentrate on actually trying not to think of anything, so just spend five minutes trying to just follow my breath and, because it's amazing, it makes you realize how busy your mind is all the time. It's always thinking of stuff and that's quite, I'm not very good at it, but it's quite good to do.

Interviewer What is your attitude to modern gadgets? Would you say you were more of a technophile or technophobe?

Tony I think I'm probably more of a technophobe really. I mean I'm aware of the amazing advances that we've had and how they can improve our lives, possibly, but I almost feel, to some extent, we'd be better off without them because we would then not be reliant upon them. So my problem is I am now utterly reliant on email. I find it incredibly convenient, I can get so much done. It is actually fantastic. However, if the Internet goes down, or the connection goes down, I'm like a baby without parents, or food, you know, I'm 'errr', I have to go to, sort of, get on my bike, cycle to an Internet café try to, so, and I see the same with people who have kind of satellite navigation in their cars, which I haven't gone for for this reason alone, is because if that goes down, I know they don't even have maps in their cars half the time, they're completely lost and they just sit there and get weepy, and you think, 'How did you allow that to happen?'

2.16 **Interviewer** Are there any gadgets you'd like to ban?

Tony Well, I don't know whether I'd ban it, but I'd certainly like to, you wouldn't expect me to say this probably, but I would like manufacturers to stop making things with remote controls. I don't know what was going on with that, I mean, the idea, just take a television. If you can't be bothered to get up and walk six feet to turn over the channel, you don't deserve a television, you know. OK, if you're disabled or something like that, then that's different, but for the general members of the public sitting there and just flicking round the channels, that I think has been disastrous for our attention spans, because, they're, people are so impatient, they want things immediately, they want entertainment, they want everything instantly and I think that remote control was the beginning of this. And the worst thing about remote controls is that because they have them for everything, you go into somebody's house, and they say, 'Oh, just watch television, or we're going out now'. I went to someone's house once and they went out and there was a football match I really wanted to watch and they had a great big television and there were five remote controls sitting on this table, one was for the stereo, one was for the VCR, one was for the, all these things, and I didn't know which remote control worked what, and I missed the entire football match because I couldn't turn on the television, it was on BBC1, it was on our main terrestrial channel and I couldn't watch it. And from then on I've had it in for remote controls.

Interviewer Do you ever feel nostalgic for simpler times, when there was less technology?

Tony I do, well, I feel very nostalgic for, I think it's something that you have to be careful of because I think it's something to watch as we get older, we can become nostalgic just for the sake of it, we go, 'Oh I remember', because I remember when I was going to school, television, there was no television in the daytime, and in a way I am sort of nostalgic for the fact that there was so little television. I read a while ago that in Iceland in possibly the 70s or 80s they had no television at all on Thursdays, because there wasn't enough power or whatever to deal with it, and I thought that was a fantastic idea that we should introduce. We should just have a day of the week where there's no television, so everyone would have to go to the theatre, they'd have to go round their friends' houses, make their own entertainment, all of that sort of stuff.

Interviewer How do you imagine the future? Do you think we'll become more dependent on technology or do you think there will be a backlash against it?

Tony I don't think there'll be a backlash against technology, I think we'll, and we'll keep on growing and we'll keep wanting more and more, but I can foresee a time, maybe not in my lifetime where there's a kind of a meltdown, where we simply can't cope any more, the Internet, kind of explodes or whatever, I don't even know how it works, but it, it gets full up and starts to overflow or satellites bash into each other, all the things that we rely on, all the things that we build our whole system around, just, they were predicting it a bit in 2000, weren't they, when in 1999 they thought things couldn't cope, they were wrong, but I do think there may well be a kind of meltdown and then we'll have to rely on people with simple skills and farmers and people that can grow things, build things, make things will be the new, new heroes.

2.18 **Interviewer** What piece of technology has most improved your life?

Matt I'd have to say the computer for the ease of information and able to get as much of an unbiased opinion as possible, as opposed to some of the older technologies.

Interviewer If you could, what piece of technology would you 'disinvent'?

Matt The television. I think it's completely harmful to our society. It causes people to stop thinking as a whole. It's easy just to shut off and, you know, be told what to do. Instead of actually thinking on your own and deciding what you want to do for your own life.

Interviewer What gadget or piece of technology do you waste most time with?

Matt Do I waste most of the time with? Definitely the Blackberry™. It's for work and for my personal use, so it probably consumes about 18 hours a day.

Interviewer What piece of technology has most improved your life?

Brian I think the Internet and just being able to stay in touch with people who are far far away from me. So either talking to them or sending messages to them or sharing pictures and movies. I think it's really brought, my family is all over the place and so it's been nice to be able to keep in touch using the Internet.

Interviewer If you could, what piece of technology would you 'disinvent'?

Brian 'Disinvent'? Well, probably any warfare technology, I think we've gotten a little over our heads with regard to weapons and some of the privacy issues I think. There's cameras everywhere and I think you have to be careful with how pervasive your cameras are and who gets to see what turns up on cameras.

Interviewer What gadget or piece of technology do you waste most time with?

Brian Do I waste most time with? It's probably the television. It's great to learn new things, but it's on more than I would probably like to admit. So television, I think. If I could just get rid of it, I would.

Interviewer What piece of technology has most improved your life?

Amy It's quite a typical answer, but it will have to be the mobile phone, because I feel a lot more in contact with friends and it's so much easier to communicate and as a girl you feel a lot safer being on your own. So having a mobile phone has definitely revolutionized life for me.

Interviewer If you could, what piece of technology would you 'disinvent'?

Amy It's really useful, but I think email has actually made people a lot more lax in the way they communicate with each other. So it stops people talking directly, so I would probably monitor the use of email rather than completely 'disinvent' it.

Interviewer What gadget or piece of technology do you waste most time with?

Amy The Internet, definitely. I go on lots of social networking sites and just browse in the web all the time in the evenings and it wastes a lot of time when you don't realize how long the time it takes up.

Interviewer What piece of technology has most improved your life?

Mark I would probably say bicycle, the bicycle, simply because it's my means of transport for getting to work, it's much faster than the car or the bus, and, you know, it's a healthy option, it's environmentally friendly as well. So all in all, I'd say yeah, it's certainly improved my life.

Interviewer If you could, what piece of technology would you 'disinvent'?

Mark That's very tricky really. I think it's probably, I think it's more not about the technology, it's more about the way in which people use pieces of technology, to be honest. There are lots of, you know, people speaking on their phones in public, that sort of thing, it's quite irritating, but it's how people are using the phone, not the actual phone itself. So, if I really had to think of something to 'disinvent' then, I don't know, a weapon of war perhaps or something like that.

Interviewer What gadget or piece of technology do you waste most time with?

Mark The Internet, definitely, the amount of time I spend Googling pointless, pointless things...

3.6 **Presenter 1** Companies are losing millions of pounds by making the wrong noises. Greg Wood, who always makes the right ones, is here.

Presenter 2 Thank you so much, Ed. Some noises can be really annoying. I'm sure we all like or dislike inappropriate music in shops for example – most of them made by companies. A new book called *Sound Business* claims that businesses which spend enormous amounts on their images are doing nothing about the way they sound. We sent its author, Julian Treasure, out onto the streets to explain.

Julian This is a typical London street scene. So we've stepped into a well-known mobile phone retailer. There is quite a lot of street noise intruding into this store when the cars go past and they've got, over the top of a very nasty hum from the air-conditioning system, there's some music playing – I don't know who chose it. I don't know what it's got to do with this brand. So we've stepped in for a quiet coffee which unfortunately is a contradiction in terms in most of London. And this coffee bar has got no absorbent

surfaces at all, everything is hard and reflective so all the sound is crashing and bashing around inside. There's a lovely buzz in the background, you can hear, from a huge chiller cabinet, which is rattling and vibrating. On top of that when the barista makes a coffee, your nerves get shredded and your brain gets fried, so I'm afraid this is a long way from a relaxing coffee that really it should be.

Presenter 2 Espresso machines feature with chiller cabinets and diesel engines as the top three most annoying noises, but the important consideration for any business is that sound changes the way people think and act, the speed at which they shop or eat in restaurants for example. According to independent academic research, appropriate sound can boost sales in a shop by 30%. Bad music has the opposite effect on shoppers.

Speaker 1 I hate most of the music they play in shops and it's a very good way of getting me out the store very very quickly.

Speaker 2 I kind of switch off when I go into shops, and often I have headphones on.

Speaker 3 Well, it depends on the kind of music. It's kind of relaxing.

Speaker 4 I don't like it. I think it's too noisy. You can't think anything so you just go out again.

Presenter 2 And then, there's the office. It's claimed that the noise in open-plan offices can cut the productivity of knowledge workers by two thirds.

Julian So we're walking now into what I think is a fairly typical BBC office and it's filled with the most distracting sound in the whole world, which is other people's conversation. As a business, sound is an enormously powerful tool, and at the moment, it's like just firing a machine gun at random. There's noise and sound coming out of businesses in all directions, nobody is conscious of it, nobody's managing it, nobody is aware of the effect it's having on the people that they're trying to affect. Many organizations spend millions on how they look and nothing at all on how they sound.

Presenter 2 This is what the experts consider to be the right sort of noise: randomly generated from a computer-based selection, and used in this case to soothe the nerves of passengers at Glasgow airport. Sales at the airport shops rose by up to 10%, demonstrating that good sound can also be good business.

3.7

1 All I knew of the man with the beard and the Panama hat was that our paths crossed at about twenty past eight in the morning on the street I walked down daily. The rest of his story was my own invention, until I spoke to him last week. Eiran is a self-taught jeweller and artist. He passes me each day on his way back from the synagogue at the end of the street where he's training to be a rabbi.

2 I pass number 220 once or twice a day depending on my route and from time to time I see an older gentleman standing outside it leaning on the gatepost. I wonder when I pass him what he sees and what he has seen. When I talk to him he tells me his name is Clarence, and he's from Barbados. He arrived in Britain in 1957 and has been here ever since. He is in his 80s and has close family who live nearby.

3 As I leave for work each morning, the man who cleans my street is usually positioned with his cart at the corner of the first junction I pass and he never fails to smile and say 'Good morning.' When I introduced myself to him, he told me that his name is Gerard and he's from Ireland. He moved to London when he was a child.

4 Always together, the young man and the dog who work at the hardware store are regularly to be found in the doorway of the shop, side by side, observing the comings and goings on the street. Shyan is from Iran and his dog is German. Both have lived in London for many years. Shyan tells me that he's not sure if he is a Londoner, but says that he kisses the ground every

time he returns to the city from a trip abroad.

5 The bun shop at the end of the road is an old-fashioned bakery where you can get a no-nonsense cup of instant coffee and a doughnut covered in hundreds and thousands. When I pass it, the two ladies behind the counter are always busy feeding the local community. Tara is from St Lucia though her accent has faded. Her nickname at work is Cleopatra because she spends so long on her hair. Rita is from the Philippines and she does not like eating buns.

3.11 **Interviewer** What made you want to be a translator?

Translator It was something that I'd done when I was at university and when I moved to Spain it was difficult to get a job that wasn't teaching English, so I went back to England and I did a postgraduate course in translation. After doing the course I swore that I would never be a translator, I thought it would be too boring, but I kept doing the odd translation, and eventually I came round to the idea because I liked the idea of working for myself, and it didn't require too much investment to get started. And actually, I enjoy working with words, and it's very satisfying when you feel that you've produced a reasonable translation of the original text.

Interviewer What do you think is the most difficult kind of text to translate?

Translator Literary texts, like novels, poetry, or drama because you've got to give a lot of consideration to the author, and to the way it's been written in the original language.

Interviewer In order to translate a novel well, do you think you need to be a novelist yourself?

Translator I think that's true ideally, yes.

Interviewer And is that the case? I mean are most of the well-known translators of novels, generally speaking, novelists in their own right?

Translator Yes, I think in English anyway. People who translate into English tend to be published authors, and they tend to specialize in a particular author in the other language. And of course if it's a living author, then it's so much easier because you can actually communicate with the author and say, you know, like, 'What did you really mean here?'

Interviewer Another thing I've heard that is very hard to translate is advertising, for example slogans.

Translator Well, with advertising, the problem is that it's got to be something punchy, and it's very difficult to translate that. For example, one of the Coca-Cola™ adverts, the slogan in English was 'the real thing', but you just couldn't translate that literally into Spanish, it just wouldn't have had the same power. In fact, it became *Sensación de vivir*, which is 'sensation of living', which sounds really good in Spanish but it would sound weird in English.

Interviewer What about film titles?

Translator They're horrific too. People always complain that they've not been translated accurately, but of course it's impossible because sometimes a literal translation just doesn't work.

Interviewer For example?

Translator OK, well, think of, you know, the Julie Andrews film, *The Sound of Music*. Well, that works in English because it's a phrase that you know, you know like 'I can hear the sound of music'. But it doesn't work at all in other languages, and in Spanish it was called 'Sonrisas y lagrimas' which means 'Smiles and tears', in German it was called 'Meine Lieder – meine Träume', which means 'My songs, my dreams', and in Italian it was 'Tutti insieme appassionatamente', which means I think 'All together passionately' or I don't know, something like that! In fact, I think it was translated differently all over the world.

Interviewer Do you think there are special problems translating film scripts for the subtitles?

Translator Yes, a lot. There are special constraints, for example the translation has to fit on the screen as the actor is speaking, and so sometimes the translation is a paraphrase rather than a direct translation, and of course, well, going back to untranslatable things, really the big problems are cultural, and humour, because they're just not the same. You can get across the idea, but you might need pages to explain it, and, you know, by that time the film's moved on. I also sometimes think that the translators are given the film on DVD, I mean, you know, rather than a written script, and that sometimes they've simply misheard or they didn't understand what the people said. And that's the only explanation I can come up with for some of the mistranslations that I've seen. Although sometimes it might be that some things like humour and jokes, especially ones which depend on wordplay are just, you know, they're simply untranslatable. And often it's very difficult to get the right register, for example with slang and swear words, because if you literally translate taboo words or swear words, even if they exist in the other language, they may well be far more offensive.

Interviewer What are the pros and cons of being a translator?

Translator Well, it's a lonely job I suppose, you know, you're on your own most of the time, it's hard work, you're sitting there and, you know, you're working long hours, and you can't programme things because you don't know when more work is going to come in, and people have always got tight deadlines. You know, it's really rare that somebody'll ring you up and say 'I want this translation in three months' time.' That just doesn't really happen.

Interviewer And the pros?

Translator Well, the pros are that it gives you freedom, because you can do it anywhere if you've got an Internet connection and electricity, and I suppose you can organize your time, because you're freelance, you know, you're your own boss, which is good. I like that.

Interviewer What advice would you give someone who's thinking of going into translation?

Translator I'd say that in addition to the language, get a speciality. Do another course in anything that interests you, like economics, law, history, art, because you really need to know about the subjects that you're translating into.

3.14 One of the most puzzling paradoxes in social science is that although people spend so much of their time trying to make more money, having more money doesn't seem to make them that much happier. My colleagues Liz Dunn and Lara Aknin – both at the University of British Columbia – and I wondered if the issue was not that money *couldn't* buy happiness, but that people simply weren't spending it in the right way to make themselves happier. Liz had the great idea of exploring whether, if we encouraged people to spend money in different ways, we could uncover the domains in which money might lead to happiness. We conducted a number of studies in which we showed that money *can* buy happiness, when people spend that money prosocially on others (for example, giving gifts to friends, donating to charities, etc) rather than on themselves (say, buying flat-screen televisions).

3.15 So what are the psychological factors involved when it comes to individuals and the feelings they encounter when they are giving away their money? Does it matter how wealthy you are? We found that it was the relative percentage of their money that people spend on others – rather than the absolute amount – that predicted their happiness. We did a study to look at the happiness of 16 employees of a Boston-based company before and after they received bonuses of between \$3,000 and \$8,000. This showed that the size of the bonus that people received had no impact on their long-term happiness. It was the percentage of that bonus they spent on others that increased their well-being. In another study, we showed that spending as little as \$5 over the course of a day, on another person, led to demonstrable increases in happiness. In other words, people needn't be wealthy and donate hundreds of thousands of dollars to charity to experience the benefits of prosocial spending; small changes – a few dollars reallocated from oneself to another – can make a difference. Of course many of us equate having money with happiness, and a large body of research does show that people become happier as they move from being very poor to lower middle class, but after this point the impact of income on happiness is much weaker. Think of someone who makes \$100,000 one year and \$110,000 the next – do we really expect this additional income suddenly to make this person fulfilled, without a care in the world? Being informed about a raise certainly makes us happy, but the \$10,000 doesn't make our siblings or in-laws any less difficult to deal with over the course of the following year. Although people believe that having money leads to happiness, our research suggests that this is only the case if at least some of that money is given to others. We had one final question. We wanted to know whether *knowing* about the effect of prosocial spending might erase it, if people engaged in prosocial spending in a calculated manner in order to 'get happy'. We conducted a research project in conjunction with the *New York Times* in which readers who had been told about our findings were invited to complete a brief survey in which they reported their happiness, as well as how much money they'd spent on others and on themselves so far that day. Consistent with our previous research, we found that spending more on others was associated with greater happiness among this sample of approximately 1,000 *New York Times* readers, even though the respondents had been exposed to our previous findings.

3.17 **Interviewer** Could you tell me who founded Women's World Banking and why?

Sarita The idea behind Women's World Banking came out in a meeting that was held in Mexico in 1975. It was a United Nations first International Year of the Woman and really they were gathering women from around the world to discuss women and human rights and there was a small group that started to think if we could work on only one issue, because they were discussing domestic violence, you know, economic access, education, the whole plethora of human rights. So if we could only discuss one issue, sort of focus on one issue, put all our energies behind it, what would that be, what would be that catalyst? And they decided that it would be economic independence for women. So that if a women has the access to financial independence, then she can choose, and she can have greater access to education, opportunity, well-being, and that's where the idea came about and Women's World Banking was really set up, the first mission was to give women all over the world greater access to the economies in their own countries.

Interviewer Where did the idea of microfinance come from?

Sarita The idea behind microfinance again goes back to the mid-70s. There had been, by that time, several decades of what we call 'the Western World' giving massive amounts of aid to the developing world and a realization that a lot of it was not working, there were still many people who were left poor. So, you know, Muhammad Yunus is credited as being the father of microfinance. He's an economist living in Bangladesh, a very poor country, and he looked around and he said, 'What is it that the poor lack? What is it that they need?' And the answer is obvious: they need money. And all of us, in order to get started, have had access to credit. So the poor can't get access to credit, they can't go to relatives to borrow because generally the relatives are as poor as they themselves are, and they certainly cannot go into a bank and borrow because they have no collateral.

Interviewer How did Dr Yunus solve these problems?

Sarita There are really three innovations that he came up with that are brilliant in hindsight. One was, OK the poor have no collateral, but let's figure out a way to create collateral, which means collateral is basically if you're not going to pay back the loan that somebody's held responsible. So he came up with a lending methodology where there was a group of peers that were given the loan and they would be lending to each other and the group held each member accountable for paying back. The second innovation that he came up with is that it is very difficult for the poor to gather a lump sum to pay back a loan, but if you can break up that payment into very small regular payments that are coming out of your daily income, then it's feasible to pay back the loan. So what microcredit did was to break up the non-payment into these very, sort of, regular small payments. And the third was really an incentive system, that the poor were not encouraged to borrow a large amount, they only borrowed what they could use in their business and then pay back, and if they paid back successfully, then they were eligible for a larger loan.

3.18 **Interviewer** Do you have any examples of individual success stories?

Sarita Oh, I love talking about individual success stories, because this is what sort of gets us up in the morning and, you know, gets us to come to work and stay late, and do this, this work. Since I've been at Women's World Banking I've been to the Dominican Republic, Jordan, and India, so I'm happy to give you a story from each of the three countries. The DR is a more established economy, if you will, and so the woman I met had already had successive loans that she had taken from our partner in the DR and what she did was to start out, she was basically selling food from her kitchen, making excess food and selling it to the factory workers, took out a loan, sort of increased that business and then set up a little cantina out of her living room. So that along with food, she was selling cigarettes, beer, candy, etc. That business did well, took out another loan and built a room on top of her house and started to rent it out. And so over seven years what she's been able to do is to completely build a new home for herself and rent out the old one and this is going to ensure income in her old age, because at some point she's going to be too old to work in the kitchen and to be, you know, standing on her feet behind the cantina counter and she's looking at these rental rooms that she has been able to put on as her, her old age security.

In Jordan, I'll tell you about a young women that we met. You know, sort of the cultural norm in Jordan is that a fairly old husband can marry again and marry a fairly young woman, so the one that we met, her husband was now too old and sick so while he took care of having a roof over her head, she had absolutely no means of earning more money for herself or her kids, and at her socio-economic level it's not considered proper for a woman to go out and work. So the only thing that she was able to do, was she had taken a loan to buy cosmetics, and was selling them from her living room to her neighbours and this was considered to be an OK business for her because primarily she was dealing with other women, but it gave her that sort of extra money to use for herself.

And then in India where I was recently in the city of Hyderabad, and Hyderabad is this up-and-coming city, you know, it's gleaming. Indians themselves are thinking of it as the next cyber city. But across town they have slums, where even now, both men and women have not gone to school, they're not educated, and their only recourse is to work in the informal economy. So the family that we met, the husband was a vegetable cart, a vegetable seller, so he took his cart and went out into the more affluent neighbourhoods. The son had dropped out of school to join his father to push a similar cart, and the mother had taken a loan to embroider saris. And she did this at home, sort of in her spare time and what she really wanted to do was to amass enough income so that she would cut out the middle man, because she basically got half of what the sari was worth, because she was handing it over to a middle man. So that if she could buy the materials herself, embroider it herself, and sell it herself to the store, she could in effect double her income without doubling her labour.

3.20 **Interviewer** Do you consider yourself good with money?

Ian No, I think I'm pretty bad on the whole. It makes me anxious. It freaks me out. Yeah.

Interviewer Do you think that women are better at managing money than men?

Ian On the whole, probably, yeah. I certainly think my wife's better. I think she and many women are better planners, I think. More sensible about these things.

Interviewer Do you think that having more money would make you happier?

Ian In a kind of banal way, I could get to do certain things more easily, yes, but maybe not in the bigger picture.

Interviewer Do you consider yourself good with money?

Sheila Yeah, I think so. I've never been in debt, so I think that's pretty good going seeing as I'm quite old now. And yeah, I spend a lot on shoes, that's my only weakness, I think.

Interviewer Do you think women are better at managing money than men?

Sheila I don't really think it's a gender issue. I mean, I'm pretty good with my money, but my brother's rubbish, he's always in debt, but my husband's fine, so I'm not sure that there's a gender thing going on there.

Interviewer Do you think having more money would make you happier?

Sheila Pretty happy as I am actually, so no.

Interviewer Do you consider yourself good with money?

Jerry I do actually, yeah. No, I do.

Interviewer Why?

Jerry Because I never go overdrawn, I pay off my credit card, I try to make sure my savings get a reasonable rate of interest, I never run out of cash, I'm just kind of an organized person, money-wise.

Interviewer Do you think women are better at managing money than men?

Jerry That's a tricky one. In some respects I think so. I wouldn't want to fall into stereotyping. I think men and women spend money on different things. I mean I do a lot of cycling, and if you see a man and woman out cycling together, the man always has a better bike. Always. It's quite amazing. So I think men like spending money on their things, whereas women might spend money more on family things, I don't know. So in that sense I think probably women have more of a perspective on money than men do.

Interviewer Do you think having more money would make you happier?

Jerry I think having a bit more might. I think having a lot more it's difficult to say. I think a lot of people find large sums of money, if you won the lottery say, that would be quite hard to deal with, I think. But you know, an extra 10,000 a year I think would be just about right, yeah.

Interviewer Do you consider yourself good with money?

Kate No, not at all. I spend it without thinking and just I'm very lazy looking for bargains and things, whereas I have friends who look really carefully for the cheapest option. I just can't be bothered to do that so I tend to spend money like water. It's awful.

Interviewer Do you think that women are better at managing money than men?

Kate Not necessarily, but now I think about it I think maybe women go, I know it's stereotypical to say, but maybe women go shopping more together as a sort of social activity, whereas men tend to, you know, I don't know, stay in their rooms or work or something. I don't know.

Interviewer Do you think that having more money would make you happier?

Kate I think it might, yes. I think I might be very happy with more money, I can, yeah, just not think about money at all, and spend all the money I want and go out, have nice meals, and go on holiday. That would be great.

Interviewer Do you consider yourself good with money?

Jason Not good enough, no.

Interviewer Why not?

Jason Why not? I'm not very good at making budgets and sticking to them.

Interviewer Do you think women are better at managing money than men?

Jason I think that depends. The ones I know probably are not.

Interviewer Do you think that having more money would make you happier?

Jason In New York, yes. In most places no.

4.3 In the book *History Goes to the Movies*, the author Joseph Roquemore gives films stars according to their historical accuracy on a one-to-five scale – five stars means a film's very accurate, and no stars means it's very inaccurate. I'm going to look at two of the best-known films that Roquemore features in his book. The first film is the Oscar-winning movie *Titanic*, which was directed by James Cameron in 1997. The film *is* historically accurate as regards the events leading up to the collision with the iceberg – the Titanic was sailing too fast and the captain ignored warnings about ice. The collision and sinking are also very accurately portrayed with amazing special effects. However, where the film falls down is in its characterization. I must say I entirely agree with Roquemore when he criticizes director James Cameron for what he calls 'class-conscious overkill'. What he means by that is Cameron depicts all the third-class passengers in the film as brave and good, and all the first-class passengers as selfish, stupid, cowardly, or downright evil. And this can't have been the case. Then a large part of the film centres on the love story between Jack, a third-class passenger, played by Leo DiCaprio, and Rose, a first-class passenger, played by Kate Winslet. Obviously, these characters and their story are fictitious and were just added, presumably to sell the film to a younger audience. But many historians have pointed out that a romance between Jack and Rose is totally improbable, because at that time there was complete class segregation on board ship. Roquemore also criticizes the film's portrayal of Captain Smith. He's made out to be indecisive and frankly useless throughout the disaster. But this contradicts everything which was said about him by survivors of the sinking. And for me, though, even more indefensible was the film's portrayal of the ship's First Officer, William Murdoch. On the night of the sinking he behaved heroically. In his home town in Scotland there's even a memorial to him, but in the film he's shown taking a bribe from a passenger (in exchange for a place in a lifeboat), shooting passengers dead, and finally shooting himself in the head. In fact, the film company 20th Century Fox, who produced *Titanic*, were eventually forced to admit that there was no historical evidence that Murdoch did any of these things, and that they'd included these details purely and simply to make the story more interesting. Roquemore gives *Titanic* three stars, describing it as 'Great pyrotechnics – mediocre history'. All in all, I think his assessment is about right. The main events are true but the characterization is definitely the weak point in the film.

Moving on to the second film, *Braveheart*, this is one of the films to which Roquemore gives five stars for historical accuracy. He gives the film five stars because despite what he calls some 'small fictions' he thinks *Braveheart* is, I quote, 'true to the spirit of William Wallace'. Well, that may be the case, but I'm afraid I have to take exception to the phrase 'small fictions'. The historian Elizabeth Ewan described *Braveheart* as a film which 'almost totally sacrifices historical accuracy for epic adventure.' William Wallace is portrayed as a kind of poor primitive tribesman living in a village. In fact, he was the son of a rich landowner and he later became a knight. You'll remember too that in the film Mel Gibson wears woad, a kind of blue face paint. Apparently, the Scots stopped wearing woad hundreds of years earlier. And while we're on the subject of costume, in the film the Scottish soldiers wear kilts. No surprises there you might think, but in the 13th century, which is when the events of the film are set, the Scots did not wear kilts, and in fact, they didn't start wearing them until four centuries later. Another of these 'fictions' is that in *Braveheart*, William Wallace has a romance with the beautiful French princess, Isabelle. However, the historical reality is that Wallace never met Isabelle and even if he had, she would only have been nine years old at the time! Finally, anyone who's seen the film will remember the famous battle scene. The battle was the Battle of Stirling, so called because it was fought on Stirling Bridge in Scotland. Basically, the reason why the Scots won the battle is because the English soldiers got trapped on the narrow bridge. In *Braveheart* the bridge does not appear at all in the battle. In fact, Mel Gibson originally planned to film the scene on the actual bridge, but he found that the bridge kept 'getting in the way'. Apparently, when he mentioned this to one of the Scottish history advisors on the film, the man's reply was 'Aye, that's what the English found'. Mel Gibson defended all the inaccuracies in the film saying that the film's version of history was more 'compelling cinematically'. Admittedly, it *is* a very entertaining film, and it does give you a strong feeling for William Wallace and how he must have inspired his countrymen, but I don't think you can give this film five stars or even two stars for historical accuracy.

4.8 **Presenter** Hello, good afternoon and welcome to today's edition of the *Book Programme*. Did you know that in every list of best-sellers, there's always one kind of book that's guaranteed to be there, and that's a self-help book? From how to make a fortune to how to bring up your children, there's a book that can give you advice on any problem you might possibly have. Today, our four contributors have each chosen a best-selling self-help book to talk about. First, Matt Crossley. What did you choose, Matt?

Matt Well, I have quite a few friends who are into psychology, and when I'm chatting to them I always wish I could make an intelligent comment which would show that I know something about psychology too – which, in fact, I don't. So I chose *The Bluffer's Guide to Psychology*. *The Bluffer's Guides* are a series of books which are supposed to help you to talk about a subject even if you don't really know anything about it. So there are *Bluffer's Guides* to economics, to opera, to wine, all sorts of things.

Presenter And what did you think?

Matt Well, I have to say I was really impressed. It's a light-hearted introduction to psychology, which is both funny but at the same time extremely informative and scientifically-based. My feeling is that even people who really do know about psychology would find it a good read, and speaking personally, it actually made me want to find out some more about certain things, like the gestalt theory....

Presenter So you'd recommend it?

Matt Absolutely! I now understand some of the terminology of psychology and a little about the main theories, but above all I had a great time reading it. I actually laughed out loud at one point just reading one of the glossary entries.

Presenter So, *The Bluffer's Guide to Psychology* recommended. Anita, how about you?

Anita Well, I chose a fairly recent diet book called *Neris and India's Idiot-Proof Diet*. I chose it firstly because India Knight is a journalist I like, and I often read her articles in *The Sunday Times*, which are usually very witty, and also because I see myself as a bit of an expert on diet books, I mean I've read them all and I've tried them all over the last ten years.

Presenter And your verdict?

Anita Well, I'll just start by saying that I haven't actually done the diet yet…

Presenter Obviously!

Anita Cheeky! I don't know if it really works, but I thought that the book was great. As Matt said about *The Bluffer's Guide*, this book was also, it was a good laugh, which is not something you can usually say about a diet book. But for me the two best points were that firstly, it's written by two women who are both extremely large, and they did the diet themselves. Most diet books seem to be written either by men or by stick-thin women who've never had a weight problem in their lives. So the fact that the authors had done the diet themselves gave it credibility for me. And then the second reason is that really more than half the book is these two women talking about all the reasons that made them put on weight in the first place, and I'm sure that all these psychological reasons are at the heart of most people's weight problems.

Presenter So, might you give the diet a try? Not that you need to of course.

Anita Well, I don't know, I might actually. The diet obviously worked for them, because they're honest enough to include photos in the book of them at their fattest, and then how they ended up after doing the diet. So…

Presenter Thank you Anita. So it's thumbs up for the *Idiot-proof Diet*. Kate, what was your choice?

Kate Well, as you know James and I recently got married, and when I saw the title of this book, it's called *The Rules of Marriage* – 'time-tested secrets for making marriage work', I thought, 'That's the book for me'.

Presenter And was it?

Kate Definitely not. To tell you the truth, I was actually horrified. The book is supposed to be a kind of manual of dos and don'ts for what to do from the engagement onwards, and if you ask me it was something that could have been written fifty years ago, or more. The message is more or less that once you've *caught* your husband, you have to keep him satisfied in every possible way. And if you don't like it, then all they suggest is that you complain and moan to your girlfriends. According to this book, making a marriage work is entirely up to the wife, the husband doesn't have to anything at all. The wife just has to try to be exactly what her husband wants her to be, and then everything will be just fine. I can't believe that in the 21st century such horrendous advice as this is being published and presumably, as it's a best-seller, being read by women in their thousands.

Presenter So you wouldn't recommend *The Rules of Marriage*?

Kate Absolutely not! In fact, I think it should be banned.

Presenter So to our last guest today, Daniel. And your book is…?

Daniel My book is Paul McKenna's latest, which is called *I Can Make You Rich*. And I don't need to give any explanations about why I chose this book.

Presenter So are we going to see you on the next list of the hundred richest people in Britain?

Daniel No, I don't think so. In fact, I feel a bit like Kate did about her book. I couldn't take it seriously at all. The book promises to help you see the world in a different way, which will make you 'think rich' and eventually 'live rich', all through doing mental exercises, which are supposed to help you find out what you want and focus on it. It has a sort of hypnosis-style CD with it, and I can't actually tell you much about it because I fell asleep after the first five minutes. Yeah, still I suppose that means it's relaxing. But after reading it, my suggestion would be, if you want to get rich, start by not wasting money on buying this book.

Presenter So a big thumbs down for Paul McKenna too. Matt, Anita, Kate, and Daniel, thank you very much.

4.10 It's Monday. Just five minutes after I'd agreed to abandon my phone, I got a text! But of course officially I didn't have a mobile any more, so I had to switch it off without reading the text and then I spent all afternoon wondering what crucial information there was in the message. After work I missed my train, and I'd arranged to meet my flatmate for dinner. I knew I was going to be late – and I hate being late but there was just nothing I could do about it. I made it in time for dinner, but in the restaurant I kept feeling an urge to check my phone for messages or missed calls. It was weird and really stressful. And on top of it all, my flatmate had her phone sitting on the table in front of her. It's Tuesday. When I was on the way home, I suddenly thought that I *had* to ring my mother. If I'd had my phone, I'd have called her there and then, and it made me realize now that I always speak to my parents when I'm on the move. They're always complaining that we never have a conversation without traffic noise in the background. So for once, when I got home, I called her on the landline, and we had a whole half-hour of conversation without any interruptions. I have to say it was one of the most relaxing conversations we'd ever had in recent years. A real pleasure! It's Wednesday. The morning started badly because I needed to make a doctor's appointment before I went to work, but the surgery was engaged for half an hour. I eventually got through, but it meant I was late for work, and I felt under pressure all day. In the evening, I'd planned to go climbing with some friends at the climbing centre, so I rushed to get home early because one of my friends said he would need to call me to check the arrangements. I waited around for him to call, which he did, but late, so we both got to the climbing centre late and didn't enjoy it as much as we might have if we'd had more time. It's Thursday. After work I went to a friend's house which was about an hour away. I actually had a good feeling about being without my mobile because it meant having a whole hour for me to relax and when no one could disturb me. The feeling lasted until I got off the bus and realized that I didn't know exactly where her street was and I got completely lost looking for it. So I was late for the fourth time. It's Friday. Well, this was the day when I ended up calling the bar trying to find my friends. First I went to the theatre with my friend Alice. I got very panicky when I was waiting for her in the foyer, because we hadn't specified exactly where we were going to meet, and there were a lot of people, and she had the tickets. If I'd had my phone, I would just have sent her a text saying exactly where I was. Luckily, we did see each other. But then after the theatre the idea was to meet up with some friends and that's when I ended up spending nearly five pounds what with trying to get the number of the bar from directory enquiries, and then doing the whole thing again for a second bar. In the end we went to have a drink on our own. So that wasn't just being late, it was a social occasion that just didn't happen.

4.13 **Speaker 1** What's the question? Do I have any obsessions? Well, I don't consider them obsessions, but I do have a habit of organizing myself in ways that other people might consider obsessive. I've walked into a friend's flat where I was staying for a week or two, and instantly alphabetized their collection of CDs or DVDs of maybe a hundred or so because if I was going to be there, and I needed to find a piece of music, it just means …it was a lot easier to find it when it's alphabetized.

Interviewer Are all your book collections and record collections at home alphabetized?

Speaker 1 Absolutely. It just saves…I do it once and it saves a lot of time in finding things afterwards. I find it practical. I don't find it obsessive.

Interviewer Do you have any private obsessions, for example, you know, collecting things, exercise, tidiness, that stuff?

Speaker 2 Well, I do, I've got a complete obsession about cleaning, and it's awful, it's the bane of my life, it's absolutely awful, I cannot relax unless everything is absolutely, you know, clean and tidy. I've had to let it go a bit because my husband's an Aussie and he's very laid-back and I just haven't been allowed to be as obsessed as I have been in the past, and of course having children stops the obsession a little bit because there's toys and stuff everywhere…

Interviewer Yeah, where did it come from?

Speaker 2 Well, I think it's just, it's a security thing, and I feel when everything's clean and tidy I feel safe and comfortable, and I think it's because when I was an early teenager my parents split up, they divorced, and that's when it started, I started cleaning. We had a smoked glass coffee table with chrome legs and I used to clean that because I couldn't stand the fingerprints on it and that's where it began, that then escalated and I started cleaning the kitchen and the bathroom…

Interviewer Oh my God, as a teenager?

Speaker 2 Yeah, I was absolutely, and then hoovering came into play, and I started hoovering, but ironically I've got a couple of friends, and their obsession with cleaning started as well with the same thing, their parents split up, at around about the same age, early teenagers, and they have obsessions with cleaning as well. One who I work with, not very far from here today, and another girlfriend who, I went on a course, met on a course, and she has the same problems, so I don't know whether it's, there's anything in that.

Interviewer Do you clean when you're upset or do you…?

Speaker 2 Yes.

Interviewer Or do you just clean all the time… when you're upset?

Speaker 2 Particularly when I'm upset. Yeah, it occupies me and everything is all nice, but I have got a handle on it now and I'm a lot better than I used to be.

Interviewer Will you come over to my place and clean?

Speaker 2 Yes, that's what everybody says.

Speaker 3 Well, my mother is completely, pathologically addicted to checking her hair in the mirror all the time, she's got a real hang-up about her hair, completely obsessed by it, spends hours and hours checking out her hair and…

Interviewer 1 Does it interfere with her life?

Speaker 3 I think it's quite time consuming and yes, I think it does, I mean she can get really upset, and if she goes to the hairdresser and sort of has anything done, she becomes really upset for days if it's slightly wrong, or she's really self-conscious about it.

Interviewer 1 Just about her hair?

Speaker 3 Yeah.

Interviewer How long has it been going on for?

Speaker 3 Ever since she was a child. I discovered that her brother had curly hair when he was a child, beautiful curly hair, and big brown eyes, and I think he was the sort of favourite child, I think he was the favoured one…

Interviewer 2 And she has straight hair…

Speaker 3 And she has straight hair, and I think that's where it comes from. But she's absolutely, is really hung up about it.

Speaker 4 There's a name for this condition but I can't remember what it is and I'm not sure what it's called but I do count things. If I come into a room, I will count the number of lights on the ceiling. The only thing is, I don't know how many there really are, because I count things so that they turn out to be in multiples of threes or nines, and I also count panes in windows, I will count panels in doors. But I like them always to get up to a 3 or a 30 or a 90 so it's a fairly useless thing, but it's just something I just do.

Speaker 5 Yeah, my friend is obsessed with healthy eating, absolutely obsessed, and it makes going out for dinner with her really quite boring because you can't… anything on the menu she just goes on and on about how this is bad, that's bad, allergy to this, allergy to that, getting the waiter over to talk and, you know about certain things that are in each dish and it's just so, it really actually does interfere with like her social life, having fun with her because she's just completely obsessed by what she eats and it's just a bit, I don't know, it's a bit boring.

4.15 **Interviewer** You've written a number of screenplays for historical dramas, for example, *Rome*, why do you think there is so much demand for historical drama and film?

Adrian Well, film and TV is always about good stories. I know that seems a fairly obvious thing to say, but the thing about history is it's jam-packed full with good stories, many of which people know, part, or at least vaguely know. If you say, 'I'm going to do a film about Robin Hood,' you know that part of your audience at the very least will already have some knowledge of that story and they will think, 'Oh yeah, I quite like that story, so maybe there is something in there that, for me in that film'. And there are many other examples, Rome is a, you know, is a canvas full of stories that have, you know, lasted for 2000 years. So, you know, many people have vaguely heard about Julius Caesar, some of them know that story very very well, and so on and so on, or Caligula or whoever. So history is just an endlessly useful way of telling great stories from the past in a way that means something in the present. In a perfect world, you get a double hit, you, you tell a classic story, but you also tell it in a way that makes it resonate with the present.

Interviewer Are historical films necessarily any more expensive than films set in the modern day?

Adrian Yeah, period is always more expensive. It's just something about the fact that you have to dress the film in a way that you don't have to dress a contemporary film. By 'dress' I mean, not just dress people who have to wear costumes that are authentic to the period. If your film is set in 1800 they all have to look as though they were, you know, dressed exactly as in that period. That all costs money. But 'dressed' also in terms of the way you make the houses look, the way you make all your decorations look, your furniture, everything has to be authentic to the period. You have to make sure there are no cars, no aeroplanes, every shot has to be weighed up to make sure that there's nothing in it which, which betrays the period. There's nothing more ridiculous than a period film where you see a glaring anachronism, some detail that's horribly wrong. So unfortunately, all of that costs money and you have to have bigger crowds in many cases. *Rome* was a case in point. We needed big crowds. In the Senate you have to have, a certain number of Senators, all of them have to be dressed in, you know, in togas and so on. So I'm afraid it is just an expensive way of making films, yeah.

4.16 **Interviewer** How important is historical accuracy in a historical film?

Adrian The notion of accuracy in history is a really difficult one in drama because, you know, it's like saying, you know, was *Macbeth* accurate, was a Shakespearean drama accurate. The thing is it's not about historical accuracy; it's about whether you can make a drama work from history that means something to an audience now. So I tend to take the view that in a way accuracy isn't the issue when it comes to the drama. If you're writing a drama, you have the right as a writer to create the drama that works for you, so you can certainly change details. The truth is nobody really knows how people spoke in Rome or how people spoke in the courts of Charles II or William the Conqueror or Victoria, or whoever. You have an idea from writing, from books, plays, and so on. We know when certain things happened, what sort of dates happened. I think it's really a question of judgement. If you make history ridiculous, if you change detail to the point where history is an absurdity, then obviously things become more difficult. The truth is that the more recent history is, the more difficult it is not to be authentic to it.

In a way, it's much easier to play fast and loose with the details of what happened in Rome than it is to play fast and loose with the details of what happened in the Iraq War, say, you know. So it's all a matter of perspective in some ways. It's something that you have to be aware of and which you try to be faithful to, but you can't ultimately say a drama has to be bound by the rules of history, because that's not what drama is.

Interviewer Do you think the writer has a responsibility to represent any kind of historical truth?

Adrian Not unless that's his intention. If it's your intention to be truthful to history and you put a piece out saying this is the true story of, say, the murder of Julius Caesar exactly as the historical record has it, then of course, you do have an obligation, because if you then deliberately tell lies about it, you are, you know, you're deceiving your audience. If, however, you say you're writing a drama about the assassination of Julius Caesar purely from your own perspective and entirely in a fictional context, then you have the right to tell the story however you like. I don't think you have any obligation except to the story that you're telling. What you can't be is deliberately dishonest. You can't say this is true when you know full well it isn't.

Interviewer Can you think of any examples where you feel the facts have been twisted too far?

Adrian Well, I think the notion of whether a film, a historical film has gone too far in presenting a dramatized fictional version of the truth is really a matter of personal taste. The danger is with any historical film that if that becomes the only thing that the audience sees on that subject, if it becomes the received version of the truth, as it were, because people don't always make the distinction between movies and reality in history, then obviously if that film is grossly irresponsible or grossly fantastic in its presentation of the truth, that could, I suppose, become controversial. I mean, you know, I think that the only thing anybody is ever likely to know about *Spartacus*, for example, the movie, is Kirk Douglas and all his friends standing up and saying, 'I am Spartacus, I am Spartacus', which is a wonderful moment and it stands for the notion of freedom, of individual choice and so on. So *Spartacus* the film, made in 1962, I think, if memory serves, has become, I think, for nearly everybody who knows anything about Spartacus the only version of the truth. Now in fact, we don't know if any of that is true really. There are some accounts of the historical Spartacus, but very very few and what, virtually the only thing that's known about it is that there was a man called Spartacus and there was a rebellion and many people were, you know, were crucified at the end of it, as in the film. Whether that's irresponsible I don't know, I can't say that I think it is, I think in a way it's, *Spartacus* is a film that had a resonance in the modern era. There are other examples, you know, a lot of people felt that the version of William Wallace that was presented in *Braveheart* was really pushing the limits of what history could stand, the whole, in effect, his whole career was invented in the film, or at least, you know, built on to such a degree that some people felt that perhaps it was more about the notion of Scotland as an independent country than it was about history as an authentic spectacle. But you know, again these things are a matter of purely personal taste. I mean, I enjoyed *Braveheart* immensely.

4.18 **Interviewer** If you could have lived in another historical period, which period would you choose?

Tim I would have chosen the 60s and 70s because of the music of that time. I thought the musical revolution, you know, you had the Beatles coming over to America. And, just the music, and it was a different culture at that time. I would have liked to experience that.

Interviewer Which historical figure do you particularly admire?

Tim Admire? I'd have to say Abraham Lincoln. He was pretty impactful on our country. You know, he had a lot of revolutionary viewpoints at that point in time that really put this country in a direction that I thought was pretty unique and necessary at the time.

Interviewer If you could have lived in another historical period, which period would you choose?

Edmund I think probably ancient Rome, probably the 1st, 2nd century AD, I think, because I'm most interested in that sort of period. And I quite like the idea of living in Italy, so…

Interviewer Which historical figure do you particularly admire?

Edmund So many. I suppose I've always had a fondness for, sort of, the great generals, like Alexander, or Wellington, or people like that, I suppose.

Interviewer If you could have lived in another historical period, which period would you choose?

Mark I think, sort of, ancient Greece quite appeals, I have to say. Sort of, I don't know, sitting around in a toga doing lots of thinking. Yeah, ancient Greece.

Interviewer Which historical figure do you particularly admire?

Mark I would say Leonardo da Vinci, principally because he is that archetypal Renaissance man. You know, a true polymath, genius really.

Interviewer If you could have lived in another historical period, which period would you choose?

Amy I think it would probably be the Victorian period because they always used to dress up so magnificently during the day and I just, I look around the streets nowadays and see people wearing jeans and that seems very normal so I think it would be very interesting to go back to a period like Victorian England when they dressed very elaborately and see if that's normal and what's casual and what's well dressed. I think that would be really interesting. So nothing historical.

Interviewer Which historical figure do you particularly admire?

Amy Gosh, I'm not really sure. I do very much admire Shakespeare. It's probably a very typical answer, but I think his writing's absolutely phenomenal and very much ahead of its time when he was writing it. So I'd say that's the most influential person I can think of.

Interviewer If you could have lived in another historical period, which period would you choose?

Jerry I think maybe, maybe the 1950s. I wouldn't want to go very far back. I think the 1950s.

Interviewer Why?

Jerry I think it was quite a, at least in Britain, it was quite an optimistic time. I think society seemed to be progressing well and science seemed to be progressing well. And it seemed to be a time of hope, a sort of optimistic sort of time, unlike now, I think, where a lot of things like social developments and scientific developments seem more sort of ambivalent and unclear. I think that was a good time to be around.

Interviewer Which historical figure do you particularly admire?

Jerry I've just read a book about Darwin, about Charles Darwin, and I think he was an amazing figure. I think to come up with an idea so simple and so brilliant and to have the courage to publish it. I think he was an amazing chap.

5.1 Why is it that so many children don't seem to learn anything at school? A TV producer-turned-writer has come up with some very revolutionary ideas. A few years ago TV producer John Lloyd thought up a formula for a new quiz show. The show is called *QI*, which stands for 'Quite Interesting', and which is also IQ backwards. It's a comedy quiz hosted by actor Stephen Fry, where panellists have to answer unusual general knowledge questions, and it's perhaps surprising that it's particularly popular among 15- to 25-year-olds. Along with co-author John Mitchinson, Lloyd has since written a number of *QI* books, for example *The Book of General Ignorance*, and these have also been incredibly successful. Lloyd's basic principle is very simple: everything you think you know is probably wrong, and everything is interesting. The *QI Book of General Ignorance*, for example, poses 240 questions, all of which reveal surprising answers. So we learn, for example, that goldfish have quite long memories, that you're more likely to be killed by an asteroid than by lightning, or that Julius Caesar was not, in fact, born by Caesarian section. The popularity of these books proves Lloyd's other thesis: that human beings, and children in particular, are naturally curious and have a desire to learn. And this, he believes, has several implications for education. According to Lloyd and Mitchinson, there are two reasons why children, in spite of being curious, tend to do badly at school. Firstly, even the best schools can take a fascinating subject, such as electricity or classical civilization, and make it boring, by turning it into facts which have to be learnt by heart and then regurgitated for exams. Secondly, *QI*'s popularity seems to prove that learning takes place most effectively when it's done voluntarily. The same teenagers who will happily choose to read a *QI* book will often sit at the back of a geography class and go to sleep, or worse still, disrupt the rest of the class.

5.2 So how could we change our schools so that children would enjoy learning? What would a '*QI* school' be like? These are Lloyd and Mitchinson's basic suggestions. The first principle is that education should be more play than work. The more learning involves things like story-telling and making things, the more interested children will become. Secondly, they believe that the best people to control what children learn are the children themselves. Children should be encouraged to follow their curiosity. They will end up learning to read, for example, because they want to, in order to read about something they're interested in. Thirdly, they argue that children should be in control of when and how they learn. The *QI* school would not be compulsory, so pupils wouldn't have to go if they didn't want to, and there would be no exams. There would only be projects, or goals that children set themselves with the teacher helping them. So a project could be something like making a film or building a chair. Fourthly, there should never be theory without practice. You can't learn about vegetables and what kind of plants they are from books and pictures; you need to go and plant them and watch them grow. The fifth and last point Lloyd and Mitchinson make is there's no reason why school has to stop dead at 17 or 18. The *QI* school would be a place where you would be able to carry on learning all your life, a mini-university where the young and old could continue to find out about all the things they are naturally curious about.

5.4 **Interviewer** For most people, art for the last few centuries has meant paintings and sculptures, and suddenly there are all these new kinds of sculptures and installations, that for most people don't mean art. First of all, could you just explain exactly what these kinds of sculptures and installations are?

Expert Well, installations are really mixed-media artworks which take up a whole gallery or space, and sculptures, these kind of modern sculptures are assemblies of objects which may take up a little less space, but which you would perhaps not think of as a traditional work of art when you first saw them.

Interviewer So how would you explain to people that installations are also art?

Expert Well, an installation, or this new kind of modern sculpture, is really no different from a painting or a traditional sculpture if you think about where the artist starts from, and that is they have an idea about something they want to communicate, and then they decide how to communicate that idea, so that could be in paint, or it could be in stone, or it could be in wood or metal, or it could be through an installation, which could be this kind of assembly of different types of object. In all three methods, in all these different media, they would still be trying to say the same thing. They would then choose the medium that was suitable for them, or for which they'd been trained in, or which was suitable for that particular idea they wanted to communicate. A lot of artists will have been trained in how to make an installation perhaps more than they will have been trained in how to draw today.

Interviewer But I think a lot of people would think that whereas drawing and painting requires an expertise, which the average person doesn't have, when people look at some installations, they think, 'Well, I could do that'. They don't see that there's any expertise involved at all.

Expert Well, it's just different skills. For example, take Damien Hirst and *Away from the Flock*, which is a sheep in some formaldehyde, in a case. First of all, he had to have the idea, and this was a very original idea, no-one had ever done anything like that before. He came up with the idea of an animal, a sheep, and it's isolated from its flock, and he came up with the idea of preserving this animal in formaldehyde, which is of course something that scientists have done, but artists haven't done. And then he had to research how this animal could be properly preserved in this substance, the formaldehyde, and how in ten or twenty years it would still be there and in good condition for people to look at, so there is a technical side to it as well. And then of course he had to arrange it in a particular way, this animal in a particular pose, so that it looks as if it's quite alive, although of course we all know that it isn't. So it's a combination of an original idea and some very specific skills.

Interviewer And what is he trying to communicate to us through it?

Expert Well, as I said, the sheep looks alive, yet we all know it isn't, and so I think it's a kind of statement about death and life, just as lots of more classical kinds of art, paintings, are about life and death, and it's not really different from those, it's just that it's expressed in a different way. I think the important thing is what it gets the viewers to think about and to reflect on, and that's the same with all art. I mean there isn't really any difference.

Interviewer OK so I can understand that you need a certain amount of technical ability to create the sheep in formaldehyde, but what about the bed? I mean the bed is something that you look at and you think, 'Yeah, that looks like my bed in the morning'.

Expert Well, Tracey Emin's bed isn't actually her bed as it is in the morning when she gets up every day; it is a bed, and there are sheets and pillows, and lots of other objects, but she has assembled these objects to represent her self, this is an autobiographical piece just like a self-portrait, without her face or her body in it, but it still represents her. It's the story of her life, it's her relationship with all the men in her life and other people. You look on the floor and there are lots of bits of her, there are her slippers, her toy dog, and newspapers that she's read, and bottles of water. So it's a story of her life, and it's arranged in a very particular way, it's not random, not just like your bed or my bed, it's a bed that she's very specifically organized to communicate something about herself. I mean it's a different set of skills, from painting a self-portrait, but actually maybe it communicates a whole lot more to us, to viewers, than some self-portraits do, because actually we can look at it and understand, as contemporary viewers, a lot about her life. And incidentally, Tracey Emin is, in fact, very very skilled at drawing, so if she'd wanted to say draw a self-portrait she could have done that. But she chose this way of communicating her message.

5.16 **Interviewer** We have in the studio Dr Linda Blakey, who is helping us sort out the medical facts from all the myths and old wives' tales that are out there. So, first one, Linda, is there any truth in the belief that if you eat a large meal in the evening, you're more likely to put on weight than if you eat the same amount of food earlier in the day?

Doctor Well, there's a clear answer there: if you're watching your weight, what matters is *what* you eat, not *when* you eat it. A calorie at midday is no different from a calorie at midnight, and the idea that your metabolism slows down in the evening is actually a myth. As a matter of fact, there is a medical condition called 'night-eating syndrome', which affects 2% of the population, and people who suffer from this eat very little during the day, but often wake up and eat during the night. These people on average are no more overweight than people who do not suffer from this syndrome.

Interviewer So I can go out for a big meal in the evening and not feel guilty about it?

Doctor Absolutely – as long as you don't have a big lunch as well.

Interviewer Well, that's good. The next one I'd like to ask you about is catching colds. It's always seemed obvious to me that if you stay out in the cold and wind, you're more likely to catch a cold. But I also remember reading somewhere that this was a myth. What's the truth about this one?

Doctor Well, colds, we know, are caused by viruses, which you catch from an infected person, for example, when they cough or sneeze. Now for many years doctors believed that the only reason why it was more common to catch a cold in the winter was because people stayed indoors more, and so they infected each other. But recent research has found that being exposed to cold temperatures does in fact lower our body's defences, so that means that if you get cold, you're more likely to become infected by a cold virus, or to develop a cold if you've already been infected. It's not a myth, it's true.

Interviewer OK. That all makes sense to me. Now something my parents used to tell me was that it was dangerous to have a bath or a shower during a thunderstorm, because I might get electrocuted. I've always thought this was crazy. Is this an old wives' tale?

Doctor In fact, this one is quite true. Between ten and twenty people a year get an electric shock while having a bath or shower during a thunderstorm, and some of these die as a result. This is due to the fact that metal pipes are excellent conductors of electricity, as is tap water. So even though statistically it's not very likely to happen to you, especially if you live in a building with a lightning conductor, it is probably best to avoid showering during a storm.

Interviewer OK, I'll remember that! Now the next one is something I'm always saying to my children: 'Turn the light on. You can't possibly read in that light!' And they always tell me they can read perfectly well. But surely reading in dim light is bad for their eyes?

Doctor Well, this is one that parents around the world have been telling their children for generations, but it actually has very little scientific backing. Reading in the dark or in bad light can cause a temporary strain on the eyes, but it rapidly goes away once you return to bright light.

Interviewer Well, now I know. Now the next one affects me directly. Every summer in the mosquito season, I get really badly bitten, even when I put insect repellent on, but my husband never gets bitten at all. He says that mosquitoes don't like him. Is that possible?

Doctor It is irritating, isn't it? As it happens, it seems to be true. Female mosquitoes, which are the ones that bite, are attracted to the carbon dioxide we exhale, our body heat, and certain chemicals in our sweat. But some lucky people produce chemicals which either prevent mosquitoes from detecting them or which actually drive them away. Unfortunately, I'm not one of those lucky people either, but your husband obviously is.

Interviewer The last thing I would like you to clarify for us is the idea that bottled water is purer than tap water. Now I know it's one thing to drink bottled water if you're travelling in a country where the water hasn't been treated and isn't safe to drink. But what about here in the UK, or in the States?

Doctor We're all a bit suspicious of what comes out of our taps, and that's why sales of bottled water have risen so much over the last decade. But what many people don't realize is that bottled water, so-called mineral water, isn't subjected to the same regular testing that tap water is, and in some tests that were done in the United States, for example, a third of the samples of bottled water analysed were contaminated. In any case a quarter of all bottled water sold is just filtered tap water.

5.22 **Interviewer** Have you ever used alternative medicine?

Speaker A Yes.

Interviewer What did you use?

Speaker A Acupuncture.

Interviewer And did it work?

Speaker A Well, it did actually. I had a terrible time of, I lost my sense of taste and smell…

Interviewer Wow!

Speaker A …which started off with a cold and then I completely lost my sense of taste and smell for about three or four months, and it was very debilitating, and it was really quite frightening.

Interviewer I'm sure.

Speaker A You suddenly realize that there is no point in eating at all because it's just fodder, and all the beauty of life kind of goes, it's an extraordinary thing of not having one of your senses. And somebody recommended to me acupuncture, and I went along and I said, 'Do you think you can do anything about it?' and she said, 'Yes, I think I can.' She said, 'So, here's a rose', which was in her room.

Interviewer Right…

Speaker A.. and she said, 'Put your nose into it and tell me what you can smell.' I put my nose into it and I couldn't smell a thing at all, absolutely nothing at all. And she laid me down and half an hour of needles later, I got up and she said, 'Have a smell of the rose again,' and I put my nose into it and there was this faint, faint odour of rose, which was quite the most beautiful thing I've ever smelt in my entire life.

Interviewer It came straight away then?

Speaker A No, well, over the course of the next two weeks, very, very slowly it came back. I was walking down Old Compton Street and a woman walked past and I went 'Ooh perfume', and I literally turned and followed her, if she'd seen me she would have thought I was rather weird because I was sort of, had my nose into her hair like that, so, and it all came back.

Interviewer Wow!

Speaker B Ever since my children were born, well, even before my children were born, which is a very very long time ago now, we've used alternative medicine, or I like to call it complementary medicine, we use homeopathy. And none of my children ever had an antibiotic when they were growing up, and I think that's quite a good claim, actually. They have used them since they've been adult, for various things because of work and having to get their voices back, but apart from that no antibiotics, and I don't think I've had one in the last thirty-odd years.

Interviewer Kate, have you ever taken alternative medicine?

Speaker C Well, the time I remember was when my second child, childbirth of my second, because my first was a pretty dramatic experience, so I thought I'd go and find out if I could make it easier, so I went to a homeopath who gave me a lot of pills, and said that when contractions started I should take one and then, you know, an hour later take another one, and an hour later take two, but within half an hour, I'd taken all three bottles and was still in agony.

Interviewer No.

Speaker C Yeah.

Interviewer Not having done anything?

Speaker C No.

Interviewer So did you call the person? 'These aren't working!'
Speaker C No, I never did, but I wouldn't recommend homeopathy for childbirth.
Interviewer No, good conclusion.
Interviewer So Adam what's your take on alternative medicine, do you have any experience?
Speaker D One, just one, and I was taking a very long flight from London to Vancouver and I don't like flying, but I don't take anything for that, but when I got there I was only there for a very few days and I wanted to enjoy my waking hours, and the jet lag was crazy so I bought some herbal sleeping pills.
Interviewer Oh, right.
Speaker D So I didn't want to use really heavy, real sleeping pills, I've never used those, so I went to buy some herbal sleeping pills and put them in my bag and then I got there and I look at the package and it says, 'Take eight half an hour before bedtime,' so I thought that was quite a lot, but that's what it said, so I took eight, but it was a bit like having a lot of grass in my mouth, it was like swallowing a lot of grass before bed and then it made me a little windy, so I was like burping up, like a lot of grass and I was burping so I wasn't sleeping, so I wasn't really convinced about them.
Interviewer So a great night's sleep.
Speaker D It was wonderful. A lot of grass.

5.23 **Interviewer** What is it about New York that inspires you?
Patricia I was born here and raised nearby and so I have memories of New York City from my early childhood and to me it was always a magical place. Anything is possible here and everything seems to happen here. As my aunt once said to me, she said, 'People who live in New York even if they've only been here for one year, they feel like they own the place,' and I think that it's because New York is almost more of an event than a place, where everything's changing and becoming something new all the time, and I think that's why it draws creative people and it's very inspiring.
Interviewer Do you always paint in situ or do you sometimes use photos?
Patricia I always paint in situ, almost always. I use sketches and I work a little from memory and from sketches. I touch things up a little in the studio sometimes or finish things. But I like to be in the location because it's always changing and I take pieces of the scene, things that happen at different times, a bird flying by might be very beautiful or a person walking in the street and assuming a certain gesture or pose that's perfect for the composition. Things like that happen over the course of a painting and they can be just perfect. But a photo is very static and kind of flat and it doesn't interest me to work from that.
Interviewer Does that mean you have to work very fast?
Patricia Actually I do, I have learnt to work very fast because there are so many things that change on the street including being blocked by trucks and I do often work very fast, the seasons are constantly changing. People think of the four seasons but really nature changes almost every day, or every day so if I started painting at one point, it's hard to finish it later in a different season or later on in the same season.
Interviewer What techniques do you use?
Patricia I use the traditional technique. I use oil paint and brushes and canvas.
Interviewer How long does it normally take you to finish a painting from start to finish?
Patricia Oh, there, every painting is different, they can take a few hours or a few years. I've worked on some paintings for years and years and sometimes I'll come back to a painting the following year when the season and the different light is right for that painting.
Interviewer As well as the city pictures, you also paint outside New York in the countryside. What similarities and differences are there in painting the city and painting the countryside?
Patricia The city is very geometric and I love, I happen to love geometry, I love angles criss-crossing on the composition and different shapes, geometric shapes but the countryside, when I first started painting it was very difficult for me for that reason, because you don't have the perspective of the streets and the angles of the roofs and so on to lead your eye through the painting. It's, it was wonderful experience to learn how to make your eye move across a grassy field as opposed to down a street where it is so clear and easy kind of, to figure out.
Interviewer So what are the advantages and disadvantages of painting in the country and the city?
Patricia The countryside is a wonderful place for me to paint. I love it because I'm usually alone, pretty much alone there and I'm not distracted by passers-by. In New York City there are just so many distractions with people coming up to me and they're usually well-meaning but it's just an interruption, it's a distraction from my work. And the countryside is so beautiful that I love painting there.
Interviewer Do you ever paint portraits?
Patricia I do occasionally. I love painting portraits, but it's very rare to find someone who will sit for a few hours, for a couple of sessions, and I don't like to do portraits from photos. I've tried it and I don't like the results.

5.24 **Interviewer** What kinds of things have influenced you as an artist?
Patricia I think one of the greatest influences on me was growing up on the banks of the Hudson, which is such a beautiful place in the different light and different times of year. I think that was a main influence on me to want to be a landscape painter. Also there were lots of paintings in the house where I grew up and my parents loved painting very much and also my mother painted some, so I, especially after we all grew up, she painted, so, there were a lot of influences on me.
Interviewer What's your favourite time of day for painting?
Patricia Actually my favourite time of day is sunrise, but I don't always get up in time for that, so early morning and also late afternoon.
Interviewer Do you have a favourite time of year or season?
Patricia Yes, I do actually. I love to paint just before the spring when the air is so crisp and clear, and there aren't yet any leaves on the trees, so that I can really see down the streets, so there's something magical in New York about that time of year, around March and then of course, when spring comes and the blossoms and the trees start to come out, it's just magical, but it lasts a very short time.
Interviewer Are there any other cities that you'd like to go and paint in?
Patricia Oh, there are thousands of cities I'd love to go to paint in, the ancient cities, the older cities, Paris, Amsterdam, Florence, Venice, many places in Sicily, in Greece, I'd love to go to Turkey and paint on the Mediterranean and any place where there's antiquity and where there's water or mountains. But it is hard to travel and paint, it's much better to go to one place and settle in and paint for a while in one place to get to really know the landscape. That's what I prefer to do.
Interviewer What do you think are the pros and cons of an artist's life?
Patricia I think to be an artist usually it requires a lot of sacrifice and I know that sounds like a cliché, but it's true. It requires an enormous amount of time, it requires being free to suddenly change your plans at a moment's notice. For example, being a landscape painter is completely insane, I could be going out the door with one painting under my arm to work on it and the weather could change and I'd be working on a different painting, or I could have plans with someone and suddenly change them, or drop the plans because the weather's right for a particular painting, and that's a real big sacrifice in terms of your social life and also, of course, finances, if, as I do, I tend to put painting before anything else. So I'm not, well, it's hard to earn money and be a dedicated artist at the same time, I think. They contradict one another to some degree.

5.26 **Interviewer** Do you often go to art galleries?
Jason I try to, yeah.
Interviewer What kind of art do you like?
Jason I like a lot of different art. My favourite is probably landscapes. Things involving the ocean.
Interviewer Do you have a favourite painting or poster in your house?
Jason Do I have a favourite? I have a Kandinsky that I'm quite fond of.
Interviewer Can you describe it?
Jason It's hard to describe and I don't even know the name of it, but it's just, it's beautiful and colourful and it's in motion.
Interviewer Do you often go to art galleries?
Jerry No, almost never in fact. Almost never.
Interviewer What kind of art do you like?
Jerry Not, well, not one kind I don't think. I like art which has a sort of emotional effect on me, I suppose. But it could be anything. I mean it's not a particular style, it's more a sort of, what I see in it. If it means something to me, then I think I appreciate it.
Interviewer Do you have a favourite painting or poster in your house?
Jerry Most of the art in my house is actually painted by my father. I've got, I must have 20 or 30 paintings by him. He paints, I take holiday snaps and he sort of improves them and paints them, you know, a photograph of Florence, say, and he'll take out some buildings and invent some replacements, and I, you know, I rather like that. It's almost like a sort of version of holiday photos, but with his personality superimposed, which is quite interesting.
Interviewer Do you often go to art galleries?
Amy I don't go as often as I should actually. A lot of my friends go quite a bit and I never seem to find the time. It might be because I'm outside London. I think if you live in London, you spend more time, or it's more available to you to go to them. So I don't go as much as I should.
Interviewer What kind of art do you like?
Amy I like art that feels very accessible, that you can understand. So portraiture and photography as well. Travel photography I find really interesting.
Interviewer Do you have a favourite painting or poster in your house?
Amy I do actually and it's in my parents' house. It's a painting that my best friend did for our family because she's an artist by profession. And she painted a picture of my mum and I, a photo that we took when I was very young and painted it as if from the point of view of the person taking the picture and it's a really interesting picture and she set it on the cliffs in Cornwall, which is where our family used to spend a lot of time. And it's a really lovely picture that she painted for us as a gift. So, yeah, that's it.
Interviewer Do you often go to art galleries?
Ian Yeah, fairly often, whenever I'm in a new town and there's a good gallery there I'll try and go. Yeah, I'm quite keen.
Interviewer What kind of art do you like?
Ian Generally 20th century and generally not figurative, not representational, a bit abstract I quite like, yeah.
Interviewer Do you have a favourite painting or poster in your house?
Ian Gosh! I have a Rothko poster that I really like, yes.
Interviewer Can you describe it?
Ian It's blocks of colour basically, sort of large blocks of a sort of magenta and grey. Very stark, but I like it, yeah.

6.4 I was in Warsaw in Poland for a week because I had rehearsals and a concert there, but on the Wednesday, Thursday, and Friday of that week I also had to do rehearsals in Berlin. I needed to be able to have the rehearsal in Warsaw in the morning, then fly to Berlin for the rehearsal there in the late afternoon, and then straight back to Warsaw late at night in time for the next morning rehearsal. The only way to get to Berlin and back in time was to fly. So I hired an air taxi. As soon as I left the rehearsal, there was a car waiting to take me to the airport, and when I arrived at the airport my heart sank because the weather was not so good, and the operations manager said, 'Look, I'm terribly sorry. We can't fly at the moment because of the weather.' Finally, the weather cleared and they said we could fly, so I was still hoping to make it in time for my rehearsal. However, we got into the plane and I didn't have a very good impression of it: it looked a bit old, and there was a little hole where the air was coming through where the door had been shut on my side.

6.5 I thought, 'Well, never mind,' and I put on my seat belt and finally we took off.
The weather was not good, and after about five or ten minutes I was terribly cold and I thought, well, I know it can be cold – and it was also very noisy – normally they give you headphones but for some reason they didn't, so the noise was very loud and it got very very cold, and then to my horror I realized that the co-pilot's door wasn't shut properly! By this point the co-pilot himself had realized that the door wasn't shut, so he turned to me and said 'Problema' and then he started gesticulating to the pilot, who was already having difficulties because the weather was very bad and it was raining very hard and there was a bit of a storm. I was feeling extremely uncomfortable by now, wishing that I was on the ground, but then came the real drama because the pilot was trying to indicate to the co-pilot how to shut the door properly. Now what do you do if you're driving a car and you realize that you haven't shut the door properly? You usually stop, open the door again and then shut it with a bang or sometimes you don't even stop, you just while you're driving slowly, you do that. Anyway, this idiotic co-pilot, he proceeded to do precisely that. He then opened the door completely, in order to shut it properly, and I was just behind them, as this is a small plane, so right in front of me was just open air, this open door – I was absolutely terrified, cold air rushing in, and then he tried to shut it properly, but presumably because of the pressure or the cold I don't know what, he couldn't do so, and had he not had his seat belt on he would have fallen out of the plane, so he was holding on, partly for dear life, partly to try and shut it, unsuccessfully. The pilot was shouting at him but he couldn't correct the situation because, you know, he had to keep the plane in the air which was now extremely precarious and the plane was going up and down.

6.6 Then suddenly I felt that we were going right down and I prayed that we were going to land. To my relief we landed in one piece, so at least my life was no longer in danger, but as far as the rehearsal was concerned, I realized with horror that because of this emergency in the air the pilot had had to land at the nearest town, which was still quite a long way from Berlin. I had to phone the rehearsal people to say I was going to be late and I was feeling thoroughly miserable. However, we eventually took off and arrived in Berlin and I did my rehearsal, and fortunately it had been the type of rehearsal where my lateness had not caused a real problem. Then on the way back, the pilots were waiting for me at the airport – this was now about ten o'clock at night or 9.30. So this time we took off, and I said, 'Are you quite sure the door is properly shut? Quite sure?' and they said, 'Yes, yes,' and I said 'We're very late now, I want you to get back to Warsaw as fast as possible,' and they said 'Yes, the wind is in our favour, this aircraft can go very fast. We should be back soon in Warsaw, don't worry, everything will go fine,' so we took off, and things were, well, nothing was going particularly wrong, but I noticed that they were going rather slowly, but it was still so noisy that I couldn't communicate with them and ask, 'Why are you going so slowly?' Eventually when we landed I said 'Why were you going so slowly? I told you to go as fast as possible,' and the pilot said, 'I'm terribly sorry, I didn't know this plane very well and we were having a fuel problem, so we were running out of fuel.' So on the way there I'd nearly fallen to the ground through an open door and now we'd been in danger of falling to the ground because of lack of fuel.

6.8 And finally wolves or dogs? Which is more dangerous to mountain walkers?

Jean-Luc Renaud was on a mountain-walking holiday in the French Alps when he saw a bloodstained man staggering towards him. The man's shorts were torn, he had been bitten badly in both buttocks, and he was in a state of complete shock.

The man, who was a tourist from Belgium, had been attacked by a notoriously ferocious breed of mountain dog, Le Chien de Montagne des Pyrénées or the Pyrenean Mountain dog. This breed is white and fluffy and looks like a cuddly family pet – but it is anything but. Fearless and ferocious, it can weigh up to 60kg and will fight to the death against wolves and bears to save a flock of sheep. So why are there so many of these dogs around? They've been brought into the French Alps to defend sheep from wolves. Wolves were reintroduced into the Alps in 1992 and there are now about 150 of them. They're protected by European Union law, but Alpine farmers say that they've killed thousands of sheep and are a threat to their livelihoods.

In an attempt to pacify the farmers, the EU has spent millions of euros on fences and sheep dogs. The plan appeared to be working. The arrival of about 1,000 Pyrenean Mountain dogs in the Alps coincided with a sharp fall in the number of sheep deaths.

But it has also brought about an alarming rise in attacks on holidaymakers by these dogs. The attacks are driving tourists away and are further splitting the community, who were already divided over the reintroduction of the wolf in France. To add to the controversy, several shepherds have been taken to court by holidaymakers who have been attacked, and 17 dogs have been poisoned in the Maurienne region of the Alps.

6.9 **Presenter** And to finish the local news for London today, what's your view on foxes? Are they pests or should they be a protected species? There are now approximately 10,000 foxes living in London parks, squares, and gardens, and in Hampstead in North London, their barking is keeping the residents awake at night. Carol Martin is one such sufferer. What happened to you last week, Carol?
Carol Well, I came down in the morning after *another* bad night's sleep and I saw a large fox on my lawn, which didn't look very well at all – it had bits of fur hanging off it. I was worried that it might have some infectious disease, so I phoned the local council.
Presenter And what did they say?
Carol Well, first I asked for pest control, and they said, 'What pest?' And I said, 'A fox,' but the woman from the council told me that foxes aren't pests, and she put me through to the 'fox project' department.
Presenter 'The fox project department'? So then what happened?
Carol Well, the man from the fox project asked me to find out if the fox was really ill, and he said that once they knew what was wrong with it, they could supply me with some medicine. So I said that, first of all I didn't speak fox language, and secondly I had no intention of going anywhere near it. I said that I would like the fox dead and the only medicine I was interested in was poison.
Presenter I see – and how did they respond to that?
Carol Well, the fox project man got a bit annoyed, and told me that this was not a caring attitude at all, and he suggested that it might be best to send an ambulance to take the animal to a vet or, if it wasn't seriously ill, to take it to the country and release it back into the wild.
Presenter That's what the man from the council suggested?
Carol Those were his very words. At this point I couldn't believe what I was hearing. Luckily, when I looked out of the window again, the fox had disappeared, so I hung up. It does seem absolutely ridiculous to me. Camden Council have problems getting ambulances to sick people, because of staff shortages, but they *are* able to provide ambulances to take sick foxes to the vet.
Presenter Well, thank you Carol. Incredible! So, does anyone else have a story about foxes in London? Do give us a ring on…

6.11

Interviewer Why did you decide to come to Spain?
Renata Well, it's a bit complicated. It was a bit of a fluke really. In fact, it was my husband who first came up with the idea of moving here. He's from Peru, and when I met him he was studying catering in Poland, in Poznan where I live, and he could sort of speak a bit of Polish, but not very well. So it would have been very difficult for him to get a job in Poland. Not to mention the paperwork, which would have been very complicated too. At that time, when we got married I mean, I'd just finished university, where I'd studied Spanish, and I'd got a job teaching Spanish in a school. So we thought about what we were going to do because if we'd stayed in Poland, I would have to be the one that worked. So as I spoke Spanish, and of course he did too, we decided to try living in Spain.
Interviewer When was this?
Renata About four years ago. We came with nothing, with just a bit of money and two suitcases – and that was it. But bit by bit, we managed to find jobs and somewhere to live. We were very lucky, the guy who rented us our first flat was a chef and he gave my husband a job, and I managed to get a job teaching Spanish to Polish immigrants here.
Interviewer What's the plus side for you about living in Spain?
Renata What I like best is that if you're prepared to work hard, you can get what you want, you can get a good standard of living quite easily. Then the weather is nice, it's not as cold as in Poland – though actually I really miss the snow. Here in Valencia it never snows. Another good thing here is that you have the sea and mountains quite close by, which we didn't have in Poznan.
Interviewer What about the downside?
Renata The traffic. I absolutely hate driving here, nobody obeys the traffic rules, they drive really crazily. And what else? The food is different, but it's OK. My husband would say the noise, the people here are so noisy. In Peru people aren't nearly as noisy– they live in their houses – if you want to see someone, you go to their house – they're not in the street all the time like they are here. I agree with him. And I think people gossip a lot here too. They're always talking about what everyone else is doing, and I don't like that.
Interviewer There must be things you miss about Poland.
Renata Of course – loads of things! The food! My family and my friends. The little corners of my town that I love, my favourite cafés and cinemas. That's what I miss most.
Interviewer Might you go back to Poland one day?
Renata I personally would love to go back, but I'm not sure if we ever will. It would be very difficult, especially for my husband. But you never know – or maybe we'll end up in Peru!

6.12 I've been living in Milan for just over 15 years now. The reason why I first came here was because I'd always wanted to go and live abroad. I'd always had this picture in my mind of me having aperitifs at a café on some exotic seafront promenade in the South of France or somewhere like that, although I must admit I never imagined staying abroad for so long. Even when I married my Italian girlfriend, I always thought we'd eventually go back to the UK. You see, what I like best about living here is that in some way I'm still 'living the dream'. Even though I have a demanding job with a multinational company, and a young child, both of which have their own stresses, somewhere in my brain there's a little voice that reminds me that I'm living abroad as I always wanted to be. Something which I think is very true is what another Brit said to me some time ago – he said, 'Despite everything, it's almost as if you were still on holiday'. And although Milan isn't half as exotic as people might imagine – I mean it's a bit grey and industrial, it's a bit like Manchester in that way – the food is a million times better, and you're only 40 kilometres of motorway away from the Alps, and about 130 from the Mediterranean. The problems I have here are mainly to do with the bureaucracy, which can be incredibly frustrating. For instance the other day, the doctor told me I needed a chest X-ray and just to *book* the appointment involved me queuing in two different places for an hour and a half! The practicalities of life can be frustrating too. Socially, Italy has changed enormously in the last 15 years, but the state hasn't realized it yet. Most Italian women work these days, but nursery schools are still only open from 8.30 in the morning till about 4.00 in the afternoon. So who goes to pick your child up when both parents work full-time? The things I miss most about the UK are the countryside, and the BBC – I find the Italian news too politically biased. But I can't really see myself going back. I'm a foreigner here, but I think I'm also a foreigner in the UK now too. When I go back to the UK, and that's maybe twice a year, and watch the TV, I understand the language, but the words or constructions are not what I would say. It isn't just language, though; it's the way of life. The UK has changed a lot and I can't say that I like it. It seems a much more violent place than it used to be, and it seems too, well it's too politically correct. For example, on the news I notice they never say 'actress' now for women because it's supposed to be sexist – they say 'actor' for both men and women. I think it's all getting a bit out of hand. Italy still hasn't gone too far down that road, thank goodness!

6.16 **Interviewer** What made you decide to become a vet?

Peter I was always interested in animals and originally when I was at school, I was hoping to become a zoologist. I wanted to study animals and their behaviour. And because my father was working at a university at the time, I said to him, 'Do you know anybody there that I can go and talk to in the zoology department?' and he arranged for me to meet the Professor of Zoology, and I went to the university and he said to me, 'Do you want to teach?' and I said, 'No, I don't think I do.' He said, 'Well, 80% of the people who do the zoology course teach. Have you ever thought of being a vet?' And I thought that's a rather good idea.

Interviewer Do you prefer treating farm animals or pets?

Peter Personally I'm, I do probably a little bit more with the farm work but I don't mind, I like treating them all. I like being involved with them all. And I'm in general practice, so I don't have a specialization in one particular species or one particular discipline within that.

Interviewer So why do you tend to prefer farm animals?

Peter I quite like meeting the people on the farm, I'm living in the countryside, where we are today, in this surgery right in a little village in the countryside on the border of England and Wales and if you look around and look out there, you'd understand why it's nice to be able to go round and drive round a bit of that country and see the animals there.

Interviewer What's the most difficult animal to treat?

Peter It's surprising what people turn up with in the surgery. So some time, most of the animals that we would see belong to a certain group, say dogs, cats, maybe rabbits, guinea pigs, hamsters, ferrets. But now we're starting to see cameloids. That is llamas – certainly we've got llamas locally – and other members of that same group. Those suddenly present a challenge because you're looking at an animal that you haven't really dealt with and is different because every species is different. Even within a species, we sometimes have variations between breeds. So the most difficult is really just one that you're not used to and you suddenly find yourself thinking, 'What are the peculiarities, what's the anatomy, what's the anatomical variation, how will particular medicines react, what is the dosage?' And you sincerely hope that either you've got a book or there's something somewhere or somebody you can ring up and find out. But I can assure you that when somebody brought a tarantula spider in one day, I did have a moment there where I thought to myself, 'Now what are we going to do with that?' It's the dreaded cardboard box. Somebody comes in with a little cardboard box and they put it down very proudly on the table and you're waiting in expectation and then they open it up and you look at it and go, 'Ah, very interesting. Now what is that?'

Interviewer What do you think is the most intelligent animal of all the ones you treat?

Peter I suppose when we're dealing with intelligence it's a question that you can have intelligent animals within a particular species. So I've met some extremely intelligent dogs, particularly collies, working collies. They are amazing, how they get the sheep in, how they sort them out or work with the cattle. Marvellous! People always say pigs are very intelligent and I had a professor at college who always maintained that why do we keep dogs and cats; we should keep pigs as pets. He reckoned they were very clean and they were wonderful animals to have as a pet – highly intelligent.

Interviewer What's the best and worst thing about your job?

Peter I think the best is always birth. It doesn't matter what species, birth is brilliant, amazing every time it happens, one marvels at it, whatever the species. I suppose the worst is always having to put an animal down, put it to sleep.

6.17 **Interviewer** How do you feel about animals being used in experiments?

Peter Well, the whole principle of using animals in experiments has been reviewed certainly in this country very, very strongly. And the principle has been to try to reduce the number of animals used. Now, unfortunately, there seems to be no other way of achieving always the result that we require in testing a particular substance. I do find myself a little bit uncomfortable with the wish that there is to test substances other than medicines. When we start to get testing cosmetics and things that are somewhat ephemeral in the needs of the human population, I'm not sure that's a good use of animals.

Interviewer How do you feel about people having large dangerous dogs as pets?

Peter All dogs can be dangerous. If you look at where deaths have occurred in babies and small children, it's surprising, sometimes it's been very small dogs that have been involved. It hasn't always been the big dogs. Unfortunately, it's not really the dog's problem and fault, it's usually the owner's problem and fault. And so if the owner can't restrain, keep control, have a proper care of that animal, then any dog can become more dangerous. And the principle of leaving children with dogs is one that should not on any occasion occur, no matter how good anybody believes a particular dog is. Dogs can be dangerous.

Interviewer Are there any animals or insects that you are afraid of?

Peter I suppose that 'afraid' is one word, 'being extremely cautious of', is another. I've been attacked by cows, not uncommonly unfortunately over the years, picked up and thrown across the room and so on. Now everybody thinks cows are rather nice creatures and so on but when they've got a calf at foot, they are very protective and they can be extremely dangerous. A sow with its piglets will be very dangerous and possibly one of the most dangerous species that we deal with. I've treated tigers, I've treated chimpanzees, and in their own right those are extremely dangerous, so I think it's a question of assessing the animal, the risk, and taking the suitable precautions because sometimes it's the small ones that bite you when you're not thinking about it rather than the big one that you are watching and thinking was going to be dangerous.

Interviewer Do you have pets yourself?

Peter Yes, over the years we've had various animals. At the moment we've got a dog, 40 sheep, a couple of ponies, and a snake. And it sits in its, in its vivarium on the landing at home, and it's my son's snake and I think he uses it purposely to terrify some of the young ladies who visit and others, and my daughter's boyfriend, is not at all keen on it and walks round the landing to try and avoid it.

Interviewer Has it ever escaped?

Peter On one occasion it did escape briefly, but was rapidly recaptured I hasten to add.

Interviewer Would you recommend becoming a vet?

Peter Yes, I think that it's been a good life. I certainly have enjoyed it. It's meant it's very challenging, very demanding. You never stop learning and, in fact, you can't stop learning because medicine – whether it be veterinary medicine or human medicine – the changes are immense over the years. So you're constantly having to be kept up to date by reading, attending lectures, talking to colleagues, and also by your clients. Because these days with the Internet, they very often will come in with a whole sheaf of papers and say, 'We think our dog has got so and so. Here you are Mr Vet, look at all this information.' And you then sort of go, 'Thank you very much,' and put it gently to one side and have a look at the animal and decide that this extraordinary disease that they've just found on the Internet doesn't have any relation to what's in front of you. But that's one of the challenges of today.

6.19 **Interviewer** Are there any animals or insects that you are afraid of or feel uncomfortable with?

Priti Mosquitoes, just they bite me a lot and I'm really really allergic to their bites.

Interviewer Have you ever had a frightening experience involving an animal?

Priti There was one time in India on a tiger safari and we were in an open 4x4 going down this steep hill when we came across a tiger in the middle of the path coming up towards us so we had to try and reverse up whilst this tiger was stalking towards us. That was pretty scary.

Interviewer Are there any animals or insects that you are afraid of or feel uncomfortable with?

Sheila Snakes. I hate them.

Interviewer Have you always felt like this?

Sheila Yes, I've seen a few snakes in the wild and really don't like them. I have had a boa constrictor put around my neck, but I didn't like it very much.

Interviewer Have you ever had a frightening experience involving an animal?

Sheila A few! The elephant was probably the most frightening. I was on safari with my husband and we were having lunch in the camp and he said, 'Oh, I'm just going to pop up to the office', there's a little office in a hut, because they can charge your batteries at certain times of the day. So he said, 'I'll just pop up and get my battery for the camera,' and off he went. Five minutes later he came running back into the lunch area and said, 'There's an elephant out there. Come on, come and have a look!' So the guy in the restaurant said, 'Just be careful, don't get too close,' but he didn't say what he meant by 'don't get too close' so out we went, and we walked around the corner and we looked up the pathway and there was a massive elephant. And it saw us and it just came charging towards us. Thank God, behind us the waiter had come out and we were just about to turn and run, because the elephant was very very close, probably about 10, 15 feet away. We were just about to run and the waiter said, 'Whatever you do, don't run!' So we just stood our ground and the elephant swung its trunk a bit and then walked away. But my heart was beating so fast. It was really quite frightening.

Interviewer Are there any animals or insects that you are afraid of or feel uncomfortable with?

Jerry I'm afraid of spiders, I must confess. I mean above a certain size I'm afraid of them. Small ones I can cope with, larger ones I don't like very much. Even pictures of spiders in a book, you know, or a magazine. If I turn a page and see a picture of a spider, I kind of, a little shudder of fear passes through me.

Interviewer Have you always felt like this?

Jerry Yeah. Yeah, I mean it's getting better but when I was a child it was really quite bad. You know, I'd run screaming from the room. I don't do that any more.

Interviewer Have you ever had a frightening experience involving an animal?

Jerry I've had an encounter with a bear in a national park in California, where I was having, camping with a friend and we were eating dinner round a campfire and he looked over my shoulder and said, 'Jerry, there's a bear behind you,' and it was standing up on its hind legs about ten feet away so we had to withdraw and it ate our dinner and then walked off. So there was no damage done, but it was quite frightening.

7.4 **Speaker 1** Just after I left drama school, I was cooking supper for my boyfriend and another bloke who we were working with in the theatre, and I was going to do spaghetti bolognese and I wanted some green peppers. And I didn't realize then that there was a difference between green peppers and green chilli peppers and so I cooked the spaghetti bolognese and I couldn't quite understand why my, underneath my nails was burning so terribly, but I just kept washing my hands and ignored it. And then we sat down to eat and Jeff, the friend who'd come, took one mouthful of the spaghetti bolognese before either of us did and fell off his chair onto the floor. And I'm afraid the whole lot had to go into the bin, it was the most horrendous experience.

Interviewer Have you had any awful, memorable disasters in the kitchen?

Speaker 2 One particular one when I'd just bought a new oven, and I'd invited some friends round and I was going to cook a piece of roast meat, and I put it in my new oven, and turned it on and left it for an hour to cook. And when I opened the oven door, I realized that I'd put the grill on, not the oven, so that the top of the meat was completely charred, and underneath it was completely raw, so the meal was completely ruined. So I had to send out for a takeaway.

Interviewer Ah, that's a shame.

Interviewer Katie, have you had a bad cooking experience?

Speaker 3 Well, it didn't really involve cooking as such, but it was certainly a bad, preparing food experience. My family, we went to Italy, and everybody in my family enjoyed the antipasti, the bruschetta, so I thought when I came home that I would re-invent this, it is very simple, basically it's little bits of bread with lovely tomato sauce on top and garlic. And I'd asked an Italian waiter and my Italian isn't very good, so I thought that I'd interpreted well what he'd said. However, you're supposed to rub the garlic on the bread, the sort of slightly toasted bread, just a little on one side, However, I went mad and was rubbing for a minute on both sides of the bread, and I put the tomato sauce on and handed it to my family, and they all spat it out, it was inedible.

Interviewer So did you, did you recycle it or did you throw it away?

Speaker 3 I think we threw it away.

7.6 **Interviewer** There's a deeply held belief that sport teaches us valuable lessons about life and ultimately makes us better people. In your view, is there any justification for that?

Mike Some, it can do. Sport involves, well, there are two types of sport, there's team sport and individual sport, but team sport most clearly involves both competition and cooperation and the advantages of cooperation, you can't do it well without the support of other people. The football striker can't score goals if he doesn't get passes. And the whole team relies on each other, and part of building up a good team is building up a good sense of cooperation. Now, secondly, in individual sport as well as team sport, there are all sorts of individual qualities that you have to have to be good at sport, you have to have guts, you have to have persistence, you have to overcome difficulties, loss, bad form, injury, you have to overcome or deal with your fear of success and your fear of failure. So there's a terrific number of qualities there, that people in general would respect and would like to develop in themselves. And sport, it seems to me does develop them.

Interviewer On balance would you say that sport brings about more happiness or unhappiness in the world?

Mike I saw a picture in *The Observer* some years ago of someone scoring a goal, and the picture was taken so that behind the netting you could see the crowd, and there must have been a hundred faces in this crowd, and every single one of them was totally, intently observing the point where the ball was, which was, I don't know if it was in the picture, I can't remember, and it seems to me that that kind of intensity, of attention and focus is something that the crowd shares with the players, and has a passion for and I would say that, it may not increase happiness, I mean happiness is a very difficult concept anyway, but it certainly increases living one's life, it is a way of living one's life to the full in the moment. And I would say that sport is like a mass form of art, certainly of culture. Sport has its ways of bringing unhappiness too. Some people can become too depressed at losing, or not doing well, or losing their form, some people find it very hard to move on from sport, say they're professionals, into another form of life. But nevertheless, I would say it increases happiness, it increases living in the moment, it increases, it develops a passionate interest which goes beyond success and failure.

Interviewer Do you think there is a sense that sport has replaced religion in modern society?

Mike It can become a religion in a bad sense for people, and it can become, as it were, the thing that gives meaning to life, and if something is the only thing that gives meaning to life I think it's rather disappointing. It can become a religion in the sense of a sort of tribal, partisanship, which the worst forms of religion have. Religion has been the source of many disastrous conflicts but it's also brought out the best in people, and I'd say a similar thing is true of sport.

Interviewer Do you think there is any difference between using new technology to gain an advantage for example hi-tech swimming suits, and doping, I mean taking performance-enhancing drugs?

Mike It seems to me there is a, a radical difference, between say, having a good diet, training better, getting better shoes and, on the one hand and taking performance-enhancing drugs on the other, which seems like a form of cheating, it seems like a form of, well, the word 'artificial', artificial transformation of the body into a different shape or outcome without the necessary work that usually goes into it. If you're going to build muscles, you have to work at it. If you build muscles by steroids, you don't work at it, it's sort of magical and it's, it's something that, it goes against the idea, which is only partially true in sport, but the idea that success is related to hard work, and you don't achieve anything without hard work.

Interviewer We seem to expect athletes to be positive role models in society, is there any reason that we should?

Mike We hope that they're going to be role models on the field of play, that's what they're especially gifted at. Now as to off the field, if they play for England or Manchester United, they are going to be in the public eye, and if they do something that an ordinary person does at the same age, stupid, gets drunk, is late out at a night club, is found to be gambling, you know those kinds of things, the focus on him's going to be much higher than it is on most people. And that's something that they have to learn to accept. They get the benefits of being celebrities but there are disadvantages too. And it seems to me that it is hard to expect them to be much better than the rest of us, but we do and they have to know that they're going to pay a heavier price if they're caught out. So I think it's part of the coach's job, or the senior players' job, to warn people, to guide people, to encourage them, but you, again you can't expect, it's wrong to expect too much.

Interviewer I've noticed this morning that the results of last night's football match are all over the front pages of the newspapers as well as the back pages. Does that suggest that we may have lost a sense of proportion when it comes to sport?

Mike You have to think that sport actually, whether you like it or not, matters a very great deal to a lot of people today and it gets a great deal of publicity and it's a talking point for many, many people. People will be talking about that match at work today, the Manchester United versus Barcelona match, they'll be fed up about it, they'll be critical, they'll be disappointed, they'll have their theories, they'll have arguments about it, it will be a talking point of a major kind. Now if you have something that's a talking point of a major kind, you're going to get extreme coverage of it, and if you get extreme coverage of it, you're going to have more of a talking point, so it's a kind of circle that goes round and round. And in a way, it's crazy, in another way it's inevitable, and if people are so passionately involved, then it's reflected by the newspapers.

7.10 **Interviewer** What was the purpose of Professor Wiseman's research? Was it simply to find the funniest joke?

Journalist No, it was much more than that. He wanted to take what he calls 'a scientific look' at what makes us laugh and this included finding answers to questions like 'Do people from different countries find the same things funny?' or 'Do men and women laugh at different types of jokes?'

Interviewer And could you tell us something about the results of his research?

Journalist Well, the first thing that came out clearly was that the jokes which people generally found the funniest had one thing in common – they create a sense of superiority in the person hearing or reading the joke, usually because the person in the joke appears to be stupid. This is clearly illustrated in the Sherlock Holmes joke, where Watson is the one who is shown to be stupid. Generally speaking, the more superior a joke makes us feel, the more we laugh. And it seems that we especially enjoy jokes where people in authority are made to look stupid, which is why there are so many jokes all over the world about policemen.

Interviewer And is there an explanation for this?

Journalist Yes, there is. According to Professor Wiseman, telling this kind of joke is simply our way of getting our own back on people in authority, people who have power over us in our daily lives.

Interviewer What about the jokes people tell about other nationalities being stupid?

Journalist Well, again this is the superiority theory in action. The English traditionally tell jokes about the Irish, the Mexicans make fun of the Americans, the French laugh at the Belgians, etc., etc., and in each case, it's a question of one group of people trying to make themselves feel good at the expense of another, by laughing about how stupid they are.

Interviewer I think it was Sigmund Freud who said that we laugh at things which are subconsciously making us feel anxious. Is this true?

Journalist Well, Professor Wiseman's research definitely supported this theory. For example, older people tend to find jokes about the problems of getting old much funnier than young people do. Everybody worries to a greater or lesser extent about getting an incurable illness, which is why we laugh at the joke about the man who has an incurable disease, which of course in reality is not a laughing matter. And for the same reason there are many many jokes about loveless marriages, family problems, and even death.

Interviewer Why do we find wordplay funny?

Journalist Professor Wiseman's research found that wordplay was enjoyed by many nationalities. The joke about the 'cereal killer' is an example of the most basic kind of joke, what we call 'a pun', where we play with words which have different meanings, or different words which are pronounced the same. It seems that we find puns funny because the first line of the joke usually sets up a situation; then the second line (the 'punchline') at first seems strange, but then suddenly we get the joke, we understand it, and this feeling of surprise makes us laugh. Surprise is a very important element in humour.

Interviewer Do men and women laugh at the same things?

Journalist Apparently not. Generally speaking, women find jokes with wordplay more amusing, whereas men often prefer jokes which involve some element of aggression or sex. Perhaps not surprisingly, women find jokes about men being stupid far funnier than jokes about women being stupid. And of course the opposite is true. So for example a woman will probably find the joke about the man doing the jigsaw funnier than the man does. That's the superiority theory in action again.

Interviewer Do different nationalities find the same kind of jokes funny?

Journalist Well, the answer it seems is no. Professor Wiseman's research found clear differences between different countries and cultures as to what they found amusing. For example, people from Britain, Ireland, and Australia enjoyed jokes based on wordplay. Whereas Americans and Canadians preferred jokes where there was a strong sense of superiority – either because a character looks stupid, or is made to look stupid by someone else. And many European countries preferred jokes which were more surreal.

7.11 Interviewer So which joke *was* voted the funniest?

Journalist Well, in second place was the joke about Sherlock Holmes and the tent. But in first place was the joke about the two hunters. This joke won because it was universal – it appealed to people in many countries, to men and women, and young and old people alike. And it also combined the classic three elements of humour – it makes us feel superior, it makes us laugh at an anxiety-provoking situation – an accident and death, and it has a strong element of surprise.

Interviewer Who submitted the winning joke?

Journalist It was sent in by a British psychiatrist from Manchester. Apparently, he told Professor Wiseman that he sometimes tells it to his patients to make them feel better 'because it reminds them that there's always someone who is doing something more stupid than they are'.

Interviewer And did Professor Wiseman think that he really had found the world's funniest joke?

Journalist No, he didn't. According to him, the funniest joke in the world doesn't exist. In the conclusion to his research, he said, 'If our research into humour tells us anything, it's that different people find different things funny. Women laugh at jokes in which men look stupid; the elderly laugh at jokes about memory loss or hearing difficulties; people who don't have power laugh at those who are in power. There is no *one* joke that will make everyone laugh.'

7.14 Interviewer Who taught you to cook?

Chantelle It would probably be my parents when I was younger. It was more, it was always something that I was interested in from an early age and I used to be in the kitchen quite a lot.

Interviewer How did you end up as a chef in London?

Chantelle One kind of afternoon when I was reading the, a foodie magazine in New Zealand, and it mentioned the Gordon Ramsay scholarship and we had to submit a menu kind of a three-course menu and talk about the food, talk about what you'd done, so I thought, 'Well, why not give that a go?' So I submitted an entry and then got a phone call kind of six weeks later saying I'd got into the semi final, which was basically 12 people, 11 of them all chefs, so I kind of felt a bit like a fish out of water, but you know, whilst I was there I met Josh Emmet, who was the head chef at the Savoy Grill, which was run by Marcus, and at the end of it he said 'Well, you know, there's a job at the Savoy Grill if you want one,' and it was just too good an opportunity to turn down, um, so it all kind of happened relatively quickly because I thought well, I can't turn this opportunity down. I was kind of at a point in my career where I was looking for another job anyway. So I just thought, 'Well, I'll do it.'

Interviewer Top chefs have a reputation of being difficult. What's Marcus Wareing like to work for?

Chantelle He is very, he's quite, I mean I wouldn't want to work for any other chef of that high calibre really. He's a very, he's a person that's very, he's got a real eye for detail and a perfectionist. But he's also got a very good business sense, which is a great thing to learn from as well, because he oversees the whole operation. So in that sense he's a great kind of mentor, I guess. I mean if he gets upset with people, it's because of what's going on on the plate or in the restaurant. There's no kind of, there's no ego there at all, it's all about what goes out on the plate and what happens, and how the guests are treated, he's very much a person that people, when people come to the restaurant he wants them to have an amazing experience, no matter if they're kind of buying a £30 bottle of wine or £3,000 bottle of wine,

Interviewer Is this restaurant into the new tendencies in cooking, using science in the kitchen and things like that?

Chantelle We are more, not traditional but we use traditional techniques, classic techniques. We, I

guess in a sense, we're more about, Marcus, Marcus is a person that's very respectful of ingredients and basically treats, you know, will treat a carrot the same way as a piece of foie gras in the sense they're both great things that need to be looked after and treated in the right way to get the maximum kind of flavour out of them and I guess we're more about making a carrot taste like a carrot as opposed to making a carrot taste like a beetroot, which, in a sense, I think some people get a little carried away with.

7.15 Interviewer You are the sous-chef here. Can you tell us what exactly is the difference between a chef and a sous-chef?

Chantelle Basically a sous-chef is, it basically translates to a second chef, so you have the head chef and then you have the sous-chefs under the head chef, so they run the kitchen in the head chef's absence.

Interviewer How many hours do you work?

Chantelle We, they are long days for most people. I mean, we start at about 7.00 in the morning and we normally finish, kind of, between 12.00 and 1.00 in the morning, so it's a long day, but in a sense it's something that you get used to the more you do it.

Interviewer Does it get very stressful in the kitchen?

Chantelle It can do. The biggest thing is organization. It can be, it makes a big difference, kind of the way diners come in as well, if they all come in at once then it does get a bit, because you, you're always conscious of the fact that you don't want to keep people waiting too long but you don't want to, in the other sense just push out the food because they're here for the experience. So it can get stressful in some situations and when, if you cook something and something, and it's not right and you can't serve it, the time it takes to kind of begin the whole process again, a) for those, the guests that have ordered that particular dish, they have to wait a long time, but also it creates a backlog in a sense, so it can get stressful but again it's something that's managed and if you're organized and kind of a bit forward-thinking and always one step ahead then it becomes, it minimizes the stress completely.

Interviewer And presumably the long hours don't help?

Chantelle Again the hours don't, don't help the stress because obviously the more tired people are, then the more stressed they can get. But in a sense the people that work here are quite, very focused, very, very passionate about what they do, you kind of have to be to be able to put in the time that we all put in. So the stress is, I think it's something that can be managed.

Interviewer Do you cook at home, if so what kind of food?

Chantelle Ah, not much, I don't cook at home much, a) because I'm not really there a huge amount and b) when you have what we have here to go to a kind of small, small kitchen it's a bit, I find it a bit difficult, in a sense because you're used to having such great equipment and kind of ovens, and everything around you and then you go back to a little flat and kind of trying to do it it's just not quite the same. But when I have time off if I'm on holiday or something like that, I of course enjoy kind of going to a market or even a supermarket and getting kind of local ingredients and doing it that way.

Interviewer What would you have as your last meal on earth?

Chantelle Wow, it's a big question, probably would start with, something like foie gras, because it is such a kind of delicacy and then a seafood, probably scallops, main course would probably be some beef, a rib of beef with some beautiful vegetables, seasonal vegetables, then I'd definitely have to have cheese, I because I'm a big fan of cheeses, especially the European cheeses, they're just, that's one thing that I really love about the, kind of, the UK and Europe and then probably to finish, probably a pear tarte Tatin.

7.17 Interviewer Do you think in general people from your country are good cooks?

Sheila I think there are some fantastic cooks in the UK, but if we talk about people in general, there are some pretty bad cooks as well. So it's, I think people are getting better. I think people are taking a

lot more interest in cooking, there's a lot of cooking programmes, and we are leading the world in some respects, in being adventurous about our cooking. So people are getting more interested, but still there's a long way to go before we can say, in general people in the UK are good cooks.

Interviewer How healthy do you think the cuisine in your country is?

Sheila There's a balance I think. Again, people are trying to be healthier or are being encouraged to be healthier, but if you go to a restaurant, there'll be a great selection of healthy and non-healthy foods on the menu. But there are also an awful lot of really awful fast food outlets encouraging you to eat junk. So it's a balance and I think the balance tips towards junk food rather than healthy food.

Interviewer What other cuisines do you really like?

Sheila Thai food is my favourite. I also love Italian, but Thai most definitely up at the top there.

Interviewer Why is that?

Sheila Because there are so many different flavours. Even in one dish, you can taste a variety of flavours and it's all very fresh, so Indian food is spicy, but it's made with a lot of dried spices so sometimes it feels very heavy and you can taste the spices afterwards, and you can smell the spices afterwards. But with Thai food, it's very very fresh and zingy and you don't feel full or heavy afterwards, you just feel exhilarated.

Interviewer Do you think in general people from your country are good cooks?

Liz I think so, yeah.

Interviewer How healthy do you think the cuisine in your country is?

Liz In general, not very healthy at all.

Interviewer Why is that?

Liz Because people eat a lot of fast food and it's very processed, and full of fat, and salt, and all that kind of stuff.

Interviewer What other cuisines do you really like?

Liz What other cuisines do I like? I like, well, I'm a vegetarian so I like vegetables and fruit and fresh food, and I like Italian, I like Thai, I like a lot of stuff.

Interviewer What do you like about Thai food?

Liz Thai, I like how spicy it is, I like the curries, and I like, I really like the curried vegetables.

Interviewer Do you think in general people from your country are good cooks?

Naomi Yeah, I think so. New Zealand's had a sort of a food revolution. It used to be very English in its food style. But over recent years, it's taken on a strong Asian feel and it's quite eclectic so I think people in New Zealand do like to cook and experiment with food. And they enjoy food.

Interviewer How healthy do you think the cuisine in your country is?

Naomi I think it's pretty healthy. We are an outdoor country, lots of fruit and vegetables and home-grown things. So, yeah, I think overall it's a pretty healthy place.

Interviewer What other cuisines do you really like?

Naomi I really like Indian, but also all types of curries, so Malaysian, Thai, Indonesian curries. I like the heat and the flavour that you get in those sorts of cuisines.

1A discourse markers (1): linkers

result

> 1 It was freezing cold, **so** I wore a thick coat.
> 2 It snowed hard all night. **As a result** the airport was closed the following morning.
> We regret that you do not have the necessary qualifications, and **therefore / consequently** we are unable to offer you the job.

1 *So* is the most common way of introducing a clause of result.
2 *As a result*, *therefore*, and *consequently* (more formal than *so*) are often used at the beginning of a sentence or clause.
• When the marker is at the beginning of a clause, it is usually preceded by a comma, or comma + *and*.
• *Therefore* and *consequently* can also be used before a main verb,
e.g. *We have therefore / consequently decided not to offer you the job.*

reason

> 1 I have stopped writing to her, **because / as / since** she never answers me.
> 2 The plane was late **because of** the fog.
> Flight 341 has been delayed **due to / owing to** adverse weather conditions.

1 *Because*, *as*, and *since* (more formal) are used to introduce clauses giving a reason and are synonyms. *As* is often used at the beginning of a sentence, e.g. *As the weather is so awful, we've decided not to go out.*
2 *Because of*, *due to*, and *owing to* also express the reason for something. They are usually followed by a noun.
• *Due to* and *owing to* are more formal than *because of*.

purpose

> 1 I did a language course **to / in order to / so as to** improve my English.
> 2 She closed the door quietly **so as not to / in order not to** wake the baby.
> 3 They moved to London **so (that)** they could see their grandchildren more often.
> 4 I'm not going to tell Ann **in case** she tells everyone else.

1 *To*, *in order to* and *so as to* introduce a clause of purpose and are all followed by an infinitive. *So as to* and *in order to* are more formal.
2 For negative purpose use *in order not to* or *so as not to*, NOT ~~She closed the door quietly not to wake the baby.~~
3 You can also use *so (that)* + *can / could* + verb or *will / would* + verb to express purpose. You can leave out *that* in informal speech and writing.
• You must use *so (that)* when there is a change of subject in the result clause, e.g. *She put a rug over the baby so (that) he wouldn't be cold.*
4 Use *in case* + clause when we do something in order to be ready for future situations / problems or to avoid them.

contrast

> 1 We enjoyed the concert, **but** we didn't have very good seats.
> Agnes was attracted to the stranger, **yet** something in her head was telling her not to get close to him.
> We enjoyed the concert. **However**, we didn't have very good seats.
> Agnes was attracted to the stranger. **Nevertheless**, something in her head was telling her not to get close to him.
> 2 We enjoyed the concert **although / even though / though** we didn't have very good seats.
> 3 **In spite of** being attracted to the stranger, something in Agnes's head was telling her not to get close to him.
> **Despite** her attraction to the stranger…
> **Despite the fact that** she was attracted to the stranger…

1 *But* is the most common and informal way of introducing contrast, and is normally used to link two contrasting points within a sentence.
Yet is used in the same way, but is more formal / literary.
However and *nevertheless* are normally used at the beginning of a sentence, to connect it to the previous one. They are usually followed by a comma.
• *Nevertheless* (or *nonetheless*) is more formal / literary than *however*.
2 *Even though* is more emphatic than *although*. *Though* is more common in informal speech.

> ⚠ *Though* can also be used at the end of a phrase as a comment adverb, e.g. *He's very friendly – a bit mean, though.*

3 After *in spite of* and *despite* you must use a gerund, a noun, or *the fact that* + clause.

---

a Circle the right connector in each sentence.

(Even though) / *Despite* she's working really hard, I don't think she'll be able to catch up with the rest of the class.
1 We can't afford to have a holiday this year *as / so* we've got an overdraft at the bank.
2 Could we rearrange my timetable *so that / in case* I don't have so many classes on a Friday afternoon?
3 At the meeting Carla stuck to her guns *due to / in spite of* the fact that everybody was against her.
4 The restaurant chain has had a very difficult year. *Nevertheless / As a result*, they haven't had to close any of their restaurants.
5 He gets a good salary *though / since* the job itself is quite monotonous.

b Circle the correct option according to register.

Sales have decreased over the last three months. *So /* (Therefore) we will not be taking on any new staff.
1 I've been off work for the last three days *because of / owing to* this nasty cough I've got.
2 Jane texted me to say she's going to be a bit late *so / consequently* let's start without her.
3 The company has reported declining sales this year. *Nevertheless / But* they have so far managed to avoid any staff cuts.
4 I stopped at a service station *to / in order to* fill up with petrol.
5 I thought it was an amazing film. It was quite depressing, *though / however*.
6 We sincerely apologize for the delay, which was *due to / because of* the late arrival of the incoming aircraft.

c Combine the two sentences using the **bold** word(s), making any necessary changes.

We always switch off the TV at night. We don't want to waste electricity. **so as**
We always switch off the TV at night so as not to waste electricity.

1 Our seats were a long way from the stage. We enjoyed the play. **In spite**
2 We took ages to get there. The traffic was heavy. **because of**
3 I took the price off the bag. I didn't want her to know how much it had cost. **so that**
4 Keep the receipt for the sweater. Your dad might not like it. **in case**
5 Susanna is an only child. She isn't at all spoilt. **Even though**
6 Prices have increased because production costs have risen. **due to**

have

> 1 They **have** a large, rather dilapidated country house in Norfolk.
> 2 He **doesn't have** lunch at home. **Are** you **having** lunch?
> 3 They**'ve been** married for 15 years.
>   How long **has** Anna **been going out** with James?
> 4 **Do we** really **have to** spend Christmas with your parents again?
> 5 We're going to **have** the kitchen **repainted** next week.
>   I **had** my eyes **tested** when I got my new glasses.

1 Use *have* as a **main verb** for possession.
   Have with this meaning is a stative (non-action) verb and is not used in continuous tenses. Use auxiliaries *do / did* to make questions and negatives.
2 Use *have* + object as a **main verb** for actions, e.g. *have a bath, a drink, a chat*, etc.
   Have with this meaning is a dynamic (action) verb and can be used in continuous tenses.
3 Use *have* as the **auxiliary verb** to form the present perfect simple and continuous. Make questions by inverting *have* and the subject, and negatives with *haven't / hasn't*.
• We also use *have* for other perfect forms, e.g. the future perfect, the perfect infinitive, etc.
4 Use *have to* to express obligation, especially obligation imposed by others, and rules and regulations. *Have to* is a **main verb**.
5 Use *have* + object + past participle to say that you ask or pay another person to do something for you.
• *Have* here is a **main verb**, not an auxiliary verb, e.g. *Where do you have your hair cut?*

have got

> 1 How many children **have you got**? **I've got** three, two boys and a girl.
> 2 **I've got to** go now – I'm meeting my girlfriend for lunch.

1 You can also use *have got* for possession. The meaning is exactly the same as *have*.
• *Have* here is an **auxiliary verb** so make questions by inverting *have* and the subject and negatives with *haven't / hasn't*.
• *Have got* has a present meaning. We use *had* for the past, NOT ~~had got~~.
• *Have got* is very common in informal spoken and written English.
2 Use *have got to* to express obligation, especially in informal spoken and written English.
• *Have got to* is normally used for a specific obligation rather than a general or repeated obligation. Compare:
   I've got to make a quick phone call (specific) and *I have to wear a suit to work* (general).

See **5A permission, obligation, and necessity** on page 148 for more information on *have to* and *have got to*.

---

a Right (✓) or wrong (✗)? Correct the mistakes in the highlighted phrases.

> **A** You look exhausted.
> **B** Yes, I've been having meetings all day with the marketing people. ✓

1 Are you going to have your nails done when you go to the hairdresser's?
2 **A** Why don't you want to come?
   B I haven't got any money.
3 Has your husband to work tomorrow or is he taking the day off too?
4 The staff don't have to dress formally in this company – they can wear what they like.
5 How long have you been having your flat in London?
6 What time are we having dinner tonight?
7 My parents had got many problems with my sister when she was a teenager.
8 I don't have a holiday for 18 months. I really need a break.
9 Have we got to do this exercise now, or can we do it later for homework?

b Rewrite the sentences using a form of *have* or *have got*.

> I started working for Microsoft in 2001 and I still work there.
> *I've been working for Microsoft since 2001.*

1 She's an only child.
   She _____.

2 We used to pay someone to take a family photograph every year.
   We used _____.

3 Wearing a hard hat is obligatory for all visitors to this site.
   All _____.

4 He last saw his father in 2009.
   He _____.

5 He lacks the right qualifications for this job.
   He _____.

6 It's not necessary for us to do it now. We can do it later.
   We _____.

7 The sea water was amazingly clear and warm – we swam every morning.
   The sea water was amazingly clear and warm – we _____.

8 When did you start to get on badly?
   How long _____ badly?

9 I need someone to fix the central heating. I think the thermostat is broken.
   I need _____
   I think the thermostat is broken.

generic pronouns

1 **You** can learn a language faster if you go to live in a country where it is spoken.
2 **One** should never criticize without being sure of the facts.
3 When **we** talk about an accent, **we** must not confuse this with pronunciation.
4 **They** always say that it's never too late to learn a new language.
   They should make it compulsory for people to learn two foreign languages at school.
5 If someone goes to live in a foreign country, **they** will have to get used to a different way of life.
   Could the person who left **their** bag in the library please come and see me?

1 We often use *you* to mean people in general.
2 We can also use *one* + 3rd person singular of the verb to mean people in general. *One* is more formal than *you* and is rarely used in spoken English.
3 *We* can also be used to make a general statement which includes the reader / listener.
4 In informal English, we also often use *they* to talk about other people in general, or people in authority, e.g. ***They** always say…* (*they* = people in general), ***They** should make it compulsory…* (*they* = the government).
5 We often use *they*, *them*, and *their* to refer to one person who may be male or female, instead of using *he or she*, *his or her*, etc.

reflexive and reciprocal pronouns

1 You need to look after **yourself** with that cold.
   He's very egocentric. He always talks about **himself**.
2 I managed to complete the crossword! I was really pleased with **myself**.
3 We decorated the house **ourselves**.
   There's no way I'm going to do it for you. Do it **yourself**!
4 I don't feel very comfortable going to the cinema **by myself**.
5 My ex-husband and I don't talk to **each other** any more.
   My mother and sister don't understand **one another** at all.

1 We often use reflexive pronouns when the subject and object of a verb are the same person. We don't usually use reflexive pronouns with *wash, shave, feel, relax, concentrate* NOT *relax yourself*.
2 We also use reflexive pronouns after most prepositions when the complement is the same as the subject.

⚠ After prepositions of place, we use object pronouns, not reflexive pronouns, e.g. *She put the bag next to her on the seat* NOT *next to herself*.

3 We can also use reflexive pronouns to emphasize the subject, e.g. *We decorated the house ourselves* (= we did it, not professional decorators).
4 *By* + reflexive pronoun = alone, on your own.
5 We use *each other* or *one another* for reciprocal actions, i.e. A does the action to B and B does the action to A.
• Compare *They bought themselves some new shoes* (= A bought some for A, and B bought some for B).
   They bought each other some new shoes (= A bought some for B and B bought some for A).

it and there

1 **It's** five miles to London. **It's** 10 o'clock.
2 **It was** great to hear that you and Martina are getting married!
   It used to be difficult to buy fresh pasta in the UK, but now you can get it everywhere.
3 **There's** a big crowd of people in the town centre.
   There used to be a cinema in that street, but there isn't one any more.
   There are three meetings this week.

1 We use *it* + *be* to talk about time, temperature, and distance.
2 We also use *it* + *be* as a 'preparatory' subject before adjectives. *It was great to hear from you* is more natural than *To hear from you was great*.
3 We use *there* + *be* + *noun* to say if people and things are present or exist (or not). You cannot use *It…* here. NOT *It used to be a cinema in that street*.

---

a Circle the right pronoun. Tick if you think both are possible.

They hurt *one another* / (*themselves*) quite badly when they fell off their motorbike.

1 *One* / *You* can often tell where people are from by the way they dress.
2 Can you put my case on the rack above *yourself* / *you*?
3 Marga and her sister look incredibly like *each other* / *one another*. Are they twins?
4 Anna is very unselfish – she never puts *her* / *herself* first.
5 Either Suzie or Mark has left *her* / *their* bag behind, because there's only one in the back of the car.
6 When a person goes to live abroad, it may take *them* / *him* a while to pick up the language.
7 *They* / *One* say that eating tomatoes can help protect the body against certain diseases.

b Complete the sentence with a pronoun where necessary.

In most circumstances *you* should address people by their title and surname.

1 If anyone has not yet paid _____ course fees, _____ should go to registration immediately.
2 Isabel is very quick-tempered. She finds it very hard to control _____.
3 I wouldn't stay in that hotel. _____ say the rooms are tiny and the service is awful.
4 There is a total lack of communication. They don't understand _____ at all.
5 Mila gets distracted too easily. She doesn't concentrate _____ very well.
6 Are you going to have the flat repainted or will you do it _____?
7 There are loads of bookshelves in the flat, which is great as _____ can never have too many!

c Complete the sentences with *it* or *there*.

There was a very interesting article about modern lifestyle in *The Times* yesterday.

1 Nowadays _____'s illegal to text from your mobile while you're driving. _____ have been a lot of accidents caused by this.
2 Look. _____'s a spelling mistake in this word. _____ should be *j*, not *g*.
3 How many miles is _____ to Manchester from here?
4 _____'s scorching today. _____ must be at least 35 degrees.
5 _____'s no need to hurry. The train doesn't leave for ages.
6 _____'s not worth buying the paper today. _____'s absolutely nothing interesting in it.

narrative tenses: describing specific incidents in the past

> This **happened** when I **was** about five years old. My father **had gone away** on business for a few days and my brother and I **were sleeping** in my parents' bedroom. Before we **went** to bed that night, I **had been reading** a very scary story about a wicked witch. In the middle of the night I **woke up** with a start and **saw** that a figure in a dark coat **was standing** at the end of my bed. I **screamed** at the top of my voice.

- When we describe specific incidents in the past, we use **narrative tenses**, i.e. the past simple, past continuous, and past perfect simple or continuous.
- Use the past simple to talk about the main actions in a story (*We went to bed... I woke up... I screamed*).
- Use the past continuous to set the scene (*We were sleeping in my parents' bedroom*) and to describe actions in progress in the past (*Somebody was standing at the end of my bed*).
- Use the past perfect and the past perfect continuous to talk about the earlier past, i.e. things which happened before the main events (*My father had gone away... I had been reading a story*).

used to and *would*: describing repeated actions in the past

> 1 Every summer my family **rented** an old house in the South of France. My sister and I **used to walk** to the harbour every morning and watch the fishermen cleaning their nets.
> 2 Every night before we went to bed my mother **would tell** us a story, but she **would never read** them from a book – she **would always make them up** herself.
> 3 When I was a teenager, my friends **were always teasing** me because of my red hair.

1 We often use *used to* + infinitive as an alternative to the past simple to talk about things that we did repeatedly in the past.
- We can also use *used to* + infinitive to talk about situations or states which have changed, e.g. *I used to have much longer hair when I was younger.*
2 We also use *would* + infinitive as an alternative to *used to* to talk about things that we did repeatedly in the past.
- However, we <u>don't</u> use *would* with stative verbs, i.e. to talk about situations or states which have changed NOT ~~I would have much longer hair when I was younger.~~
3 We can also use *always* + past continuous for things that happened repeatedly, especially when they were irritating habits.

> ⚠ When we describe past habits or repeated past actions we tend, for stylistic reasons, to use a mixture of *used to*, *would*, or the past simple (with adverbs of frequency). *Used to* and *would* make it clear that you are talking about something that happened regularly and often convey a sense of nostalgia.

a Circle the right form. Tick if both are correct.

> Corinne and I (*used to be*) / *would be* very close, but recently we've grown apart.

1 When I came into the room, my aunt *sat* / *was sitting* with her back to me. When she turned round, I could see that her eyes were rather red and I was sure that she *had been crying* / *had cried*.
2 Our grandmother *always used to have* / *would always have* a little surprise waiting for us when we visited.
3 My uncle *lived* / *used to live* on his own because his wife *died* / *had died* several years earlier.
4 When my brother was a child, *he didn't use to look* / *he wouldn't look* at all like my father, but the older he gets the more he looks like him.
5 When I was small, *I was always getting* / *I always used to get* into trouble at school and my parents *used to punish* / *would punish* me by not letting me play with my friends at the weekend.
6 Suddenly we heard a tremendous crash and we saw that a car *crashed* / *had crashed* into a tree and petrol *poured* / *was pouring* out of the car onto the road.

b Put the verbs in the right form, using a narrative tense or *would* / *used to*.

My earliest memory

When I was about four or five, my grandmother, who was Polish, *was living* (live) in London, and we children often ¹_____ (spend) weekends at her flat. My grandfather ²_____ (die) a couple of years earlier, so I suppose she was in need of company. We loved going there, as my grandmother ³_____ (cook) special meals for us and ⁴_____ (take) us for lovely walks in Regent's Park, which was quite nearby. One occasion that I remember really well was when I ⁵_____ (invite) to stay with her on my own, without my brothers and sisters. On the first day, after lunch, my grandmother ⁶_____ (tell) me that she ⁷_____ (go) to have a rest, and that I should have a rest too. I ⁸_____ (try) to sleep but I couldn't, so after a while I ⁹_____ (get) up and ¹⁰_____ (decide) to explore the flat. Everything was very quiet so I was convinced that my grandmother ¹¹_____ (sleep). The room I most ¹²_____ (want) to explore was my grandfather's study, I imagine, precisely because I ¹³_____ (tell) not to go in there. I opened the door and went in, and was immediately drawn to his large old desk. I ¹⁴_____ (climb) onto the chair, and ¹⁵_____ (see) on the desk a green pen in a kind of stand, with a bottle of ink. I ¹⁶_____ (ask) my parents for a real pen for a long time, but they ¹⁷_____ (refuse), foreseeing the mess that I was almost bound to make with the ink. I picked up the pen and then tried to open the bottle of ink. At that moment I ¹⁸_____ (hear) my grandmother's voice saying 'Christina? Where are you? What are you doing?' To my horror I ¹⁹_____ (realize) that my grandmother ²⁰_____ (get up) out of bed and ²¹_____ (come) towards the study. Two seconds later she ²²_____ (open) the door. I will never forget the awful feeling of shame that she ²³_____ (catch) me doing something that she ²⁴_____ (forbid) me to do.

seem / appear

> 1 **It seems / appears** (that) there is a direct relation between your position in the family and your personality.
> The new head of department **seems / appears to be** quite friendly.
> Excuse me. **There seems to be** a mistake with the bill.
> 2 **It would seem / appear** (that) Mr Young had been using the company's assets to pay off his private debts.

1 We often use *seem* and *appear* to give information without stating that we definitely know it is true, and in this way distancing ourselves from the information.
We can use *It seems / appears* + *that* + clause, or subject + *seem / appear* + infinitive.

2 We use *It would seem / appear* + *that* + clause to distance us even further from the information, and to make it sound less sure. This is more formal than *It seems / appears…*

the passive with verbs of saying and reporting

> 1 **It is said that** using a washing machine saves people on average 47 minutes a day.
> **It has been announced** by a White House spokesman **that** the President has been taken to hospital.
> 2 The company director **is expected to resign** in the next few days.
> The missing couple **are understood to have been living** in Panama for the last five years.
> 3 **There are thought to be** over a thousand species in danger of extinction.

Another way of distancing ourselves from the facts, especially in formal written English, is to use the passive form of verbs like *say*, *think*, etc. to introduce them. We can use:
1 *It* + passive verb + *that* + clause.
• Verbs commonly used in this pattern are: *agree, announce, believe, expect, hope, report, say, suggest, think,* and *understand.*
2 subject + passive verb + *to* + infinitive.
• Verbs commonly used in this pattern are *believe, expect, report, say, think,* and *understand.*
3 *There* can also be used + passive verb + *to* + infinitive.
Compare:
It is said that there are more than five million people living in poverty in this country.
There are said to be more than five million people living in poverty in this country.

other distancing expressions: *apparently, according to, may / might*

> 1 **Apparently,** Maurice and Yvette have separated.
> 2 **According to** new research, the idea that we have to drink two litres of water a day is a myth.
> 3 Dinosaurs **may** have died out due to extremely rapid climate change.
> There are rumours that the band, who disbanded in the late 80s, **might** be planning to re-form and record a new album.

1 We can use *apparently* (usually either at the beginning or the end of a phrase) to mean that we have heard / read something, but that it may not be true. This is very common in informal conversation.
2 We can use *according to* to specify where information has come from. We use it to attribute opinions to somebody else NOT *According to me…*
3 Using *may / might* also suggests that something is a possibility, but not necessarily true.

---

a Complete the sentences with one word to distance the speaker from the information. Sometimes there is more than one possibility.

> *Apparently,* Lisa and Dani are going to get married. Have you heard anything?

1 It _____ that the less children sleep, the more likely they are to behave badly.
2 It _____ appear that someone has been stealing personal items from the changing rooms.
3 Mark _____ to have aged a lot over the last year.
4 He may not look it, but he is _____ to be one of the wealthiest people in the country.
5 _____ to some sources, the latest research is seriously flawed.
6 Despite the fact that there will be an autopsy, his death _____ have been from natural causes.
7 _____ are thought to be several reasons why the species died out.
8 The missing couple are believed _____ have had financial difficulties.
9 It is understood _____ the minister will be resigning in the near future.

b Rewrite the second sentence so that it means the same as the first.

> People say that eating garlic stops you catching colds.
> It is *said that eating garlic stops you catching colds.*

1 Apparently, people who work night shifts die younger.
It would _____.

2 It is possible that the prisoners escaped to France.
The prisoners may _____.

3 We expect that the Prime Minister will make a statement this afternoon.
The Prime Minister is _____.

4 The company has announced that the new drug will go on sale shortly.
It _____.

5 People believe that improvements in diet and lifestyle are responsible for the rise in life expectancy.
Improvements in diet and lifestyle _____
_____.

6 The manual says you have to charge the phone for at least 12 hours.
According _____.

7 It appears that the government is intending to lower interest rates.
The government _____.

8 People have suggested that the painting is a fake.
It _____.

9 It seems that there are more cyclists around than there used to be.
There _____.

1 I **got** an email from Marc today.
If you're going to the post office, could you **get** me some stamps?
When do you think we'll **get** to Paris?
Let's not bother with a taxi – we can **get** the bus.

2 We'd better go home. It's **getting dark**.
I seem to have **got very forgetful** recently.
The traffic **gets worse** in the city centre every day.
I don't think my mother will ever **get used to** living on her own.

3 We need to **get someone to fix** the central heating – it's not working properly.
Could you **get Jane to finish** the report? I'm too busy to do it this afternoon.

4 I'm going to **get my hair cut** next week.
I need to **get my passport renewed** – it runs out in a couple of months.

5 Did you know Dan **got sacked** last week?
My husband **got caught** driving at 150 km/h. He got three points on his licence.

Get is one of the most common verbs in English and can be used in many different ways.

1 *Get* + noun / pronoun can mean 'receive', 'bring', 'fetch', 'obtain', 'buy', or 'catch', and with *to* + a place it means 'arrive at / in'.

2 We use *get* + adjective or comparative adjective to mean 'become'.
• Compare *be* + adjective and *get* + adjective.
 It's dark. It's getting dark.
 I'm used to the climate in England now. I'm getting used to the climate in England.

3 We can use *get* + object + infinitive to mean 'make somebody do something' or 'persuade somebody to do something'.

4 In informal spoken English we sometimes use *get* (+ object + past participle) instead of *have* (+ object + past participle) to say that you ask or pay another person to do something for you.
See 1B *have* on page 137.

5 We can use *get* (+ past participle) instead of *be* to make a passive structure. This is more informal than using *be*.

a Replace *get* with another verb so that the sentence means the same.

I **got** fined yesterday for breaking the speed limit. *was*

1 My father is **getting** increasingly forgetful in his old age. _____

2 Do you know anywhere near here where I can **get** a newspaper? _____

3 Could you try to **get** your brother to come tonight too? _____

4 We had to **get** the roof repaired, as it was damaged in the storm. _____

5 I **got** an email out of the blue today from an old school friend. _____

6 If I **get** the 7.30 train, would you be able to pick me up at the station? _____

7 Do you think they'll **get** here in time for lunch? _____

8 If you're going upstairs, could you **get** me my jacket, which is on my bed? _____

9 She's going to **get** caught if she's not careful. _____

10 How can I **get** you to change your mind? _____

b Complete the sentence with the right form of *get* and the word in brackets. You may need to change the form of the verbs in brackets.

I *always get lost* (always / lose) when I'm driving. I think I'm going to get a satnav.

1 I only just _____ in time. It was about to run out. (my work permit / renew)

2 My husband has only been in the UK for two months and he just can't _____ on the left. He gets very confused at roundabouts. (used / drive)

3 Monica's fiancé _____ in a car crash. He was lucky to survive. (nearly / kill)

4 I can _____ tomorrow night so we can go out. (my sister / babysit)

5 If you can't find your keys, we'll have to _____. (all the locks / change)

6 We _____ by the police just before we crossed the bridge. They were looking for a stolen car. (stop)

7 I went to the optician's yesterday to _____. (eyes / test)

8 **A** What happened to your eye?
 B I _____ by a mosquito last night. (bite)

modal verbs: *must / may / might / can't / should*

1 Mel and Trudy **must be** very well off – they've got an enormous house.
   You **must have seen** him – he was standing right in front of you!
2 They **can't be playing** very well – they're losing 0-3.
   You **can't / couldn't have spent** very long on this essay – you've only written 100 words.
3 I haven't seen the sales manager today. He **may / might / could be** off sick.
   The keys of the store cupboard have disappeared. Do you think someone **may / might / could have taken** them?
   He **may / might not have heard** the message I left on his voicemail.
4 If I post the letter today, it **should arrive** on Friday.
   I posted the letter a week ago. It **should have arrived** by now.

1 As well as for obligation, we also use *must* + infinitive to say that we are almost sure something is true about the present, and *must have* + past participle to say that we are almost sure something was true or happened in the past.
2 We use *can't* and *can't / couldn't* + perfect infinitive (NOT *mustn't / mustn't have*) to say that we are almost sure that something isn't true in the present or didn't happen / wasn't true in the past.
3 We use *may / might / could* + infinitive and *may / might / could* + perfect infinitive to say that we think it's possible that something is true in the present or was true / happened in the past.
• Compare:
   He might not have done it. (= Maybe he didn't do it.)
   He couldn't have done it. (= It is impossible that he did it.)
4 Use *should* + infinitive (or *should have* + participle) to describe a situation you expect to happen (or would expect to have happened in the past).

⚠ Compare the use of the infinitive and the continuous infinitive after these modals.
   He must work really hard. He never gets home before 9.00 p.m.
   = deduction about a habitual action
   There's a light on in his office. He must still be working.
   = deduction about an action in progress at the moment of speaking

adjectives and adverbs for speculation

1 He**'s bound / sure to** be here in a minute. He left an hour ago.
   She**'s sure to** know. She's an expert on the subject.
2 I think she**'s likely to** agree to our proposal – we've given her some very good reasons.
   The doctors say that at his age he**'s unlikely to** recover.
   I think **it's very likely that** the meeting will be over by 6.00.
   It's unlikely that the government will raise interest rates this year.
3 She**'ll definitely pass** the exam. She's worked really hard.
   She **definitely won't pass** the exam. She hasn't done any work at all.
   He**'ll probably be here** around 8.00. He usually leaves work at 7.30.
   He **probably won't be here** until about 8.15. He's stuck in a traffic jam.

1 *Bound* and *sure* are adjectives. We use *be bound* or *be sure* + infinitive to say that we think something is certain to be true or to happen.
2 *Likely / unlikely* are also adjectives (not adverbs). We can use subject + *be likely / unlikely* + infinitive, or *it is likely / unlikely* + *that* + clause.
3 *Definitely* and *probably* are adverbs. They go before a main verb and after the auxiliary (if there is one) in ⊞ sentences and before the auxiliary verb in ⊟ sentences.
• With *be* they go after the verb in ⊞ sentences and before it in ⊟ sentences, e.g. *He's probably British. The painting definitely isn't genuine.*

⚠ *be likely to* and *will probably* are very similar in meaning, but *be likely to* is more formal. Compare:
   The new coach is likely to be appointed today.
   The new coach will probably be appointed today.

a Right (✓) or wrong (✗)? Correct the mistakes in the highlighted phrases.
   A When's Jim arriving?
   B I'm not sure, but he won't likely be here before 7.00.
      ✗ *isn't likely to be here*
1 My glasses aren't in their usual place. Someone must move them.
2 **A** Do you know where Ann is?
   B She should be in the library. That's where she said she was going.
3 **A** What's that noise in the garage?
   B I think it can be the neighbour's cat.
4 I'm sure Barcelona will win tonight. They're unlikely to lose three times running.
5 I don't think we should use that photo of Tina in the brochure. She won't definitely like it.
6 Julian is bound be late – he always is.
7 No one's answering the phone at the shop. They've probably gone home.
8 I don't think Marta has gone to bed yet. I think she must still study.
9 It's quite likely that the boss will retire in a year or two.

b Rewrite the sentences using the **bold** word.
   Perhaps Luke has got lost. He has no sense of direction.
   MIGHT
   Luke *might have got lost*. He has no sense of direction.
1 I don't think he'll have time to call in and see us. He's got a very tight schedule.
   PROBABLY
   He _____. He has a very tight schedule.
2 I'm not sure she'll ever get over the break-up.
   MAY
   She _____ the break-up.
3 They will probably have heard the news by now.
   SHOULD
   They _____ now.
4 I'm sure I didn't leave my credit card in the restaurant. I remember putting it in my wallet.
   CAN'T
   I _____. I remember putting it in my wallet.
5 I'm sure your sister will like the scarf. It's just her style.
   BOUND
   Your sister _____. It's just her style.
6 The company director probably won't resign, despite the disastrous sales figures.
   UNLIKELY
   The company director _____, despite the disastrous sales figures.
7 I'm sure he was in love with her otherwise he wouldn't have married her.
   MUST
   He _____ otherwise he wouldn't have married her.
8 Are you sure you locked the back door?
   DEFINITELY
   Did _____ the back door?
9 According to press reports, the couple will probably get divorced soon.
   LIKELY
   According to press reports, it's _____ soon.

Study Link MultiROM www.oup.com/elt/englishfile/advanced

1 **Not only is** my brother lazy, (but) he's also very selfish.
Not until you can behave like an adult **will we treat** you like an adult.
Never have I heard such a ridiculous argument.
No sooner had the football match **started than** it began to snow heavily.
2 **Not only did you forget** to shut the window, (but) you also forgot to lock the door!
Not until you become a parent yourself **do you understand** what it really means.
3 The train began to move. **Only then was I able to** relax.
Only when you leave home **do you realize** how expensive everything is.
Hardly had I sat down when the train began to move.
Rarely have I met a more irritating person.

In formal English, especially in writing, we sometimes change the normal word order to make the sentence more emphatic or dramatic.
1 This structure is common with negative adverbial expressions such as *Not only…*, *Not until…*, *Never…*, and *No sooner… than* (= a formal way of saying *as soon as*).
• When we use inversion after the above expressions, we change the order of the subject and (auxiliary) verb NOT ~~Not only my brother is lazy…~~ .
Compare:
My brother is not only lazy, but he's also very selfish.
(= normal word order)
Not only is my brother lazy, but he's also very selfish.
(= inversion to make the sentence more emphatic)
2 In the present simple and past simple tense, rather than simply inverting the subject and verb we use *do / does / did* + subject + main verb NOT ~~Not only forgot you to shut the window.~~
3 Inversion is also used after the expressions *Only then…*, *Only when…*, *Hardly / Scarcely… when*, and *Rarely…*

> ⚠ Inversion should only be used occasionally for dramatic effect. Overusing it will make your English sound unnatural.

Rewrite the sentences to make them more emphatic.
I had just sat down when the train left.
No sooner *had I sat down than the train left*.

1 I didn't realize my mistake until years later.
Not until _____.

2 We had never seen such magnificent scenery.
Never _____.

3 They not only disliked her, but they also hated her family.
Not only _____.

4 We only understood what he had really suffered when we read his autobiography.
Only when _____.

5 We had just started to eat when we heard someone knocking at the door.
Hardly _____.

6 I have rarely read such a badly written novel.
Rarely _____.

7 We did not put down our tools and rest until the sun set.
Not until _____.

8 The hotel room was not only depressing, but it was cold as well.
Not only _____.

9 They only lit the fire when it was unusually cold.
Only when _____.

10 Shortly after he had gone to sleep there was a knock on the door.
No sooner _____.

11 I only realized the full scale of the disaster when I watched the six o'clock news.
I watched the six o'clock news. **Only then** _____.

12 I had only just destroyed the evidence when the police arrived.
Scarcely _____.

13 He has never regretted the decision he took on that day.
Never _____.

14 I spoke to the manager and the problem was sorted out.
Only when _____.

1 It's a difficult problem. I **wish** I **knew** the answer to it!
I **wish** I **hadn't spoken** to Jane like that – you know how sensitive she is.
2 **If only** I **knew** the answer!
If only you **hadn't forgotten** the map, we'd be there by now.
3 **I'd rather you left** your dog outside – I'm allergic to animals.
Are you sure this is a good time to talk? **Would you rather I called** back later?
4 Don't you think **it's time** you **found** a job? It's six months since you finished university!
It's (high) time the government did something about unemployment.

1 We use *wish* + past simple to talk about things we would like to be different in the present / future (but which are impossible or unlikely).
We use *wish* + past perfect to talk about things which happened / didn't happen in the past and which we now regret.
• We sometimes use *that* after *wish*, e.g. *I wish that I knew the answer*.
2 You can also use *If only…* instead of *wish* with the past simple and past perfect. This can be used by itself (*If only I knew!*) or with another clause.
• *If only* is more emphatic than *wish*.

⚠ When we want to talk about things we want to happen or stop happening because they annoy us, we use *wish* or *If only* + person / thing + *would* + infinitive, e.g. *I wish the bus would come! If only he wouldn't keep whistling when I'm working!*

3 We use *would rather* + subject + past tense to express a preference.
• We can also use *would rather* + infinitive without *to* when there is no change of subject, e.g. *I'd rather **not talk** about it*. However, we cannot use this structure when the subject changes after *would rather*, e.g. *I'd rather **you didn't talk** about it* NOT *I'd rather you not talk about it.*
4 We use the past simple after *It's time* + subject to say that something has to be done now or in the near future.
• We can also use *It's time* + *to* + infinitive when we don't want to specify the subject, e.g. *It's time to go now.*
• We sometimes use *high* before *time* for emphasis.

a Put the verbs in brackets in the right form.

I wish I *hadn't lent* Gary that money now. Who knows when he'll pay it back? (not lend)

1 It's time the government _____ that interest rates are far too high. (realize)
2 My wife would rather we _____ nearer the city centre. (live)
3 I wish you _____ to stay a bit longer – we're having such a good time! (be able)
4 Would you rather we _____ the subject now? (not discuss)
5 I think it's time the company _____ expecting us to do so much overtime for no extra pay. (stop)
6 If only I _____ a bit more when I was earning a regular salary, I wouldn't be so hard up now. (save)
7 I'd rather you _____ me in cash, if you don't mind. (pay)
8 If only we _____ the name of the shop, we could Google it and see where it is. (know)
9 Do you wish you _____ to university or do you think you made the right decision to leave school and start work? (go)

b Rewrite the sentences using the **bold** word(s).

The children ought to go to bed. It's nearly nine o'clock.
TIME
It's time the children went to bed. It's nearly nine o'clock.

1 I'd prefer you not to smoke in here, if you don't mind.
RATHER
_____, if you don't mind.

2 I would like to be able to afford to travel more.
WISH
_____ travel more.

3 We shouldn't have painted the room blue – it looks awful.
IF ONLY
_____ – it looks awful.

4 Don't you think you should start to look for a job?
TIME
Don't you think _____ for a job?

5 He should be less tight-fisted! Then he'd enjoy life more.
IF ONLY
_____, he'd enjoy life more.

6 Would you prefer us to come another day?
RATHER
_____ another day?

7 I should have bought the maroon sweater and not the beige one.
WISH
_____ the maroon sweater and not the beige one.

A I really like your shirt. Hasn't Harry got one just like it? **B** **Talking of** Harry, did he get the job he applied for?	To change the direction of a conversation, but making a link with what has just been said.
So let's meet at five o'clock then. **By the way / Incidentally**, could you possibly lend me some money until the weekend?	To introduce something you have just thought of, or to change the subject completely.
A Did you see the match last night? **B** No, I didn't. **Actually / In fact / As a matter of fact** I don't really like football.	To introduce additional surprising or unexpected information.
We didn't go away at the weekend because I had too much work. **In any case / Anyway** the weather was awful, so we didn't miss anything.	To introduce the idea that what you said before is less important than what you are going to say. To return to the main topic after a digression.
Yes, it was a bad accident. **At least** nobody was killed, though. Tom's coming to the meeting, or **at least** he said he was.	To introduce a positive point after some negative information. To make what you have just said less definite.
As I was saying, if Mark gets the job we'll have to reorganize the department.	To return to a previous subject, often after you have been interrupted.
On the whole, I think that women make better journalists than men.	To generalize.
I like both flats, but **all in all**, I think I prefer the one next to the cathedral.	To say that you are taking everything into consideration.
I think we should buy them. **After all**, we'll never find them anywhere cheaper than this.	To introduce a strong argument that the other person may not have taken into consideration.
I don't think I'll come to Nick's party. It will finish very late. **Besides**, I won't know many people there.	To add additional information or arguments.
Basically, my job involves computer skills and people skills.	To introduce the most important or fundamental point.
Obviously you can't get a real idea of life in Japan unless you can speak the language.	To introduce a fact that is very clear to see or understand.
She's very selfish. **I mean**, she never thinks about other people at all.	To make things clearer or give more details.
A lot of people booed, and some people even left early. **In other words**, it was a complete disaster.	To say something again in another way.
Please try not to make a mess when you make the cake. **Otherwise** I'm going to have to clean the kitchen again.	To say what the result would be if something did not happen or if the situation were different.
That's all you need to know about the travel arrangements. **As far as** accommodation **is concerned**, **As regards / Regarding** accommodation, the options are living with a family or living in a hall of residence.	To introduce a new topic or to announce a change of subject.
The government are going to help first-time buyers. **That is to say**, they are going to make mortgages more easily available.	To introduce an explanation or clarification of a point you have just made.
On (the) one hand, more young people today carry knives. **On (the) other hand**, the total number of violent crimes has dropped.	To balance contrasting facts or points. *On the other hand* is also used alone to introduce a contrasting fact or point.

a Circle the appropriate discourse markers in the dialogue.

A What a good film! I really enjoyed it. Didn't you?
B (Actually) / Incidentally, I didn't like it very much.
A Why not?
B [1]Basically / After all I thought it was incredibly far-fetched. I couldn't believe in the characters at all, and the plot was totally implausible.
A I wouldn't call it far-fetched. [2]At least / In any case it wasn't supposed to be a true story.
B I know, but it was set in a very specific historical period. [3]Otherwise / Obviously you can't expect the dialogue to be totally authentic, [4]I mean / on the other hand nobody knows exactly how people spoke in the 17th century, but [5]at least / anyway the period details should be right. There was a clock in the king's palace and they didn't have clocks until the eighteenth century! [6]All in all / That is to say I thought it was a pretty awful film.
A We'll have to agree to disagree then. [7]By the way / As a matter of fact, do you know what time the last train leaves? I don't want to miss it. [8]Otherwise / In any case I'll have to get a taxi home.
B 11.40. Don't worry, we've got plenty of time. [9]In fact / Besides, I think we've even got time to have something to eat. Do you fancy a quick pizza? There's a good Italian restaurant just round the corner.
A Yes, let's go. [10]As I was saying / Talking of Italian food I made a wonderful risotto with mushrooms last night…

b Complete the sentences with appropriate discourse markers. Sometimes more than one answer may be possible.

The food was delicious and the service was excellent. *All in all* the meal was a great success.

1 Jason is an excellent teacher, although _____ I think female teachers are usually better with four- and five-year-olds.
2 **A** Did you buy the shoes in the end?
  B No, they were too expensive. And _____ I decided that I didn't really like them that much.
3 I really think you ought to apply for the post of head of department. _____ you've got nothing to lose, and you might just get it, who knows?
4 **A** I've just read a brilliant book that Simon lent me.
  B _____ Simon, did you know he's moving to New York?
5 **A** How was your day?
  B Fine. I finished work a bit earlier than usual. _____, did you remember to get a birthday present for your mum?
6 It was a very grey, overcast day, but _____ it didn't rain.
7 **A** Do your wife's parents live near you then?
  B _____, they live in the flat below us. It's not ideal but it does have some advantages.
8 They've employed me as a kind of troubleshooter – _____ somebody who sorts out problems whenever they occur.
9 _____ salary _____, you will be paid on the 30th or 31st of each month, with a bonus in December and in July.
10 You'd better hurry up with your homework. _____ you won't be able to watch TV tonight.
11 I'm not sure what the best solution is. _____ buying our own place would mean not having to waste money paying rent, but _____ I'm not sure we can really afford a mortgage.

verb + object + *to* + infinitive

> 1 We **expect the flight to arrive** at 19.50.
> It **took me ages to get** there.
> She **advised him not to travel** by train.
> 2 I **would hate you to think** that I don't appreciate your offer of help.
> I'**d like you to send** me the bill.
> 3 I'm **waiting for my friend to arrive**.
> We've **arranged for a taxi to come** at 6.30.

1 We often use the following verbs + object + *to* + infinitive: *ask, advise, allow, beg, cause, enable, encourage, expect, force, help, intend, invite, mean, order, persuade, recommend, remind, take (time), teach, tell, warn.*
- After *advise, persuade, remind, teach, tell,* and *warn* you can also use an object + *that* clause, e.g. *He advised me that I should stay off work for two weeks.*

> ⚠ After *recommend* you can use
> – object + *to* + infinitive, e.g. *He recommended me to take some cash.*
> – a *that* clause, e.g. *He recommended that I took some cash.*
> You can't use *recommend* + object + *that* clause, e.g. NOT *He recommended me that I took some cash.*

2 We also often use object + infinitive with *want, would like, would love, would prefer, would hate.*
- After these verbs a *that* clause is impossible. NOT *I would hate that you think.*
3 After some verbs including *arrange, ask, plan,* and *wait* we put *for* immediately after the verb before the object + *to* + infinitive.

verb + object + infinitive without *to*

> Please **let me explain**!
> He **made me feel** really guilty.
> Can you **help me do** the washing up?

We can use object + infinitive <u>without</u> *to* after *let, make,* and *help.*
- *Help* can be followed by object + infinitive with or without *to*, e.g. *She helped me (to) make the dinner.*

> ⚠ When *make sb do sth* is used in the passive, it is followed by the infinitive with *to*, e.g. *We were made to clean our rooms every morning.*

verb + object + gerund

> Please don't **keep me waiting**!
> I **dislike people telling** me what to do.
> I **don't mind you smoking** in the garden, but please don't smoke in the house.

Complete the second sentence so that it means the same as the first.

> 'Take special care because of the snow and ice,' the police told motorists.
>
> The police warned <u>motorists</u> <u>to</u> <u>take</u> <u>special</u> care because of the snow and ice.

1 I don't like it when people answer their mobiles in restaurants.
   I dislike people _____ _____ _____ in restaurants.
2 I felt uncomfortable because of the situation at work.
   The situation at work made _____ _____ _____.
3 You are going to stay with a British family. We have made the arrangements.
   We have arranged _____ _____ _____ _____ with a British family.
4 I don't have a problem if Jane comes, but I'd rather her boyfriend didn't.
   I don't mind _____ _____ , but I'd rather her boyfriend didn't.
5 Please don't think I didn't enjoy myself, because I did!
   I would hate _____ _____ _____ I didn't enjoy myself, because I did!
6 You paid for everything, which wasn't what I expected.
   I didn't expect _____ _____ _____ everything.
7 It would be wonderful if you stayed for a few days.
   I would love _____ _____ _____ for a few days.
8 If you get this job, you will have to travel a lot.
   This job will involve _____ _____ _____ _____.
9 I told Hannah not to forget to do the washing up.
   I reminded _____ _____ _____ the washing up.
10 Did you really use to be shy? I can't imagine it!
   I can't imagine _____ _____ shy!
11 We were able to buy a bigger flat thanks to the money my uncle left me.
   The money my uncle left me enabled _____ _____ _____ a bigger flat.
12 The guards wouldn't let us cross the border.
   The guards prevented _____ _____ _____ the border.
13 I could call back later if you're busy now.
   Would you prefer _____ _____ _____ _____ later?
14 The car might break down on holiday. We don't want to take the risk.
   We don't want to risk _____ _____ _____ _____ while we're on holiday.

real and unreal

1 They **won't get** a table unless they**'ve** already **booked**.
 Can I **borrow** your dictionary a moment if you**'re not using** it?
 If it **stops** raining, I**'m going to** walk into town.
2 How **would** you **know** if he **wasn't telling** the truth?
 If we **had** a bit more time here, we **could go** on an all-day river trip.
3 I **would have picked** you up if **I had known** what time your flight arrived.
 If I**'d been looking** where I was going, I **would've seen** the hole in the road.

1 Type 1 conditional sentences are used to talk about a possible present or future situation and its result.
 You can use any present tense in the *if* clause and any form of the future in the other clause.
2 Type 2 conditional sentences are used to talk about hypothetical or improbable situations in the present or future.
 You can use the past tense (simple or continuous) in the *if* clause and *would* + infinitive (or *could* / *might*) in the other clause.
3 Type 3 conditional sentences are used to talk about a hypothetical situation in the past.
 You can use the past perfect (simple or continuous) in the *if* clause and *would have* + past participle (or *could* / *might have*) in the other clause.

mixed conditionals

I **wouldn't be** in this mess if I **had listened** to your advice.
Jane **would have left** Mike by now if she **didn't** still **love** him.

If we want to refer to the present and the past in the same sentence, we can mix tenses from two different types of conditional, e.g.
I wouldn't be in this mess (type 2) *if I had listened to your advice* (type 3).
Jane would have left Mike by now (type 3) *if she didn't still love him* (type 2).

alternatives to *if* in conditional sentences

1 I'll tell you what happened **as long as** / **so long as** you promise not to tell anyone else.
 Provided / **Providing (that)** the bank lends us all the money we need, we're going to buy that flat we liked.
 They agreed to lend us the car **on condition (that)** we returned it by the weekend.
2 I'm going to sell the car **whether** you agree with me **or not**.
3 **Even if** I get the job, I'm going to carry on living with my parents for a while.
4 **Supposing** you lost your job, what would you do?
5 **Had I known** that you were coming, I would have bought a bottle of wine.

a Right (✓) or wrong (✗)? Correct the mistakes in the highlighted phrases.

> If you hadn't been here last night, I don't know what I would do. *what I would have done*

1 They wouldn't have made you Marketing Manager if they didn't think you were right for the job.
2 The government would accept more refugees if the camp isn't so crowded.
3 If you've done all your homework, you can go out this evening.
4 We wouldn't be living in Singapore now if my company hadn't been taken over by a multinational.
5 Hannah would be in the first team if she didn't get injured last month.
6 If you've ever been to New York, you will know exactly what I'm talking about.
7 They would get divorced ages ago if they didn't have young children.
8 If the storm wasn't at night, more people would have died.
9 If their flight hasn't been delayed, they will have arrived by now.

b Complete the sentences with *one* word. Don't use *if*.

> *Supposing* we missed the last train, how would we get home?

1 My father has agreed to lend me the money _____ I pay it back by the end of the year.
2 _____ if I had played my best, I still wouldn't have beaten him.
3 I'll tell you exactly what happened as _____ as you promise not to tell anyone.
4 _____ the rebels not surrendered, there would have been a lot more casualties.
5 The company will only employ me on _____ that I sign a two-year contract.
6 We've decided we're going to go ahead with the event _____ we sell all the tickets or not.
7 I'm convinced Amy won't get back with her boyfriend, _____ if he apologizes.
8 You can go to the party _____ long as you are home by midnight at the latest.
9 _____ we do buy a dog, who's going to take it for walks?
10 I'm going to make an appointment for you at the doctor's _____ you like it or not.
11 _____ the plane not caught fire, there would have been more survivors.

can, must, should, ought to, had better

> 1 I **couldn't** take any photos in the gallery, so I bought some postcards of the paintings.
> Passengers on the bus **mustn't** distract the driver.
> We **should / ought to** go home on the motorway – it's much quicker.
> 2 We **should have / ought to have** gone home on the motorway – it would have been quicker.
> 3 You**'d better** post the parcels today or they won't get there in time.

1 The most common modal verbs for talking about permission and obligation are *can / could, must*, and *should / ought to*.
2 We can use *should have* or *ought to have* + past participle to talk about past events which did not happen and which we regret.
3 *Had better* is stronger and more urgent than *should / ought to* and is often used to give strong advice or a warning. It normally refers to the immediate future.
• The negative is *had better not* NOT *hadn't better*.

have to / have got to

> 1 All passengers **will have to** fill in an immigration form on arrival.
> You **don't have to** tip here unless you think the service was especially good.
> 2 I**'ve got to** buy a birthday present for my brother.

1 We also use *have to* to express obligations. It can be used in any tense.
2 We can also use *have got to* to express obligation, but it is normally used for specific occasions rather than repeated or general obligations.

need

> 1 You usually **need to** check in at least two hours before a flight leaves.
> I **don't need to** take a jacket. It's going to be hot today.
> 2 You **needn't** lock the car. Nobody will steal it in this village.
> 3 We **needn't have booked / didn't need to book** a table. The restaurant is empty!
> 4 We had plenty of petrol so we **didn't need** to stop, which saved time.

1 We use *need / don't need* + *to* + infinitive to say that something is necessary / unnecessary. You can use these forms for habitual, general, and specific necessity.
2 When we want to say that something is unnecessary on a specific occasion, we can also use *needn't* + infinitive without *to*.
• We use *don't need to* (NOT *needn't*) for habitual or general necessity, e.g. *I don't need to wear glasses. My eyesight is still good.* NOT *I needn't wear glasses.*
3 When something was not necessary, but you did it, we can use either *needn't have* + past participle or *didn't need to* + infinitive.
4 When something was not necessary, so you did **not** do it, you must use *didn't need to* NOT *We had plenty of petrol so we needn't have stopped, which saved time.*

be able to, be allowed to, be permitted to, be supposed to

> 1 From tomorrow we **won't be able to** park in this street.
> You**'re not allowed to** smoke in any public buildings in our country.
> 2 It **is not permitted to** take mobiles into the exam room.
> 3 We **are supposed to** check in at 3.30. What's the time now?
> You **aren't supposed to** park here – it's a hospital entrance.

1 We often use *be able to* or *be allowed to* + infinitive to talk about what is possible or permitted instead of *can*, particularly when we want to use a form which *can* does not have.
2 *be permitted to* + infinitive is used in formal situations, e.g. notices and announcements, to say what can / can't be done according to the law or to rules and regulations.

> ⚠ We do not use *it* followed by *be allowed to* NOT *It isn't allowed to take mobiles into the exam room.*

3 We can also use *be supposed to* + infinitive to say what people should or shouldn't do, often because of rules. There is often a suggestion that the rules are not necessarily obeyed, e.g. *Students are not supposed to have guests after 12.00, but everyone does.*

---

a Complete the second sentence so that it means the same as the first.

> We couldn't go out at night when we were at boarding school.
> We weren't *allowed to go out at night when we were at boarding school*.

1 Officially you mustn't park here – but everyone does.
You aren't _____ here.

2 Put that cigarette out. This is a no-smoking area.
You'd _____. This is a no-smoking area.

3 I regret losing my temper last night.
I shouldn't _____ last night.

4 You can't take flash photographs in this museum.
Flash photography is _____ in this museum.

5 Wearing a seat belt in the back seat of the car is compulsory.
You _____ in the back seat of the car.

6 Swimming in the lake is strictly prohibited.
You aren't _____ in the lake.

7 Wearing a tie is optional in this restaurant.
You don't _____ in this restaurant.

8 The best thing to do would be to get specialist advice.
You really _____ specialist advice.

9 I must finish the sales report by Friday.
I've _____ by Friday.

10 You don't have to bring your car – we can go in mine.
You _____ – we can go in mine.

b Complete the sentences with **three** words.

> If you don't finish your homework, you won't be *able to watch* TV.

1 You don't _____ to go into the art gallery. Entrance is free.

2 Smoking _____ anywhere on the aircraft. Anyone caught smoking will be severely punished.

3 You'd _____ late – you know what Jane is like about punctuality!

4 You _____ back before next month. I'm in no hurry for the money.

5 You _____ you didn't like the pasta. You know how sensitive he is about his cooking.

6 It was a difficult journey because we _____ trains three times.

7 A lot of people think that governments _____ more to protect young people's health.

8 You aren't _____ your mobile phone when you are driving.

9 We _____ sweaters after all – it's really warm!

10 Am I _____ a suit to the wedding or is it quite informal?

Study Link **MultiROM** www.oup.com/elt/englishfile/advanced

hear, see, smell, feel, taste

> I **can hear** a noise downstairs.
> **Can you see** the blue circle at the top of the painting?
> I **can smell** burning. Are you sure you turned the gas off?
> I **can feel** a draught. Is there a window open?
> I **can't taste** the garlic in the soup.

- The five basic verbs of the senses, *hear, see, smell, feel*, and *taste* are stative (non action) verbs. We normally use *can* with these verbs to refer to something happening at the moment.
- We don't usually use verbs of the senses in the continuous form NOT ~~I am hearing a noise. I'm feeling a pain behind my eye.~~
- *hear* and *see* can also be dynamic verbs and used in the continuous form, but with a different meaning:
  I've been hearing good things about you recently. (= I have been receiving information.)
  I'm seeing James tonight. = (I have arranged to meet him.)

see / hear + infinitive or gerund

> 1 I **heard** the girl **play** a piece by Chopin.
>   I **saw** the man **hit** his dog.
> 2 I **heard** the girl **playing** a piece by Chopin.
>   I **saw** the man **hitting** his dog.

- We often use *see / hear* + an object + verb in the infinitive or gerund. The meaning is slightly different:
1 *see / hear* + object + verb in infinitive = you saw or heard the whole action.
2 *see / hear* + object + verb in gerund = you saw / heard an action in progress or a repeated action.
- The same distinction also applies to verbs after *watch* and *notice*.

look, feel, smell, sound, taste + adjective / noun

> 1 You **look** tired. That **smells** delicious. This music **sounds** awful.
>   These shoes **feel** uncomfortable. The soup **tastes** a bit salty.
> 2 You **look like** your mother. It **sounds like** thunder. This **tastes like** tea, not coffee.
> 3 She looked **as if / as though** she had been crying.
>   It sounds **as if / as though** someone is trying to open the door.
> 4 This smells / tastes **of** garlic. This smells / tastes **like** garlic.

When we talk about the impression something or someone gives us through the senses, we use *look, feel, smell, sound*, and *taste*.
- After these verbs we can use
1 an adjective.
2 *like* + a noun.
3 *as if / as though* + a clause.
4 Compare *smell / taste of* and *smell / taste like*.
  It tastes / smells of garlic (= it has the taste / smell of garlic).
  It tastes / smells like garlic (= it has a similar taste / smell to garlic, but it probably isn't garlic).

seem

> 1 You **seem** worried. Is something wrong?
> 2 You **seem to be** a bit down today. Are you OK?
>   The waiter **seems to have made** a mistake with the bill.
> 3 It **seemed like** a good idea at the time, but in fact it wasn't.
>   It **seems as if / as though** every time I clean the car it rains.

- We use *seem* when something / somebody gives us an impression of being or doing something through a combination of the senses and what we know, but not purely through one sense, e.g. the visual sense. Compare *seem* and *look*:
  You look worried. (= I get this impression from your face.)
  You seem worried. (= I get this impression from the way you are behaving in general, e.g. voice, actions, etc.)
- After *seem* we can use
1 an adjective.
2 an infinitive (simple or perfect or continuous).
3 *like* + noun or *as if / as though* + a verb phrase.
- *seem* is not used in the continuous form.

a Right (✓) or wrong (✗)? Correct the mistakes in the highlighted phrases.

> I'm smelling something funny in here. What on earth is it? ✗ *I can smell something funny*

1 Kerry says she hasn't been feeling very well recently – do you know what's the matter with her?
2 We could hardly sleep at all, as we could hear the wind howling in the trees all night.
3 I was very near where it happened. I actually heard the bomb exploding.
4 Do you know what this piece is? It sounds of Beethoven's 7th, but I'm not quite sure.
5 I think we should send the wine back. It tastes like vinegar.
6 They said this bag was leather, but it's feeling more like plastic.
7 You and Raquel seemed to be getting on very well last night. What did you think of her?

b Circle the right form. Tick if both are possible.

> The shop assistant *looks* / (*seems*) to have forgotten about us.

1 He *looked* / *seemed* very angry about something.
2 It *looks* / *seems* as if children today are only interested in playing with gadgets.
3 It doesn't *look* / *seem* possible that ten years have passed since we last met.
4 Jane *is looking* / *is seeming* very tired, don't you think?
5 You *look* / *seem* much more like your father than your mother.

c Complete the sentences with one word.

> The clouds are very low. It looks *as* if it's going to snow.

1 This tastes a bit _____ a soup my mother used to make. What's in it?
2 I haven't met the boss yet. I've only spoken to him on the phone. He _____ quite nice, though.
3 She must have gone out because I heard the front door _____ about five minutes ago.
4 The engine sounds as _____ there's something wrong with it. I think we should stop at the next petrol station.
5 My mother's favourite perfume is one that smells _____ roses. Apparently it's made from thousands of petals.
6 We stopped for a moment and watched the men _____ on the edge of the pier, but as they didn't seem to be catching anything, we walked on.
7 Could you possibly speak up a bit? I _____ hear you very well.

149

complex gerunds and infinitives

> 1 She loves **being told** how pretty she is.
> I'm tired of **being lied to**. I want the truth.
> It's very difficult **to get promoted** in this company.
> My car needs **to be serviced**.
> 2 He thanked them for **having helped** him.
> **Having studied** one language before makes it easier to learn another.
> How wonderful **to have finished** all our exams!
> By the time I'm 30, I hope **to have started** a family.
> 3 I would like **to have seen** your face when they told you you'd won the competition!
> We would rather **have stayed** in a more central hotel, but they were all full.
> 4 I'd like **to be lying** on the beach right now.
> She seems **to be coughing** a lot – do you think she's OK?

1 We use a passive gerund (*being done*) or a passive infinitive (*to be done*) to describe actions which are done to the subject.

2 We use a perfect gerund (*having done*) or a perfect infinitive (*to have done*) if we want to emphasize that an action is completed or in the past.

• Often there is no difference between using a simple gerund or infinitive and a perfect gerund or infinitive, e.g.
He denied stealing / having stolen the money.
It was our fault. We were silly not to lock / not to have locked the car.

3 We use the perfect infinitive after *would like, would love, would hate, would prefer*, and *would rather* to talk about an earlier action.
Compare:
I would like to see the Eiffel Tower. (= when I go to Paris in the future.)
I would like to have seen the Eiffel Tower. (= I was in Paris, but I didn't see it.)

4 We use a continuous infinitive (*to be* + verb + *-ing*) to say that an action / event is in progress around the time we are talking about.

other uses of gerunds and infinitives

> 1 **It's no use worrying.** There's nothing you can do.
> **Is there any point (in) asking** him? He never has anything useful to say.
> **It's no good talking** to my dad because he doesn't listen to me.
> 2 We had **an agreement to share** the costs.
> Our **plan** is **to leave** on Saturday.
> 3 You can't visit the Louvre in a day – there's **too much to see**.
> There wasn't **enough** snow for us **to ski**.
> 4 Is there **anything to eat**? There's **nowhere to go** at night.
> 5 I don't know **where to go** or **what to do**.
> 6 He's the **youngest** player ever **to play** for England.

1 We use the gerund after certain expressions with *it* or *there*, e.g. *It's no use, There's no point, It's not worth*, etc.
We use the infinitive with *to*:

2 after nouns formed from verbs which take the infinitive, e.g. *agree, plan, hope*, etc.

3 after expressions with quantifiers, e.g. *enough, too much, a lot, plenty of*, etc.

• When we want to refer to the subject of the infinitive verb we use *for* + person or object pronoun before the infinitive. This can be used before any infinitive structure, e.g. after adjectives:
*It's very difficult **for me to decide**.*

4 after *something, anywhere*, etc.

5 after question words (except *why*).

6 after superlatives and *first, second, last*, etc., e.g. *Who was the first person to walk on the moon?*

a Put the verbs in brackets in the correct form of the gerund or infinitive.

> I hate *being told* (tell) what to do. I prefer to take my own decisions.

1 I was really stupid _____ (follow) my mother's advice. She was totally wrong.

2 I'd love _____ (be) there when you told him you were leaving.

3 If I had a serious illness, I would prefer _____ (tell) the truth.

4 It's no use _____ (run). The train will have left by now.

5 Mark seems _____ (work) too hard at the moment. He looks very tired.

6 By the time I'm 55, I expect _____ (save) enough to be able to just work part-time.

7 The man denied _____ (commit) the crime.

8 There will be plenty of time to have something _____ (eat) at the airport.

9 It's no good _____ (phone) him because he didn't take his mobile with him.

10 Who was the second man _____ (walk) on the moon?

11 There wasn't enough room for us _____ (sit down).

b Rewrite the sentences with the **bold** word.

> Don't get angry. That won't help.
> **POINT**
> *There's no point getting* angry.

1 We haven't got many eggs so we can't make an omelette.
ENOUGH
We _____ make an omelette.

2 I hate it when people wake me up from a siesta.
WOKEN
I _____ from a siesta.

3 Are you sorry you didn't have more children?
REGRET
_____ more children?

4 It's amazing what she's managed to achieve considering she didn't finish school.
WITHOUT
It's amazing what she's managed to achieve _____.

5 I really wish I'd been able to go to your birthday party.
LOVE
I _____ to your birthday party.

6 The children look as if they're having a good time, don't you think?
SEEM
_____, don't you think?

7 We're not planning to redecorate the kitchen until we've finished the rest of the house.
PLAN
Our _____ until we've finished the rest of the house.

present and future forms

> 1 I'm **seeing** Sarah tomorrow. We're **having** lunch together.
> 2 I'm **going to** have my hair cut tomorrow.
>   She's **going to** get the last train home.
> 3 I'm **meeting** Cathy this evening. I'm **going to** tell her that it's all over.
> 4 I'll **be going** to the supermarket later – do you want anything?
>   **Will** we **be having** dinner at the usual time? I'm going to see a film and it starts at 8.00.
> 5 The train **leaves** in five minutes. Our classes **start** next Tuesday.

1 The present continuous is the most common way to talk about arrangements, i.e. fixed plans for the future, when the time and place have been decided.

2 *be going to* is the most common way to express future plans and intentions, and to imply that a decision has been made.

3 In most cases you can use either *going to* or the present continuous, but there is a subtle change of emphasis. The present continuous emphasizes that a time and place to do something has been decided; *going to* emphasizes the intention. Compare:
I'm meeting Cathy. (= We've arranged to meet.)
I'm going to meet Cathy. (= It's my intention, but arrangements may or may not have been made.)
We do not use the present continuous when it is clear that something is just an intention, not something that has been arranged NOT ~~I'm telling her that it's all over.~~

4 The future continuous can often be used instead of the present continuous to refer to future arrangements.

• We sometimes use it to emphasize that we are talking about something that will happen anyway rather than something we have arranged. Compare:
I'm seeing Sarah tomorrow. (= I have arranged it.)
I'll be seeing Sarah at the party tomorrow. (= It will happen anyway, but I didn't arrange it.)

• It is often used to make polite enquiries about arrangements, e.g. *Will you be meeting us at the airport?*

5 We can also use the present simple to talk about future events which are part of a timetable or a regular schedule.

other ways of expressing future arrangements

> 1 My sister **is due to** arrive at 7.30. Can you meet her at the station?
> 2 My sister **is about to** have a baby, so I need to keep my mobile switched on.
>   It is believed that the chancellor **is on the point of** resigning.
> 3 It has been announced that the Prime Minister **is to visit** Malaysia next month.

1 *be due to* + infinitive can be used to say that something is arranged or expected.

• We also use *due* on its own to mean 'expected', e.g. *The next train is due in five minutes.*

2 We use *be about to* + infinitive to say that something is going to happen very soon.

• We can also use *be on the point of* + gerund with a similar meaning, but this is slightly more formal and implies something is more imminent.

3 We can use *be + to* + infinitive in a formal style to talk about official plans and arrangements.

a Circle the right form. Tick if both are possible.

I see /(I'm seeing) some friends after class tonight.

1 The train *is going to leave soon / is about to leave.*
2 Don't call me between 5.00 and 6.00 as *I'll be having / I'll have* a massage.
3 **A** What are you going to do this evening?
   B I'm not sure. I'm probably *going to watch / watching* the match.
4 When are you *going to pay me / paying me* back the money I lent you?
5 My dad *is retiring / will be retiring* at the end of this year.
6 My flight *is due to arrive / arrives* at 6.00.
7 You'll easily recognize me. *I'll be wearing / I wear* a white suit.
8 The King *is to open / is going to open* the new gallery on Saturday.
9 *I'll be seeing / I'm going to see* John at work tomorrow. I can give him your message then.

b Look at the sentences you have ticked. Is there any difference in meaning or register between the two forms?

c Rewrite the sentences with the **bold** word.

I'm meeting Myriam tonight.
GOING
I'm *going to meet* Myriam tonight.

1 We're going to go out in a minute. Could you ring me back later?
ABOUT
_____. Could you ring me back later?

2 Our head of department is going to be promoted in the next few months.
DUE
_____ in the next few months.

3 Are you going to the canteen at lunchtime? If so, could you get me a sandwich?
WILL
_____? If so, could you get me a sandwich?

4 The ministers are about to sign a new agreement.
POINT
_____ a new agreement.

5 James will be at the meeting so I'll see him there.
SEEING
_____ at the meeting.

ellipsis: leaving out subjects and auxiliaries

> 1 He got up **and (he) had** a shower.
> She came to the meeting **but (she) didn't say** anything.
> We should phone him **or (we should) send** him an email.
> We usually have dinner at 10.00, and **then (we) watch** TV.
> 2 They locked the door and windows **before they left**.
> We'll have a look at the photos **after we finish** dinner.
> He's stressed **because he has** too much work.
> She was horrified **when she saw** the mess he had left.
> I met Sam **while I was working** in Italy.

1 After *and*, *but*, and *or* we often leave out a repeated subject or a repeated subject and auxiliary verb, especially when the clauses are short.
- After *then* we can also leave out a repeated subject pronoun.
2 You cannot leave out the subject pronoun after *before*, *after*, *because*, *when*, and *while*.

ellipsis: leaving out verb phrases or adjectives

> 1 Laura has never been to the States, but her sister **has**.
> Gary thinks he's right, but he **isn't**.
> I didn't like the film, but Mike **did**.
> They said I would love the film, but I don't think I **would**.
> 2 I thought I **would be able to** come tonight, but in fact I **can't**.
> I know you**'ve** never **learned** to drive, but I really think you **should have**.
> **A** You **must** see his latest film!
> **B** I already **have**.
> 3 I haven't been to Egypt, but I**'d love to**.
> The students cheated in the exam, even though I **told** them **not to**.

1 We often leave out a repeated verb phrase or adjective, and just repeat the auxiliary or modal verb, or the verb *be*, e.g. *Laura has never been to the States but her sister has ~~been there~~; Gary thinks he's right, but he isn't ~~right~~.*
- If the verb we don't want to repeat is the present or past simple, we substitute the verb with *do / does / did*.
2 We can use a different auxiliary or modal verb from that used in the first part of the sentence.
3 We can also leave out a repeated verb phrase after the infinitive with *to*. This is called a reduced infinitive, e.g. *I haven't been to Egypt, but I'd love to (go)*.

substitution: *so* and *not*

> 1 I'll have finished the work by Friday, or at least I **hope so**.
> **A** Will you be working on Saturday?
> **B** I **suppose so**, unless we get everything done tomorrow.
> Mark loves animals, and his sister **even more so**.
> 2 **A** Do you think it'll rain tonight?
> **B** I **hope not**.
> **A** She's not very likely to pass, is she?
> **B** No, I**'m afraid not**.
> The children may be back, but I **don't think so**.
> I know she liked the present, even though she **didn't say so**.

1 We often use *so* instead of repeating a whole ⊞ clause after verbs of thinking (*assume, believe, expect, guess, hope, imagine, presume, suppose, think*) and also after *be afraid, appear / seem*, and *say*.
2 With negative clauses we use ⊞ verb + *not* (e.g. *I hope not*) with *be afraid, assume, guess, hope, presume*, and *suspect*.
- We normally use ⊟ verb + *so* (e.g. *I don't think so*) with *believe, expect, imagine*, and *think*.

---

a Cross out the words / phrases which could be left out.

> They look happy, but they aren't really ~~happy~~.

1 Everyone else loved the hotel we stayed in, but I didn't like it.
2 Nobody expects us to win, but you never know, we might win.
3 I didn't take the job in the end, but now I think that I should have taken it.
4 I got into the car and I turned the radio on.
5 **A** Would you like to come for dinner tomorrow night?
  B I'd love to come to dinner, but I'm afraid I can't come.
6 We don't go to the theatre very often now but we used to go before we had children.
7 I won't be able to go to the exhibition, but my wife will be able to go.
8 We met in 2009 and then we got married in 2010.

b Complete the sentences with a modal or an auxiliary verb in the right form.

> I'd like to help you this week, but I *can't*.

1 I'm not vegetarian, but my wife _____.
2 I would love to fly a plane, but I know that I never _____.
3 Nobody believes me when I say that I'm going to resign, but I _____.
4 We thought that Karen would get the job, but she _____.
5 In the end they didn't come, even though they had promised that they _____.
6 If you haven't seen the film yet, you _____. It's absolutely fantastic!
7 If I could help you, I would, but I'm afraid I _____.
8 I don't speak French, but my friend _____.

c Write the responses using the right form of the verb in brackets and a reduced infinitive or adding *so* or *not*.

> **A** Would you like to come round for dinner tomorrow?
> **B** I*'d love to*. (love)

1 **A** The weather forecast said it would snow at the weekend.
  B I _____. I was planning to do some gardening. (hope)
2 **A** Do you smoke?
  B I _____, but I gave up last month. (use)
3 **A** If you think she's coming down with flu, you shouldn't send her to school tomorrow.
  B I _____. She might infect the other children. (suppose)
4 **A** Have you spoken to Martin yet?
  B No, but I _____ after the meeting. (try)
5 **A** Do you think we should leave early to miss the traffic?
  B I _____, though I'm really enjoying myself. (guess)
6 **A** Why are you going to do a parachute jump?
  B I don't know. I _____. (always / want)

When we want to focus attention on or emphasize one part of a sentence, we can do this by adding certain words or phrases to the beginning of the sentence. This is sometimes called a 'cleft sentence'.

More emphatic sentence

1 beginning with *What* or *All*	
I need a coffee.	**What I need is** a coffee.
I don't like the weather here.	**What I don't like here is** the weather.
I just want to travel.	**All I want is** to travel.
I only touched it!	**All I did was** touch it.

2 beginning with *What happens is...* / *What happened was...*	
You do a test and then you have an interview.	**What happens is** (that) you do a test and then you have an interview.
We left our passports at home.	**What happened was** (that) we left our passports at home.

3 beginning with *The person who...*, *The place where...*, *The first / last time...*, *The reason why...*, etc.	
I spoke to the manager.	**The person (who / that) I spoke to was** the manager.
We stayed in a five-star hotel.	**The place where we stayed was** a five-star hotel.
I last saw him on Saturday.	**The last time I saw him was** on Saturday.
I bought it because it was cheap.	**The reason (why / that) I bought it was** that / because it was cheap.

4 beginning with *It*	
A boy in my class won the prize.	**It was a boy in my class who** won the prize.
We had the meeting last Friday.	**It was last Friday when** we had the meeting.
They charged us extra for the wine.	**It was the wine (that)** they charged us extra for.

1 We can make some kinds of sentences more emphatic by beginning with *What* (= the thing) or *All* (= the only thing) + clause + *be*, and then the part of the sentence we want to emphasize.

2 To emphasize an event or sequence of events, we can begin with *What happens is (that)...What happened was (that)...*

3 We can also make part of a sentence more emphatic by beginning with an expression like *The person who..., The place where..., The first / last time that..., The reason why...*, etc. + clause + *be*, with the emphasized part of the sentence at the end.

4 We can also use *It is / was* + the emphasized part of the sentence + a relative clause.

> ⚠ If the emphasized part is a pronoun, we normally use the object pronoun after *It is / was*, e.g. *It was me who paid the bill.* NOT ~~It was I who paid the bill.~~

a Complete the sentences with one word.

The *last* time I saw my brother was at his 40th birthday party.

1 _____ was my father who told me not to marry him.

2 _____ I hate about Sundays is knowing you have to work the next day.

3 The _____ why I want you to come early is so that we can have some time on our own before the others arrive.

4 After you've sent in your CV, what _____ next is that you get called for an interview.

5 It's not my fault you can't find them! _____ I did was tidy up your desk a bit.

6 The _____ where we're going to have lunch is a sort of artist's café near the theatre.

7 _____ happened was that I lost the piece of paper with my flight details on it.

8 It was _____ who told Angela about the party. I'm terribly sorry. I didn't know you hadn't invited her.

b Rewrite the sentences with the **bold** word.

I only need a small piece of paper.
ALL
All I need is a small piece of paper.

1 She left her husband because he cheated on her.
REASON
_____ he cheated on her.

2 We stopped in an absolutely beautiful place for lunch.
PLACE
_____ was absolutely beautiful.

3 We got stuck in an enormous traffic jam.
HAPPENED
_____ we got stuck in an enormous traffic jam.

4 They didn't apologize for arriving late, which really annoyed me.
WHAT
_____ they didn't apologize for arriving late.

5 A girl from my town won the silver medal.
IT
_____ won the silver medal.

6 I only said that I didn't like her dress.
ALL
_____ that I didn't like her dress.

7 I like my Aunt Emily best of all my relatives.
PERSON
_____ is my Aunt Emily.

8 You pick up your tickets at the box office.
HAPPENS
_____ you pick up your tickets at the box office.

9 Right now you need to sit down and put your feet up.
WHAT
_____ to sit down and put your feet up.

10 I first met Serena at a conference in Berlin.
TIME
_____ at a conference in Berlin.

apostrophe s

> 1 I borrowed my **father's** car. I trod on the cat's tail.
> The **company's** head office is in New York.
> The **government's** decision to raise taxes has not been well received.
> *Zalacain* is one of **Madrid's** most famous restaurants.
> 2 It's **Chris's** book.
> It's my **friends'** wedding.
> That's the **children's** room.
> The blonde girl is **Alex** and **Maria's** daughter.
> 3 We had dinner at **Tom's** last night. My mother is at the hairdresser**'s**.

Possessive forms express the idea of 'having' (in a very general sense) which exists between two nouns.

1 We normally use a possessive (+ *'s*) when something belongs to a particular person or thing, e.g. a person, an animal, an organization, a group of people, or a place.
• With places we can also say, e.g. Zalacain *is one of the most famous restaurants in Madrid*.
2 If a name (or singular noun) finishes in *s*, we either add *'s*, e.g *Chris's book* or put an apostrophe at the end of the word, e.g. *Chris' book*. With plural nouns we put the apostrophe after the *s*, e.g. *friends'*. With irregular plurals which don't end in *s* (*people, children, men*, etc.) we add *'s*.
• If there are two people, we put the *'s* on the second name.
3 When *'s* refers to 'the house of' or 'the shop of', we often omit the word *house* or *shop*.

using *of* (instead of apostrophe s)

> 1 Can you remember the name **of** the film?
> My brother lives at the end **of** the road.
> The problems **of** old age are many and varied.
> 2 Helen is the sister **of** my cousin in Rome I told you about.
> 3 Jim is a friend **of** my brother's.

1 We normally use an *of* phrase, not *'s*, with things or abstract nouns, especially when one thing is part of another.
2 We use *of* to express possession with a long phrase, e.g. NOT ~~my cousin in Rome I told you about's sister.~~
3 With *friend*, we often say *a friend of* + name / noun + *'s*.

compound nouns

> 1 I need the **tin opener**. Do you know where it is?
> I bought a huge **flower pot** in a **garden centre** near my house.
> My brother is a **company director** and my sister is a **history teacher**.
> I opened the **car door**, got in, and put on my **seat belt**.
> 2 There was a **wine bottle** on the table and two empty **wine glasses**.

1 We use compound nouns, not possessive forms, to refer to people or things in terms of what they are for, what they are made of, what work they do, or what kind they are. The second noun is the main thing or person, and can be singular or plural. The first noun gives more information about the second noun. It is usually singular, unless it has no singular form, e.g. *clothes shop*.
tin opener = an opener for tins, *history teacher* = a teacher of history

> ⚠ Compound nouns are usually two separate words, but they are occasionally joined together as one word, e.g. *sunglasses, bathroom* or hyphenated, e.g. *house-husband, letter-box*.

2 With containers, a compound noun (*a wine bottle*) focuses on the container (usually empty), whereas the container + a possessive noun (*a bottle of wine*) focuses on the contents (the container is usually full).
• Other common examples are *a wine glass / a glass of wine, a jam jar / a jar of jam, a petrol can / a can of petrol, a matchbox / a box of matches*, etc.

---

a Circle the right phrase. Tick if both are possible.

Shall I make (chicken soup) / soup of chicken for dinner tonight?

1 I enjoy spending time with *my friend's children / my friends' children*.
2 Didn't I meet you *at Jenny's / at Jenny's house* one night?
3 The hero dies at *the end of the film / the film's end*.
4 She's *the wife of my friend who lives in Australia / my friend who lives in Australia's wife*.
5 I want to introduce you to Jake. He's *a colleague of my sister's / a my sister's colleague*.
6 When you go to the supermarket, can you buy me *a milk bottle / a bottle of milk*?
7 The *photo of the house / house's photo* made me want to buy it.
8 I'm looking for a *stories book / story book* that would be right for an eight-year-old.
9 We bought a beautiful *table of glass / glass table* for the living room.
10 The Tower of London is *London's most popular tourist attraction / the most popular tourist attraction in London*.
11 There's *a wine glass / a glass of wine* on the table. Did you leave it there?

b What difference, if any, is there between the two phrases in the sentence(s) you have ticked?

c Combine a word from each list to make compound or possessive nouns to fill the gaps, adding *'s* or ' where necessary.

Alice and James	bottle	cats	~~children~~	garage
government	marketing	sea	wine	woman

~~bedroom~~	bowls	door	film	list	manager
opener	proposal	view	wedding		

I always leave the light on in the <u>children's bedroom</u> – my youngest child is a bit scared of the dark.

1 I can't find the _____. It's usually in this drawer, but it's not there now.
2 It's _____ next week and I don't have anything to wear yet.
3 We'd like to order something to drink. Could we see the _____, please?
4 My husband refused to go and see *Bridget Jones' Diary* with me. He said it was a _____.
5 Can I introduce you to Jenny White, our _____? She's been with our company for six years.
6 Don't forget to lock the _____ when you go out.
7 We would like a room with a _____, if that's possible.
8 The _____ to freeze MPs' salaries has been met with criticism by the opposition.
9 Make sure you fill the _____ with water every day.

1 It was **so cold** (that) we decided not to play tennis.
Agatha plays **so well** now (that) it's very difficult to beat her.

2 There was **so much noise** (that) the players couldn't concentrate.
There were **so many people** outside the stadium (that) we couldn't find each other.
I had **such a lot of work / such a lot of things to do** (that) I had to stay at the office late.

3 It was **such an exciting match** (that) I didn't want it to end.
It was **such awful weather** (that) the match had to be cancelled.
They were both **such great players** (that) everyone wanted to see the final.

4 It was **such a lovely day**!
She's **so mean**!
They're **such nice people**!

We often use *so* and *such* followed by a *that* clause to talk about a consequence or an effect. We often omit *that* in informal situations.

1 We use *so* before an adjective or adverb.

2 We use *so much* with uncountable nouns and *so many* with plural nouns.

• We can also use *such a lot of* instead of *so much / many*.

3 We use *such a / an* + adjective + a singular countable noun, and *such* + adjective + an uncountable or plural noun.

4 We often use *so* + adjective and *such* + noun or noun phrase without the *that* clause as exclamations.

> ⚠ We can use *so* + adjective / adverb at the beginning of a clause for emphasis. When we do this the subject and verb are inverted.
> *So successful was the first night that people flocked to see the play.*
> This is much more formal than saying *The first night was so successful that…* .

> ⚠ *such as* = 'for example'.
> *He loves winter sports, such as skiing and skating.*

a Complete the sentences with *so, so much / many*, or *such (a / an)*.

Nico is <u>*such an*</u> inspiring personal trainer that there is a waiting list to be with him.

1 She eats _____ healthily and does _____ exercise that she never puts on any weight.

2 The stadium is _____ near our house you can hear the roar of the crowd.

3 We made _____ mistakes in the second half that we didn't deserve to win.

4 They're both _____ fantastic players that the final should be a classic.

5 There was _____ snow on the pitch that the match was postponed.

6 It was _____ shock to find out that I wasn't in the team for the next match!

7 I'm _____ exhausted! I don't think I can do any more press-ups today.

8 Squash is _____ intensive sport that people don't usually play for more than half an hour.

9 There are _____ sports channels on TV now that you could be watching sport 24 hours a day if you wanted to.

b Rewrite the sentences using the **bold** word.

There was a lot of traffic and we were late for training.
SO
There was so much traffic that we were late for training.

1 It was so windy that we couldn't play tennis.
SUCH
_____ that we couldn't play tennis.

2 I have so many things to do that I don't have time to do exercise.
SUCH
_____ that I don't have time to do exercise.

3 It was such dirty water that we couldn't drink it.
SO
_____ that we couldn't drink it.

4 My colleagues are fantastic, so I really enjoy going to work.
SUCH
_____ I really enjoy going to work.

5 It was such a gripping match that the crowd were on the edge of their seats.
SO
_____ that the crowd were on the edge of their seats.

6 There was such a lot of noise that we couldn't have a proper conversation.
MUCH
_____ that we couldn't have a proper conversation.

7 He does a lot of water sports, for example sailing and windsurfing.
SUCH
He does a lot of water sports, _____ .

8 He's such a dangerous driver that no one ever wants to go in the car with him.
SO
_____ that no one ever wants to go in the car with him.

modifiers with *as...as...*

My sister's **almost as tall as** me / **almost as tall as** I am.
She's **just as bossy** now as when she was a child.
Their house is **nearly as big as** yours.
His latest film isn't **half as good as** his previous one.
Our new flat is **twice as big as** our old one.
The holiday cost **three times as much as** I'd expected.

We often use the modifiers *almost, just,* and *nearly,* and *half, twice, three times,* etc. with *as...as...*
- You can use *so* instead of the first *as* in negative sentences, e.g. *She's not nearly so difficult as people say.*
- After *as...as...* we can either use a subject pronoun + auxiliary verb, or an object pronoun, e.g. *She drives as fast as I do* OR *She drives as fast as me.*

> ⚠ *Twice* can only be used before *as...as...* NOT ~~Our new flat is twice bigger than our old one.~~
> However *three times, four times,* etc. can be used with *as... as...* or with a comparative adjective or adverb, e.g. *The holiday cost three times more than I'd expected.*

modifiers with comparative adjectives or adverbs

1 The French wine is **far more expensive** than the South African one.
The play was **much better** than I'd expected.
He's driving **a lot more carefully** since he got points on his licence.
2 She earns **much more money** than I do.
Women today have **many more opportunities** than they used to.
3 She's **a little better** than she was yesterday.
The later train is **slightly cheaper** than the earlier one.
Could you two talk **a bit more quietly**, please? I'm trying to concentrate.
4 **A** Would you like some more coffee? **B** Just **a little more**, please.
We've only got **a few more minutes** before the show starts.
5 The taxi driver drove **faster and faster**.
It's getting **more and more difficult** to make ends meet nowadays.

1 We use *far, much,* or *a lot* (informal) + comparative adjective or adverb for a big difference.
2 When we use *more* + noun for big differences we use *much / far / a lot more* + an uncountable noun and *many / far / a lot more* + a plural countable noun.
3 We use *slightly, a little,* or *a bit* (informal) + comparative adjective or adverb for a small difference.
4 When we use *more* + noun for small differences, we use *a little / slightly / a bit more* + an uncountable noun and *a few / slightly / a bit more* + a plural countable noun.
5 We sometimes repeat a comparative adjective or adverb for emphasis. When the comparative is formed with *more*, the adjective / adverb is only used after the second *more* (NOT ~~It's getting more difficult and more difficult~~).

modifiers with superlatives

It was **by far the nicest** of all the hotels we stayed at.
She's **much the prettiest** of the three children.
That was **easily the best** fish I've had for ages.
I'm **nearly the oldest** in my class.

- We often use *by far / much / easily,* and *nearly / almost* to modify superlative adjectives or adverbs.

the...the... + comparatives

The more dangerous a sport (is), **the more exciting** it is to watch.
The bigger the car (is), **the more expensive** it is to run.
The faster I speak in English, **the more mistakes** I make.
A When do you want me to do it? **B** **The sooner the better.**

We can use comparatives with *the...the...* to say that things change or vary together.
- When the verb in the first part is *be*, it can be left out, e.g. *The more dangerous a sport (is), the more some people seem to be attracted to it.*
- We often use *more* + noun in this structure, e.g. *The more coffee you drink, the less well you sleep.*
- When the second comparative is *better*, a reduced structure can be used, e.g. *the bigger the better,* etc. and also in set phrases like *the more the merrier.*

a Add one word to make the sentence correct.

My new broadband server is twice as fast the old one. *twice as fast as*

1 You're terrible – the ruder the joke, more you laugh!
2 That was far the best meal I have ever had in any restaurant.
3 He's just good a player as he used to be.
4 The book you lent me is lot funnier than I expected it to be.
5 This morning I was almost late for work as I was yesterday.
6 Generally speaking, the earlier you book the flight, the cheaper is.
7 Fortunately, our new boss is far laid-back about punctuality than our previous one.
8 Your slice is bit bigger than mine – I don't think that's fair!
9 He's easily most intelligent in the class, in fact maybe he should move into a more advanced group.

b Circle the right word or phrase. Tick if both are possible.

That hotel is *much more expensive* / *far more expensive* than ours. ✓

1 There are twice as many cars on the road *than* / *as* there used to be.
2 I think our kitchen is *slightly bigger* / *a bit bigger* than yours.
3 I think her new film was *by far* / *by much* her best one.
4 **A** When do you need it by?
   B *The sooner better* / *The sooner the better*.
5 Their flat cost *twice as much as* / *twice more than* ours.
6 The harder I try, *the worse I do it* / *I do it worse*.
7 It's getting *easier and easier* / *every time easier* to do all your shopping online.
8 We need *a few more* / *a little more* days to think about what we're going to do.
9 There were *many more* / *much more* people at the concert than we had expected.

1 Adjectives describing a job

Match sentences 1–6 with A–F.

1 My job is very <u>challenging</u>.
2 I'm a cashier in a supermarket. I quite enjoy my job, but it can be a bit **mono<u>tonous</u> / repetitive**.
3 I'm a primary school teacher. I think working with young children is very **re<u>ward</u>ing**.
4 I work in a small graphic design company, and I find my job really **<u>motivating</u>**.
5 Being a surgeon is very **demanding**.
6 I work in the Passport Office. My job is incredibly **tedious**.

A Everything takes a long time and it's boring.
B I have to do exactly the same thing every day.
C It makes me happy because I think it's useful and important.
D It tests my abilities and keeps me motivated.
E It's very high pressure, requires a lot of skill and you have to work long hours.
F The kind of work I do and the people I work with make me want to work harder / do better.

2 Nouns that are often confused

Complete the noun column with the best word from each group. Sometimes you need to use a word twice.

Noun

career / post / profession

1 My sister has applied for the ▨ of head of human resources at a multinational company based in Berlin. _____
2 Nursing is a rewarding ▨, but one which is not usually very highly paid. _____
3 It's difficult for a woman to have a successful ▨ and bring up young children at the same time. _____

wages / salary / bonus / perks

4 The ▨ (informal **The money**) isn't fantastic – about 20,000 a year but the work is rewarding. _____
5 I'm a waiter and I get paid every Friday. The ▨ aren't very high but you can earn a lot in tips if you do your job well. _____
6 The company made a huge profit this year and so all the staff were given a ▨. _____
7 One of the ▨ (formal **benefits**) of this job is that I get free health insurance. _____

staff / employer / employee

8 The company has a ▨ of nearly 600 ▨. _____, _____
9 I wouldn't describe the factory owner as a very generous ▨. _____
10 It's a great hotel and the ▨ are very friendly. _____

skills / training / qualifications

11 All the managers were sent on a three-week ▨ course. _____
12 He left school without any ▨ at all. He failed all his exams. _____
13 There are certain ▨ you need to be a web designer, for example you need to be able to use words effectively. _____

hours / timetable

14 **A** What ▨ do you work? **B** It depends on the day but usually 8.30 to 6.00. _____
15 My husband is a university lecturer and he has a very easy ▨ – he only has eight classes a week. _____

3 Collocations

Complete the phrases with the missing words.

1 I'm a manager. **I'm in ch_____** of the sales department. I have to **d_____ with** some very difficult clients. **I'm** also **res_____ for** publicity. **I'm o_____** work at the moment. **I'm on maternity leave.**

2 I'm part of a **t_____**. I always work with other people. **I have** the **opp_____** to travel, which is something I appreciate. **I have** good **pr_____** in this job. I think I can go far. I'm hoping to **get pr_____ to** head of department next year.

3 I'm hoping to **get a r_____**. I think my salary is very low. It's a **temp_____ job** – I'm only **on a short-t_____ contract**, so **I have** no job **sec_____**.

4 **I was sa_____ / fired from** my last job. My boss didn't like the way I worked. Now **I'm self-employed. I r_____** my own business and I'm much happier. I only **work p_____-t_____**, from 10.00 to 2.00, and in the afternoon I'm doing an Open University course.

5 **I was made re_____**. There were too many workers and the company was losing money. **I've been o_____ of work** for three months now, but I hope to find a job soon. I've been **doing** some **vol_____ work** at the local community centre. **It's un_____**, but at least **I'm getting** some more work **exp_____**.

Can you remember the words on this page?
Test yourself or a partner. ⟳ p.7

Family

1 21st century families in the UK

Read the information about 21st century families in the UK. What do the **bold** expressions mean?
With a partner, say if the same is true in your country.

The **nuclear family** is no longer the norm. Because of divorce and people remarrying, many children live with **step-parents** and have **half-brothers** or **half-sisters**, or **stepbrothers** and **stepsisters**.

Members of **extended families** no longer live close to each other in the same town, but are very often **spread out** around the country or even abroad, so many people rarely see their **relatives**.

One in four families is a **single-parent** family. According to a recent survey, 91% of single parents are women. As a result many children **grow up** today without a **father figure**.

Due to the fact that people are living longer, many more children have **great-grandparents**, or even **great-great-grandparents**.

2 Describing families

Circle the right word or expression from the pair on the right. Tick the two sentences where both options are possible.

1 He ▨ his mother. They have exactly the same sense of humour.
2 Jack is a ▨ relative. He's my father's second cousin.
3 She's ▨ child. She has no brothers or sisters.
4 My sister and I are very ▨. We're both cheerful and hard-working.
5 They are a very ▨ family. They enjoy spending time together.
6 After their parents died, the ▨ rarely met.
7 His mother died when he was young. He was ▨ by his father.
8 My father was a farmer so I ▨ in the country, surrounded by animals.
9 My niece has ▨ a lot recently. She's now almost as tall as I am.
10 I have a very good ▨ with my cousins. We see a lot of each other.
11 It's going to be a small wedding. Only a few friends and ▨ have been invited.
12 My ▨ originally came from Ireland.

takes after / looks like
far / distant
a single / an only
alike / like
close / near
brothers and sisters / siblings
educated / brought up
grew / grew up
grown / grown up
relation / relationship
relations / relatives
ancestors / descendants

3 Family idioms

Match to the idioms 1–8 to their meaning A–H.

1 My sister is **the black sheep** of the family.
2 My father doesn't **see eye to eye** with my brother about politics.
3 My aunt and I are **not on speaking terms**.
4 We usually have a family **get-together** at Christmas.
5 My sister-in-law **wears the trousers** in that marriage!
6 Red hair **runs in the family**.
7 Most families **have a skeleton in the cupboard**.
8 He's your brother! How can you say that about your **own flesh and blood**?

A having very different opinions on the matter
B making the decisions and telling her husband what to do
C not talking to each other
D Something happened in the past that they would prefer to keep secret.
E You are related to each other.
F different from the rest of the family who don't approve of them
G Several people in the family have it.
H We all meet in someone's house for a meal.

Can you remember the words on this page? Test yourself or a partner.

⟳ p.11

1 Verbs with *time*

Complete the sentences with the right verb from the list.

give	have	kill	make up for	run out of	save	spare	take (x2)	take up	waste

1 I _____ **a lot of time** playing solitaire on my computer instead of studying.
2 If you go on the motorway, you'll _____ **time** – it's much quicker than going on the country roads.
3 I had three hours to wait for my flight, so I sat there doing *sudoku* puzzles to _____ **time**.
4 There's no hurry so _____ **your time**.
5 When my mother was young she never had the chance to travel. Now she has retired she wants to _____ **lost time** and she has booked a round-the-world tour.
6 The novel is 700 pages long and I'm a slow reader. It's going to _____ **me a long time** to finish it.
7 I'd better go home now. If I'm late again, my dad will _____ **me a hard time**.
8 I would like to go camping with my friends this weekend but my exams are next week so I can't _____ **the time**.
9 My children _____ **all my time** – I never seem to get to read a book or watch a film!
10 New York's such a fantastic city! You're going to _____ **the time of your life** there.
11 Don't let's spend too long at the museum or we'll _____ **time**. We have to get the train back at 10.30 and there are lots of other things I want to see.

2 Prepositional phrases with *time*

Complete the prepositions column with a preposition from the list.

at (x2)	before	by	for	from	in (x2)	off	on	to

Prepositions

1 I'm really punctual, so I hate it when other people aren't ▨ **time**. _____
2 I've never heard of that singer. He must have been ▨ **my time**. _____
3 ▨ **the time** we got to our hotel, it was nearly midnight. _____
4 I'm very excited. I'm going to New Zealand ▨ four **days' time**. _____
5 I missed the birth of my first child. I was on a plane ▨ **the time**. _____
6 He's been working too hard recently. He needs some **time** ▨. _____
7 If we don't take a taxi, we won't get to the airport ▨ **time** ▨ the flight. _____ _____
8 I don't eat out very often, but I do get a takeaway ▨ **time** ▨ **time**. _____
9 He suffers from back pain and it makes him a bit irritable ▨ **times**.

3 Expressions with *time*

Match sentences 1–10 with A–J.

1 The referee's looking at his watch. ▨
2 He hardly spoke to me at lunch. ▨
3 I'm really looking forward to my holidays. ▨
4 I'm sorry, I can't help you this week. ▨
5 I can't afford a new computer. ▨
6 She's sure to find a job in the end. ▨
7 I think I need to take up a hobby. ▨
8 Stop writing, please. ▨
9 I really thought I was going to be late. ▨
10 You look very young in that photo. ▨

A But in the end I got to the airport **with time to spare**.
B He spent **the whole time** talking on his mobile.
C **Time's up.** The exam is over.
D **I'm** a bit **short of time** (*inf* **pushed for time**).
E **I've got time on my hands** since I retired.
F I'll have to carry on with this one **for the time being**.
G It's only **a question of time**.
H It must have been taken **a long time ago**.
I **There isn't much time left**.
J **This time next week** I'll be lying on the beach.

Can you remember the expressions on this page? Test yourself or a partner.

⟳ p.27

get

1 Expressions with *get*

a Complete the sentences with an expression from the list.

| get a shock | get hold of | get into trouble | get out of the way | get rid of |
| get the chance | get the impression | get the joke | get to know | get *your* own back on |

1 I _____ you're a bit annoyed with me. Have I done something wrong?
2 You'll _____ when you see him. He looks at least ten years older.
3 Since we stopped working together we hardly ever _____ to see each other.
4 I didn't laugh because I didn't _____.
5 When you _____ him, I think you'll really like him.
6 I need to speak to Sarah urgently, but I just can't _____ her.
7 I want to _____ that awful painting, but I can't because it was a wedding present from my mother-in-law.
8 I'm going to _____ my brother for telling my parents I got back late. Next time he asks to borrow my bike, I won't lend it to him.
9 He's going to _____ with his wife if she finds out that he's been emailing his ex-girlfriend.
10 I tried to walk past him but he wouldn't _____. He just stood there, blocking the path.

'Well, I've managed to get rid of the annoying double vision effect on your T.V.'

www.CartoonStock.com

b With a partner, say what you think the expressions mean.

2 Idioms with *get*

a Match the sentence halves.

1 **Get real**!
2 **Get a life**!
3 I'm **not getting anywhere** with this crossword.
4 She really **gets on my nerves**.
5 She really needs to **get her act together**.
6 They **get on like a house on fire**.
7 When we spoke on the phone I **got the wrong end of the stick**.
8 Your grandfather must be **getting on** a bit, isn't he?
9 My boyfriend just never **gets the message**.
10 She always **gets her own way**.

A It's just too difficult for me.
B Is he in his eighties now?
C They seem to have exactly the same tastes and interests.
D Her exam is in two weeks and she hasn't even started studying.
E I thought the party was at their house, but it isn't – it's at Mike and Jane's
F Everything about her irritates me, her voice, her smile – everything!
G He just does whatever she tells him to.
H I keep dropping hints about his awful cooking but he takes no notice
I There's no way you can afford that car!
J You're 35 and you're still living with your parents!

b With a partner, say what you think the idioms mean.

3 Phrasal verbs with *get*

Match the phrasal verbs to their meaning.

1 Shall we try to **get together** for dinner next weekend?
2 I hope my brother **gets over** his break-up soon. He's very depressed.
3 I can't help you now. I need to **get on with** the cooking.
4 I've tried to talk about it, but I just can't **get through to** him.
5 How did you **get into** journalism?
6 The best way to **get around** the city is by taxi – they're very cheap here.
7 She's cheated in exams several times but she always **gets away with** it.
8 My wife is out of work so we'll just have to **get by** on less money.
9 I've **got** a bit **behind** with my work – I may have to do some at the weekend.
10 This terrible weather is really **getting** me **down**.
11 I want to **get out of** going to Ann's party. Can you think of a good excuse?
12 Thanks for your email. I'll **get back to** you as soon as possible.

A recover from
B start a career or profession
C move from place to place
D make someone understand
E manage with what you have
F fail to make enough progress
G depress
H write or speak to sb again later
I avoid a responsibility or obligation
J meet socially
K continue doing
L do something wrong without getting caught or punished

Can you remember the expressions on this page? Test yourself or a partner.

◐ p.29

1 Sounds

a **3.2** All the words in the list can be both nouns and regular verbs, and they describe sounds. Many of the words are onomatopoeic, (i.e. they sound like the sound they describe). Listen to the sounds and the words.

bang	buzz	click	crash	creak	crunch	drip	hiss
hoot	hum	<u>ra</u>ttle	roar	screech	slam	slurp	sniff
snore	splash	tap	tick	<u>whi</u>stle			

b Now complete the **Sounds** column with a word from the list.

Sounds

1 This clock has a very loud ▨. _____
2 Don't ▨! Get a handkerchief and blow your nose. _____
3 To download the new software just ▨ on the 'download' icon. _____
4 There was a ▨ as he jumped into the swimming pool. _____
5 Did you hear that ▨? It sounded like a gun. _____
6 I heard a floorboard ▨ and I knew somebody had come into the room. _____
7 I lay there hearing the ▨ of a mosquito but I couldn't see it anywhere. _____
8 I hate people who ▨ at me when I slow down at an amber light. _____
9 When I'm nervous I often ▨ my fingers on the table. _____
10 Don't ▨ your soup! Eat it quietly. _____
11 The snake reared its head and gave an angry ▨. _____
12 Please turn the tap off properly otherwise it'll ▨. _____
13 We could hear the ▨ of the crowd in the football stadium from our hotel. _____
14 Some of the players carried on playing because they hadn't heard the ▨. _____
15 I don't remember the words of the song, but I can ▨ the tune. _____
16 Please don't ▨ the door. Close it gently. _____
17 I heard the ▨ of their feet walking through the crisp snow. _____
18 I can't share a room with you if you ▨ – I won't be able to sleep. _____
19 Every time a bus or lorry goes past, the windows ▨. _____
20 I heard the ▨ of brakes as the driver tried to stop and then a loud ▨. _____ , _____

2 The human voice

a Match the verbs and definitions.

<u>gi</u>ggle	groan	<u>mum</u>ble	scream	sigh
sob	<u>stam</u>mer	<u>whi</u>sper	yell	

1 _____ to make a loud high cry because you are hurt, frightened, or excited
2 _____ (*at sb*) to shout loudly, e.g. because you are angry
3 _____ (*at sth*) to laugh in a silly way
4 _____ (*to sb*) to speak very quietly so that other people can't hear what you are saying
5 _____ to speak or say sth in a quiet voice in a way that is not clear
6 _____ to make a long deep sound because you are in pain or annoyed
7 _____ to speak with difficulty, often repeating sounds or words
8 _____ to cry noisily, taking sudden sharp breaths
9 _____ to take in and then let out a long deep breath that can be heard, e.g. to show that you are disappointed

b Answer the questions using one of the verbs above. What do people do…?
- when they are nervous
- when they are terrified
- when they lose their temper
- when they are not supposed to be making a noise
- when they speak without opening their mouth enough
- when they are relieved
- when a player in their team misses a penalty
- when they are very unhappy about something

Can you remember the words on this page? Test yourself or a partner.
⟲ p.36

1 Nouns for money or payments

Match the words and definitions.

budget	charge	deposit
donation	fare	fees	fine	grant
instalment	loan	lump sum
overdraft	savings	will

1 _____ the money that is available to a person or organization

2 _____ a sum of money that is given by the government or another organization to be used for a particular purpose, e.g. education

3 _____ money that a bank lends and somebody borrows

4 _____ an amount of money you pay for professional advice or services, e.g. to a lawyer or architect

5 _____ the money you pay to travel by bus, plane, taxi, etc.

6 _____ the amount of money sb asks for goods and services, etc.

7 _____ money that you keep in the bank and don't spend

8 _____ money that you give to an organization such as a charity in order to help them

9 _____ a sum of money that must be paid as punishment for breaking a law or a rule

10 _____ one of a number of payments that are paid regularly until sth has been paid for

11 _____ a sum of money that is given as the first part of a larger payment

12 _____ a legal document that says what is to happen to sb's money and property after they die

13 _____ the amount of money that you owe to a bank when you have spent more than is in your bank account

14 _____ an amount of money that is paid at one time and not on separate occasions

2 Money in today's society

a With a partner, say what you think the **bold** phrases mean.

1 We live in **a consumer society**, which is dominated by spending money and buying material possessions.

2 The **standard of living** has risen a lot over the last ten years.

3 People's **income** has gone up, but **inflation** is high, so the **cost of living** has also risen.

4 House prices are rising and many young people **can't afford** to buy somewhere to live.

5 People who have mortgages or loans have to pay high **interest rates**.

6 A lot of people are **in debt** /det/, and have problems paying their **mortgages** /ˈmɔːɡɪdʒɪz/.

7 Some people make money by buying and selling **shares** on the **stock market**.

8 Our **currency** is unstable and **exchange rates** fluctuate a lot.

b Which aspects of the sentences above are true in your country?

3 Adjectives related to money

Look at the *Oxford Learner's Thesaurus* entries for *rich* and *poor*. Match the synonyms to their definitions.

> **rich** *adj.* **rich, affluent, loaded, wealthy, well-off**
>
> 1 _____ / _____ having a lot of money, property, or valuable possessions
>
> 2 _____ (*rather formal*) rich and with a good standard of living. *The ~ Western countries are better equipped to face the problems of global warming.*
>
> 3 _____ (often used in negative sentences) rich: *His parents are not very ~ .*
>
> 4 _____ [not before noun] (*very informal*) very rich: *Let her pay. She's ~ .*
>
> **poor** *adj.* **poor, broke, hard up, penniless**
>
> 1 _____ having very little money; not having enough money for basic needs
>
> 2 _____ (*literary*) having no money, very poor: *She arrived in 1978 as a virtually ~ refugee.*
>
> 3 _____ (*informal*) having very little money, especially for a short period of time: *After he lost his job he was so ~ he couldn't afford the price of a beer.*
>
> 4 _____ [not before noun] (*informal*) having no money: *I'm always ~ by the end of the month.*

4 Idioms related to money

a Match sentences 1–8 with A–H.

1 They've got a ten-bedroomed house.

2 Jack's broke again.

3 That restaurant has good food at a reasonable price.

4 Their income doesn't cover their basic expenses.

5 I have an overdraft at the bank.

6 Do you think Mark will lend me the money?

7 Dan has bought two sports cars.

8 They have a luxurious lifestyle which they can't really afford.

A He's got more **money than sense**.

B No way. He's really **tight-fisted**.

C I'm **in the red** (*opp* **in the black**).

D It must have **cost a fortune**.

E It's **good value for money**.

F I'm not surprised. He **spends money like water**.

G They're **living beyond their means**.

H They **can't make ends meet**.

b With a partner say what you think the **bold** idioms mean.

Can you remember the words and expressions on this page? Test yourself or a partner.

⊙ p.45

Study Link MultiROM www.oup.com/elt/englishfile/advanced

1 Weapons

Match the words and pictures.

arrow	<u>mi</u>ssile
bow /bəʊ/	shield /ʃiːld/
<u>bu</u>llet	spear
<u>ca</u>nnon	sword /sɔːd/
ma<u>chi</u>ne gun	

2 People and events

a Match the nouns with the definitions for people.

ally /ˈælaɪ/   <u>ca</u>sualties   ci<u>vi</u>lians
<u>for</u>ces   refu<u>gees</u>   <u>sni</u>pers
sur<u>vi</u>vors   troops
the <u>woun</u>ded /ˈwuːndɪd/

1 _____ people who are forced to leave their country or home because there is a war, or for political or religious reasons

2 _____ people who have been killed or wounded in a war, e.g. *Both sides suffered heavy ~.*

3 _____ a group of people who have been trained to protect other people, usually by using weapons, e.g. *armed ~, security ~, peace keeping ~*

4 _____ soldiers, especially in large groups

5 _____ people who shoot at someone from a hidden position

6 _____ people who are not members of the armed forces or the police

7 _____ people who have been injured by weapons, e.g. in a war, e.g. *They evacuated ~ from the war zone.*

8 _____ people who have managed to stay alive in a war or accident, especially despite being nearly killed

9 _____ a country that has agreed to help and support another country, especially in time of war

b Match the words with the definitions for events.

<u>cease</u>fire   coup /kuː/   civil <u>war</u>   revo<u>lu</u>tion   siege /siːdʒ/   <u>treaty</u>

1 _____ when a very large number of people in a country use violence to try to change the government

2 _____ a sudden, illegal, often violent change of government often forced by a specific group of people, e.g. *a military ~*

3 _____ when two armies agree to stop fighting temporarily

4 _____ a war between groups of people in the same country

5 _____ when an army try to take a town by surrounding it and stopping the food supply

6 _____ a formal agreement between two or more countries, e.g. *They signed a peace ~*

3 Verbs describing warfare

Complete the verb column with the past simple of a verb from the list.

blow up   break out   <u>ca</u>pture   de<u>clare</u>   de<u>feat</u>   loot
over<u>throw</u>   re<u>treat</u>   shell   su<u>rren</u>der   with<u>draw</u>

	Verbs
1 The rebels ▨ the government. (They removed them from power using force.)	_____
2 Fighting ▨ between the rebels and the army. (It started.)	_____
3 The rebels ▨ the government building. (They made it explode.)	_____
4 The army ▨ from the city. (They moved back to another position for tactical reasons.)	_____
5 The army ▨ the city all night. (They fired shells (explosives) at them.)	_____
6 The rebels ▨. (They moved away from the enemy because they were in danger.)	_____
7 Some of the rebels ▨. (They admitted that they had lost and wanted to stop fighting.)	_____
8 The army ▨ the rebels. (They beat them.)	_____
9 They ▨ over 300 rebels. (They took them prisoner.)	_____
10 Some soldiers ▨ the city. (They stole things from shops and buildings.)	_____
11 The government ▨ war on the rebels. (They announced their intention to go to war with them.)	_____

⚠ *capture, defeat, overthrow, retreat,* and *surrender* can also be used as nouns.

Can you remember the words on this page? Test yourself or a partner.
⟳ p.53

a Complete the column on the right with one of the words. Sometimes there is more than one possibility.

1 **above / over**
  a She lives in a flat ▨ a shop.
  b In a few minutes we'll be flying ▨ Paris.
  c Liverpool are three places ▨ Aston Villa in the Premier League.

2 **below / under**
  a We kept an eye open for speed cameras as we drove ▨ the bridge.
  b She lives on the floor ▨ us.
  c There's a wastepaper basket ▨ the table.

  ⚠ beneath (*formal*) = below, e.g. *He considered such jobs beneath him.*

3 **off / away**
  a I fell ▨ my bike and cut my knee.
  b She walked ▨ from me, and didn't look back.
  c The thief ran ▨ with her camera.

4 **in / inside / into**
  a We decided to eat ▨ because it was cold on the terrace.
  b He poured some wine ▨ his glass, and raised it.
  c Please keep this document ▨ a safe place.

5 **on / on top / on top of / onto**
  a Don't leave the towel ▨ the floor. Pick it up.
  b I'm going to put your suitcase ▨ the wardrobe so it's not in the way.
  c The toddler climbed ▨ the chair and then stood up.
  d It's a chocolate cake with cream ▨.

  ⚠ upon (*formal*) = on, e.g. *He lay upon the bed.*

6 **outside / out / out of**
  a Take your hands ▨ your pockets.
  b Let's meet ▨ the cinema.
  c He took his wallet ▨ and gave the driver a five-pound note.

7 **across / through**
  a We walked ▨ a very dense forest until we came out into a clearing.
  b He was walking ▨ the road on a zebra crossing when he was hit by a car.
  c We can go ▨ the park to get to Kate's house. It's a short cut.

8 **along / past / round**
  a He walked ▨ the corridor until he reached the door.
  b If you go ▨ the supermarket, the church is on your left.
  c She drove ▨ the roundabout twice because she wasn't sure which exit to take.

9 **to / towards**
  a Jane has gone ▨ the hairdresser's.
  b If you walk ▨ the beach, you'll see the hairdresser's on the right after about 200m.

10 **in / at**
  a I called David at home but they told me he was ▨ the pub.
  b There are some sofas and armchairs ▨ the pub, so we can relax and read the papers.
  c Turn left ▨ the lights, and you'll see it on your right.

b Test yourself with the words on the page by covering the right-hand column
and trying to remember the missing words in the sentences.

◀ p.75

1 Nouns and noun phrases

a Complete the missing words. What do you think they mean?

1 **City b_____** – three days in **Prague** €157.

2 Eight-day **p_____** holiday to **CHINA** including flights, hotels (half-board) and excursions.

3 **Flight to Australia** with one night **s_____** in Singapore (4-star hotel).

4 **Day t_____ to Hampton Court** – Henry VIII castle – coach leaves at 9.00 a.m., return approx 6.30 p.m.

5 **Hever Castle** – guided **t_____** 10.00 a.m. – 6.00 p.m. Visits last approx one hour.

6 Visit **Thingvellir National Park,** located 50 kilometres east of Reykjavik, this is one of Iceland's most spectacular landscapes and the **s_____** of the ancient Icelandic parliament.

7 **FLY,** the new **l_____-c_____ airline** that offers cheap flights to hundreds of destinations.

8 Cheap **l_____-haul** flights to Australia and the Far East. **AUSTRALIA** from €399, **JAPAN** from €250.

b Complete each definition with the correct word.

_____ [c] an act of travelling from one place to another, and usually back again: *a business ~ , a school ~ to France, Tomorrow there will be a boat ~ to the island. They had to make several ~ to bring all the equipment over.*

_____ [c] an act of travelling from one place to another, especially when they are a long way apart: *It was a long and difficult ~ across the mountains. They continued their ~ on foot. We broke our ~ (stopped for a short time) in Madrid.*

_____ [u] the activity of going to different places for business or pleasure, especially over long distances: *Her interests include music and foreign ~ . Continued fighting makes ~ in the area dangerous. air / rail / space ~. ~ insurance / ~ documents / ~ guide / ~ sickness.*

Oxford Learner's Thesaurus

2 Verb phrases

Match the verbs with their collocates.

cancel   cut short   go   go on   postpone / put off
set off / set out   take out

1 _____ travel insurance
2 _____ on a journey / early
3 _____ a trip / a visit (= finish earlier than planned)
4 _____ camping / backpacking / sightseeing
5 _____ an outing (or excursion) / a trip / holiday / a safari / a cruise
6 _____ a trip / a visit (= reschedule it for a later time)
7 _____ a trip / a flight / a visit (= decide not to go)

3 Adjectives and phrases to describe places

Match the adjectives and definitions.

breathtaking   dull   lively   off the beaten track
overcrowded   overrated   picturesque   spoilt   touristy

1 _____ with a better reputation than it really deserves
2 _____ boring
3 _____ designed to attract a lot of tourists
4 _____ changed for the worse
5 _____ full of life and energy
6 _____ far away from other people, houses, etc.
7 _____ with too many people or things in it
8 _____ very impressive or surprising, spectacular
9 _____ pretty, especially in a way which looks old-fashioned

Can you remember the words on this page? Test yourself or a partner.
🔵 p.85

The natural world

1 Animals, birds, and insects

a Match the words and pictures.

wings
a shell
paws
a beak
horns
a tail
claws
fur
fins

b Can you name an animal or insect which can…?

a bite _____
b sting _____
c scratch _____
d kick _____
e spit _____

2 Issues relating to animals

a Look at the **bold** words and phrases with a partner and say what they mean.

In your country are there…?

1 any organizations which **protect** animals and their **environment**, or **animal charities**
2 **animal activists**, who make violent protests against the use of animals for entertainment, product testing or in medical research
3 national or regional celebrations where animals are **treated cruelly**
4 national parks or conservation areas where animals **live in the wild**
5 **endangered species** /ˈspiːʃiːz/
6 animals which are **hunted for sport**
7 animals which are being **bred in captivity** in order to reintroduce them into the wild
8 animals which are kept or transported in inhumane conditions, e.g. **battery hens**

b Answer the questions. Give examples.

3 Animal idioms

a Read the sentences and try to guess the meaning of the **bold** idioms. Then match them to definitions A–O.

1 I did all **the donkey work** on this project, so I hope I'm going to get the credit for it.
2 I told him what I thought of him but it's **like water off a duck's back** for him.
3 He was **like a fish out of water** when he left the village and went to live in London.
4 You *think* you've passed the exam but **don't count your chickens (before they hatch)**.
5 I decided to **take the bull by the horns** and went to see my boss.
6 When they divorced, Nick's wife got **the lion's share** of everything they owned.
7 I think James was married before, but I'm not sure. He's a bit of **a dark horse**.
8 I'm **in the doghouse** because I forgot our wedding anniversary.
9 He **made a** real **pig of himself** at the dinner. He had second helpings of everything.
10 When my car broke down at the end of such an awful day it was just **the last straw** (that breaks the camel's back).
11 The company say they're not going to make anyone redundant with the restructuring, but **I smell a rat**.
12 If we have the meeting in London, we can go and visit my mother at the same time and **kill two birds with one stone**.
13 My boss can seem quite aggressive but in fact **her bark is worse than her bite**.
14 After playing so badly he walked off **with his tail between his legs**.
15 I wouldn't bring up the subject again if I were you. I'd **let sleeping dogs lie**.

A face a difficult situation directly and with courage
B the hard boring part
C not mention something that happened in the past to avoid arguments or problems
D criticism doesn't affect him
E manage to achieve two things by doing one action
F a person who doesn't tell others much about their life (but sometimes surprises them)
G the largest or best part
H not be <u>too</u> confident that something will be successful
I eat and drink too much, be very greedy
J the last in a series of bad events that makes you unable to accept the situation any longer
K feeling ashamed, embarrassed, or unhappy because you have been defeated or punished
L somebody (usually your partner) is annoyed with you about something
M sb whose words are worse than their actions
N think that sth is wrong or that sb is trying to deceive you
O feel uncomfortable or awkward in unfamiliar surroundings

b Do you have the same or similar idioms in your language?

Can you remember the words and phrases on this page? Test yourself or a partner.

⊙ p.90

Match the words and the pictures.

- heat (sth in the microwave)
- beat (eggs)
- stir (a sauce)
- mix (the ingredients)
- drain (the pasta)
- pour
- simmer
- a saucepan /ˈsɔːspən/
- a frying pan
- a chopping board
- a baking tray
- an oven

- baked figs
- poached eggs
- melted chocolate
- steamed mussels
- mashed potatoes
- roast lamb
- stuffed peppers
- scrambled eggs
- grated cheese
- chopped onions
- peeled prawns / shrimps
- whipped cream
- sliced bread
- toasted sandwich
- minced beef
- pork ribs
- turkey breast
- shellfish
- herbs
- spices

**Can you remember the words
and phrases on this page?
Test yourself or a partner.**
➲ p.100

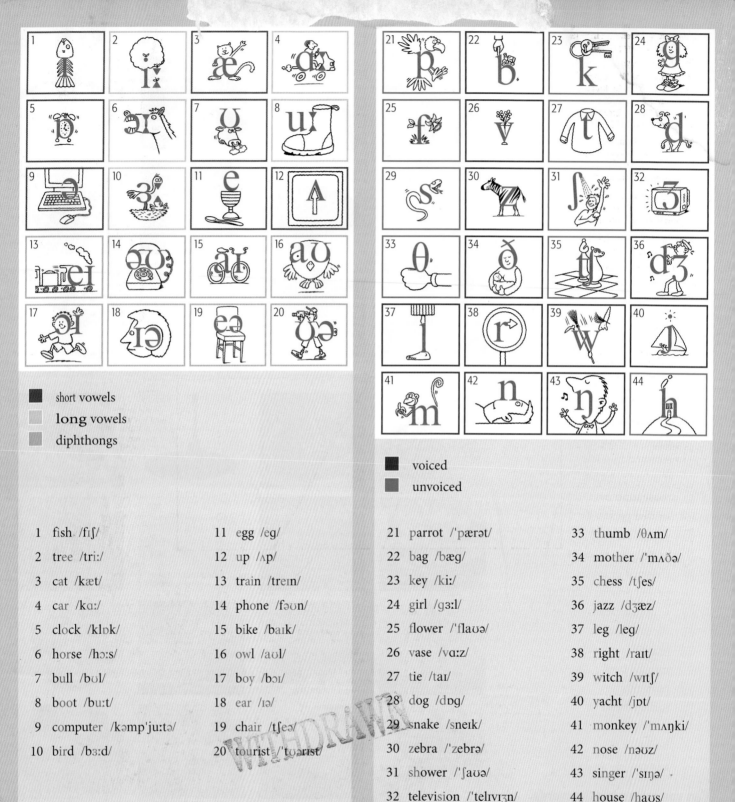

- short vowels
- **long** vowels
- diphthongs

- voiced
- unvoiced

1 fish /fɪʃ/	11 egg /eg/	21 parrot /ˈpærət/	33 thumb /θʌm/
2 tree /triː/	12 up /ʌp/	22 bag /bæg/	34 mother /ˈmʌðə/
3 cat /kæt/	13 train /treɪn/	23 key /kiː/	35 chess /tʃes/
4 car /kɑː/	14 phone /fəʊn/	24 girl /gɜːl/	36 jazz /dʒæz/
5 clock /klɒk/	15 bike /baɪk/	25 flower /ˈflaʊə/	37 leg /leg/
6 horse /hɔːs/	16 owl /aʊl/	26 vase /vɑːz/	38 right /raɪt/
7 bull /bʊl/	17 boy /bɔɪ/	27 tie /taɪ/	39 witch /wɪtʃ/
8 boot /buːt/	18 ear /ɪə/	28 dog /dɒg/	40 yacht /jɒt/
9 computer /kəmpˈjuːtə/	19 chair /tʃeə/	29 snake /sneɪk/	41 monkey /ˈmʌŋki/
10 bird /bɜːd/	20 tourist /ˈtʊərɪst/	30 zebra /ˈzebrə/	42 nose /nəʊz/
		31 shower /ˈʃaʊə/	43 singer /ˈsɪŋə/
		32 television /ˈtelɪvɪʒn/	44 house /haʊs/

197382

www.oup.com/elt/englishfile/advanced